DEATH
EDUCATION

DEATH EDUCATION

JAMES M. EDDY, D.Ed.

Assistant Professor, Health Education Department,
The Pennsylvania State University,
University Park, Pennsylvania

WESLEY F. ALLES, Ph.D.

Associate Professor, Health Education Department,
The Pennsylvania State University,
University Park, Pennsylvania

Illustrated

The C. V. Mosby Company

ST. LOUIS • TORONTO • LONDON   1983

MOSBY

A TRADITION OF PUBLISHING EXCELLENCE

Editor: Charles K. Hirsch
Assistant editor: Michelle A. Turenne
Editing supervisor: Lin Dempsey Hallgren
Manuscript editor: Robert A. Kelly
Book design: Kay M. Kramer
Cover design: Diane Beasley
Production: Barbara Merritt

The C.V. Mosby Company
11830 Westline Industrial Drive, St. Louis, Missouri 63141

Library of Congress Cataloging in Publication Data

Eddy, James M.
    Death education.

    Bibliography: p.
    Includes index.
    1. Death—Psychological aspects.   2. Death—
Social aspects.   3. Death.   I. Alles, W. F.
II. Title.
BF789.D4E32   306'.9'07   82-2122
ISBN 0-8016-1497-X   AACR2

SS/VH/VH   9 8 7 6 5 4 3 2 1   02/C/278

Preface

Many books have been written on topics related to death, typically by sociologists, psychologists, health professionals, philosophers, and members of the clergy. Both content and perspective display the professional orientation of these authors. *Death Education* is a unique work in the field of thanatology. It was written by educators whose intent was to provide a useful textbook for the other educators. For this reason, the first three chapters focus on the modalities of death education and the last five chapters provide course content. Traditionally, educators have used a variety of books to provide course content. From these books, chapters are carefully selected to form an anthology, and content is arranged to give the student a coordinated progression of material. From an educational point of view, this is adequate if the objective of a course on death is only to provide information.

Most people would agree that death education has more to offer than content. Therefore the primary objective of this work was to provide teachers with a comprehensive book that provides a variety of learning strategies for classroom use and to encourage dialogue among students and instructors. The underlying premise is that people across the life span need to be educated about death to more fully appreciate themselves and their relationships with others. Whether death education is taught to preschoolers or adults, by professional educators or lay teachers who come from one of the helping professions, or for academic credit or personal interest, the course should have an underlying philosophy based on the needs of the target audience. We hope this textbook will engender a unified perspective with which the teacher can plan a purposeful death education course.

This objective is achieved in several ways. Each chapter that covers a death education content area provides a list of major concepts on which to focus attention. Additionally, sample learning activities have been provided. These activities can be used as they appear in the text, or they can stimulate spin-off activities appropriate for the audience. The annotated bibliography of key books, journals, and documents dealing with death offers substantial guidance. The appendixes are extensive. By progressing from the key concepts to the chapter content and eventually to the annotated bibliography and appendix, the reader will be able to formulate a broad perspective toward each issue.

Benjamin Franklin once remarked, "Were it offered to my choice, I should have no objection to a repetition of the same life from its beginning, only asking the advantage authors have in a second edition to correct some faults in the first." If a second edition of this book should come to pass, we hope as Franklin once hoped to be able to correct some of the faults observed in our first edition. We solicit your input and would be happy to receive comments from readers for the purpose of improving the quality of death education.

At this time it is appropriate to acknowledge some of the people who have contributed to this book. Charles Hirsch and Michelle Turenne provided continuous encouragement, and their expertise guided the progress of the text without delay. The considerable administrative support provided by Dick St. Pierre and Karl Stoedefalke is greatly appreciated. We gratefully acknowledge the assistance of the publisher's reviewers: Charles R. Carroll, Ph.D., Ball State University; Darrell Crase, Ph.D., Memphis State University; Mal Goldsmith, Ph.D., Southern Illinois University–Edwardsville; Robert F. Guthmann, Jr., M.S., Centennial Area Health Education Center–Greeley, Colorado; Rick Guyton, Ph.D., University of Arkansas; Patricia Hess, Ph.D., San Francisco State University; Carol Ann Holcomb, Ph.D., Kansas State University of Agriculture and Applied Science; Janice Litwack, Ed.S., Kent State University; Carole Lou Roberts, University of Dayton; Catherine Salveson, R.N., M.S., Cancer Outreach Program (New Mexico Department of Health and Environment); and Dr. William L. Yarber, Purdue University. Beth Musser, Peg Krumrine, and Anne Jacobs typed the many drafts that preceded the final copy, and their secretarial skills and personal qualities made the challenges of manuscript preparation substantially easier for us. David Bower, a health educator in the Williamsport, Pennsylvania, school district, helped to compile the annotated bibliography. Guidance Associates kindly granted permission to use illustrations from the filmstrip series *Death and Dying: Closing the Circle.* Finally, we wish to thank our wives for being so understanding while the manuscript was being researched and prepared.

James M. Eddy
Wesley F. Alles

Contents

DEATH
EDUCATION

The ways in which society responds to death influence our mourning customs.

CHAPTER ONE

Introduction:
the evolution of death education
in the United States

Death is the horizon which places the possibilities of life in perspective.*
CHARLES R. MOJOCK

For a person who has never seriously tried to define death it would seem to be a simple matter. People are alive, and we can tell they are alive by observing them. Human beings move, speak, and respond to stimuli. Dead bodies do not. However, as will be demonstrated, the matter of determining death is extraordinarily complex, having medical, legal, philosophical, moral, religious, and economic considerations. For example, knowing that a person has died permits the termination of treatment, the performance of postmortem examination (if necessary), the removal of organs for transplantation when designated, the initiation of paperwork to proceed with the transfer of property, and the initiation of sociocultural and religious ceremony.

Common law defined death as the moment when life ceased. Physicians considered the person to have died when the vital functions of blood circulation and respiration were no longer in evidence. For hundreds of years a simple medical judgment was able to determine the fact of death. The judgment was rendered on the basis of irreversible cessation of spontaneous respiration and heartbeat. The criteria were easily understood, the examination was performed expeditiously, and the judgment was seldom questioned. Diagnosis was determined by palpation of the pulse, and auscultation of the heartbeat and observation of breathing, fixed dilation of the pupils, and discoloration of the skin (cyanosis).

Recent advances in two areas of medical care have been largely responsible for the controversy surrounding the determination of death. The first of these is the ability to maintain artificially the vital body functions of respiration and circulation. Medical technology has made it possible to nourish the body with oxygenated blood indefinitely. Cells, organs, and body systems can be kept alive for years even though

---

*From Mojock, Charles R.: A course in death education as a factor in influencing attitudes toward death of juniors enrolled in a parochial high school, Pub. No. ERIC #160593, Washington, D.C., 1979, Resources In Education.

the heart and central nervous system have suffered irreversible and irreparable damage.

The second medical advance is the ability to transplant organs from one person to another. Although the organism has died, the organs themselves remain alive. Obviously, there is only a short period of time between the cessation of blood supply and the death of an organ that depends on circulation. The need for functioning organs from a lifeless body has promoted a serious concern as to whether some physicians may pronounce a person dead prematurely to use the organs for transplantation. These two factors, artificial circulation and transplantation, have clouded the formerly acceptable criteria used by physicians to determine death.

Attempts have been made to resolve the issue by being more precise. New terms were created to replace the traditional, but somewhat vague, concept of death. The current literature speaks of *clinical death, physiological death, biological death, spiritual death, mind death, cerebral death, brain death, somatic death, body death, heart death,* and *organismic death.* But these terms proved to be even more confusing. What was once a simple medical judgment has now become a controversial matter with profound medical-legal implications. So much turmoil has been created, in fact, that a number of states have passed legislative mandates that specify the criteria to be used by physicians to determine whether a person is dead or alive.

Of the new terms, one stands out as having fueled the controversy. The very mention of brain death evokes a strong reaction from doctors, lawyers, and legislators. Principally because of the publicity that arose from several cases in the mid-1970s, a few states legislated that brain death should be used as the legal test for death; some states specified *total brain death,* as endorsed by the American Bar Association; other states and organizations opted for the use of cerebral death (also known as *cortical death*). The rationale for using cerebral death is that death of the cerebrum means death of the "person." The cerebrum is the section of the brain that makes us human, since it houses our rational and moral thoughts, our sense of identity, and our memories. The importance of the distinction between cerebral death and total brain death has to do with the physician's decision to terminate treatment. For those who believe that personhood resides in the cerebral cortex, the destruction of this area means there is no longer a person to be kept alive. Even though other parts of the brain, and indeed, the organism itself, do not require a cerebrum to maintain the vital functions necessary to support cellular life, cerebral brain death allows the machinery that artificially circulates oxygenated blood to be turned off. Those who use total brain death as the criterion argue that as long as the organism remains alive, artificially or not, the very fact of cellular life prohibits a declaration of death. For them, a pronouncement of death can only be issued when the total organism has expired.

4

The central focus of the issue is quality of life. *Cellular death* refers to the cessation of simple life processes of cells, tissues, and organs; however, biological death is more difficult to determine, since it refers to the cessation of integrated life functions. In other words, while individual organs may remain alive, the sum function of these organs or systems does not result in an integrated whole that is capable of supporting life on its own. An illustration of this point, is a person who loses the use of a kidney (clinical death of the organ) but still enjoys a happy, normal life. Organismic function continues even though the kidney itself is dead. In this situation no one would argue that the person is less alive than another person who has two healthy kidneys. The issue, however, is whether there comes a point when cellular death is so tremendous, when capacity is replaced by incapacity, when life can only be supported with continuous medical intervention, that life of the organism is no longer worthwhile. Is there a point when cellular death becomes so pervasive that biological death should be allowed to occur by withholding the necessary medical techniques? For those who favor the criterion of total brain death, there is no such point. Those who use cerebral death as the criterion believe that the point is reached when the living organism is no longer a "person."

Another facet of the "determination of death" controversy is in relation to the question, "Is death a process or an event?" The legal profession and the courts usually need to know the exact moment of death. The instant of death can change the outcome of cases related to homicide, inheritance, the legal right to receive constitutional and civil benefits, and even the right to receive medical treatment. Physicians are extremely cautious about stating that death occurred at a precise moment in time. This is because each organ or system has a varying ability to survive without oxygen. The brain is the most vulnerable organ and normally cannot survive much longer than 4 minutes without oxygen. The heart may continue to survive for an additional 3 to 4 minutes. Ligaments may remain alive for hours after the heart has stopped beating and blood has ceased circulating throughout the body.

The physician recognizes that life is supported by the interdependent activities of the respiratory, circulatory, and central nervous systems. If any of these systems ceases to function, the destruction of the other two will shortly follow. With the technology of the heart/lung machine, however, it is possible to circulate artificially oxygenated blood. Without this machine, heartbeat and respiration would cease when the brain dies. With this machine, however, heartbeat and respiration are maintained by artificial means to keep the organs and even the organism alive. This situation renders invalid the traditional criteria of pulse, heartbeat, and respiration for determining death. In a substantial number of cases it also raises the haunting question of whether the person is alive or dead. If the organism is considered to be alive, how many systems must fail before it can be said, with certainty, that death has occurred? Does every cell in the body have to be void of life before death can be declared? If not, at what point does it become reasonable to certify that a person has died?

The establishment of a standardized set of criteria for determining death would seem to benefit all parties concerned. Without a standardized list of criteria, among other possible sources of confusion, a person could be declared dead in one hospital but alive in another. To date, the most widely accepted criteria for the determination of death were developed in 1968 by the Harvard Medical School's Ad Hoc Committee to Examine the Definition of Brain Death. The purpose of the committee was to define irreversible coma as a new criterion for death. The intention of the committee was not to replace existing criteria, but rather to deal with the confusion and controversy brought about by the ability to sustain life even though the brain was irreversibly dead. The committee identified four criteria[1]:

1. Unreceptivity and unresponsivity: A total unawareness of the patient to externally applied stimuli and inner need satisfies this criterion. Even the most painful stimuli evoke no response.
2. No movement or breathing: Observation by a physician for at least 1 hour satisfies the criterion of no muscular movement. If the patient has been on a respirator, the total absence of spontaneous breathing may be established by removing the respirator for 3 minutes and observing the patient.
3. No reflexes: This criterion is satisfied by no response to a direct source of bright light from pupils, which remain fixed and dilated; no swallowing, yawning, vocalization, or tendon reflexes; and no response to noxious stimulation.
4. Flat electroencephalogram: This provides confirmatory data.

Each of these tests must be repeated at least 24 hours later with no change. The diagnosis must be rendered by a physician, and the committee recommended that when all of the criteria have been met, the family of the patient, all colleagues who participated in major decisions, and all nurses involved should be informed. Death is then declared and the respirator turned off.

Four years later, in an effort to clarify the state of affairs, an interdisciplinary task force conducted an evaluation of the new criteria for determining death. The Institute of Society, Ethics, and Life Sciences was founded in 1969 to study the ethical impact of the biological revolution. The resulting report represents the unanimous agreement of a group composed of physicians, lawyers, social scientists, philosophers, biologists, theologians, and laymen who deliberated for 18 months. The task force of the institute indicated that the criteria to determine death should include the following[2]:

1. Results should be clear, distinct, and unambiguous. Tests of presence or absence of function are preferred to gradations of function.

2. Tests should be simple, easily performed, and interpretable by an ordinary physician or nurse. They should not require consultation with specialized practitioners.
3. The permanence and irreversibility of the absence of function should be evaluated.
4. The determination should not rely exclusively on a single criterion.
5. When artificial maintenance of vital functions has not been in use, the criteria should be compatible with the continued use of the traditional criteria. The revised criteria should be seen as providing an alternative means for recognizing death.
6. The criteria should determine the physician's actions; that is, all people who fulfill the criteria should be declared dead as soon as it is determined the criteria are fulfilled.
7. The criteria should be easily communicable both to laymen and to physicians. They should be acceptable to the medical profession; that is, a person determined to be dead in one location will not be considered alive in another.
8. The reasonableness and adequacy of the criteria should be vindicated by experience and by autopsy findings.

After developing these recommendations, the task force observed that the Harvard Committee Report satisfied the criteria. The task force further noted that the criteria of the Harvard Committee were meant to complement the traditional criteria of heartbeat and breathing, which are still useful in the majority of cases, and were intended to be used only for the small number of cases involving irreversible coma in which the traditional signs of death are no longer valid because of life-support equipment. The task force also believed that the criteria were reasonable and that postmortem examinations validated the fact of brain destruction. In conclusion, the task force found no medical, logical, or moral objection to the criteria prepared by the Harvard Committee but did take issue with some of the other proposals that place exclusive reliance on the electroencephalograph.

To date, statutes pertaining to brain death have been enacted in 18 states. In 1970, Kansas became the first state to enact legislation that established a legal test for the determination of death. In addition to Kansas, four other states (Maryland, Virginia, New Mexico, and Alaska) have laws that permit brain death to be used as an alternative to the traditional criteria of heartbeat and respiration. In other words, either standard may be used. Five states have chosen to make brain death a supplement to the traditional criteria. In Michigan, West Virginia, Louisiana, Iowa, and Montana, the traditional definition is used in the majority of cases, but the law permits another possibility in exceptional cases. Six states have substituted the criterion of brain death

7

for traditional criteria. These states followed the recommendation of the Law and Medicine Committee of the American Bar Association, which stated that for all legal purposes a human body with irreversible cessation of total brain function shall be declared dead. California, Georgia, Illinois, Oklahoma, Tennessee, and Idaho have statutes of this type. For the remaining 32 states the issue must be determined on a case by case basis.[3] The determination will vary depending on the doctor, the hospital and the particulars of the case itself.

The concept of death is similar to the concept of death education in that both are difficult to define. Death education has been a part of civilization for centuries. Rituals related to death were certainly passed from generation to generation. To be sure, philosophers and theologians such as Socrates and St. Thomas Aquinas wrote about death, and their writings were educational to those who read or heard their messages. But formal academic courses dealing with death are a recent development, having come into existence only since the 1960s.

It would be nice to be able to offer a definition of death education that is widely accepted among educators. However, death education has many different meanings that vary according to the source. It is probable that a universally accepted definition will never be created because death education does not belong exclusively to health educators, health practitioners, sociologists, funeral directors, phychologists, or the clergy. Courses in death education do not have a standardized body of knowledge or a common focus of content. The nature of death education is determined largely by who is offering the course, where it is being conducted, and who is the intended audience. A seminary student enrolling in a death education course will have a vastly different educational experience than an undergraduate sociology major. Likewise, a community-sponsored death education seminar will have little in common with a seminar intended for fourth-year medical students.

Death Education, has been written to serve two major audiences. We recognize that death is a subject that has gained tremendous public fascination. Therefore it can be used by the interested reader as a source for death-related topics. The second audience is the professionals, who not only want to learn about death but who also want to communicate their knowledge to others. Public school teachers, community educators, nurses, physicians, and academicians will find the book to be a useful textbook and an authortative reference for personal use.

The focus of this work is somewhat different from other books that have served as death education textbooks. Some manuscripts focus on the medical and legal issues that surround death. Much has been written about the psychosocial needs of the dying patient. Still other literature focuses on religious and cultural aspects of death. Typically, the person who wants to offer a course, workshop, or seminar on death has to rely on a combination of books and select particular chapters from each to fit the purpose of the course. This book has been written primarily to serve the needs of those who want to teach death education regardless of their professional background or the setting in which the educational experience takes place. In addition to content, it offers an organization of material that is suitable for the classroom study of death. The broad purposes of this textbook are (1) to inform the public and replace misinformation (myth) with accurate information (fact), (2) to help professionals fulfill their roles as compassionate caregivers, and (3) to serve death educators in their quest to stimulate, challenge, and inspire the students who seek an understanding of death.

WHY SHOULD DEATH EDUCATION BE TAUGHT?

We know that people of all age groups, including children, have both conscious and unconscious attitudes about death. Many experts believe the primary reason for offering contemporary courses in dying and death is to help people cope with their own mortailty. Superstitions and myths of the unknown contribute to fears and denial of death. By examining death, individuals often develop a greater understanding, appreciation, and reverence for life. When individuals are given the opportunity to examine factual information and to clarify personal values, it is probable that their anxiety will be reduced, which will enable them to pursue life with enthusiasm and confidence. Discussion of death can help to legitimize one's inner feelings toward death. It is hoped that through death education the denial of death can be replaced with a personal philosophy that accepts death as a fact of life. Death education helps to place the experience of dying within the natural realm of human experience as a necessary part of the human life cycle. This perception can give new meaning to life and may enhance precious human relationships.

Some people have expressed the thought that death education is morbid and frightful and that it should not be offered in public forum and certainly should not be made available to school-aged children. But why should information about death be different from information on any other topic? Our society as well as most civilizations believe that an informed, intelligent, and educated person can better decide how to live than a misinformed person. Knowledge applied to problem solving is both advantageous and healthful. Ignorance is rarely blissful and is the substance from which superstition is created. Hiding death in a shroud of mysticism will not change the inexorable fact that death is the end of the line for every living thing.

Many adults in our society have not fully accepted the fact that someday they will die. Their life-styles make this statement obvious. Contributing to the false sense of immortality is the fact that we learn about death and we develop beliefs and attitudes toward death whether or not we ever enroll in a course entitled "death education." We witness thousands of deaths each year on television and in movies. Some deaths are thrust on us with insensitivity for human empathy, some in a humorous vein, and still others in brutal detail. Death is part of our folklore, music, art, and even our fairy tales. The advertising industry exploits death by using it in subtle ways to subliminally influence our minds and our choice of products. Our everyday expressions such as, "These shoes are killing me," or, "You'll be the death of me yet," convey messages that carry a double meaning. It is appropriate to ask whether the outcome of these experiences is likely to help the individual develop a realistic concept of death. The challenge for death education is to present information, facilitate the examination of alternatives, and help promote a life-style conducive to health and happiness.

Our quality of life often depends on our ability to deal with reality. Effective coping strategies are essential to a productive way of life. To cope effectively, however, one must be informed. In our society an understanding of death poses a serious challenge when the very definition of the word has been disarranged by advances in medical technology. Scientific accomplishments that raise questions about the power of God versus the power of man have shaken religious dogma. Existential philosophies have impugned the traditional views of life, death, and the human experience. Reports of transcendence and near-death recollection have helped to pique human curiosity. In our culture we witness death on a daily baisis, but we receive conflicting messages about the meaning of death. Should we be insensitive to the death of another? Is death humorous? Is death brutal? Education has the potential to help the individual sort through all of the mixed messages and arrive at conclusions that make sense. For the individual, coping with reality may be more satisfying than coping with unexpressed anxiety and unknown fears about death.

At the turn of the twentieth century the prediction of death was rarely possible for any given person. Death occurred shortly after the symptoms of disease became apparent. This meant that people grieved the loss of a loved one only after the event of death. Today, people often know of their terminal condition months, even years, before the actual event. This results in what psychologists have called *anticipatory grief.* People look to others who are close to them for help. The clergy do not have to be the only source of spiritual support and counsel to the bereaved. Family and friends are capable of helping others who are going through the grieving process. In addition, the changing nature of death in modern America in which terminal diagnosis precedes death requires that grieving family and friends be able to provide sustenance throughout the dying process. Effective moral support is much more likely to occur, however, when the people involved have reflected on the meaning of death and have

10

come to grips with their own mortality. An examination of personal feelings about death, perhaps stimulated by a death education course, helps to make the discussion of death a more approachable topic.

In addition to the many psychosocial issues related to death, educational experiences may be justified on the basis of some rather practical concerns. For instance, the study of death has popularized a whole new vocabulary. Terminology such as bereavement and euthanasia is used in everyday conversation but may be used inappropriately. Many people in our country neglect to prepare a will, even though the legal and financial consequences in certain instances may be severe. Most people do not discuss funeral and burial practices, organ donation, and issues related to autopsy. This leaves the tremendous burden of decison making to the survivors. It is much more practical, and not the least bit morbid, to consider these issues prior to one's own death. Choosing the type of funeral one wants and preparing a will increases the probability that a person's final wishes will be known and honored.

Doctors, nurses, counselors, and the clergy have been given the descriptive title of caregivers. They provide professional services to others who must face death. Death education has obvious benefits for these professions. Being aware of one's own feelings toward death can help to diminish the fear, anxiety, aggression, and conflict described by Kubler-Ross.[4] Students who have completed course work in death education commonly report that they are better able to face death, that they are more comfortable talking about death, and that they are better able to communicate with dying patients and their families. Furthermore, students report that course work has enabled them to achieve a greater appreciation of life and human dignity. Death is considered less as a biological fact and more as a human experience. Presumably, these internalized changes that allow the student to view death in a human context will enhance the relationship between those offering support and those having to face death.

The first part of this chapter examines the concept of death and outlines the reasons for offering death education. Briefly, the reasons include the following:

1. Helping people to deal with their own mortality; to use effective problem-solving skills and coping strategies that are helpful in dealing with inner conflict and personal fear of death.
2. Helping people put into perspective the conflicting messages about death that are found in everyday life as part of our music, art, literature, and media.
3. Helping people to value life and encouraging them to adopt a life-style that promotes health and happiness.
4. Helping nonprofessional as well as professional caregivers feel comfortable about providing emotional support to the dying patient and the bereaved.

11

5. Helping laymen to understand terminology, issues, and trends related to death and dying.
6. Helping the public to take action in the preparation of a will and the initiation of open conversation about the choice of funeral ceremony, mode of body disposal, and medical treatment intended to prolong life.

Although a person may not benefit from a death education course in all of these ways, it seems reasonable to expect that every student will achieve some satisfaction from the study of death.

WHEN AND WHERE SHOULD DEATH EDUCATION BE TAUGHT?

The recent evolution of death education as a legitimate topic of scholarly study has created a rather large body of literature known as thanatology. These writings offer a multitude of issues, conceptualizations, and philosophical perspectives. Because of this, it is important for the death educator to adapt both content and methodology to the needs and interests of the student. Learning outcomes must be targeted for the audience. The challenge for death education, no less than for other topics of study, is to recognize the needs of the learner; to select the appropriate content, methodology, and resources; to apply known learning principles; and to evaluate the effectiveness of the effort.

Most of the early interest in thanatology evolved from the social sciences. Students preparing to work in the human service professions selected death education courses to strengthen professional preparation and individual competency. The focus of these courses was to provide information considered important for future job success. Syllabi reflected this professional orientation. While these courses may have been beneficial for social science majors, it would be wrong to assume that the content and methods are appropriate for other audiences.

More recently death education courses offered in a community setting for the general public have become popular. Typically a person who has superior knowledge about death, by virtue of training or experience, arranges a series of public lectures. The programs are sponsored by churches, community groups, hospitals, or local institutions of higher learning. Announcements are made through the media or may go directly to interested civic groups. People in attendance are usually a diverse population. Most are elderly or middle aged; many are professionals in search of new information; some have been sparked by a recent movie or television show; a few may have had to face death recently and are looking for helpful coping strategies. The important implication is that a skilled educator will have a much better chance of satisfying the variety of needs than will a person who is knowledgable about death but ignorant of effective educational techniques. Whether the instructor is a nurse or a nun, a physician or a philosopher, death education requires a nucleus of skills that are commonly found among professional educators. Successful programs rarely occur by chance. Knowledge of the subject is no substitute for good planning and effective teaching.

Dying and death education courses have begun to emerge in the curricula of both elementary and secondary public schools. Previously the only information students received occurred during "teachable moments." Today death education is planned in advance with specific learning outcomes stated in behavioral terms and with sufficient time allocated to achieve the objectives. The study of death has been formalized as part of science, social studies, English, and health education classes. Literature courses have begun to study death through books such as *The Death of Ivan Illych, Love Story, The Shadow Box,* and *The Garden is Doing Fine.* In elementary schools teachers are using *My Grandpa Died Today, Why Did He Die,* and *The Tenth Good Thing About Barney.* Public school teachers are generally competent when it comes to methodology. If there is a deficiency, it probably lies in the area of content. It is recommended that all teachers have completed at least one course in death education before they consider giving instruction to others.

Death education has become popular on the college campus. It is estimated that more than 1,000 courses are currently being offered at institutions of higher learning. Many students undoubtedly enroll for professional preparation, but thousands of students each year select dying and death education courses as an elective. Since most college programs permit only a few electives, it is noteworthy that students are able to recognize the personal value of the course experience and are willing to allocate their elective credits for the study of death. No less than in the community setting or the public school classroom, instructors at the college level need to be sensitive to educational planning as well as to content. The scientific study of death and publication of research findings in a professional journal cannot replace effective teaching technique. The college professor needs to blend educational expertise with content expertise.

WHO SHOULD TEACH DEATH EDUCATION?

Historically death educators have come from a variety of academic and professional backgrounds. The general public may actually believe that death education is taught by a certified death educator. Teachers are often described by the

13

content of their courses. Thus people have been called sex educators, alcohol educators, consumer educators, and so on, when their academic and professional preparation does not support such a title. Formal certification standards (credentials) do not exist for death education. As a result anyone wishing to teach death education can use the term *death educator* regardless of his or her professional competence. The Forum of Death Education and Counseling has been attempting to standardize criteria that would certify individuals who wish to teach death education. This type of certification process would help to improve the overall quality of instruction.

Death education has emerged from the scholarly activity of many academic disciplines. Since each discipline generally approaches the subject from a different point of reference, the standards for certification will come into conflict. If those with an education background were solely responsible for certification standards, it is probable that the criteria would reflect those skills commonly found among educators. Certification as a death educator would probably require courses in methods and materials, audiovisual aids, and educational psychology and a student practicum with a certified teacher. On the other hand, psychologists would see the value of courses related to counseling and would probably require a practicum under the supervision of an experienced therapist. Physicians would probably focus on courses dealing with the biology of death, pathology, and medical ethics. This dilemma makes it interesting to speculate about the ideal professional preparation for a death educator.

An examination of university catalogs demonstrates the difficulty in establishing standards for certification. Death education appears as a course in many departments; health education, nursing, and sociology departments all may offer death education. It is not uncommon to find that a college actually offers several courses about death with the courses being located in different departments. The issue of course prerequisites further compounds the problem since the nursing course may define a specific prerequisite while the health education course demands a different one. The end result is that a nursing major, for example, will enroll in the nursing course but not in the health education course. For the health education major the situation will be reversed. When these two individuals come together to consider a common set of criteria for certification, the collaborative effort will obviously require compromise.

HISTORICAL PERSPECTIVE

Many people would probably speculate that the impetus for dying and death education grew out of medical school curricula. Actually, since its inception as a recognized separate course in the college curriculum beginning in the early 1960s, death education has been an interdisciplinary evolution. Most experts believe that the momentum for course development was the 1959 publication of *Meanings of Death* by Herman Feifel. This book legitimized the academic study of death. As researchers began to study death, and as their findings began to appear in the professional and popular literature, scientific knowledge was translated into commonly understood terms and gradually began to attract the attention of the general public.

It is widely believed that the first formal university course was offered at the University of Minnesota in 1963 by Robert Fulton. Between 1963 and 1970 expansion was slow and only a few courses existed nationwide. Most were not affiliated with medical schools, but instead the courses were part of the curriculum for the professional preparation of sociologists and psychologists.

Several factors are responsible for the tremendous surge of death education courses that began to appear during the decade of the 1970s. In 1966 the publication *Omega: The Journal of Death and Dying,* edited by Robert Kastenbaum, first appeared. This publication provided a vehicle for social scholars to publish their research findings. In 1969 Kastenbaum also established the Center for Psychological Studies of Dying and Lethal Behavior at Wayne State University. In the same year Robert Fulton organized the Center for Death Education and Bereavement at the University of Minnesota. Also in 1969 Elisabeth Kubler-Ross published *On Death and Dying,* a work that has had tremendous popular appeal. Kubler-Ross offered a sensitive portrayal of the problems experienced by dying people and the means by which they cope with the diagnosis of terminal illness.

In 1970 *Psychology Today* published the results of a questionnaire entitled "You and Death." The reader response of 30,000 was the largest ever for a *Psychology Today* survey. In the same year, the first conference on death education was held at Hamline University. By 1973 there were an estimated 600 courses being offered by the university level and literally thousands of seminars were available in communities everywhere.[5] In 1976 Worden and Procter wrote a book entitled *PDA: Personal Death Awareness.* Its primary contribution was to help readers put life into perspective by encouraging them to consider death in personal terms. In 1977 an international quarterly entitled *Death Education* was begun. By the end of the decade death education had become an acceptable topic for discussion both inside and outside of the classroom.

Courtesy Guidance Associates, Mt. Kisco, N.Y.

SOCIOLOGICAL ORIENTATION

The sociological approach to death education examines the ways in which the American culture (or any other culture) deals with death, bereavement, grief, and mourning. As individuals our views are shaped by cultural and societal influences. For instance, a variety of authors have suggested that Americans live in a death-denying society. One manifestation of denial is the use of euphemistic phrases, such as "going to your great reward," "the eternal sleep," and "kicking the bucket," to refer to death. In addition to euphemisms the denial of death in American society takes other forms:

The shielding of children from the trauma of death

The funeral practice of making the dead look lifelike

The medical emphasis on prolonging the life span rather than improving the quality of life

The large percentage of people who never prepare a will

The belief in immortality through life after death

The isolation and rejection of the elderly because they remind us of our own mortality

A trend that has fostered the cultural denial of death in contemporary American society is the occurrence of death in the hospital rather than in the home. Perhaps this situation has given children an unrealistic concept of death. A century ago when infant mortality rates were higher and life expectancy was shorter, people were exposed to death earlier and more often throughout their life spans. In an era when extended families were the rule rather than the exception, children were more likely to observe the aging process and subsequent death. Children were participants in the emotional and ceremonial aspects related to death. Today many children are shielded from death. When grandparents become ill they are usually taken to institutions that prohibit visitation by children. In this situation the child is protected from the death experience. The denial of death serves as a means to avoid the painful perception of mortality. In practical terms, this denial of death appears to operate as an inhibiting factor to the development of a realistic concept of death.

An integral component of the sociological approach to death education is seen in the ways in which our society responds to the death of a friend or relative. The term used to describe the societal response to death is *mourning*. Mourning is the expression of grief and the sharing of emotions and ceremony within a cultural framework. Traditionally, mourning in the United States occurs as part of funeral and burial customs.

In 1963 Jessica Mitford[6] wrote a book entitled *The American Way of Death*. The book was an expose of the funeral industry. It alerted the public to the questionable and sometimes unethical business practices of some funeral directors. Mitford expressed the belief that the funeral industry was exploiting the American public by encouraging mourning practices that were unnecessary and excessively expensive. Funeral directors were marketing services and products to consumers who knew little about what was customary, reasonable, and required by law. Although some of the examples in *The American Way of Death* may have been overgeneralized, the text did pave the way for increased awareness in areas such as funeral consumerism, the preparation of wills, the existence of memorial services and prepaid funeral plans.

In 1976 Yaffa Draznin[7] wrote a book entitled *How to Prepare for Death: A Practical Guide*. This work was also consumer oriented with an emphasis on personal decision making and planning for the future. Draznin suggested that the bereaved may be less in need of clergy or counseling than in need of accountants, lawyers, and insurance experts. There are obviously social aspects related to death that go beyond the individual and family bereavement. Death is a consumer issue in terms of services rendered and the cost of those services. The state, the church, the legal system, and the insurance industry are all a part of death in America.

Richard Kalish[8] presented a concise overview of the meaning of death in American

17

society in his 1976 article entitled, "Death and Dying in a Social Context." Kalish offered three conceptualizations of death in America. First, death is an organizer of time. We tend to view life simplistically as conception, birth and life, and finally death. We organize our lives using death as the marker against which all other events are located. In this sense death helps us to recognize that all possessions and experiences are temporary. The finality of death helps to determine the ways in which we use our time. Acceptance of the fact that death will come eventually to each of us may help the individual to establish priorities for living. The second conceptualization offered by Kalish is that death is a form of loss. Throughout life we are confronted with losses related to the aging process, such as the loss of family and friends, the loss of social roles and status, the loss of health, and the loss of independence, but death is the ultimate loss. A third concept of death in America as identified by Kalish indicates that death is seen as punishment for our sins. A large proportion of people in our society maintain the belief that human behavior is either rewarded or punished after life has ended.

Sociologists have researched and written about many topics related to death. The following list of topics will demonstrate the recent concerns of scholars in the field. The listing also serves as an excellent inventory of topics that are suitable for term papers, independent study, or interest reading:

Problems associated with defining death
Historical aspects of death, illness, and the church
Role analysis defined within various cultures
Terminology shifts
Residence within nursing homes, hospitals, hospices
Voodoo death and witchcraft
Social networks
Western and Eastern philosophical tradition
The concept of wrongness
Social fictions and taboos surrounding death
The social effect of medical technology on death
Political, social, and economic consequences of death
Moral theories
Violence, murder, suicide, abortion, and euthanasia
American funeral and mortuary products
Folk balladry and death themes
Symbology of death
Revival movements
Organ transplantation

Cryonics
Attitudes toward capital punishment
The right to die

PSYCHOLOGICAL ORIENTATION

The focal point of the psychological study of death is an attempt to understand the dying person and those who are bereaved. The necessity to understand the psychological aspects of death was made vivid by Kubler-Ross in her book *On Death and Dying*. Her research indicated that terminally ill patients progress through five psychological stages: denial and isolation, anger, bargaining, depression, and acceptance.[4] Although her findings have been criticized because the research design lacked scientific control, her work prompted a deluge of other studies. Chapter 4 provides a more thorough discussion of Kubler-Ross and her research with dying patients.

Hutschnecker[9] found that dying patients seem to remain true to their basic personality even when faced with death. The term *personality* refers to the individual's habitual behavior pattern and total response to the environment. He also found that when people initially learn they have a terminal illness, they may develop a pessimistic outlook of failure and unfulfillment. As they progress toward death, however, many of these patients develop a positive acceptance of the end of life. This research supports the findings of Kubler-Ross that acceptance does occur, but it does not support the finding that people progress sequentially through four stages on the way to acceptance.

Austin Kutscher[10] noted that life is full of major and minor preparations for death even though few people recognize these preparations. The experience of superficial losses can help the individual to develop effective coping strategies when confronted with loss or failure. The availability of the coping strategies that are used to deal with losses of lesser significance should not be underestimated. More important losses such as divorce, being fired from a job, and loss of social status can also help the individual to prepare for death. Each of these losses can be accompanied by grief that may produce the same psychological and physiological responses brought about by the death of a friend or relative.

Other cognate areas that are usually included under the broad category of the psychology of death are the terms *bereavement* and *grief.* Bereavement is an objective and a social fact that occurs as a result of a death or other personal loss. Grief is a response to bereavement. Lindemann[11] described the characteristic grief syndrome as somatic distress, a feeling of tightness in the throat, choking with shortness of breath, an

19

empty feeling in the stomach, loss of muscular power, and intense distress manifested by tension or pain. Perhaps the most striking characteristics of grief are weeping, a tendency toward sighing respiration, complaints about lack of strength and energy, and digestive disturbances. In addition the person may be restless and unable to initiate meaningful activity. The grief response can be so overwhelming that biological changes cause permanent harm. Those who wish to comfort grief-stricken individuals need to understand the seriousness of this psychological and physiological reaction to bereavement.

The psychological approach to death uses observation to gain information. Observational studies are appropriate within the context of psychological and sociological research. This type of research can take many forms. Participant observers may keep diaries or otherwise record the events of daily life. Psychologists may examine thoughts as they are expressed through art forms. Philosophical writings can be useful when thoughts about the meaning of life and death are being interpreted. While the study of the psychology of death should concentrate on primary source information, it is appropriate to draw auxiliary information from other observational sources.

A search through various indexes and professional journals indicates that current research in the field of psychology can be divided into four basic concerns. The first of these is fear and anxiety toward death. Studies have been conducted to determine anxiety among the following:

Dying patients

Counselors, nurses, university students

Police officers, military officers, and their spouses

Elderly individuals

Suicide attemptors

Additional studies about fear and anxiety have analyzed the relationship between the following:

Anxiety and ordinal position

Anxiety and self esteem

Fear of death and belief in afterlife

Fear of death and personality correlates

Fear of death and fantasy correlates

Fear of death and church membership

The second category of research deals with coping and adjustment. Psychologists study the following questions:

What effect do family support systems have on coping and adjustment?

What is the nature of conjugal bereavement?

What are the psychological responses of family members to suicide?

Are there differences in the way men and women cope with death?

What kind of emotional attachments remain to the dead spouse, parent, or friend?

Are there typologies of bereavement?

How do urban people or rural people cope with death?

How do doctors, nurses, and counselors cope with terminally ill patients?

How do people adapt to cancer and the threat of death?

What kind of dreams do terminally ill patients experience?

For the psychological researchers, the third area of study is concerned with counselor intervention. The following questions deal with this category:

What are the effects of peer counseling?

What are the effects of death education on emotional stability?

What are the clinical implications of spiritual values held by the patient?

What are the clinical implications of the "dying role" among patients?

What is the effect of using the cancer patient as a counselor?

How should death be reported to family members?

What is the effect of hyposensitization of death among adolescents?

How do stress management techniques affect cancer patients?

The fourth area of study among psychologists represents an attempt to understand the ideations people have about death. Research has attempted to understand viewpoints about death based on the following:

Age

Locus of control

Educational level

Socioeconomic status

Occupation

Interaction with the elderly

Health status

Religious affiliation

Near-death experiences

Altered states of consciousness

MEDICAL-LEGAL ORIENTATION

The medical-legal approach to death education addresses three major areas of concern. First, it emphasizes the need to clarify the terminology related to the definition of death. Historically, death referred to the cessation of respiration and heartbeat that deprived the brain of blood circulation and oxygen. When this definition was used, it was fairly simple to decide whether a person was alive or dead even though the brain itself continued to live for a short time after breathing and heartbeat ceased.

The concept of brain death has become a recent and controversial alternative to the traditional definition of death. The concept is recent because the technology that allows heart and lung function to be maintained through artificial means is a new scientific development. The concept is controversial because artificial heartbeat and respiration can supply the brain with oxygen indefinitely. Questions pertaining to humanity itself arise from the issue. However, the most pressing question at this time is whether meaningful existence can be defined within the medical-legal context.

The second concern of the medical-legal approach focuses on the issue of euthanasia. Although the term has been used synonymously with mercy killing, it actually means *good death,* or a painless, happy, easy death. Euthanasia has been categorized as direct and indirect. Direct (active) euthanasia refers to the administration of a fatal dose of a drug or the use of other means to deliberately terminate a suffering person's life. This form of euthanasia is not legal in any civilized nation. Indirect (passive) euthanasia is a process in which specific medical procedures are withheld from a terminally ill person. Indirect euthanasia is practiced by a substantial number of physicians.

Draznin[7] provides an extensive description of the third concern, which is the combination of legal and financial concerns brought about by death. Although a large percentage of people agree that steps should be taken to plan for their own death, only about one in four complete such plans. There is a need to educate people to prepare for death because if they do not make plans, their suvivors must make arrangements on behalf of the deceased. This can be a traumatic, costly, and frightening event for the survivors. Death education should help people to prepare for their own deaths, to appreciate the necessary decisions when death is imminent, and to help family members cope with death. Considerations include a variety of financial, legal, and practical concerns such as body disposal, funeral cemetery arrangements, and the disposal of worldly possessions.

The medical and legal professions have responsibilities in death that extend beyond the definition and preservation of life. Current research interests within the medical-legal professions include the following:

Physician responsibilities to family members after the death of a patient

How to communicate with the dying patient

Preventive care for the terminally ill

Giving-up syndrome as it facilitates premature death among terminally ill patients

Physiological impact of grief

Organ procurement

The doctor as a grief counselor

The cost and quality of dying at home versus dying in a hospital

Biorhythmic cycles of death

Informed consent of dying patients

Completion of death certificates

Near-death experiences

HEALTH EDUCATION ORIENTATION

The goal of health education is to help people enjoy life by encouraging them to adopt a life-style that promotes good health. The educational effort is intended to bridge the gap between scientific knowledge and personal acceptance of the information. Therefore health education must be relevant to the learner. Health education also helps people to search for alternatives when decisions related to health are made. The process of the educational experience is as important as the factual information being presented. Health is the goal and education is the process.

In the area of death there is much information that is not currently being received by the general public. Obviously the content is relevant for every human being. Each death-related issue offers a variety of alternatives that the general public should consider since the outcome of the decision can have an impact on physical and mental health. Decisions related to death have legal, economic, social, and psychological implications. For this reason people should have the benefit of factual information and should understand the alternatives available to them. The health education approach, then, is to gather information about the issue, to demonstrate the relevancy of the content, to select learning strategies that facilitate examination of personal values, and to encourage individual choices that improve health and quality of life.

GOALS OF DEATH EDUCATION

Knott[12] believed the basic goals of death education are formed by a triad of overlapping objectives. The first of these is information sharing, which includes the dissemination of relevant concepts related to thanatology. The second objective deals with values clarification, which involves activities what enable individuals to consider a variety of alternatives and then to incorporate their choices into healthful behavior. The third objective relates to coping behaviors. Problem-solving skills are valuable for

23

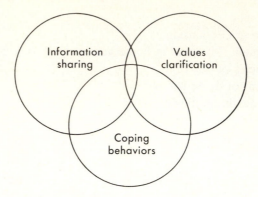

Figure 1. Knott's goals of death education.

self-reliance and for helping others to make appropriate adjustments. A conceptuali-zation of these overlapping objectives is presented in Figure 1.

With this triad, Knott provided a concise picture of the basic goals of death education. Knott's triad emphasized the notion that knowledge alone is insufficient to bring about positive behavior changes. For death education to be effective, instruction related to attitude formation and coping behaviors is necessary, For example, most adults are fully aware of the need to write a will, but a large number of people in the United States die without writing this document. The simple knowledge that writing a will may save their relatives from needless financial, legal, and emotional problems is enough to motivate some people to take action. However, others may need to be motivated by a values clarification process, in which alternatives and trade-offs of writing a will are identified. If the person decides that he or she values a reduction of financial, legal, and emotional problems that may surround the death of a person, then drawing up a will would be a logical course of action. In some cases, these two approaches may still not be sufficient to bring out the desired behavior, that is, writing a will. The person may need information related to coping behaviors. In addition to knowledge and values, there is often a need to outline procedures for drawing up a will, the nature of information to be included in a will, and how and when to contact a lawyer if legal assistance is necessary.

While Knott provided a theoretical framework for the goals of death education, Gordon and Klass[13] provided four practical goals for death education:

To inform students of facts not currently widespread in the culture

To help students deal effectively with the idea of personal death and the death of significant others

To help the students become informed consumers of medical and funeral services

One of the goals of death education is to help students become
informed consumers in funeral services.

Courtesy Guidance Associates, Mt. Kisco, N.Y.

To help the students consider socioethical issues related to death and to define
  value judgments that these issues raise

The person teaching death education should possess certain competencies and
personal qualities whether the programming is intended for children, adults, or the
elderly. Leviton[14] identified five criteria that extend beyond the minimum skills
required of a licensed teacher:

1. The teacher must have come to terms with his or her own feelings about death.
2. The teacher needs to know the content and process of death education.
3. The teacher needs to be able to communicate easily and naturally.
4. The teacher needs to be familiar with the sequences of developmental events of
   life and be sympathetic to the problems associated with these events.
5. The teacher needs to be aware of social changes and their implication for
   shaping our cultural attitudes, practices, laws, and institutions.

Another seven competencies were more recently identified by Leviton[15]:

1. The teacher must be able to communicate with students, parents, and resource persons in managing grief and bereavement and in handling other sensitive issues.
2. The teacher should be sophisticated about counseling and crisis intervention techniques.
3. Teachers need to know about the availability of pertinent resources including literature, audiovisual, and professional associations.
4. The teacher needs to be able to integrate community resources into the instructional/counseling process.
5. The teacher needs to be committed to interdisciplinary involvement and to problem solving.
6. The teacher should be able to assess student progress as it relates to predetermined course objectives.
7. The teacher should possess a spirit of scientific inquiry to keep abreast of current research and contribute to the knowledge base through research.

Grollman[16] identified five principles for teaching death education to children. Not only are these suggestions useful for professional educators but they can serve as a good point of reference for parents who want to discuss death with children.

1. Questions should be answered truthfully and children should not be overprotected. It is appropriate to assume that the child will be able to deal with the truth. Accurate information provides a base for building sophisticated concepts. False information, on the other hand, leads to misconceptions that eventually need to be changed. A few examples illustrate how misinformation presented to children can develop into a problem:
   A. "God took Grandma because he loves her." This implies that God must not love the rest of us, for if God loved us, we too would not be alive.
   B. "God took your sister because she was good." This implies that the person asking the question must be bad, or it could be interpreted that if you don't want to die you must avoid good behavior.
   C. "Joe went on a long trip." This implies that dying is a voluntary event and the coming back to life must also be possible. Or knowing that Joe will never return, the youngster may be afraid to take a trip.
2. One needs to be certain the question is understood. Sometimes an adult's interpretation of a question assigns greater meaning to the question than was intended by the child. It is also possible that the question is really a way to approach a problem. The function may be a way of saying that an unresolved need within the child should be discussed. For example, if the child asks, "What

will happen if Mommy dies?" the question may not seek information about afterlife, but rather, who will care for the child should Mother die. The motivation may be a serious concern about security.

3. It is better to begin explanations with basic information and progress toward more complex concepts. Confusing explanations can be harmful. Once formed, misconceptions can be difficult to correct.

4. Children should be encouraged to feel free to communicate their questions, observations, and concerns. They should be allowed to experience the human response to death, which we know as grief. Overprotection may stifle the normal emotions that surround personal loss. For example, if a child's pet dies, some parents immediately purchase another pet to help the child forget about the loss. In this situation the child is not permitted to resolve his or her emotions. It also creates the impression that loss can be easily replaced.

5. When discussing issues of a religious or philosophical nature, one should be sure to mention that other points of view exist. An illustration of this point is the child who becomes confused after he or she discusses heaven in detail and then learns from others that they do not believe in heaven.

Research in death education tends to focus on the following:

Evaluating the effectiveness of educational strategies

The impact of death education offered to specific target groups

The influence of the teacher on student knowledge, attitudes and behavior

Common misconceptions about death and dying

Readiness of children to study death and dying

Professional competencies of the death educator

Designing learning units for death education

SUMMARY

The first part of the chapter conceptualized death and offered a rationale for instruction about death. The second part of the chapter presented information about when and where death education is being offered, the people who are actually teaching death education, the development of thanatology, and the orientation of death education by behavioral scientists, the medical and legal professions, and health educators.

It would appear that the study of death is not only fashionable but necessary. Even though a variety of perspectives exist with regard to the character of death education, the benefits of study outweigh the differences of opinion about what is necessary for the effective study of death. It is probable that agreement cannot be achieved among disciplines about content, methods of instruction, or evaluation of teaching effectiveness. Of greater importance, though, is the realization that Americans have begun to study death and to convey the information to the general public as a means of enabling people to make healthful decisions.

Regardless of the educational setting or the target audience, the people offering instruction in death education need to possess certain knowledge, skills, and personal qualities. As a prerequisite they need to have established for themselves a measure of comfort with the subject matter. They must also be willing to answer questions truthfully, to utilize community resources, to be sensitive to alternative philosophies, and to be helpful in counseling others who are trying to cope with unresolved conflict.

REFERENCES

1. Harvard Medical Schools's Ad Hoc Committee to Examine the Definition of Brain Death: A definition of irreversible coma, Journal of the American Medical Association **205:**337-340, 1968.
2. Institute of Society, Ethics and the Life Sciences (Task Force on Death and Dying), Journal of the American Medical Association, **221:**48-53, 1972.
3. Isaacs, Leonard: Death, where is thy distinguishing? Hastings Center Report, **8**(1): 5-8, 1978.
4. Kubler-Ross, Elisabeth: On death and dying, New York, 1973, Macmillan Publishing Co., Inc.
5. Pine, Vanderlyn: A socio-historical portrait of death education, Death Education, **1:**57-84, 1977.
6. Mitford, Jessica: The American way of death, New York, 1963, Simon & Schuster, Inc.
7. Draznin, Yaffa: How to prepare for death: a practical guide, New York, 1976, Hawthorn Books, Inc.
8. Kalish, Richard: Death and dying in a social context. In Binstock, R., and Shanas, E., editors; Handbook of aging in the social sciences, New York, 1976, Van Nostrand Reinhold Co.
9. Hutschnecker, A.: Personality factors in the dying patient. In Feifel, H., editor: The meaning of death, New York, 1959, McGraw-Hill Book Co.
10. Kutscher, Austin: Anticipatory grief, death and bereavement: A continuum. In Wychograd, E., editor: The phenomena of death: faces of mortality, New York, 1973, Harper & Row, Publishers, Inc.
11. Lindemann, E.: The symptomology and management of acute grief, American Journal of Psychiatry **101:**141-148, 1944.
12. Knott, J.E.: Death education for all. In Wass, H., editor: Dying: facing the facts, New York, McGraw-Hill Book Co., pp. 389-391.
13. Gordon, A.D., and Klass, D.: The need to know: how to teach children about death, Englewood Cliffs, N.J., 1979, Prentice-Hall, Inc.
14. Leviton, Daniel: The scope of death education, Death Education, **1:**41-56, Spring, 1977.
15. Leviton, Daniel: Death education. In Feifel, H., editor: New meanings of death, New York, 1977, McGraw-Hill Book Co., pp. 253-272.
16. Grollman, Earl: Explaining death to children The Journal of School Health **47:**336, June 1977.

Courtesy Guidance Associates, Mt. Kisco, N.Y.

CHAPTER TWO

Death education across the life span

We are not free to choose whether anyone will learn about death, though we have some choice about how they will learn.*

MICHAEL SIMPSON

It has often been stated that America is a death-denying society. Americans certainly spend a greater proportion of time thinking about life than death. In a nation that has the potential to offer an abundance of life-styles as well as longevity of life, it is reasonable to expect that personal thoughts about death will be infrequent. Unlike many societies in the world and quite dissimilar from American life in the eighteenth and nineteenth centuries, American society reserves the event of death for those who have experienced a full life of many years. Our standard of living and the availability of excellent health care services have encouraged us to think of death as a distant event. The rejection of death is not a cultural belief in immortality, but rather it is a personal expectation for a long life.

A child born in this country in the year 1900 had a life expectancy of 50 years. Today the life expectancy at birth is around 73 years. A couple giving birth to a child just 30 years ago had twice the risk that the infant would die during the first year of life than a couple whose child is born today. These trends illustrate the point that death in the United States occurs to adults and predominantly to those adults beyond the fifth decade of life. At the turn of the century one of every five deaths was caused by infection and parasitic disease such as tuberculosis, pneumonia, and dysentery. Children were victims as often as adults. However, since 1950 cardiovascular disease and cancer have been the leading causes of death. These diseases are usually the result of personal life-style and exposure to risk factors over many years. Since these two diseases account for more than half of all deaths in this country each year, we have learned to associate death and dying with old age.

Another factor that has permitted death to be concealed from many Americans is the institutionalization of people who are seriously ill. Death used to be an event in which the dying person was surrounded by family members and close friends in the

---

*From Simpson, Michael: Death education: where is thy sting? Death Education 3:165, 1979.

home. Now death has become an event that takes place in a hospital or nursing home with care being provided by professionals. Furthermore, a century ago the extended family was typical. Aunts, uncles, cousins, and grandparents all resided in close proximity. When families worked, played, and celebrated together, children established meaningful relationships with people of all ages. Children could observe the aging process and begin to form impressions early in life about the human life cycle. When death occurred, it was an event that had deep personal impact on every member of the extended family. Children were forced to cope with death early and often, thus enabling them to form realistic concepts about the meaning of death. It was not feasible for adults to tell children that "Grandpa went on a long trip," or that "Aunt Becky went to sleep." It was also considered inappropriate to protect children from bereavement and to exclude them from the ritual of mourning or the ceremony of body disposal.

The situation today is markedly different. As this country shifted from a rural agrarian society to an urban industrialized society, the experiences related to death also changed. For instance, it is probable today that when death occurs in a family, at least one generation separates the deceased and the younger family members. Since most people today live in a nuclear family structure, grandparents, aunts, and uncles may be distant acquaintances rather than persons of intimate importance. Death takes place in a distant hospital, and the event itself may be the first time the child has had to face the prospect of never again being able to see a grandparent. Because childhood is viewed as a time of innocence and happiness, we have adopted the attitude that children should not be forced to cope with the loss of another human being. We attempt to reserve the emotion of grief for those who are strong enough (or old enough) to deal with it in an effective way. Therefore children are often excluded from the emotional aspects of death and may not be permitted to attend the ritual ceremony, which is intended to help the grieving family cope with severe loss. Accordingly, children may not have the ability to comprehend death or to understand their own feelings. Childhood inexperience with death helps to explain why adults often deny death and find it difficult to resolve the emotional impact created by the death of another.

THE CHILD'S CONCEPT OF DEATH

Numerous authors have provided a description of the child's concept of death, but few research studies have actually been conducted. In this section of the chapter some research findings will be discussed to provide a framework for studying the child's concept of death. Current literature seems to favor the viewpoint that children progress through stages of maturity that place limitations on their ability to comprehend the meaning of death. As if moving along a continuum, children gradually replace fantasy-oriented concepts with increasingly more sophisticated and abstract understanding. The work of Maria Nagy,[1] published in 1948, is often considered a pioneering effort to study this progression. Nagy's findings were based on a study of 378 Hungarian children in the years immediately following World War II. She concluded that children tend to evolve through three stages of understanding, and each stage more closely approximates the adult concept of death.

Stage one (ages 3 to 5 years)

At 3 to 5 years, children see death as a departure or sleeplike state that is reversible. They are unable to comprehend the finality of death. Instead they view the dead person as breathing, thinking, and feeling. Death is a temporary form of sleep and the deceased will eventually return to life. For the young child who has yet to develop a concrete perception of time, "forever" is an impossible concept to grasp.

Stage two (ages 5 to 9 years)

Nagy found the 5- to 9-year-old children were able to understand the finality of death. However, they had a tendency to personify death in the form of the "big bad wolf," the "bogeyman," a skeleton, or an angel. They believe death is caused by an external force that is determined by the imagination. Because death is brought about by some external force, it can be avoided by those who are clever and those who are able to outsmart the "death man." Children often play games in which they are being killed or in which they act out scenes in which they pretend to confront the image of death.

Stage three (ages 9 years and above)

Nagy found that once children reach the age of 9 or 10 years they begin to see death as a part of the life cycle; that is, all living things are created, grow old, and die. At this age children have accepted the fact that death can occur to anyone at any time throughout the life-span. They begin to realize that death is inescapable and that someday they too will cease to be alive. Beliefs about magical power to control death have been replaced. Most developmentalists agree with Nagy that children at this age have the ability to think abstractly and are able to grasp the meaning of words such as life, forever, and death.

A comparison of Nagy's work to more current studies demonstrates that even though her conclusions were derived more than 40 years ago in a different country, there is still much similarity in her description and present descriptions of how children at various ages view death. The recent research of Menig-Peterson and McCabe is a good example.[2] Their study analyzed the narratives of children between the ages of 3½ and 9½ years. They observed that discussion of death was practically nonexistent for children below the age of 6 years but was a popular topic for children above this age. Most of the narratives focused on the death of pets, which is apparently an experience fairly common among young children. Interestingly, the narratives did not convey the impression that death caused an affective response for children between the ages of 6 and 8 years. Death was described as physical absence. The 8- and 9-year-old children, however, explicitly stated feelings about the death of their animals. Menig-Peterson and McCabe concluded that the dramatic shifts in dialogue were the result of developmental changes rather than experience with death.

Anthony[3] inserted death items on an intelligence test that was intended to correlate the child's age with the child's concept of death. Anthony then developed a continuum of the maturational understanding of death as follows:

1. Apparent ignorance of the word *dead*.
2. Interest in the word or fact of death combined with limited or erroneous concepts.
3. No evidence of noncomprehension of the meaning of the word *dead*, but definition of the word is given by reference to (1) associated phenomena not biologically or logically essential, or (2) human death.
4. Essentially correct definition, but limited reference.
5. Generally logical or biological definition or description.

Anthony believed that our vocabulary and the unique ways we refer to words such as dead, die, and kill may influence the child's concept of death. The child's mind is both curious and imaginative. When children hear statements such as "kill the umpire," "I'm dead tired," "John is dead wrong," "Beth is dying to be asked out," "Joe is a dead head," or "dead end street," their imagination may generate a host of misconceptions. This is further complicated by the many euphemisms we have chosen to use instead of saying the word *dead*. False impressions may be created by the use of phrases such as "passed on," "went to his great reward," "expired," "went to sleep," or "joined the maker." From her research, Anthony found that no child under the mental age of 8 years was classified into category 4 or 5 (above). In other words, children below this mental age were not able to formulate a correct or logical concept of death. Similarly, no child above the mental age of 8 years was classified into category 1 or 2. Therefore Anthony concluded that the development of a correct and logical concept of death is dependent on the mental age of the child.

Bluebond-Langner[4] studied leukemic children and found them to be capable of acquiring a vast amount of information based on their experiences with the health care delivery system. Interactions with physicians and other patients facilitated an early understanding of death among children who were terminally ill. Bluebond-Langner found that 3- and 4-year-old children were as knowledgeable of death as typical 9- and 10-year-old children. They recognized that their illness was serious and began to understand the vocabulary related to therapy and side effects. Eventually they synthesized information and perceived that they were going to die. They knew that they would no longer be able to play with friends or watch television. Because they were able to conceptualize the finality of life, they did not want to waste time. Time itself took on a new meaning in which every minute was important. The terminally ill children avoided talking about their own future and what they wanted to be when they grew up. One child anticipated Christmas gifts in October for fear he would not be alive in December. Bluebond-Langner reached the conclusion that experiences of life among young children can promote a realistic, more adult view of death.

Childhood experiences that concern the death of another person can have profound, lifelong effects. Children may develop a fear of physicians, nurses, or hospitals. After experiencing the death of a sibling, the child may carry a lifelong burden of guilt thinking he or she was responsible for the death or believing he or she should have died instead. Self-esteem, confidence, and a willingness to seek adventure may be lacking in a person who lived through the death of a significant other at an early age. The effects may last well beyond the initial reaction, especially if the person has difficulty coping with the death. It is known, for instance, that during their childhood, adults with psychiatric problems often experienced the death of a parent. On this basis it would seem appropriate to encourage youngsters to face and resolve emotional conflict rather than to repress their feelings and suffer the consequences in adulthood.

THE CHILD'S REACTION TO DEATH

Children may react to the death of a close friend, relative, or pet in ways that are difficult for adults to understand. It is important for educators to be aware of how the child perceives death to help children cope more effectively with death. Like adults, children need to be able to understand the death of a person and to try to handle their emotional reactions. As an example, one obvious response to death is crying. This reaction is sometimes protected by adults because of the basic notion that childhood should be a carefree, happy time for the child and free of worry and strife. Since death is a traumatic experience, some parents would rather shield the child from it or at least protect the child from the hurt associated with grief. Therefore some parents mistakenly believe that if they can keep the child from crying in response to death, they are offering protection from the grief that surrounds death. Conversely, Grollman believes that:

Children should be allowed to express their grief. It is natural. . . . So often parents and teachers deliberately attempt to veer the conversation away from the deceased. They are apprehensive of the tears that might start to flow. They do not understand that expressing grief through crying is normal and helpful.[5]

Other childhood responses to death cited by Grollman (although adults may also respond in these same ways) include the following:

Denial. The lack of response by children may be an indication that they have found the death too traumatic to accept. Therefore the child secretly pretends that the person is still alive or is going to return in the near future. Parents and teachers may feel that the child is unaffected or unconcerned, but the child is actually trying to protect himself or herself from the death by denying that it ever happened.

Bodily distress. Some of the same physical responses found in the normal grieving

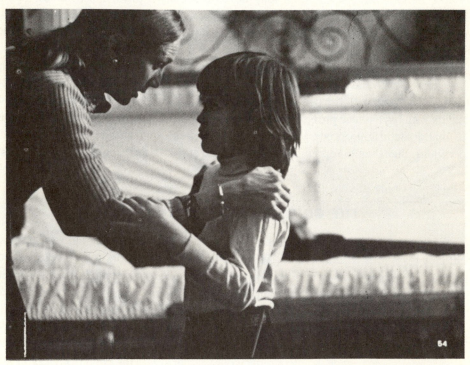

Children may react to death in ways difficult for adults to understand.

Courtesy Guidance Associates, Mt. Kisco, N.Y.

process of adults are found in children. The anxiety over the death of a friend or relative often expresses itself in the following physical and emotional symptoms: (1) a tightness in throat or difficulty in swallowing, (2) a difficulty in breathing, (3) a need to sigh, (4) a lack of appetite, (5) a weak or exhausted feeling, and (6) an inability to sleep.

Hostile reaction toward deceased. Children may believe that the deceased has deserted or abandoned them. They may express this anger by saying "How could Mommy leave me alone like this?" or "If Daddy really cared for me, he would not have left." These hostile reactions toward the deceased may be compounded by parents who tell children that the deceased went on a long trip. Going on such a trip implies that the person has gone voluntarily and can return at any time but has chosen instead to remain away.

Hostile reaction toward others. The child may perceive that someone else is responsible for the death. The child may believe that "The doctors didn't do all they could to make Grandma well" or "If mother would have taken better care of Grandma, she would not have died." Projecting these feelings of resentment and hostility on others may help to ease the child's feelings of guilt.

Replacement. The child may seek someone to take the place or at least assume the role of the deceased. The child may seek the affections of other adult friends or relatives as a substitute for a parent who has died. The child may also seek others to assume the roles of the deceased parent, such as playing ball, reading stories, and helping with homework.

Assumption of mannerisms of deceased. The child may attempt to imitate the characteristics of the deceased. The child may even try to assume some of the roles commonly performed by the deceased.

Idealization. In an attempt to eliminate unpleasant thoughts of the deceased, children may be obsessed with only the good qualities of the deceased. This idealization is often not an accurate characterization of the real-life behavior traits of the deceased.

Panic. Children may wonder who is going to take care of them now that Mommy or Daddy is gone. Children need to be assured that they are still loved and will be taken care of in the same fashion to which they have grown accustomed.

Guilt. Children often believe something they did or did not do may have caused the death because they have learned from past experience that bad things seem to happen when children are naughty. The mother who says, "Johnny, clean your room. . . . You're going to be the death of me" may cause the child to develop the notion that his or her behavior can have an influence on death.

LIFE-SPAN DEVELOPMENT

The life-span theory of human development is based on the notion that development occurs at all ages (infancy, childhood, adolescence, adulthood, and old age) with specific critical characteristics becoming present at each stage. In essence, the life-span view of human development suggests that behavior of the individual as well as differences between the individual and others are a function of the developmental history of the person. Therefore the ability of adults to cope with concerns related to death and dying is to a large extent dependent on the types of coping skills they have learned throughout the course of their lives.

The life-span human development orientation provides a unique method through which a teacher can integrate death concepts into the school curriculum. This orientation also provides other health professionals with a unique method for promoting lifelong competence in concerns related to death and dying. This model stresses the need for educators or counselors to help individuals confront and successfully deal with death and dying throughout all of the developmental stages rather than trying to develop new coping strategies in adulthood. Life-span development education, then, tries to promote emotional stability through effective coping strategies learned in an earlier developmental stage. Basically, this philosophy views development as an integrated, articulated series of stages. How well we learn to adapt to various death- and loss-related events early in our lives can influence our ability to make positive adaptations at a later date.

An appropriate view of life-span human development recognizes that growth and development of the individual is preceded by a crisis, stress encounter, or state of imbalance (also referred to as a life event), and without these crises or life events, development cannot occur. The goal of life-span development education or intervention is not to prevent crises, but to enhance the individual's ability to deal constructively with these life events. In other words, helping children deal with death and dying–related events can serve as a means to help them grow and develop into emotionally stable adults.

Implications for death education

Death education programs provide an ideal setting for intervention education related to death and dying concerns. Intervention education across the life span serves two purposes. First, preventive intervention aids in the development of positive health behaviors that can be sustained throughout the course of life. Second, by discussing the role and impact of life events (either actual or simulated), the educator can enhance a person's ability to cope with analogous problems in the future by maximizing the

The life-span theory is based on the notion that development occurs at all ages.

Courtesy Guidance Associates, Mt. Kisco, N.Y.

transfer value of the existing problem. Most educators would agree that it is preferable to help students develop positive coping behaviors early in life rather than to attempt subsequent behavior change. Therefore with respect to death education, it is important for the educational program to equip students with knowledge and coping skills they can use throughout their total life span.

For example, there are various life events occurring throughout the school-age years that can serve as a foundation for subsequent death-related events. The death of a pet can serve as a life event that helps prepare the child for the death of friends and relatives at a later time in life. From an educational standpoint, this would be an appropriate time to intervene and discuss the common reactions to death and the coping skills needed to deal with the death situation.

Table 2-1 provides a brief outline of some common life events related to death and dying and suggests appropriate intervention strategies.

Table 2-1: Childhood life events that can be useful in developing effective coping strategies for dealing with loss

Life event	Possible death education intervention strategy
Loss of baby teeth	This provides an excellent opportunity to discuss concepts of physiological change across the life span. This life event provides an opportunity to begin discussion that can help the child develop a life-cycle perspective of death and dying; that is, all living things are born, grow old, and die.
Loss of baby role when younger sibling is born	There are a variety of life events that help prepare us for death and the losses involved. This life event provides a setting to discuss the changes in roles that occur across the life span. The role change that Grandma experienced when Grandpa died is an analogous death-related situation.
Death of pet	The death of a pet is another life event that helps prepare the individual for death. The emotional response to the death of a pet can be discussed in the context of death occurring at various times throughout the life span. Again, this life event provides an opportunity to discuss the cycle of life for all living organisms.
Loss of childhood body at puberty	This life event provides an opportunity to discuss the notion that physiological and psychological changes occur throughout the life course and that these changes are part of the normal human life cycle.
Death of major public figure	Viewing the rituals following the death of a major public figure provides an excellent time for intervention and discussion about bereavement, grief, and mourning. Concepts related to loss and the response to loss can also be discussed.

Table 2-1: Childhood life events that can be useful in developing effective coping strategies for dealing with loss—cont'd

Life event	Possible death education intervention strategy
Birth of first child	As a life event, the birth of the first child often begins in motion a wide range of role and expectation changes. The parents begin to think in terms of providing for their future and the future of their children. This would be an appropriate time to intervene to discuss the need to plan for one's own death with actions such as writing a will, and providing appropriate insurance coverage.
Loss of job	Although not everyone loses a job of significance during his or her life course, this life event can provide an analogous death-related experience. The loss of role, purpose, and expectation may be analogous, although on a much smaller scale, to the loss that the terminally ill person experiences.
Death of close friend or relative	Although the frequency and timing of this life event varies greatly among individuals, it is another example of how life prepares us for our own death. Intervention at this point may provide an opportunity to discuss common reactions to the death of a close friend or relative.
Retirement	Retirement is often a time when there is a change or loss of certain roles and expectations. Similarly, when there is a death in the family, often the roles of the family members change. Also, the terminally ill person experiences changes in roles and expectations analogous to those of the retired person.

The death of a pet serves as a life event in which the educator can intervene to discuss concepts related to dying and death.

Illustration at top by Strix Pix. Illustration above, courtesy Guidance Associates, Mt. Kisco, N.Y.

THE ADOLESCENT'S CONCEPT OF AND REACTION TO DEATH

Statistical data indicate that adolescents themselves do not have a high risk of dying. The vast majority of adolescents will survive into adulthood. The primary threat to the life of an adolescent is automobile accidents rather than disease. By the time they have reached this stage of life, people have generally developed a realistic concept of death. From a life-span development perspective, adolescents have encountered a variety of life experiences that were useful in shaping their concept of death. Nevertheless most adolescents equate the aging process with the dying process. As they look around and observe life, adolescents learn that most people who die are older than adolescents. Because most of their life is ahead of them, adolescents do not fear death but see it as being able to steal away their future. They are not afraid of death per se, but they are afraid of not being able to achieve specific life goals that have been identified.

This transition from a child's limited or inappropriate understanding of death to a more mature and realistic understanding of death may challenge adolescents to seek ways to prove their immunity to death. Adolescents engage in a variety of dangerous or self-destructive types of behavior such as drug abuse, smoking, reckless driving, and

Table 2-2: Adolescent attitudes toward death

Attitude item	Agree		Uncertain		Disagree	
	No.	(%)	No.	(%)	No.	(%)
1. I believe in life after death.	73	(48)	37	(24)	42	(28)
2. I feel that death is the end, the final process of life.	52	(34)	37	(24)	63	(42)
3. I believe that death is sometimes a good thing for both society and individuals.	93	(61)	23	(16)	34	(23)
4. I feel that every person should have the freedom to die.	91	(60)	24	(16)	36	(24)
5. I feel that suicide is a crime.	50	(33)	22	(15)	80	(52)
6. I believe that every person has a right to die with dignity.	91	(60)	30	(20)	31	(20)
7. I seldom think about my own death.	62	(41)	24	(16)	66	(43)
8. When I think of my own death, I feel fearful.	35	(23)	20	(13)	97	(64)
9. I believe that I want to donate my body to science.	37	(24)	60	(40)	55	(36)

Modified from Perkes, A. C., and Schlidt, R.: Death Education 2:359, 1979.

hitchhiking. At this age adolescents tend to joke about death in a defiant way, as if to prove to themselves that death cannot happen to them.

The emotional responses to death that are common in adulthood are often seen in adolescents. The adolescent may display an intensely emotional response or a grief response that is bitter and prolonged. Or in an effort to avoid an outpouring of emotions that may appear childlike, adolescents may adopt a stoic, unemotional state to hide their inner feelings.

In 1979 Perkes and Schlidt[6] conducted one of the few studies that examined adolescent attitudes toward death. Table 2-2 provides a synopsis of their work. It is interesting to observe that a significant percentage of the adolescent study population were not fearful of their own death. For the death educator, this finding may serve as an indication that the adolescent is capable of logically conceptualizing principles covered in a death education experience.

THE YOUNG AND MIDDLE-AGED ADULT'S CONCEPT OF DEATH

Young adults begin to take on a somewhat more philosophical thinking about death. For them, the most distasteful aspect of death is the loss of fulfillment in life. Marriage, career, and children all lie just ahead. Thoughts of death bring about questions related to the meaning of life, the significance of humanity, and the purpose of their own life. While they understand that death is inevitable, young adults usually expect their own death to occur at the end of a full and productive life. If they were terminally ill, however, many young people would want to be told of their impending death to put their lives into perspective and to be able to achieve important goals that have yet to be attained.

One way to avoid thinking about death is to consider the philosophical alternative of immortality. Lifton[7] indicated that young adults have five modes of thinking about immortality. The first of these is attached to the birth of their own children, which results in the belief that their own lives will be extended through their offspring. A second concept of immortality could be described as biological. It is believed that spiritual life transcends physical presence on Earth. Increasingly, fewer people seem to be willing to accept this notion. The third mode of immortality is even more abstract. Some people view immortality as the memory of the individual that lies in the works left behind by the deceased. Art, music, literature, and other creative accomplishments illustrate this concept. Still other young people see immortality as nature itself. The very act of living means that one never fully dies but remains as part of the matter found on Earth. Finally, some people think of immortality as a transcendence beyond the ordinary boundaries of human experience. Conceptually, one transcends death by having experiences that enable the mind to escape from the body. The rapture of the experience is so ecstatic that life is not bound by normal physical constraints.

Middle-aged adults usually have a realistic concept of death. During their course of life, most of them have experienced the death of friends or relatives. Typically, there exists a host of unresolved goals. The prospect of death is acknowledged but is repressed in an attempt to focus on fulfillment of these goals. The graduation of children from high school or college, marriage of their children, grandchildren, occupational promotions, and retirement represent a series of goals that may occur in fairly brief chronological order. The attainment of each goal creates an enthusiasm for the next in succession. Even though many people die during their fourth and fifth decades of life, the majority of people who enter middle age will live to see the sixth decade of life and enter into "old age."

THE ELDERLY ADULT'S CONCEPT OF DEATH

Contrary to popular thinking, a person's awareness of death does not automatically increase with advancing age. Since most of us grow up associating old age and dying, it would be reasonable to conjecture that the older a person becomes, the more likely is his or her preoccupation with thoughts of death. As the decades of life pass it becomes increasingly clear that death is inescapable. This truth is made obvious by the fact that the longer a person lives, the more he or she has experienced the death of lifelong friends and acquaintances. Because separation and loss are powerful catalysts of human emotion it is natural to believe that death is an intimate companion of elderly adults.

It seems axiomatic that the longer a person lives, the less time that is available for future life. One would reasonably expect that at some point during the lifetime of an individual, a perceptual shift may occur. Individuals might begin to think of how many years they have lived rather than how many years remain to fulfill personal goals. However, this transition is not a function of chronological age. For some people, "hurrying to beat death" occurs early in life, whereas for others, the focus remains essentially optimistic regardless of age. For those in the former category, each birthday brings them one step closer to death, while for the latter, each birthday is a milestone of achievement. Across the life span, some people focus on a day-to-day existence while others see each day as fitting into part of the total life experience. To be sure, death anxiety is a debilitating affliction. The chronic fear of death inhibits productivity,

45

restricts personal freedom, and prohibits the true enjoyment of life. Erikson suggested that those who develop a sense of ego integrity will not fear death but will generally be satisfied with life. For these people, it is quality of life, not quantity, that serves as the measuring stick.

Elderly adults have as much diversity of perspective about death as the younger generations. Some are oriented to the past and to who they have been, while others continually focus on the future and who they are becoming. Swenson[8] found that 45% of the elderly population he studied were optimistic about life, 44% repressed thoughts of death by making statements such as "I feel fine, so there is no reason to be concerned about death," and only about 10% were actually fearful of dying. A host of psychosocial factors rather than chronological age accounts for these differences. For instance, it has been observed that people who engage in frequent religious activity, especially if it is a fundamentalist-type religion, tend to have a positive outlook. People in good health generally have a positive approach to living and dying. Another contributing factor seems to be the development of a crude estimate of how long one will live based on the age when one's parents died.[9] If they are younger than the age at which both parents died, individuals are less likely to have conscious thoughts of their own death. People who are older than the age when both of their parents died are very much aware of personal finitude. An even greater awareness exists when individuals have also outlived siblings and most of their friends. This association between age of parental death and reference for personal death is actually a stronger relationship than chronological age and attitude toward death. In other words, the individual who is 55 years old and outlived parents and siblings will have a different (and presumably more negative) outlook on life expectancy than an older person whose parents and siblings are still alive.

Wass and associates[10] studied specific demographic characteristics in relation to attitudes toward death. They found that nearly three times as many urban elderly adults viewed death as "the end," whereas, the vast majority of rural elderly residents indicated a strong belief in afterlife. Similarly, the rural group more often felt that all possible efforts should be made to keep a seriously ill person alive. The researchers also found that while 97% of the urban group had made a will, fewer than half of the rural group had taken this action. The large majority of the rural group preferred cremation. Other important differences in attitudes were found when the levels of income, levels of education, and households in which elderly adults lived with families or lived alone were compared. It was concluded that in regard to beliefs and attitudes about death, certain life events have a greater effect on elderly adults than the commonality of advancing age. Based on this finding it can also be concluded that topics related to death and dying may be discussed among the elderly without having to fear that the discussion will necessarily create discomfort or anxiety.

It should be obvious to the reader at this point that a discussion of death and dying does not have to be a morbid, depressing, and fearful experience. Realistically, it is an area that needs to be discussed, especially among elderly adults. A variety of practical issues such as the writing of a will, preferred method of body disposal, and plans for achieving unmet goals needs to be considered. It is not the discussion of death that is distasteful, but rather it is the denial of death and the subsequent effects that the denial has on one's approach to life that is unacceptable.

SUMMARY

Death education is appropriate for people of all ages. It has been demonstrated that children as young as 3 years have begun to develop rudimentary concepts of death. In addition to their natural curiosity and inquisitiveness, children are observant. Death and the subsequent emotional reactions of survivors cannot be hidden. Futhermore, children may become confused by the various beliefs and attitudes that adults have toward death. Euphemisms often add to the confusion. The fact that young children may not be able to verbalize their concerns does not mean that the issues should be ignored. Life events during childhood can be used by parents or teachers to help children conceptualize the life cycle and to recognize that all living things must die. The development of effective coping strategies will prove useful in later life.

Attitudes about death in adulthood are shaped by childhood experiences. As such, there is no single perspective about death that is held in common by middle-aged or elderly adults. Viewpoints about death are shaped by experiences in life rather than by the number of years a person has lived. Frank and open discussion of death and dying can promote a healthy view of life and living.

REFERENCES

1. Nagy, Maria: "The child's view of death." Journal of Genetic Psychology **73**:3-27, 1948.
2. Menig-Peterson, Carole, and McCabe, Allyssa: Children talk about death, Omega **8**:305-317, 1977-1978.
3. Anthony, Sylvia: The discovery of death in childhood and after, New York, 1972. Basic Books, Inc., Publishers.
4. Bluebond-Langner, Myra: Meaning of death to children. In Feifel, H., editor: New meanings of death, New York, 1977, McGraw-Hill Book Co., pp. 48-56.
5. Grollman, Earl: Explaining death to children, The Journal of School Health **47**:336-339, June 1977.
6. Perkes, A. Cordell, and Schlidt, Roberta: Death-related activities of adolescent males and females, Death Education **2**:359-368, 1979.
7. Lifton, Robert Jay: On death and the continuity of life: a psycho-historical perspective, Omega **6**:143-159, 1975.
8. Swenson, Wendell M.: Attitudes toward death among the aged. In Feifel, H., editor: Death and identity, New York, 1965, John Wiley & Sons, Inc., pp. 105-111.
9. Marshall, Victor W.: Age and awareness of finitude in developmental gerontology. Omega **6**:113-130, 1975.
10. Wass, Hannelore, Christian, Milton, Myers, Jane, and Murphy, Milledge Jr.: Similarities in attitudes toward death in a population of the older persons, Omega **9**:337-354, 1978-1979.

A student's knowledge, attitudes, and behaviors related to death and dying are often a function of cultural and societal influences.

Courtesy Guidance Associates, Mt. Kisco, N.Y.

CHAPTER THREE

Instructional modalities
in death education

*Death education relates not only to death itself, but to our feelings about
ourselves and nature and the universe we live in.**

ERNEST MORGAN

In recent years death education has attracted the attention of health educators in
both school and community settings. Professional literature emphasizes the need for
death education to be included in the curriculum at all levels. It seems that death
education, thought to be a taboo subject a decade ago, has been gaining popularity in
many educational circles. Striking evidence that the death education taboo has been
weakened at the college and university level is reflected in the recent proliferation of
death education courses being offered. Leviton[1] reported that in colleges, as of 1970,
there were no more than 20 death education courses in existence. Four years later,
Berg and Daugherty[2] estimated that over 1,100 college courses were offered. Today,
that is a conservative estimate.

As with any successful educational endeavor, death education must be carefully
planned and organized. This chapter will discuss techniques that can be used to plan,
implement, and evaluate death education programs and teaching strategies.

CURRICULUM DEVELOPMENT

The emergence of death education as a topic worthy of instructional time has made
it imperative that educators be prepared to evaluate curricular program needs and to
develop valid instructional modules based on sound principles of curriculum
development.

There are a variety of curricular models available to assist the death educator in
program development. One such model is the rationale developed by Tyler.[3] Although
this model may not be as sophisticated as many of the more recently developed
models, it does present theories and stages that are generic to most curricular

*From A Manual of Death Education and Simple Burial, by Ernest Morgan. ($2.50 plus 50 cents postage
from Celo Press, Route 5, Burnsville, NC 28714.)

51

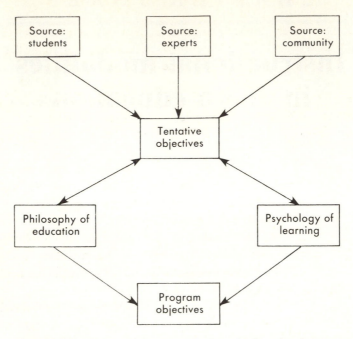

Figure 2. Tyler's rationale theory of curriculum development.

development models. Developed in 1948 by Ralph Tyler, the Tyler rationale incorporates many of the components of current curricular theory into a logical and concise framework (Figure 2).

The Tyler rationale suggests that the educator consult three sources prior to the initiation phase of curriculum development: students, experts in the field, and community representatives. Often the particular needs of students are ignored when developing a curriculum. Tyler believes that the first source to be studied prior to the initial stages of curriculum development are the students. The student population should be studied to identify the problems, needs, and interests of the students and to identify the types of behavioral changes (both cognitive and affective) for which educational institutions should strive. Because death education has been a taboo subject, it is especially important to assess student knowledge and attitudes, as well as their needs, prior to developing a curricular package. It is important to determine the developmental levels of the student and to assess levels of misinformation students possess. For example, the types of misconceptions students have related to suicide should help to shape instruction in that area. For if students believe that only insane people commit suicide or that people who talk about suicide will not actually commit suicide, the ability of students to conceptualize the scope and preventive aspects of the problem will be severely limited. In essence, this step of curricular development process, which is a form of needs assessment, is structured to determine the growth and developmental characteristics as well as the problems, needs, and interests of the learner.

The second source to be consulted is the subject matter specialists, or in this case, experts in the area of thanatology and death education. The death education experts should provide valuable assistance in the development of tentative objectives along with helpful suggestions for program goals, objectives, materials, and content. This interdisciplinary nature of death education often creates difficulty for the educator who is trying to develop a program that addresses all the cognitive, affective, and behavorial components of death education. Therefore when developing a death education curriculum, it is advisable to consult subject matter specialists who have wide-ranging expertise. Harris[4] has identified five approaches (philosophical, sociological, psychological, medical-legal, and health education) for teaching death education. The curriculum of death education course will depend on the approach (or combination of approaches) that influence the planning process.

Philosophical approach. The philosophical approach often centers on the meaning of life and death. In the philosophical approach, individuals understand their own death thoughts and feelings in an attempt to reconcile themselves with the inevitability of death. The religious views of death are often included in the philosophical approach. Although most religions accept the fact that people die, a variety of fundamental religious beliefs concerning the immortality of the spirit or soul are compared in this approach. If students are encouraged to develop a personal position or philosophy regarding death and dying, it may provide them with a greater understanding of life and serve as a focal point from which life values, priorities, and goals can be established.

Sociological approach. The sociological approach explores how the American culture as a society deals with death. Knowledge, attitudes, and behaviors related to death and dying are often a function of cultural and societal influences. An appropriate basis of the sociological approach to death is the notion that America is often considered a death-denying society. Yet in recent years, there has been increased interest in death education despite strong cultural taboos. When a death education curriculum is being developed, it is important to understand the impact that society has exerted and continues to exert on the students. Experts in sociology should help the death educator identify these societal influences. An important point to keep in mind when experts in this area are being consulted is that only a relatively small percentage of sociologists are involved in the study of dying and death. Therefore the curriculum developer should be careful to consult only those sociologists who have appropriate expertise.

53

Psychological and counseling approach. The focal point of the psychological and counseling approach to death education is understanding the dying person and the bereaved. In addition, techniques and trends in the management of grief are included in this approach. From an educational perspective it is important to understand the dying patient and the bereaved to sensitize students to their needs and feelings. The educator needs to have an awareness of the psychological aspects of the dying and bereavement process yet be sensitive to individual differences. If a goal of death education is to help students deal effectively with dying friends and relatives and eventually with their own death, an understanding of the psychological and counseling concerns is imperative. Although, historically, a systematic description of even the most basic psychological processes related to death has been lacking, this is an area of concern that has received more attention recently. Few systematic descriptions of the psychological processes related to dying and death have been proposed, yet the literature is abundant with psychological and qausi-psychological descriptions of dying and death, for example, Becker, Kubler-Ross, Moody, Feifel, and Kastenbaum.

Medical-legal approach. The medical-legal approach to death education addresses two major concerns. First, this approach stresses the need to clarify the medical terminology related to the definition of death. Second, this approach embraces the need to prepare individuals to deal with the legal and medical responsibilities they will confront when they administer the estate of a deceased relative or prepare for their own death. When developing a death education curriculum, especially with adult populations, it is important to include medical and legal concepts. In this area, students need to have accurate, up-to-date information to make wise decisions that are consistent with their personal philosophical positions on life and death.

Health education approach. Of the various approaches to death education, the health education approach is the broadest in both depth and scope. In essence, the health education approach can be considered an eclectic approach to death education. The main areas of approach are mental health concerns and education or informational concerns. The health education approach integrates the major tenets of the other approaches previously mentioned and aims at both mental and physical well-being of the total person. From an educational standpoint, this holistic approach to death education makes sense to many curriculum developers. For example, when dealing with the bereaved widow, it is very difficult to deal with the immediate need to plan the funeral (medical-legal approach) without also addressing the stage and intensity of the ordinary grief response (psychological approach) and the social and cultural factors (sociological approach) that may influence her preference of body disposal.

■ ■ ■

It can be seen that the curriculum specialist has a variety of possible disciplines to consult when a death education curriculum is being developed. It is important that the death educator assess the needs of the students and then determine the approach to death education or the subject matter specialist to consult in the developmental stages of the curriculum.

In addition, there are a variety of community resource people who may provide a specialized form of expertise to the curriculum developer. The inclusion of the community in the curriculum development process may enhance community acceptance of the death education curriculum. Using Yarber's list of resources[5] as a starting point, it is easy to demonstrate that communities have a variety of resources to help in the curriculum planning process:

1. *Attorneys:* Attorneys could be consulted for information related to the preparation of a will, estate planning, and legal aspects of death, including laws governing funeral practices in the state.

2. *Cemetery or memorial garden directors:* For information regarding costs, locations, and procedures for obtaining a plot or other appropriate space for internment, cemetery and memorial garden directors could be consulted. It is important to consult an individual who gives factual yet unbiased information. In some cases, such a person may be difficult to find.

3. *Clergy:* Representatives from various religions can provide insight into the doctrines of their churches that concern death and dying. Such opinions are especially important in funeral consumerism and euthanasia concerns. However, one should keep in mind that some religious sects have not formulated clear-cut positions on death-related concerns.

4. *Corners:* The coroner can provide information regarding the state and local laws concerning the determination of death and the rules and procedures governing autopsies.

5. *Funeral directors:* For information related to the traditional funeral process and related costs, the funeral director may be a good resource person. Again, in this case, it is important to consult a funeral director who will provide accurate and unbiased information.

6. *Physicians:* The physician can provide information concerning the causes and definitions of death. The physician may also be a source of information regarding the explanation of death to the family, although many physicians have difficulty in this area. The physician can also be a source of information on medical issues related to dying and death, such as organ donation and transplants, euthanasia, and abortion.

7. *Psychologists or psychiatrists:* Professionals in psychology or psychiatry who have worked with terminally ill persons or bereaved families can often provide valuable insights into the psychological aspects of death, grief, and mourning. In addition, the psychologist or psychiatrist can often provide useful information on how to effectively deal with the bereaved and how to come to terms with one's own death.

8. *Representatives from a euthanasia organization:* Resource persons from a euthanasia organization can provide information in support of the right of patients to make their own decision concerning euthanasia. If there is no euthanasia organization in the area, information may be obtained from Concern for Dying, 250 West 57th Street, New York, New York 10019.

9. *Representatives from a funeral and memorial society:* Funeral and memorial societies are non-profit voluntary organizations that have been created to assist members in obtaining a simple and dignified means of body disposal at a reasonable cost. Representatives from this group could provide the curriculum developer with information related to the function of their organization, alternatives to traditional funerals, and preplanning funerals. Funeral and memorial societies have been established in most major cities in the United States. More information on these organizations may be obtained from The Continental Association of Funeral and Memorial Societies, Suite 1100, 1828 L Street, N.W., Washington, D.C. 20036.

10. *Representatives from a state medical society:* As resource persons, professionals from a state medical society can provide information related to the donation of anatomical gifts to medical schools. In addition, this group can provide information on their position regarding dying and death-related issues, such as euthanasia, body donation, organ transplantation, explaining death to the family, and the patient's bill of rights.

The list of suggested community resource personnel sketches a fairly complete picture of the possible scope and parameters of a death education curriculum. As well, the community resource personnel along with the five major approaches to death education provide an outline of the wide variety of experts that can be consulted when a death education curriculum is being developed.

The third source to be consulted when a death education curriculum is being developed is community representatives. Especially when developing a curriculum for school-aged students, the curriculum developer must be cognizant of the prevalent community mores. Students are more likely to learn when they recognize the similarity between situations encountered in daily life and hypothetical situations encountered in the educational setting. Because society is rapidly changing, death education programs must focus on the critical aspects of contemporary problems in thanatology. Community input can help to delineate the nature and scope of these problems. In addition, community input ensures the most effective use of the community resource personnel mentioned previously.

Once the data from the three sources discussed above are gathered, tentative program objectives should be developed. These tentative objectives should reflect the input from the three sources: students, experts, and community representatives. Once these objectives have been developed, they should be screened through the philosophy of education of the institution that offers the course and screened through the sound principles of education psychology and learning theory. The purpose of this screening process is to develop feasible, highly consistent, and relevant program goals and objectives. For example, one of the goals of a death education program may be to enhance decision-making skills related to funeral consumerism. However, if the program is geared for an elementary age audience and research in educational psychology tells us that children below the mental age of 8 or 9 years cannot use decision-making skills, that objective should be deleted from the primary level death education curriculum.

Therefore objectives that are inconsistent or contradictory to the basic beliefs of the educational institution or do not adhere to sound principles of educational psychology should be eliminated. In addition, it is important that the death educator is aware of the educational and fiscal parameters of the institution that will offer the death education course. For example, the death educator who develops a multimedia approach to death education may be distraught to discover that the educational institution such as a public school, college, university, parochial school, or hospital does not have the audio-visual resources or the financial resources to support such a program.

Comparison of the tentative objectives with recognized principles of learning should illustrate how well the objectives articulate with "accepted" educational approaches. This review process often helps the educator distinguish between those objectives that are feasible and those that are not likely to be obtained. There are a variety of learning principles in the area of the psychology of learning that may emerge during the screening process. The following are foremost among these notions:

- Students tend to learn at their own pace. Therefore, instructional programs should be developed that allow students to progress through a planned and sequential program at their own pace. This notion is especially important when the instruction is aimed at adult populations in which the educational background may vary drastically.

- Students tend to learn more easily when they are actively involved in the learning process. Instructional programming in death education should incorporate learning strategies that involve the students. For example, to highlight the complexity of many euthanasia decision-making situations, the teacher could provide individual students or groups of students with simulated case studies and ask them to use a valid decision-making model to derive a position statement on each situation. By doing this, the teacher will have provided students with a simulated experience they may have to deal with in the future and will have actively involved them in the learning process. In essence, this notion addresses the need to center instruction on the student rather than the teacher.
- Students can learn from a variety of teaching strategies and educational media. There is no one best way to instruct students or one best way for students to learn. For example, some students learn best by listening to a lecture, some through reading, and some through instructional television. Therefore a death education course should use a variety of different types of media and instructional activities to facilitate all types of learners.
- Learning entails more than cognition. Learning includes cognitive, affective, and behavorial components. In death education information sharing is an important component, but students should be equipped with appropriate coping skills to enhance their ability to deal with life events. Although it may be difficult to measure, behavior change is still an important goal of death education. For example, through an information-sharing experience a student may learn to approximate costs of funerals and alternatives to funerals. And through a values clarification exercise, the student may become aware of his or her desire to have his or her body disposed of in a nontraditional manner. However, unless the death education course provides the student with the appropriate coping skills related to preplanning body disposal arrangement, his or her wishes may never be realized. Therefore a good death education program needs to include information sharing, values clarification, and coping behavior components.
- Students tend to learn when the instruction is part of a sequential educational program. When developing a death education course for school age populations, the curriculum developer should be aware of the need to develop a well-planned, sequential program for kindergarten through twelfth grades.

Again, these screens help to ensure that the proposed curriculum will meet the needs of the students and the sponsoring institution.

Once the tentative objectives have been passed through both screens, the program objectives can be developed. As with other educational objectives, these program objectives should be written in measurable terms and follow a format consistent with current educational philosophy. From these program objectives, the instructional program should be developed. There are a variety of ways to structure such an educational program.

APPROACHES TO STRUCTURING CURRICULUM

There are a variety of ways to structure a death education curriculum. Three approaches that have received varying degrees of popularity among the health educators are the conceptual approach, the unit approach, and the competency-based approach. Although these three approaches will be discussed, it should be noted that there are other ways to structure a death education curriculum. Prior to making these curricular decisions, the death educator should consult with appropriate administrative officials to ensure the approach is congruent with the educational philosophy of the institution.

Conceptual approach

During the 1960s, the School Health Education Study[6] popularized the conceptual approach to health education. The study demonstrated the value of teaching toward major concepts. Because of the rapidly changing nature of the health-related content, the conceptual approach advocates teaching toward concepts or major ideas rather than specific content. The basic premise of the study arose from the notion that health can be defined as being three dimensional: (1) Health as a unity of physical, mental, and social well-being, (2) health behavior as knowledge, attitudes, and practices, and (3) the focus of health education in regard to the individual, family, and community. The conceptual approach is based on three key concepts: growing and developing, interacting, and decision making. "The three key concepts serve as the unifying threads of the curriculum characterizing the process underlying health."[6] These concepts are described as follows:

1. Growing and developing represents the evolving of the continuous life process from conception to death, with all the attendant changes. Understanding this process is fundamental to the conceptualization of health. It represents a dynamic interplay of the physical, the mental, and the social aspects of the individual.

2. Interacting is the dynamic relationship of the individual to the biological and social world. This process is in a continual state of flux, and interaction may bring about balance or disrupt the stability of the relationship.
3. Decision making enables the individual to reason through life situations, to solve problems, and to some extent, to direct behavior. It is unique to humans and is based on the desire for a specific outcome in the future.

These key concepts have definite implications for death education. The first concept clearly highlights the notion that growing and developing is a continuous life process from conception to death. This notion is consistent with the life-span development theory, which also proposes that human development continues until death. Also, physical, mental, and spiritual conditions influence an individual's concept and reaction to dying and death. For example, a person suffering extreme pain may have a much different outlook on euthanasia or suicide than a person enjoying good health. A person whose mental outlook on life is one of worthlessness caused by a condition such as retirement or physical disability may also have a different view of euthanasia or suicide. And, in countries in which euthanasia or suicide is more socially acceptable, one will find an increased suicide incidence.

Interacting with the biological and social world provides the individual with some basic concepts related to the physical and emotional aspects of death and dying. Through interacting with different environmental stimuli, the individual learns the biological difference between living and nonliving organisms. At an early age, students can identify objects that possess life from objects that are lifeless. In addition, by interaction with their social environment, individuals learn coping mechanisms to deal with the social and emotional aspects of death, such as grief response, mourning rituals, and body disposal preferences. Perhaps one reason why the aged generally have lower death anxiety levels is partially a function of an extended period of interaction with environmental stimuli.

The decision concept addresses the notion that humans want and, in many cases, are able to exert some control over life events. The decision-making process in death education can be applied to many areas, such as funeral procedures, wills and estate planning, euthanasia, and to a certain extent, suicide. Decision making is an essential component of a death education program. It provides students with the skills and strategies necessary to enhance their ability to cope with life events.

The basic tenet of the conceptual approach to death education is that because knowledge is changing so rapidly, it is best to structure a curriculum around basic concepts that for the most part will not change over time. The focus of instruction is the mastery of these basic concepts.

Unit approach

The unit approach is widely used by many educators, school districts, and states because of the relative ease with which this approach can be planned and implemented. In the unit approach a series of educational units or modalities are taught for varying lengths of time throughout the school year.

There are a variety of formats and components of unit plans. Although unit plan requirements may vary considerably from one educational institution to another, there are a variety of components that appear to be generic to the development of unit plans. The sample unit plan format outlined below includes many of these essential components.

1. Rationale: The rationale should justify the need for a unit for the intended target group. In addition, the rationale should include a description of the needs of the age group along with a discussion of their emotional, social, physical, and personality characteristics.

61

2. Major concepts: The major underlying premises for the particular unit should be outlined. These foundation statements serve as guidelines for the development of behavioral objectives, learning strategies, and methods and materials.
3. Behavioral objectives: The behavioral objective clearly states what the student is expected to accomplish during the unit. The behavioral objectives should be written in the cognitive, affective, and psychomotor domains.
4. Content outline: The content outline should present the content to be covered within the unit in a logical and concise manner.
5. Key questions: The key questions necessary to facilitate meaningful classroom dialogue should be outlined.
6. Controversial issues: The controversial issues component of the unit plan highlights the issues in the particular subject matter that have conflicting viewpoints or aspects.
7. Method and materials of learning strategies: The learning strategies clearly state the types of classroom activities that can be used to enhance the achievement of the stated behavioral objectives. There are a variety of teaching methods that could be used in an educational setting. Most educators agree instructional programs that incorporate a variety of educational methodologies are the most successful.
8. Resources: Two types of resources should be included in the unit plan. Student resources outline materials (written on the students' level) that may help the students achieve the stated behavioral objectives. Teacher resources are designed to assist teachers in obtaining the necessary cognition and appropriate educational strategies to facilitate meaningful instruction. The resource component should include printed materials as well as a variety of audiovisual materials. Annotations are helpful for future reference.
9. Evaluation: The evaluative techniques stated in the behavioral objectives should be expanded and clarified in this component of the unit plan. A discussion concerning the use of teacher-made tests, educational games, question and answer sessions, and homework assignments to evaluate student progress should be included in this component of the unit plan.
10. Glossary: Important terms should be defined to ensure that teachers and students are working under the same set of assumptions.

Although the unit plan approach is widely used, it has been criticized for creating instruction based on a subject matter orientation as opposed to a learner orientation. The nature of professional preparation in education (a variety of short courses based on topics of limited scope) fosters the use of unit planning. It has been suggested that colleges and universities should reexamine their teacher preparation programs to allow students to experience a variety of approaches to curricular planning or at least students should be given the option to use unique or varied curricular development plans.

Competency-based approach

The competency-based approach to death education is based on the notion that there are certain knowledges, skills, and behaviors that students must master in any given death education area. A competency-based instructional program places the responsibility for learning on the students. The function of the teacher becomes that of a facilitator of learning. This is a concept that has gained the support of many educators.

- Students should clearly understand what is expected of them and how they can be successful in the classroom.
- Individual freedom with personal responsibility should be emphasized so that each student can work at his or her own speed and pace.
- When students receive immediate knowledge of results, they can work toward correcting mistakes and toward the completion of the specified objectives.

Although the competency-based instructional approach has been successful in a variety of educational settings, there is much disagreement concerning its educational validity. Opponents of this instructional approach believe that there is too much emphasis on achieving the stated objectives and the classroom may become a mechanical and sterile environment. In addition, it is difficult to find creative ways to measure different types of behaviors, especially those behaviors from the affective domain. Nonetheless, if properly planned, organized, and evaluated, the competency-based approach to death education can be useful in almost any educational setting.

Nature of content

The content of any death education program will vary as new health issues emerge or the needs and interests of students change. It is important, however, to remember the major purpose of a death education course is to enhance the students level of learning in three areas: information sharing, values clarification, and coping behaviors. Obviously, basic content serves as a vehicle for attainment of these goals.

Because death education is a relatively new field the content is always increasing and changing. The death educator must remain aware of these changes. Selection of content for each instructional program should be based on the growth and developmental characteristics, needs and interests, and educational level of the students. Therefore the teacher or curriculum developer must carefully select the content for each instructional program.

In 1978 Eddy and others[7] surveyed 38 death educators to determine the specific content areas that should be included in a death education course designed to prepare teachers as death educators. Based on a review of literature, 30 cognitive content areas were identified and survey participants were asked to rate each content area on a Likert scale.

The results of the survey delineated four broad categories of cognitive areas according to perceived importance. The first category consists of cognitive areas thought to be essential concepts for a death and dying professional preparation course. The five topical areas included in this category would provide the basic core of a death education course for prospective health educators:

1. An understanding of friends and relatives who are dying
2. The meaning of death in American society
3. Bereavement and mourning
4. Explaining to children the subject of death
5. Preparing for death

The second category consists of those cognitive areas that should be included in a death and dying course but are not the major concepts. It is obvious that several of these items relate closely to those key concepts identified in the first category:

1. Methods and materials of death education
2. Definitions and causes of death
3. Cross-cultural views of death
4. Curricular development in death education
5. Religious views of death
6. Euthanasia
7. The life cycle
8. Suicide (psychosocial aspects)
9. Aging (psychosocial aspects)
10. The role of the funeral home
11. Aging (biological aspects)
12. Expressing condolences to a friend or relative
13. Suicide (referral aspects)
14. The cost of funerals

The third category consists of cognitive areas that should be included in a death and dying professional preparation course if adequate time were available:

1. Organ donation and transplant
2. The history of death and dying
3. Alternatives to traditional funerals
4. Memorial services

5. Children's literature and its treatment of death
6. Cremation
7. Embalming

The fourth category consists of items that were thought to be of little importance in a professional preparation course:

1. Death as it is portrayed in music and literature
2. Cryogenics
3. Necrophilia

Although the results of the survey are subject to different interpretations, these findings may prove useful to the educator who is struggling to determine the parameters of a professional preparation course in death education. In addition, the results reflect the collective thinking of 38 practicing educators experienced in the field of death education.

APPROACHES TO TEACHING

Effective communication techniques are essential in death education. Although they may possess fascinating data, if instructors are unable to communicate that data to students, help students develop personal values, and help students to make decisions, they may be wasting their expertise. There are several ways to communicate. Most individuals possess basic communication skills: verbal, vocal, and nonverbal. It is often believed that the skill with the greatest impact on communication is nonverbal behavior. Vocal behavior is often believed to have the second greatest impact, and verbal behavior may have the least importance. Nonverbal skill refers to the use of the body, facial expressions, body movement, gestures, and especially eye contact to communicate. Verbal skill is the language part of communication or what the students hear. Verbal skill includes word choice and pronunciation. Vocal skill refers to voice quality, pitch, inflection, volume, rate of speech, articulation, fluency, and basic emphasis on specific words. This helps to explain why teachers may be saying one thing (verbal), but via the teacher's nonverbal expression or gestures, the students comprehend something entirely different. Because death education typically addresses a variety of controversial and value-laden issues, it is important that death educators be aware of these nonverbal behaviors.

It is also known that the greater number of senses involved in the learning process, the more likely the data will be retained by the learner. The now-classic study of Wittich,[8] which has since been replicated several times with similar results, found that if "telling along" (audio) was the only method of communication, such as lecture, after

3 hours the students remembered 70% of the data. Three days after the communication, students retained only 10% of the data. If "showing alone" (visual) was the only method of communication, such as silent films of labeled slides, after 3 hours, the students remembered 72% of the data. After 3 days, students recalled 20%. If "telling and showing" (audio-visual) was used together, 83% of the data was recalled after 3 hours, and 60% was retained after 3 days.

These findings emphasize the need for educational programs to include a variety of instructional modalities. If students learn more readily from multiple instructional strategies, death educators would be wise to incorporate a diversity of educational strategies into the curriculum. In addition, these data emphasize the importance of using appropriate instructional aids. There are several advantages to using aids in the classroom. Aids appeal to the senses, interest the students, help develop understanding, and save time in the classroom. There are several questions to consider when developing an aid or selecting a commercially produced aid. The most important questions are: Does the aid relate to the objective? Is it accurate? Does it say what it is supposed to say? Is it easily understood by the students, or is it so complex that many students cannot comprehend what the aid is exemplifying? Is it legible? Is the aid able to be handled or managed without too much difficulty? Is the cost of a commercial aid worth the price? Instructional aids can provide alternative modes of instruction. However, they should not be considered a panacea for instructional problems. Instructional aids should be used to assist the student to achieve the behaviors outlined in the educational objectives of the curriculum.

In essence, if death educators expect to become successful facilitators of learning in the classroom, they must develop educational programs that actively involve students in the learning process and utilize a variety of instructional methods and strategies. The section that follows will outline a variety of instructional methods to help the death educator become a successful facilitator of learning.

INSTRUCTIONAL METHODS

The method the instructor decides to use in a death education class should be based on several factors. The first and most important factor is the educational objective. The method must provide the opportunity for the students to practice the behavior specified in the objective. Therefore if the objective specifies *discuss,* then time must be alloted during the class period for the students (not the teacher) to discuss the assigned topic. The nature of the subject matter is the second factor in determining an instructional method. If it is highly complex data, the student may be asked to participate in a discussion, role play, or simulation activity. In general, the more complex the subject, the more the student should be involved in the learning experience. Student motivation is the second factor. If the students have low motivation, the instructor should try to avoid the lecture technique. If students have high motivation, lecture with scheduled class questions may be appropriate. Other factors that may influence selection of method would include the previous knowledge of the students, class size, time allotment, and the capabilities of the instructor.

Regardless of the particular method selected, the students must be involved in the learning experience and must practice the behavior specified in the objective. One of the easiest ways to involve students in class activities is through appropriate questioning. There are a variety of reasons for using the question techniques in teaching. A good question and answer session stimulates interest and attention, guides discussion and thinking, opens discussion, allows transition from one topic to another, increases understanding, gauges comprehension, checks on past learning, involves the students, checks to see if what was supposed to be taught was actually taught, helps discipline a distracted or sleepy student to maintain attention, emphasizes a main point, and develops a subject.

When initiating a question and answer session, it is often wise to begin with basic questions and progress to the more complex questions. If a student is hesitant to become involved in a question and answer session, the teacher may need to ask simple, nonthreatening questions until the student gains the self-confidence needed to answer the more complex questions. Each question should have a specific purpose and emphasize one point. All complex questions should require an explanatory answer other than "yes" or "no." Questions should be phrased in a positive manner to emphasize good habits rather than stressing what is wrong with a particular behavior. For example, a question such as "Why is it important to make out a last will and testament?" is a positvely phrased question. A negatively phrased question would be "What types of legal problems arise when someone dies intestate?" When discussion questions are being developed, the interrogative terms should be used first. These are terms such as who, what, when, where, how, and why. Questions that use the interrogative pronoun necessitate an explanation from the student. Last, the questions must be understandable and clear. If students do not understand the question, the teacher should be prepared to rephrase the question so that the students understand what the teacher is asking. The preferred technique for asking questions, is the *ask-pause-call technique*. The instructor asks the question, pauses, then calls for a response. This gives all of the students a chance to think about the answer. Emphasis here is being placed on questioning because it should be incorporated into every class session and method. Also, because of the taboo nature of death education content, it is

67

important that the death educator assess the cognitive and affective levels of the students. A good question and answer session will help in these assessments.

The *lecture technique* is the easiest method for the teacher to prepare. Lectures may be appropriately used when the educator wishes to introduce new background knowledge, to outline directions or procedures, or to handle a large class. However, if the lecture method is to be used, the teacher should try to involve students in other activities related to the subject matter. The use of audiovisual aids often helps to increase the effectiveness of a lecture because they expose students to other instructional modalities and force students to use a variety of senses. One of the greatest problems with the lecture method is student boredom, limited retention of content, and limited emphasis on affective objectives. Unfortunately, many times the boredom is justified. To avoid student boredom, the educator must actively involve students in the lecture, perhaps by asking well-prepared questions throughout the lecture. In addition, an overreliance on the lecture method may limit its effectiveness. As previously mentioned, students seem to learn best when a variety of instructional methods are utilized. If used wisely, the lecture method can be an effective educational method.

The *discussion method* is characterized as being predominately student oriented. The teacher facilitates discussion by clarifying data for the students and guiding students back to the topic. Any time the discussion method is used, the teacher must have prepared topics and questions for the students to answer and discuss. The predominate characteristic of a discussion is that there is no preplanned conclusion. Ideally, the discussion method allows the students to freely discuss a particular topic and arrive at their own conclusions.

When the teacher prefers to have the students reach a particular conclusion following a discussion, the *directed questioning* or *guided discovery method* should be used. The major difference between the conference method and discussion method is whether or not the teacher wants the students to reach a preplanned conclusion. The death educator would ask the student a carefully orchestrated series of questions that leads the students to a logical conclusion or a specific viewpoint.

The *symposium method* requires selecting a student to research a specific area and become the class expert. The expert briefly explains that topic to the class, and a group discussion follows. The teacher prepares questions for the groups to answer. If the groups need clarification or assistance, the class expert is available to provide answers.

The *problem-solving technique* is one of the most relevant methods for the students. This technique combines the concepts and principles that the student has been studying and relates them to situations that the student may encounter in real life. The value of problem solving is that it affords students the opportunity to practice decision-making skills. Problem-solving situations can be used in most death education content areas. An appropriate problem-solving situation related to death education would be to ask students to use their knowledge of funerals and alternatives to funerals and their personal values to develop a personal plan for disposal of their remains. The basic assumption of problem solving is that if students gain practice during a death education class in coping with these potential life problems, then they may use these skills when real life events occur.

Role playing is an educational strategy in which the students are given specific hypothetical roles or situations and are asked to act them out in the classroom setting. Both open-ended and structured role-playing strategies have been proven useful in death education classrooms. An open-ended role-playing situation is used when the teacher wants the students to develop their roles and when no specific points or outcomes are desired. The following is an example of an open-ended role-playing situation related to euthanasia:

First role: This student believes that euthanasia should be outlawed regardless of the condition or wishes of the patient.

Second and third roles: These students believe that euthanasia should be legal in specific situations.

Situation: All three students are friends. The two who favor euthanasia under certain circumstances try to convince the third student of the validity of their viewpoint.

In this open-ended role-playing situation, the exact methods the students use to convince the first-role student that euthanasia should be legal in certain situations are not clearly defined. It is the students' prerogative to decide in which direction this role playing will progress. In a structured role-playing situation, the teacher clearly states the parameters of the roles the students are asked to play. In structured situations, the teacher influences the direction and conclusion of the role-playing situation. The following is an example of a structured role-playing situation related to euthanasia.

First role: Student does not believe euthanasia should be legalized because once it is legalized, there would be no way to judge the intent involved in each case.

Second role: This student believes that individuals have the right to decide how they want to live and how they want to die. The legalization of euthanasia would allow for such freedom.

Third role: This student believes that euthanasia should be legalized only if the patient is of sound mind and has completed a "living will." In this way, everyone would be certain of the patient's intent.

Situation: All three students are friends. Each student tries to convince the other students that his or her position is the most logical.

Although the structured role-playing situation limits freedom of expression, it does provide a mechanism for specific points to be discussed. In addition, for the activity cited above, a role model is shown dealing with the problem of developing a personal position on euthanasia in a constructive manner.

Value clarification, valuing games, and related techniques have received a great deal of attention from many professional educators. Including values clarification techniques in the death education classroom can be an effective means of approaching the affective aspects of death and dying. Unfortunately, rather than being related to cognitive learning experiences, affective and valuing learning experiences are frequently separated from the "real learning experiences." Many educators use values clarification simply to spice up a boring section of the course. However, to be effective, it is essential that values clarification be included as a normal part of curriculum. In a death education curriculum it is appropriate to categorize one section of curriculum "thinking," that is, cognitive learning, and another "emotions and feelings," that is, affective learning. All people experience some emotional response while they are thinking. It is important that cognitive learning experiences either incorporate affective experiences or at least are followed by some form of affective learning.

Every decision or choice individuals make is based on their beliefs, attitudes, and values. However, many times people are unclear about their own personal beliefs; thus their decision-making processes are made more complicated. Valuing activities provide students with the opportunity to identify a personal set of beliefs and clarify their values. It is hoped that the result will enhance their decision-making process.

The major problem with moralizing is that the set of values used may not be appropriate for the individual or may not be well related to current trends and life-styles. In addition, there may be a variety of different sets of values. Parents may stress one set of values, the church another, peer group a third, Hollywood and popular magazines a fourth, the death education teacher a fifth, the funeral director a sixth, and social norms a seventh. Thus too often the important choices of life are made on the basis of peer pressure, unthinking submission to authority, or the power of propaganda.

The *laissez-faire attitude* is another approach. This approach acknowledges that people have different sets of values and that no one set of values is right for everyone. In this approach, no guidance is given and the students are expected to develop their own sets of values. The greatest drawback to this approach is that people often need some form of guidance. They need to know the parameters of the issue or concern. The laissez-faire attitude does not provide such parameters.

In the *modeling* approach the model sets a living example for the student to follow. It is hoped that the model practices what is taught. Unfortunately, the student is presented with many different and often conflicting models: parents, teachers, politicians, movie stars, friends, and relatives. How does the student know which model is appropriate?

Raths' *values clarification*[9] is a systematic approach to the process of valuing. According to this approach, the content of the values of students is unimportant, but the *process* of valuing is essential. Raths has broken the valuing process down into seven subprocesses.

Freely chosen values. By choosing values freely, students are allowed to make their own decisions without coercion. Students are more likely to feel comfortable when their decisions are freely selected.

Values chosen from alternatives. In any decision-making process, there have to be alternative choices. Only when a choice is possible can students engage in a values clarification or a decision-making process.

Values chosen after thoughtful consideration of the consequences of each alternative. If it is to become an intelligent and meaningful guide to the student, the decision should be derived from the careful evaluation of all the alternatives. The choosing process is the focal point of this decision-making process. Raths believes that in addition to making their choices, students should prize their decision.

Values prized and cherished. Students should feel comfortable with their decisions. They should believe that their decisions are meaningful and have the respect of teachers and peers.

Values publicly affirmed. If students are proud of their decisions, they should feel comfortable affirming their choices when asked about them. The prizing stage of this model relates closely to self concept. If students believe they are capable of making meaningful and intelligent decisions, they are likely to prize, cherish, and publicly affirm those decisions. Once their decisions have been made, students must act accordingly.

Actions based on chosen values. The actions of the students are congruent with their decisions.

Values chosen repeatedly. The student acts consistently to form a life pattern. Because of the simplicity of this model, it can be used in a wide range of situations.

Most of the values clarification strategies encourage students to progress through a varying number of stages of this seven-stage process. Raths believes that if students use this valuing process to formulate beliefs, opinions, and values, they will develop a realistic and personal system of values.

Values clarification and decision-making activities help to enhance the effectiveness of death education.

Photo by Strix Pix.

The intent of values education is to teach the students how to use factual data to make defensible, consistent decisions. A variety of activities may be used to assist students in decision making. These decision-making and value activities may fulfill the following goals:

1. To have students rate particular value objects
2. To help students make rational, defensible judgments on controversial issues
3. To have students become aware of and utilize the various procedures needed for making rational, defensible health judgments and decisions
4. To have students participate in individual decision-making activities and to practice the skills needed for operating within a group in attempting to develop common value judgments and decisions

Values clarification strategies appear to have their greatest instructional impact when incorporated into the various death education content areas. When a values strategy is used to facilitate discussion or define the parameters of a particular death education concern, students can observe how their particular value positions relate to real-life problems or situations. Death educators should also realize that incorporating values clarification strategies into the curriculum will not guarantee positive behavioral change among students. There are too many other factors that could influence student behavior for which the teacher has little or no control.

Sample values clarification strategies have been included in some of the learning strategies section of this text.

Decision making can best be defined as the process by which students select an alternative or course of action from two or more possible choices. The prime reason for using decision making in the death education classroom relates to the notion that students are more likely to be satisfied with their decision if they use such a process. There are a variety of decision-making models that have been developed. Most of these models were developed under the premise that decision-making skills can be learned by students and subsequently applied to real-life situations. This premise supports the life-span intervention concepts outlined in Chapter 2 of the text.

Kime, Schlaadt, and Tritsch[10] state that there are three basic assumptions related to decision making regardless of the model used:

- The first assumption is that there is more than one alternative. If there is only one alternative or course of action, there is no need to use a decision-making model.
- The second assumption is that for decisions there are consequences. The consequences are the results of the outcomes of decisions and vary in complexity and severity. A good or bad decision is determined by the degree of satisfaction or dissatisfaction experienced as a result of the decision.

73

- The third assumption is that for every decision, there is a degree of risk involved. The purpose of the decision-making process is to help students reduce the risk of making a bad decision.

A variety of decision-making models have been developed. Some models address the decision-making process in general while others relate to the decision-making needs of specific content areas. An examination of these models reveals that there are some basic similarities among most decision-making models. These generic components include the following:

1. *Defining the problem:* This stage includes objectives to be considered in making the decision. (for example, health and safety, environmental effects, costs, convenience, social custom, and pleasure).
2. *Observing relevant data.* Through observation, measuring, testing, poll-taking, sampling, library research, interviews, and visits, students are asked to organize and evaluate data related to the problem.
3. *Citing alternatives with their pro's and con's:* Students are asked to outline the various alternatives and the losses and gains related to each alternative.
4. *Reviewing of data:* Students are asked to determine if the data originally collected are still valid and to determine if new data are needed.
5. *Making a personal choice:* Students are then asked to cite reasons for their choices and to discuss how their choices may affect other people.
6. *Evaluating the decisions:* At some point following their decisions, students are asked to evaluate the decisions they made along with the decision-making process.
7. *Recycling the problem:* If after evaluating their decisions, students are not satisfied with the decisions made, they can recycle through the decision-making process to the first step, which is defining the problem.

Because death education is a relatively new field of study, there is a need to determine the extent to which death education programs and methodologies have been able to increase the levels of cognition, favorably enhance death attitudes, and reduce death anxieties. In addition, there is a need to assess the types of programs and methodologies that have proven to be successful in promoting knowledge and attitudes related to death.

Descriptive literature

Death education programs have been developed for a variety of target groups: nurses, health educators, social scientists, medical students, elementary and secondary students, and college and university students. Many of these programs include cognitive, affective, and experiential components. Although the writings of many death educators have addressed the need to include death education in the curriculum for these target groups, several authors have outlined a scope sequence of content that might be included in such courses.

Sadwith[11] believed that the following topics should be included in a college-level death education course:

1. Biological aspects of death
2. Anthropological aspects of death
3. Euthanasia
4. Economic aspects of death and dying, that is, funeral costs, health-care costs, and nursing home costs
5. Sociological aspects of death and dying
6. Relationship of doctor and patient concerning death
7. Process of death and denying
8. Family reaction to death
9. Sex roles, romantic love, and death

Along with the discussion of the components of this death education course, Sadwith listed some suggestions for structuring a death education course. Sadwith believed that the focal point of death education should be classroom discussions. Sadwith also believed that the course should be flexible, that a sense of humor (in an appropriate manner) should be maintained, and that the instructor should be able to discuss with the students personal problems that might arise. In addition, Sadwith suggested that the death educator use local personnel (physicians, morticians, and religious leaders) as potential classroom resources.

Leviton[12] suggested that the death education experience be broken into three basic components: (1) the nature of death, (2) attitudinal and emotional correlates of death and dying, and (3) coping with death and dying. These three basic components incorporate the following content areas:

The nature of death:
1. The view of western philosophies toward death and dying
2. The view of great religions toward death
3. Theoretical views of death
4. The medical and legal aspects of death

Attitudinal and emotional correlates of death and dying:
1. Attitudes of children and adolescents toward death and dying
2. Adult attitudes toward death and dying
3. Attitudes of death-defying athletes, soldiers, and war-torn populations toward death

Coping with death and dying:
1. Communicating with terminally ill loved ones
2. The effects of the death of a loved one on the living
3. The relationship between the style of life and the style of death
4. Explaining to children the subject of death
5. The American funeral
6. Coming to terms with the inevitability of personal death
7. The role of language in reducing the fear of death

Leviton believed that suicide and suicide prevention should also be incorporated into the death education curriculum.

Yarber[5] provided a helpful and fairly complete outline of content appropriate for a death education course. Yarber believed that death education should be interdisciplinary in nature, including medical, legal, sociological, psychological, religious, and biological aspects of death. He thought that both the health science and the biological science classrooms are logical avenues to introduce death education into the curriculum.

Yarber believed that there is an abundance of content in death education. Possible areas of study in death education include the following:
1. Definitions, causes, and stages of death
2. The meaning of death in American society
3. Cross-cultural views and practices related to death
4. The life cycle
5. Funeral ceremonies and alternatives
6. Bereavement, grief, and mourning
7. Cremation
8. Cryogenics
9. Organ donation and transplant
10. Suicide and self-destructive behavior
11. Extending condolences to a relative or friend
12. Religious viewpoints of death
13. Legal and economic aspects of death
14. Death portrayed in music and literature
15. Understanding the dying relative or friend
16. Preparing for death
17. Euthanasia

Yarber provided this list as an overview of possible topics. The topics chosen and the depth of the content should be dictated by the age, maturity, and interests of the audience.

Corr[13] provided an excellent example of a model syllabus for death and dying courses. Corr believed that as a result of the recent and rapid proliferation of death education courses, there is a definite need to step back and examine the strengths and weaknesses of such courses. The author also suggested the following course syllabus for a broad-scale, introductory level death and dying course:

Unit 1: Self-confrontation and value identification
Unit 2: Analysis of a portrait of death and dying
Unit 3: Social and cultural attitudes
Unit 4: Historical and demographic background
Unit 5: Defining and determining death
Unit 6: Euthanasia
Unit 7: Suicide
Unit 8: Socially approved deaths
Unit 9: Dealing with dying
Unit 10: Survivors and grieving
Unit 11: Body disposal, funeral practices, and other practical consequences
Unit 12: Children and death
Unit 13: Life, death, and human dignity

This model provides a comprehensive syllabus. Although it does not address the educational aspects of the discipline, such as planning, methodology, and evaluation, this model does provide a useful example for the health professional, sociologist, or psychologist who wants to develop a death education course.

Leviton[12] also outlined possible topics for inclusion in a death and dying course. Leviton arranged topics for a college level death education course from the more objective, nonaffective topics, to the more sensitive, personal, highly emotional topics. The topics that were more impersonal included the following:

The language of death
Philosophical views of death
Anthropological and historical views of death
The sociology of dying and death
Theories of death
Religious views of death
Definitions of death

The following topics were more likely to evoke an emotional response from students:

The stress of dying and death
The process of dying: the meaning of death
The life cycle: the child

Sudden infant death syndrome

The life cycle: adolescence through middle age

The life cycle: old age

Bereavement and grief

Widowhood

The funeral from the view of the funeral director

The funeral from the view of the consumer advocate

Caring for the dying person and the family

The nature of suicide

Suicide prevention

Ethical issue: euthanasia

Ethical issue: war

The syllabus outlined by Leviton compares favorably with that provided by Corr. Although Leviton has outlined the topic areas with a bit more detail than Corr, both authors have provided a complete outline of content for an introductory death and dying course.

Death education courses for medical students generally address clinical and counseling concerns from a more didactic approach. Barton [14,15] outlined a sample death education course. He thought that for this audience (medical students) the lecture approach combined with group processing and discussion techniques were the most effective techniques for this target group. A course for medical students should cover the following:

Literature on death and dying

Life-prolonging procedures

Grief and bereavement

Religious and philosophical aspects

Management of terminally ill patients

Ethical issues

Family interactions

A continued discussion of the potential content for courses related to dying and death could continue for quite some time. It is sufficient to say that the educator seeking to develop a death education course has a variety of curriculum guidelines available.

Evaluation of programs

Although many studies describe the scope and nature of death education courses, a few authors have evaluated the effectiveness of death education. These research studies have used a variety of research methodologies and designs. Because of this, the findings may be interpreted in a variety of ways. Nonetheless, the results of some of these studies are offered to provide the reader with a foundation on which to build a curriculum.

Most research on the effectiveness of death education courses has been designed to assess changes in death attitudes. Appendix E highlights some of the recent research conducted on the effectiveness of death education.

The research on death education programs and courses seems to indicate that death education can be effective in improving knowledge and attitudes and in reducing death anxiety. It is interesting to note that most programs that demonstrated these results incorporated a variety of instructional modalities (discussions, field trips, role playing, values clarification, and audiovisual devices) along with the lecture of didactic approach to death education. It seems, then, the most successful programs are those that blend personal and experiential components into the curriculum along with factual information. In the published research on death education, several limitations can be noted. First, the researchers often do not adhere to rigorous research methodologies. This is a contention and concern of many death educators who wish to elevate the status of death education. Secondly, many studies have used knowledge, attitude, and behavioral instruments for which no reliability and validity data were reported. This situation reflects the lack of reliable and valid instrumentation in the area and poses a challenge for death educators to develop such instrumentation.

Assessment of needs

As can be seen by the descriptions of health education programs and the evaluative research, most of the literature in the area deals with descriptive research and research that uses unsophisticated design methodologies. As a result, there is a need to conduct research in a variety of death education areas[16]:

1. Which educational methodologies are the most effective? There needs to be further study conducted on which types of educational methods are the most successful in positively changing cognition and affect. Before a death education curriculum is designed, it is important for the death educator to have confidence that the instructional techniques can actually facilitate cognitive and affective growth. Because death education courses are generally taught on a one-shot basis or only receive a limited amount of time in the school curriculum, it is important to make prudent use of the time allotted.

2. Which instructional materials are the most effective? As death education becomes more popular, new instructional materials will be developed and sold commercially. It will be important to assess the quality of these materials, as well as the impact of the materials related to death and dying on cognition, affect, and

behavior change. Gideon[17] provided an excellent set of criteria for evaluating death education curriculum materials that are used in grades kindergarten through 12:

A. Multiple usage of material
    1. *Age groups:* Can this child's book be useful to older students as well? Is a particular film appropriate for preteens as well as teenagers?
    2. *Topics:* What issues are addressed in this material? Most materials cover several topics. Can the same film, book, or filmstrip be used to kick off several discussions or raise several issues? For example, does a film on euthanasia include the issue of the dynamics of family relationships?
    3. *Grouping:* Would this film or book be appropriate in a history class as well as a class on death and dying?

B. Accuracy of information
    1. Is the information outdated or still current?
    2. Was the material written or produced by a group with an obvious bias? If so, will that bias be detrimental or helpful for the intended use of the material?

C. Guidelines for use of material
    1. Are there suggested warm-up activities to prepare the students for the material?
    2. Are there suggested prerequisites?
    3. Are there suggested objectives?
    4. Are there suggested follow-up activities to help the learner process what has been experienced?

D. References and bibliographies
    1. Are they available?
    2. Are they written in such a manner that an interested teacher or learner can continue to learn about the topics in the curriculum material?

E. Quality of the material
    1. Is the technical quality good? Is the sound clear? Is the printing appropriate for the age and reading level of students?
    2. Is the length appropriate? Is it too long and boring? Too short? Is too much information covered in too little time or space?
    3. Is the vocabulary appropriate for intended learners and not laden with euphemisms?
    4. Are there appropriate illustrations? Scary? Nonthreatening, yet not hiding necessary truths? Is the print large for the young reader?

F. Availability of material
    1. Can it be rented or borrowed from a public institution or must it be purchased?
    2. Can film footage be replaced?
    3. Is the book in open stock? Does the publisher have good service?

G. Past use and results of material
    1. Has the material been field tested? Can one obtain the results of that testing?
    2. Have reliable persons or reviewers recommended material for your purpose?

H. Educational quality of material, specifically for test, curriculum guides, and other related material
   1. Is there a logical scope and sequence?
   2. What is the philosophy behind the death education curriculum material?
   3. For what population was it designed? Inner city? Rural? Teenagers?
   4. Are there guidelines for adapting it to the population of the specific instructor, to special students, to gifted students, or to handicapped students?
   5. Is there a summary available?
   6. Does the producer or author suggest means of evaluating the student?
   7. Are suggested lesson plans offered?
I. Cost of material
   1. Because of today's limited budgets, cost becomes a very powerful tool for evaluating the purchase of any curriculum material. However, if a specific death education curriculum material can serve a multitude of uses over a long span of time and speak to various populations, the cost per use can be markedly decreased. In the long run, an expensive initial outlay may be less expensive than numerous small expenditures.

3. Does death education change behavior? Although a death education course may alter cognition and affect, it does not necessarily mean that it will foster positive behavior change among students. Research in this area needs to be conducted to determine whether death education reduces the incidence of suicide, increases the percentage of people who draw up wills, increases the percentage of people who preplan funeral arrangements, improves communication between parents and children regarding death, and increases the percentage of people who complete a "living will" or similar document.

4. Who teaches death education and what are their qualifications? Death education courses are taught in a variety of settings by professionals with divergent backgrounds. A systematic study needs to be conducted to determine the qualifications of death educators and the academic disciplines that foster death education.

5. What are the long-term effects of death education? Much of the knowledge, attitudes and behaviors that death educators are trying to change may not be immediately applicable to the students. It is important for research to be conducted to determine the impact of death education on the ability of students to cope with subsequent life events. For example, as a result of a death education experience in a university setting, students may conceptualize the need to preplan funeral arrangements. Research also needs to be conducted to determine whether such instruction will have an impact 20 years later.

6. What type of students enroll in death education courses? Many studies compare

students enrolled in death education courses with a randomly selected control group. Characteristics (both attitudinal and demographic) of students need to be assessed to determine the nature of students who enroll in death education courses, their attitudes toward the subject, and the types of personal life events that may predispose them to enroll in a death education course.

These research questions address only a fraction of the death education concerns and indicate the need for further study. It is sufficient to say the descriptive, experimental, and quasi-experimental research that utilizes appropriate research design, adequate sample sizes, and reliable and valid instrumentation needs to be conducted. A subsequent section of this chapter discusses the development of cognitive and affective death education instruments.

Evaluation of student progress

To this point the discussion of assessment has addressed the need to evaluate the effectiveness of death education courses and programs. Because of the uniqueness of death education, the evaluation of student progress should also be discussed. Evaluation is composed of two parts. First, a measurement must be made of student's proficiency or attitude in a particular task or content area. Second, a judgment must be made based on that measurement. For example, an individual may be measured to be 4 feet 10 inches tall. A judgment based on the height measurement might be , "You're too short to be a policeman." Or a student may receive a score of 18 on a death and dying knowledge test. That is the measurement; the judgment is the *A* grade assigned by the teacher. The evaluation process must include measurement and judgment.

There are two basic types of evaluation commonly used in educational settings: *norm-referenced evaluation* and *criterion-referenced evaluation.* Norm-referenced evaluation is used as a means of student comparison. The Scholastic Aptitude Test and American College Test commonly given to high school seniors interested in attending college are examples of norm-referenced evaluation. The students taking these tests are compared to one another and with students who have taken the tests in previous years. Criterion-reference evaluation is used to judge the performance of a student according to a previously established standard rather than as a comparison with other students. Determining if a student has successfully outlined a personal position statement related to euthanasia or if the student successfully preplanned a funeral are examples of criterion-referenced evaluation.

There are several requirements for effective evaluation. The first requirement is that the evaluation procedure be determined prior to the beginning of class. Students should be informed during the initial days of the class of the specific nature of the grading system. The most important criterion is that evaluation should be based on the educational objectives. The evaluation activity should test the behavior identified in the objective. If the evaluation activity is inconsistent with the objective, the evaluation strategy must be adapted to become consistent with the objective.

Evaluation must also be based on the emotional and physical maturity of the students. Student maturity will vary with each class. One class may be mature enough to handle a particular evaluation activity while another class may be too embarrassed or developmentally unable to complete the evaluation.

Evaluation should be as objective as possible and must facilitate the consistent scoring by the teacher. The teacher should prepare a scoring guide that specifies the criteria by which the students will be measured. Once the scoring guide is completed, consistent, reliable scoring is possible. Evaluation should also provide various experiences for the students. A teacher who only practices one format of evaluation, such as multiple-choice tests, is being unfair to the students in class who do not perform well on multiple-choice tests. Educational objectives that require students to be evaluated by a variety of techniques, such as class reports, role-playing situations, educational games and puzzles, panel discussions, group activities, and the development of posters and displays, can be used effectively to evaluate student achievement of an educational objective. It should be noted that all educational activities conducted in the classroom need to be evaluated for grading purposes.

Construction of assessment instruments

As the number of death education programs increases and as the programs become more diverse in nature, death educators should begin to evaluate the effectiveness of programming, instructional methodologies, and learning strategies. Effective research of death education programs, methods, and strategies requires the availability of reliable and valid measurement instruments. Because death education is a relatively new field of study, few such instruments have been properly developed and validated. Consequently, to properly assesss the impact of death education programs, death educators may have to develop and validate measurement instruments appropriate for the target population and educational goals.

To assist in this attempt to develop reliable instruments, a discussion of procedures that can be used to develop a knowledge instrument, an attitudinal inventory, and a behavior questionnaire will be discussed. Appendixes C and D contain examples of such instruments.

Development of knowledge test of death and dying

The development of a standardized testing instrument should adhere to sound developmental procedures. Nunnally[18] outlined several procedural steps that should be followed when a standardized evaluative instrument is being developed. Among these steps are the following:

1. *Content outline:* The outline of content for a knowledge test should be developed by experts in the field of endeavor for which the instrument is being designed. In the case of death education, this would include experts in the cognitive areas of death and dying as well as authorities in the death education curriculum development field.

2. *Curriculum research:* The curricula of death education courses should be scrutinized and compared to the content of the proposed instrument to insure content consistency.

3. *Experimental edition:* Following the specification of content, the curriculum research phase, and the formulation of test items, an experimental edition of the test should be prepared and reviewed by experts in the death education field. Inappropriate items should be deleted.

4. *Item analysis:* The item analysis should include two major components: (1) a difficulty rating for each item and (2) the discriminating power of each item.

5. *Try-out program:* The test should be administered to varied populations. This will help to develop normative data on the instrument.

Nunnally's suggestions serve as guidelines for the death educator who wants to develop a knowledge instrument. Appendix D outlines the eight-phase model used to develop a Knowledge Test of Death and Dying. This instrument has been validated by a select group of death educators and could prove useful for assessing levels of cognitions in a variety of settings.

Construction of death attitude questionnaires

Questionnaires are very popular and effective research tools. Part of their popularity is rooted in the notion that every individual assumes that he or she knows how to ask questions. However, asking the proper question to obtain the exact information one wants or to test a hypothesis is a difficult task. A poorly designed questionnaire will not achieve the stated objectives and may cause embarrassment for the researcher when colleagues point out biases in the wording and structuring of the questionnaire. If the respondent draws a different meaning from the questionnaire items than the researcher intended, the instrument will be worthless.

Questionnaires have been severely criticized for common weaknesses, of which many can be avoided. Van Dalen[19] outlines some pertinent points researchers should consider when developing a questionnaire. The following checklist highlights these points and concerns:

1. *Establishing rapport:* When establishing a rapport between the researcher and the subjects, the following questions should be addressed:
   ____ Is the study worthy of the respondent's time?
   ____ Have the researchers obtained permission at the highest level to conduct the research?
   ____ Does the cover letter clearly outline the purpose of the questionnaire?
   ____ Is the researcher's institution position and title clearly stated?
   ____ Does the questionnaire significantly contribute to the body of knowledge?
   ____ Does the questionnaire and cover letter attract the interest of the respondents?
   ____ Does the research offer to provide a summary of the results to the respondents?
2. *Framing of questions:* A properly worded question is an absolute necessity for a valid questionnaire. When developing questionnaire items, the researcher should ask the following questions:
   ____ Has the researcher thoroughly explored the literature related to the question?
   ____ Does the question relate to the stated hypothesis?
   ____ Has the researcher weighted the number of questions in accordance with the importance of the issue?
   ____ Are the questions redundant?
   ____ Does each question focus on a specific point?
   ____ Is a Likert-type scale used when appropriate?
   ____ Does the researcher provide enough alternative responses for each question?
3. *Orderly questions:* The questions should be ordered in a logical sequence with the more simple and neutral questions preceding the more difficult, controversial or personal questions.
   ____ Are similar types of questions grouped together?
   ____ Is there a smooth transition from one group of questions to the next?
   ____ Do the questions progress from simple to complex?
   ____ Are the questions ordered so that the nonpersonal and neutral questions precede the controversial and personal questions?
   ____ Are the questions ordered to arouse and maintain the interest of the respondents?
4. *Designing direction and format:* A concise, clear format with the easy to understand directions will help to improve the response rate of the questionnaire.
   ____ Are clear and concise directions given?

_____ Do the respondents know where to place responses?

_____ Does the format facilitate analysis of the data?

_____ Are any sample questions or illustrations necessary?

_____ What are the best type of questions to ask for the researcher's audience, setting, and hypothesis: dichotomous, multiple choice, short answer, Likert-type, or other type?

5. *Eliciting honest replies:* The wording of the questionnaire items, to a large extent, determines the ability of the questionnaire to elicit honest responses.

_____ Are the questions worded so as to limit embarrassment and fear on the part of the respondent?

_____ If personal questions are asked, is the anonymity of the respondent insured?

_____ Are questions leading or written in such a way to show researchers' biases?

_____ Is the researcher asking for information the respondents are not qualified to answer?

_____ Does the researcher ask parallel questions to insure consistency of responses?

The checklist outlined above highlights the notion that the development and administration of a questionnaire, if done correctly, is a complex task.

SUMMARY

The study of death and dying, once a taboo subject, has gained widespread popularity. Courses are being offered for academic credit within the public schools and on college campuses. Interest courses are frequently conducted in community settings. This chapter begins with a discussion of the planning process for educational programs. Considerations must focus on the needs and interests of the intended target population as a prerequisite to the selection of content and methodology. During the planning stage, teachers should take advantage of both human and material resources available in the community. Since knowledge gain is seldom the only objective of an educational endeavor, student attitudes, beliefs, and personal health practices must be considered by the teacher when course objectives are being developed. A professional effort requires that the teacher consider basic principles of educational psychology.

Conceptual, unit, and competency-based approaches to curriculum development are discussed. The suggested course content is based on a review of existing curricula, input by consultant experts, and current literature. Additionally, the chapter presents effective classroom techniques for presenting death education. The advantages and disadvantages of specific instructional methods are portrayed, with a special emphasis on values clarification and decision making. Finally, the chapter offers the reader information on the evaluation of educational programs, student progress, and educational materials along with an entire section devoted to the construction of assessment instruments and standardized tests.

REFERENCES

1. Leviton, D.: The scope of death education, Death Education **1**:41-56, 1977.
2. Berg, D., and Daughtery, G.: Death education: a survey of colleges and universities, DeKalb, Ill., 1974, Educational Perspectives Associates.
3. Tyler, R.W.: Basic principles of curriculum and instruction, Chicago, 1971, University of Chicago Press.
4. Harris, W.: Some reflections concerning approaches to death education, The Journal of School Health **48**:162-165, 1978.
5. Yarber, W.: Death education: a living issue, The Science Teacher, **43**:21-23, 1976.
6. School Health Education Study: Health education: a conceptual approach. St. Paul, 1967, 3M Education Press.
7. Eddy, J.M., St. Pierre, R.W., Alles, W.F., Shute, R.E.: Conceptual areas of death education, Health Education, **11**:14-15, January-February 1980.
8. Wittich, W.A. and Schyller, C.F.: Audio-visual materials, New York, 1953, Harper & Brothers.
9. Raths, L.E., Harmin, M., and Simon, S.: Values and teaching: working with values in the classroom, Columbus, Ohio, 1966, Charles E. Merrill Publishing Co.
10. Kime, R.E., Schlaadt, R.G., and Tritsch, L.E.: Health education: an action approach, Englewood Cliffs, NJ., 1977, Prentice-Hall, Inc.
11. Sadwith, J.: An interdisciplinary approach to death education, Journal of School Health, **44**: 455-458, 1974.
12. Leviton, D.: Education for Death, Journal of Health, Physical Education and Recreation **40**: 46-47, 1969.
13. Corr, C.A.: A model syllabus for death and dying courses, Death education **4**:433-457, 1978.
14. Barton, D., Flexner, J., Van Eys, J., and Scott, C.: Death and dying: a course of medical students, Journal of Medical Education **47**: 945-951, 1972.
15. Barton, D., and Crowder, M.: The use of role playing as an instructional aid in teaching about death, dying and bereavement, Omega **6**:199-205, 1975.
16. Crase, D.A.: The need to assess the impact of death education, Death education **1**: 423-432, 1978.
17. Gideon, M.: Criteria for evaluating curriculum materials in death education from grades K-12, Death Education, **1**:235-239, 1977.
18. Nunnally, J: Education measurement and evaluation, New York, 1964, McGraw-Hill Book Co.
19. Van Dalen, D.B.: Understanding educational research: an introduction, New York, 1973, McGraw-Hill Book Co., pp. 327-329.

Courtesy Guidance Associates, Mt. Kisco, N.Y.

CHAPTER FOUR

Bereavement, grief, and mourning

*We are rediscovering that expression of grief is not a sign of weakness or self-indulgence. Rather, it is a normal and necessary reaction to loss or separation from a loved or significant person, and represents a deep human need.**

HERMAN FEIFEL

The terms *bereavement, grief,* and *mourning* are often used synonymously. A recently widowed woman may be labeled as *bereaved, grief-stricken,* or *in mourning* by friends and relatives. Although these terms may be used interchangeably, they have distinct meanings. We will begin by defining these terms and citing examples of each.

Robert Kastenbaum[1] has done an excellent job conceptualizing these terms and providing definitions of each:

"Bereavement is an objective fact. We are bereaved when a person close to us dies. It is also a change in status. The child may have become an orphan, the spouse a widow or widower. Bereavement is a recognized social fact, then, as well as an objective fact."[1]

In essence, when someone we know dies, we are bereaved. There are a variety of historical examples of bereavement. The assassination of President Kennedy caused the entire nation to be bereaved. The vast majority of the populace did not personally know the late president, but because of his status, the country was bereaved. The impact of this bereavement is evident today. National sentiment following the assassination was a major factor in the passage of Kennedy-sponsored legislation by Congress and the naming of athletic stadiums, airports, schools, and streets after the late president.

"Grief is a response to bereavement. It is how the survivor feels. It is also how the survivor thinks, eats, sleeps and makes it through the day."[1] Grief is not the only possible response to bereavement, but is the most common. The state of grief is more descriptive than explanatory. Lindemann[2] provides insight in his now-classic study

---

*From Feifel, Herman, editor: New meanings of death, New York, 1977, McGraw-Hill Book Co., p. 9.

The way in which people as a culture respond to death constitutes the mourning rites. In the United States, the traditional American funeral process seems to typify the socially acceptable mourning process.

Courtesy Guidance Associates, Mt. Kisco, N.Y.

- Sensations of somatic distress occurring in waves lasting from 20 minutes to an hour at a time
- A feeling of tightness in the throat
- A need for sighing
- An empty feeling in the abdomen
- A lack of muscular power
- An intense subjective distress described as tension or mental pain

Obviously, the grief process affects all components of human function. However, not everyone responds to the death of close friends or relatives in the same manner. A variety of factors, including the relationship of the bereaved to the deceased and the circumstances surrounding the death, may affect the grief process. This is discussed in more detail later in the chapter.

Mourning, according to Kastenbaum, has been defined as the "culturally patterned expressions of the bereaved person's thoughts and feelings."[1] In essence, the way in which people as a culture respond to death constitutes the mourning rites. In the United States the traditional American funeral process seems to typify the socially acceptable mourning process. In addition, flying the flag at half-mast, wearing black arm bands, firing the 21-gun salute, and wearing black are examples of the mourning rituals in the United States.[1] Mourning might be described as a patterned expression of the behavior based on religious and cultural traditions that occurs at the death of a member of a group.

GRIEF RESPONSE

As mentioned previously, grief is a psychological and, to a certain extent, physiological response to the death of a friend or relative. It is estimated that each year in the United States 4 to 5 million people will experience the grief response. Similar to many other areas related to death and dying, the grief response has been the subject of little research until recently.

It is important for health professionals to be aware of the manifestations of the grief syndrome to assist clients and students in dealing more effectively with this most stressful of life events. Also, it is important to note here that there is no medical cure for grief. The health professional needs to be able to provide care for the bereaved. In essence, the health professional should possess the skills necessary to provide support to the bereaved and, in turn, to facilitate the natural healing process that takes place over time.

To this end, it is important to discuss the ordinary grief syndrome (Table 4-1). Although this ordinary grief syndrome may present a generally predictable course with definable stages, it should be emphasized that none of these stages is absolute. Obviously, the behavioral patterns and emotional response to the death of a loved one are dependent on a myriad of variables, including the following.

Culture. The culture that the survivors are reared in may have a significant influence on their grief response. For example, in contrast to the members of many religious sects in the United States, many Jewish people continue to observe a pattern of mourning rituals that are remarkably parallel to the stages of the ordinary grief response outlined in Table 4-1. Cognizant of the intense grief response of the first week, the bereaved are directed to remain in their own homes to cry and lament the death. Following this, friends and relatives are encouraged to visit the bereaved but to talk only of the deceased. For the first month, the bereaved generally resumes only the

Table 4-1: Hypothetical stages of ordinary grief response

Stage	Timetable	Possible manifestations	Possible behaviors
Stage I: denial, shock, and disbelief	Begins immediately after the death and lasts up to 2 weeks. This stage peaks from 4 to 14 days.	Shock, stunned numbness, anxiety, crying, confusion, denial, disbelief, stress, tightness in throat and shortness of breath.	Sighing, calling for deceased, preoccupation with thoughts of deceased, lack of attention to personal appearance, and illusions of the deceased
Stage II: despair and mental images of deceased	Generally starts 2 to 3 weeks after the death and begins to decline after 12 weeks. Can last up to a year.	Continued sadness and despair, episodic numbness and apathy, mental images of deceased, preoccupation with thoughts of deceased, loss of sense of purpose, irritability, and anger	Loss of appetite, insomnia, withdrawal, physiological sign of depression, restlessness, short tempered, and denial of self-pleasures
Stage III: recovery, resolution, and return to normalcy	Usually occurs within a year to 15 months of the death.	Decreased episodic sadness, recalled past pleasures, decreased frequency and intensity of stage II manifestations, and resolution	Return to normal activities, development of new behaviors and skills, and development of new relationships

most essential tasks. For the remainder of the year the bereaved are expected to express grief publicly but also to gradually resume and assume ordinary life activities. As discussed later, cultural mores may have a significant influence on the grief response.

Relationship of bereaved to deceased. Research has shown that the closer the relationship of the bereaved to the deceased, the higher the level of stress. Generally, the death of a spouse elicits a stronger grief response than the death of a family member. This variable of the grief response also has a qualitative component in that it is generally believed that the better the relationship is between the bereaved and the deceased, the better the bereaved is able to handle the grief syndrome. There are a variety of reasons to explain this observation, but psychologists believe that guilt may be a contributing factor.

Personal characteristics. The age of the deceased often influences the severity and duration of the grief response. Generally, a young widow has a much more difficult and prolonged grief response than does an older widow. A variety of factors could contribute to this, but it is generally thought that the older widow has had more life experiences to help her prepare for this loss and that the young widow may have experienced fewer such life events. Also, the young widow may be obsessed with the injustice of her husband being taken in the prime of his lfe. The gender of deceased (and the various roles and responsibilities) may influence the grief response. The housewife who must become the sole breadwinner for the family or the businessman who must combine his work with his new family-rearing duties has acquired new roles and responsibilities that may affect his or her ability to cope with the grief syndrome.

Other life-change events. The subsequent life-change events that could occur following a death may also influence the syndrome or ordinary grief. If the bereaved must assume new roles, change residence, or find employment, these life-change events could have an impact on the ordinary grief response. Table 4-2 presents the Holmes and Rahe scale of life-change events.[3] A few minutes should be taken to glance at this scale to look for those life events that may occur before, concurrent with, or shortly after the death of a loved one. The cumulative nature of these life-change events have a perceptible effect on the ability of the bereaved to handle the grief response. For example, following the death of a spouse, the widow or widower may experience a change in financial status, experience a foreclosure of a mortgage or loan, have to begin a new job, and change residence and also experience a change in living conditions, recreational activities, church activities, eating habits, and sleep habits. To complicate matters, the cumulative effect of these stressors may influence the personal health status of the bereaved.

Table 4-2: Stress associated with change

Life event	Scale of impact
Death of spouse	100
Divorce	73
Marital separation	65
Jail term	63
Death of close family member	63
Personal illness or injury	53
Marriage	50
Fired at work	47
Marriage reconciliation	45
Retirement	45
Change of health of family member	44
Pregnancy	40
Sex difficulty	39
Gain of new family member	39
Business adjustment	39
Change in financial state	38
Death of a close friend	37
Change to different line of work	36
Change in number of arguments with spouse	35
Mortgage or loan for major purchase (home, etc.)	31
Foreclosure of mortgage or loan	30
Change in responsibilities at work	29
Son or daughter leaving home	29
Trouble with in-laws	29
Outstanding personal achievement	28
Wife begins or stops work	26
Begin or end school	26
Change in living conditions	25
Revision of personal habits	24
Trouble with boss	23
Change in work hours or conditions	20
Change in residence	20
Change in schools	20
Change in recreation	19
Change in church activities	19
Change in social activity	18
Mortgage or loan for lesser purchase (car, television, etc.)	17
Change in sleeping habits	16
Change in number of family get-togethers	15
Change in eating habits	15
Vacation	13
Christmas	12
Minor violation of the law	11

Reprinted with permission from *Journal of Psychosomatic Research,* **11,** Holmes, T.R., and Rahe, R.H., Social readjustment scale, Copyright 1967, Pergamon Press, Ltd.

■ ■ ■

Because there are a variety of factors that influence the grief response, it is difficult to determine what a normal sequence of events should be for the bereaved. Therefore the stages of ordinary grief presented in this chapter should serve as guidlelines of what could possibly occur in the process and are not intended to convey a notion of a good or appropriate grief response.

The first stage of the ordinary grief response begins immediately after the news of the death is heard and generally lasts up to 2 weeks. This stage is characterized by denial, shock, and disbelief and may provide the bereaved with a form of psychological protection that enables them to attend to the various matters related to the death without being totally dysfunctional. Mourners at a funeral often wonder how a widow or widower can remain so remarkably composed throughout the funeral ceremony. It may relate to this concept that the widow or widower is still consciously or unconsciously denying the fact that his or her spouse has died.

There is an obvious comparison between stage I of the ordinary grief response and the study of Kubler-Ross that is related to the terminally ill patient.[4] As mentioned earlier, these denial phases allow the individual a period of time that is sometimes necessary to collect thoughts and organize a less radical response to the traumatic life event that has just occurred. During this period the bereaved will generally not seek professional help. It is important for the health professional to have a clear understanding of the wide variation of behaviors that are considered normal during this stage. Health professionals should have mastered many of their own anxieties and fears related to death before offering assistance or guidance to grief-stricken individuals immediately following the death.

The second stage of the normal grief syndrome is characterized by episodic periods of despair, numbness, and apathy coupled with preoccupations and memories or mental images of the deceased. This stage generally begins 2 to 3 weeks after the death and usually begins to decline in about 3 months, although it may last up to a year. During this time grief-stricken individuals may be angry, irritable, and apathetic and also may seem to have lost their sense of purpose. Often, the bereaved tend to deny themselves of personal pleasures and tend to withdraw socially. It should be noted that these feelings and emotions do not arrive in a predictable sequence.

The most obvious or observable aspect of stage II is the recurrent episodic bouts of sadness and tearful longings that are brought about by the memories of the deceased. It is important for the health professional to realize that various events during any given period of time can trigger a painful mental image of the deceased. All too often people assume that because a widow or widower seems to function normally on Monday and then displays overt signs and symptoms of grief response on Tuesday, the bereaved is backsliding or not progressing toward a satisfactory recovery or resolution. Again, it is important to stress the notion that although grief is a process of gradual adaptation to a loss, there may be weekly, daily, or even hourly fluctuations in overt grief symptoms. An important role of the health educator is to help students conceptualize this notion of individual variation and fluctuation in the grief response to enhance the ability of individuals to deal more effectively with their own grief responses as well as that of others.

During stage II it is important to provide the bereaved with an opportunity to express feelings of grief. Often friends and family members who are experiencing their own form of grief find it too painful to bring up the subject of the deceased for fear of witnessing another tearful episode. Nonetheless, it is important to encourage the bereaved to discuss their feelings even if the experience is painful. Parkes found that widows who experience intense, painful, yet open discussions about their grief tended to display less distress or incapacity than widows who initially expressed little or no grief. It appears then that it is healthy to discuss the grief response with the bereaved although many people feel uncomfortable doing so.

Frequently during this stage the bereaved suffer guilt concerning the death of the deceased. This guilt may arise from a feeling on the part of the bereaved that in some way they have failed the deceased. The bereaved individual may start to wonder, "What if I had been more attentive to the needs of the deceased?" "What if I would have encouraged him to stop smoking?" or "If I would have not allowed her to work so hard, she might still be alive today." Also, like many of us, the bereaved may feel guilty concerning things they did not say or do for the deceased while he or she was alive. The bereaved need to be allowed to express these guilty ruminations.

In the third stage of the ordinary grief response, the bereaved begins to show signs of recovery and resolution of their grief and to resume ordinary life functions. The third stage generally occurs within a year to 15 months of the death. However, two points need to be stressed here. First, grief does not necessarily end in any specific period of time. A variety of events, such as Christmas or anniversaries, can trigger episodic responses, although these responses generally are not as severe as those found in the early phases of stage II. Second, the stages are often intermingled. Again, grief is a gradual adaptation to the loss of a loved one; therefore it is extremely difficult to determine when one stage ends and another stage begins.

Generally, during stage III the frequency and severity of the episodic bouts of longing and despair decline. The bereaved begin to formulate fond memories of the deceased but do so with less pain and sadness. In essence, what seems to be happening is that the bereaved are gradually accepting the loss and are beginning to take positive steps to resume normal activities. In addition, during this time the bereaved begin to experiment with the development of new relationships and social roles to satisfy personal needs and expectations.

ATYPICAL GRIEF RESPONSE

The ordinary grief response previously outlined in the chapter highlights the notion that there is much variance in the grief response of individuals. Occasionally, the grief response is more prolonged or intense than normal and becomes a mental illness. This is often called the pathological, morbid, or atypical grief response. Often in the atypical grief response the mourner is obsessed with the notion that the deceased will return. In essence, the mourner has intellectually accepted the fact that the death has occurred but is emotionally denying the death.

There could be a variety of factors that may cause a pathological grief response. Some of the more salient are the following:

1. *Sudden death:* The sudden death of a friend or relative is often considered a high-grief death. As such, the ability of the mourner to cope is diminished because of the lack of an anticipatory grief period.

2. *Suicide:* There is still a stigma connected with suicide. Many believe that something they did or did not do may have been a contributing factor to suicide. In addition, suicidal persons often leave behavioral indicators of their potential for lethal behavior prior to the actual act of suicide. Therefore, in cases of suicide, the bereaved may experience high levels of guilt as a result of the belief that either they were in some way a contributing factor in the suicide or their intervention at the appropriate time could have prevented the suicide. This high level of guilt may be a causative factor in a morbid grief response.

3. *When the body was not found:* When there is no positive identification of the body or no body can be found, there may be a prolonged grief response. The bereaved is obsessed with the notion that the person did not actually die, and the individual may experience prolonged preoccupation with thoughts of the deceased, which is identified in the early stages of the ordinary grief response.

4. *When the next of kin has to make a decision on medical care:* If the next of kin has to authorize the use of a sophisticated medical procedure, the level of guilt of the bereaved may be heightened. Without knowing the wishes of the deceased, these are difficult decisions that place the next of kin in an awkward situation. If the relatives decide not to authorize the medical procedure, they may experience an increased level of guilt because they did not do everything

humanly possible to keep the loved one alive. On the other hand, if the relatives do authorize such procedures and the patient suffers through a slow, prolonged, and painful death, again the level of guilt is likely to increase. As mentioned previously, an increase in the level of guilt may increase the likelihood of experiencing a pathological or morbid grief response.

5. *Close relationship:* The closer the relationship between the deceased and the bereaved, the more likely there will be a pathological grief response. Again, guilt may be a contributing factor. For example, in couples in which there was a mature and satisfying relationship, the bereaved will experience grief but without a high level of guilt. In relationships that were less mature and not as stable, the level of guilt may increase as a result of the notion on the part of the bereaved that in some way a stormy relationship may have been a contributing factor in the death. It is important to put guilt in a proper perspective. Too much self-inflicted guilt may result from the bereaved saying, "I could or should have done more."

Lindemann[2] outlined two major manifestations of the morbid grief response in his classic study of the symptomology of grief: delay of reaction and distorted reaction. Lindemann believed that the most frequently occurring and most striking morbid grief response is this delay or postponement of the grief response. He found, "If the bereavement occurs at a time when the patient is confronted with important tasks and when there is necessity for maintaining the morale of others, he may show little or no reactions for weeks, or even longer."[2] This delayed emotional response could last several weeks or longer. During this time the bereaved may be exhibiting a state of general well-being, but the internalization of the grief response may result in a variety of psychosomatic illnesses or later mental health problems.

The distorted reactions that Lindemann and others speak of may be considered manifestations of unresolved grief.[3] Such reactions include the following:

1. *Overactivity:* Without a sense of loss and with a general sense of well-being and zeal, the bereaved may engage in adventurous activities that often bear a resemblance to those of the deceased.

2. *Acquiring of symptoms of the deceased:* The bereaved may display symptoms of the last illness of the deceased. These may be either real or imagined. The widow whose husband died of heart disease may experience symptoms of a heart problem, and in rare cases these symptoms may even show up on an electrocardiogram.

3. *Mummification:* In mummification, the personal environment and personal affects of the deceased remain unchanged for months and even years. Queen Victoria, after the death of Prince Albert, was careful to keep everything in the

palace as Albert had left it. More recently, this phenomena has been recognized in childhood death case studies. The bereaved parents keep the room of the deceased child exactly as the child left it for an extended period of time. In these case studies the cleaning and rearranging of the room is an overt admission by the parents that the child is dead and is not coming back—recognition that is too emotionally painful to endure at the time of death.

4. *Altered relationship to friends and relatives:* The bereaved may be irritable and short tempered and may seek to deny himself or herself pleasure. Because of these manifestations, the bereaved may think they will "be a bother" and consequently avoid social activities. To a certain extent this reaction may be evident in the ordinary grief response. However, if prolonged, this reaction provides an indication that the bereaved is having difficulty working through the grief response.

5. *Extreme hostility toward a specific person:* It is normal for the bereaved to question in their own minds whether the doctors, nurses, or hospital did all that was humanly possible for the deceased. However, in a morbid grief response the bereaved may have an exaggerated belief that the health care system was negligent or gave up life-saving efforts too soon.

6. *Inability to become integrated back into society:* Generally, in the recovery phase of the ordinary grief response the bereaved will begin to establish new relationships, assume new roles, and return to a normal life-style. In this example of a pathological or morbid grief response the bereaved does not become properly integrated back into society. In essence, the person is merely going through the motions of life. The bereaved may perform expected social roles, for example, care of children, clean house, and provide financial support, but they are unable to satisfy personal needs or develop meaningful interpersonal relationships. The bereaved try to function in a social setting, but their actions are formal and robotlike and may lack normal human concern.

In the atypical grief response, the bereaved experience many of the manifestations outlined in the ordinary grief response, but the timing, duration, or intensity of the response is distorted.

There are a variety of intervention strategies and counseling programs designed to help individuals cope with bereavement and grief. Some of these programs are outlined in Chapter 8. However, it should be stressed that bereavement and grief are normal responses to death and therefore not readily preventable. Most of the programs developed to help the bereaved are steeped in counseling and therefore not within the educational scope of this text.

KUBLER-ROSS AND RELATED RESEARCH

Until recently, there had been a dearth of information concerning the emotional and psychological aspects of the dying individual. There was a lack of a systematic description of the emotional aspects of the dying process along with a void of research in this area. One of the first authors to develop and popularize a systematic description of the dying process was Elisabeth Kubler-Ross.[4] In her book *On Death and Dying,* she studied approximately 200 terminally ill patients and found they progress through five psychological stages: denial and isolation, anger, bargaining, depression, and acceptance. Although the findings of Kubler-Ross have been criticized for the lack of an empirical research design, it is important to discuss her work to lay a foundation on which appropriate implications may be drawn.

In the first stage, denial and isolation, the patient expresses a "no, not me," reaction. The patient may believe there was a mix-up in the diagnosis or in the laboratory reports, and there was no possible way the medical evidence would be correct. The denial process may function as a buffer that allows the patients time to gather themselves and time to develop other, less radical defenses. Kubler-Ross believed that radical forms of denial may be caused by the patient being informed too abruptly by someone who does not know the patient or how to inform a patient about a terminal condition. An excellent example of a radical or prolonged denial stage relates to the use of laetrile. Whether or not one agrees with the use of laetrile, the cancer patient who seeks laetrile treatments is denying the prognosis that the condition is terminal and therefore incurable. Kubler-Ross' belief that terminally ill patients tend to encounter varying degrees of denial may lend credence to the notion that America is a death-denying society. If we as a culture tend to deny death when we are healthy, the likelihood exists that we would deny the reality of death when we are ill.

According to Kubler-Ross, the second stage is anger. In this stage the emotional status of the patient shifts from a "No, not me," reaction to a "Why me?" reaction. When the initial stage of denial can be maintained no longer, it is replaced by feelings of anger, rage, envy, and resentment. Kubler-Ross believed that this stage may cause difficulty for the family and medical staff because the anger may be projected at random to the enviornment surrounding the patient. This problem may be aggravated by the fact that few people can truly empathize with the terminally ill patient. Kubler-Ross states, "A patient who is respected and understood, who is given attention and a little time will soon lower his voice and reduce high angry demands."[4] In other words, the patient's anger will subside in time with empathic understanding. It is important to realize that the terminally ill patient, because of his or her condition, is going through

101

rapid change in social roles and expectations that may be contributing factors to the anger and hostility the patient displays. For example, Mr. Jones, a 42-year-old businessman, is diagnosed as a terminally ill cancer patient. Prior to this diagnosis Mr. Jones was a father, a husband, a Little League coach, a contributing member of a successful business firm, and a member of the company softball team. In addition, Mr. Jones had a variety of life goals toward which he had been striving: to see his children through college, to become company vice-president, and to become a grandparent. After the diagnosis his social roles become somewhat more limited. Because of his physical condition or subsequent treatment, he may not be able to perform all the roles and personally perceived expectations of a father, a husband, and a worker. And obviously, the life goals that Mr. Jones has established will have to be reevaluated and significantly altered. In addition, Mr. Jones, like most individuals, has a need to be in control of his life, but in a clinical setting it is difficult to exercise such control. The terminally ill patient needs to be included in discussions and decision-making processes to regain some control over his or her life.

The third stage, bargaining, is characterized by the patient's attempt to bargain with those who are perceived to have some control over their lives, such as the physician and God, to be able to live long enough to experience a personally meaningful event, for example, an upcoming anniversary, a Christmas holiday, or the wedding of a granddaughter. The notion of the "will to live" relates to this stage.

Bargaining is followed by the fourth stage, depression. During the depression stage the patient feels a sense of great loss that may be complicated by the loss of a job (and income), the accumulation of medical bills, and the rearrangement of cherished goals and expectations. Again, the change in social roles and expectations discussed in the anger stage may also be a contributing factor to depression. Kubler-Ross delineated two types of depression, reactive and preparatory. Reactive depression relates to the loss of bodily functions or the loss of social roles that have been traditionally performed. The second type of depression, preparatory, is caused by the patient's realization of his or her impending loss. Kubler-Ross also supported the notion that anger and depression may relate to loss of status, life goals, and social roles.

In the fifth stage, acceptance, Kubler-Ross believed that with time, individuals work through the other stages and accept their fate. Acceptance does not mean that the patient is happy. Rather, there appears to be almost a void of feeling. The struggle is over and the person is making appropriate practical and psychological arrangements.

The stages of dying that were advanced by Kubler-Ross have been criticized by thanatologists. The major drawback cited is that these stages have not been subjected to research utilizing an experimental research design to determine whether the clinical observations are valid. In essence, the universal applicability of these five stages is undetermined. Additionally, patients rarely progress through the five stages as if each stage were a progression resulting from the previous stage. People often move from one stage to another, which makes it difficult to label each stage. As guidelines of what might possibly occur, these stages are extremely valuable. However, to imply that these stages are the appropriate or acceptable way to die is not what Kubler-Ross intended. The popularity among health professionals and the general population of the Kubler-Ross stages may have created a self-fulfilling prophecy. If people have a preconceived notion that most people progress through five stages, then they may do the same. Research that incorporates a large random sample and utilizes an appropriate research design is obviously needed to validate or refute the Kubler-Ross observations.

The scope of literature that deals with the dying patient is not extensive. A variety of authors have dealt with issues related to the Kubler-Ross theories and their findings lend varying degrees of support and clarification of the dying process. For example, Degnan and others[5] conducted a study related to genetic counseling and found that the prospective parents experience a grief process analogous to that outlined by Kubler-Ross. Degnan found that families go through a mourning process after the birth or the identification of a handicapped child. It was observed that the parents experienced varying periods of denial of diagnosis and "shopped around" for a diagnosis they wanted to hear. This was followed by sequences of depression, rejection, and overprotection. When the work of Degnan and associates is compared to the Kubler-Ross stages, there are some similarities. Both believe that in times of stress caused by emotional trauma, the client or patient exhibits stages of denial, "shopping around," and depression. Although Degnan and associates cite some of the same stages as Kubler-Ross, these were not organized in any type of sequence.

Butler and Lewis[6] found that the dying person experiences the psychological responses outlined by Kubler-Ross but that these experiences seldom occur as clear and concise stages. Butler and Lewis also expressed concern that the health care professional who deals with the dying patient should not depend too rigorously on the Kubler-Ross stages.

In one of the early observational studies of the psychological aspects of the dying person, Hutschnecker[7] found two factors that seemed to be of special significance. First, dying patients seem to remain true to their basic personalities even when they are faced with death. Personality here refers to the habitual behavior pattern and the total response of the individual to the environment. In essence, the general interactions of individuals with their environment remained fairly consistent with the pattern developed throughout the life course. Second, many people enter a terminal illness with an already established sense of defeat, failure, and unfulfillment. Hutschnecker stated that patients generally realize when the end of their life is imminent and therefore may be somewhat prepared for the terminal prognosis. This theory compares favorably with the notion of Kubler-Ross that people tend to accept their fate and are depressed by the inability to fulfill life goals. Hutschnecker, however, believed that the dying patient remains consistent with his or her basic personality and does not progress through predetermined stages of dying; therefore prolonged periods of denial, anger, and depression may be a function of the patient's lifelong personality rather than a universal dying process.

Kutscher[8] approached the individual's preparation for death from a life-cycle perspective. He believes that life is full of major and minor preparations for death that few people realize exist. Throughout life there are a variety of superficial losses that help to prepare individuals for death. Examples of such losses are divorce, loss of a job, loss of social status, the death of a pet, and retirement. These losses can be accompanied by anticipatory grief.

Schulz[9] has distinguished qualitative differences in the grief response by categorizing death as either high-grief death or low-grief death. A high-grief death would be one that was caused by a sudden accident or a heart attack or one that occurred to a younger person. A low-grief death would be a death that was caused by a prolonged chronic illness or affected an older person. The difference in the level of grief experienced by these two conditions relates to the period of time prior to death that the bereaved were able to experience preparatory grief. In the case of a high-grief death, such as sudden heart attack, the bereaved would have little time to prepare psychologically, financially, or socially for the impending death. In the case of a low-grief death, such as a prolonged bout with cancer, the bereaved would have an opportunity to prepare themselves psychologically, to make appropriate financial arrangements, and to begin to develop new social roles and responsibilities. When the patient dies, the family and friends will progress through an ordinary grief response, but the duration may not be as long or the emotions as intense.

Several authors have discussed the anticipatory grief process. Perhaps the most well-known anticipatory grief response was outlined by Kubler-Ross. It is generally thought the family and friends of the terminally ill patient may also experience some of the stages of dying outlined by Kubler-Ross. Again, it should be noted that these stages do not represent a universal phenomenon. Nevertheless, some of the manifestations outlined by Kubler-Ross, that is, denial, depression, anger, guilt, and bargaining, also may occur in the ordinary grief response. In essence then, the bereaved are "working through" the grief process prior to the actual death. This may have an effect on the duration and intensity of the grief response following the death.

Fulton[10] identified four stages of anticipatory grief. These were depression, heightened concern for the ill person, rehearsal of death, and an attempt to adjust to the consequences of death.

Depression. The bereaved could be depressed for several reasons. Obviously, the impending death of a close friend or relative can trigger depression. However, the impending change in social status and roles also may cause depression. The wife will become a widow and consequently, have to perform some of the roles of the deceased, for example, be a father to the children, provide financial support for the family, and continue to operate the family business. The level of depression does not change the level of grief that immediately follows the death, but it may give the bereaved time to collect thoughts and organize coping strategies.

Heightened concern for the ill person. The bereaved have an opportunity to communicate feelings, thoughts, and emotions and to work out preparatory aspects of the death, such as the type of funeral desired. This heightened concern provides a better explanation for the differences between high-grief and low-grief deaths. The bereaved who have the opportunity to communicate with the deceased prior to death should experience less guilt, and therefore they should have a reduction in the negative aspects of ordinary grief response.

Rehearsal of death. The rehearsal of death also may help to explain the differences in the grief response between anticipated and unanticipated death. The ability to prepare for the death obviously will help to minimize the effects of the loss. The bereaved is able to develop coping strategies for this stressful life event that may help to diminish the impact and duration of the grief response.

An attempt to adjust to the consequences of death. Again, the bereaved is able to predict the possible consequences of the impending death and to begin to prepare plans to cope with these adjustments. The bereaved can develop strategies to cope with the emotional and economic problems that may arise following the death. If the death is anticipated, the bereaved at least is able to adjust to the consequences of the death and exercise some measure of control over the situation.

The notion that the severity and duration of the grief response will be diminished if the death is anticipated is consistent with the basic levels of the life-span theory of human development. The stress encountered by the family and friends of a terminally ill person stimulate them to develop strategies and techniques useful for coping with this stress. Therefore when the death occurs, the bereaved have already experienced an analogous situation that in turn may enhance their ability to cope with the ordinary grief response.

GRIEF IN CHILDREN

The extent to which a child may be affected by grief is dependent on three factors. First, the type of family situation influences the grief response. If children receive adequate affection and security from the family structure, their reaction to the death may differ from children reared in a family that did not provide such support. Second, as with the grief response of adults, the way in which the person died may have an effect on the child's bereavement process. For example, the sudden, unexpected death of a parent may cause a more severe grief response than an anticipated death in which the child has the time and opportunity to gradually adapt to the situation. Third, the developmental age and past experiences of children may influence their response to death. The research of Nagy[11] and Anthony[12] support the theory that a child begins to develop realistic, life-cycle concepts of death as they grow toward the age of 9 or 10 years. Thus the age of the child may be a factor in the bereavement process. In addition, the type of life experiences the child has had, as well as his or her past ability to cope with those life experiences may effect the response of the child to the death of a friend or relative. For example, if parents or teachers have enhanced the child's ability to cope with previous loss situations (the death of a pet, the death of a classroom animal, or the death of a grandparent), then the child will be better prepared to deal with the death of a friend or a member of the immediate family.

Grollman[13] identified some of the possible reactions of children toward death. The following sections use Grollman's list to describe the reactions that might be observed in children.

Denial. Denial of death in children can be the result of a variety of feelings and emotions. As Kubler-Ross hypothesized, denial may allow the child time to organize a more realistic response to the death. By pretending the death did not occur, children may be consciously or subconsciously trying to convince themselves that everything is going to be alright; the death will not be permanent, so there is no need to be upset. Adults and teachers may believe that the child's lack of concern in this situation is heartless or that the child is being strong. However, children usually care very much, but they may be having difficulty handling their feelings.

Isolation and withdrawal. One way to cope with a problem is to withdraw or isolate oneself from the source of the stress. Children generally have not developed sophisticated methods of coping with extremely stressful situations, so they may decide to stay as far away from the source of the stress as possible. The child who sees his or her parents react emotionally to a death in the family may find the reality of the situation too painful to endure. So the child may remain in his or her room or withdraw to a familiar hideout to avoid the emotional trauma.

106

Physiological distress. As discussed previously, the ordinary grief response is characterized by a variety of bodily reactions. This holds true for children as well. The anxiety the child is feeling may manifest itself in physical symptoms, such as a feeling of exhaustion, a tightness in the throat, insomnia, the loss of appetite, and an increase in the number and frequency of nightmares. In this situation, it is important for the parent and teacher to be sensitive to the change in the child's life.

Guilt. The guilt that children often experience following the death of a close friend or relative has several causes. Children may believe that not doing all the things Grandma told them to do may have some bearing on Grandma's death. Or, as with adults, children may feel guilty as a result of not expressing their true feelings toward the deceased during the deceased's lifetime. Grollman believed that

> "Children are very likely to feel guilt since in their experience, bad things happen to them because they were naughty. The desertion of the parent must be a retribution for their wrongdoing. Therefore, they search their minds for the bad deeds that caused it."[13]

Children may also believe that they have some sort of magical or mystical power that controls life events. So if Grandma says, "Johnny, chasing after you all day is going to kill me," the child may feel that his actions were in some way the cause or a contributing factor in Grandma's death.

Hostility. Children may express varying degrees of hostility toward the deceased or toward other individuals who they feel may have been able to somehow influence the outcome. First, children may feel abandoned or wonder why Grandma had to leave at this time in their life. These hostile reactions may be intensified if the parent or teacher tells the children that Grandma went on a long trip or that Grandma went to sleep. Children know that adults generally have control over these occurrences and therefore may feel that Grandma deserted them. Second, children may feel hostility toward people who they feel could have intervened to prevent the death. The child who says, "Why couldn't the doctors do something to make Grandma well?" or, "If Mother would have taken better care of her, Grandma would not have died," may be exhibiting manifestations of such hostility.

Replacement. Children may look for other people to assume the roles that the deceased played in their life. These roles can be as minor as finding someone to play baseball with or as important as finding someone to provide the emotional support and love the deceased previously provided.

Fear and Panic. The child may wonder, "Who is going to take care of me?" or, "Now that daddy has died, will we have to move?" Children often have a variety of questions that need to be answered at the appropriate time. The parent and teacher must be aware of such childhood fears and concerns and provide appropriate guidance and support for the child.

■   ■   ■

Again, it should be stressed that children will experience normal human emotions to a traumatic and stressful situation. Children should not be shielded from the reality of the situation or denied the opportunity to express their grief, anger, guilt, or despair

Helping the child cope with death is a difficult endeavor. The child needs to feel that the significant others in his or her life are caring and supportive.

Photo by Strix Pix

when a death has occurred. Children need to feel that the significant others in their lives are caring and supportive.

Helping the child cope with death is a difficult endeavor. Each child confronts death in a unique way, so there are no universal rules that can help all young people successfully understand and cope with death. However, Grollman[13] has identified some general guidelines that parents, teachers and health professionals should keep in mind when trying to help the child cope with death.

1. *Do not* avoid the subject of personal death in your classroom discussions. Clifton Fadiman writes in the afterword of Louisa M. Alcott's *Little Men,* "The most moving episode has to do with John Brooke's death and funeral. As I read it, I found myself wondering why most books for children these days are afraid to mention death."

2. *Do not* discourage the emotions of grief. Anger, tears, guilt, despair, and protest are natural reactions to family disorganization. Never be so cold to human feelings that you do not accept the emotional reactions of those young people who hurt.

3. *Do not* close the door to doubt, questioning, and differences of opinion. Respect the other's unique personality, for in the long run it is he or she who must discern the meanings to the questions of life and death.

4. *Do not* tell a child what he or she will later need to unlearn. Avoid fairy tales, half-truths, and circumspection. Honesty is the *only* policy.

5. *Do not* legislate your own convictions. Avoid abstractions. Thoughts must be translated into the language and comprehension of the child.

6. *Do* spend time with responsive listening to the needs of the student. The dedicated teacher is a perceptive listener to the spoken word and an astute discoverer of the nonverbal communication.

7. *Do* make referrals to other supportive people. There are times when even the best-informed and well-intentioned teacher and nurse are simply inadequate. Seeking further help from a guidance counselor or school psychologist is not an admission of weakness but a demonstration of your own security and ego strength.

8. *Do* remember that the process of adjustment to death is longer than the funeral. The height of depression may come many months after death. Grief may be expressed by poor grades, lack of attention, daydreaming, and hostility.

9. *Do* be human. It is not wrong to express your own emotions of grief . . . to shed a tear . . . to touch a person in pain. Just remember the words of Thornton Wilder; "There is a land of the living and a land of the dead and the bridge is *love*—the only survival, the only meaning."

10. *Do* consider death education courses. Children are already confronted with the fact of death in word and song, as well as in the natural world of plants, animals, and friends. Death education begins when life begins. And always understand that your real challenge is not just how to explain death to children but how to make peace with it yourself.*

*From Grollman, Earl A.: THE JOURNAL OF SCHOOL HEALTH **48**(6):336-339, June 1977. Copyright, 1977, American School Health Association, Kent, Ohio 44240.

It is interesting to note that these principles center around the notion that we must keep the lines of communication open between the child and parents, teachers, and health professionals. Such lines of communication are often closed in a society that believes the child should be shielded from death.

Death of a child

As with adults, the circumstances surrounding the death will dictate the approach the parent or teacher takes in discussing the death of a child. Fredlund believes that a teacher should not avoid the death of a school-aged child:

> The circumstances influence how the subject is approached, but in my opinion the death should never, never be ignored. I think that the children should be gathered together by their teacher and the death explained in simple, open, honest terms, in keeping with how old they are.[14]

Children often need to know the cause of the death to help assess and put into perspective their own vulnerability.

Children need to feel free to ask questions about death and need to be given straightforward and concise responses. They also need to be reassured that their feelings and reactions to death are normal, and therefore they should not feel ashamed.

SUMMARY

Chapter 4 begins by differentiating the concepts of bereavement, grief, and mourning, terms often used synonymously. Characteristics of the normal grief response are described as well as those factors that help to determine the nature of this response. A prolonged or intense response represent common manifestations of atypical grief response. Six examples of distorted reaction are offered. The chapter does not provide material about the possible counseling or intervention techniques that might be used to help someone who suffers from atypical grief. For the layman it is difficult to distinguish normal grief from abnormal grief, and since the textbook is directed toward educators rather than counselors, it would be inappropriate to dwell on this subject matter.

In many ways the grief response parallels the response of terminally ill patients, a description of which has been provided by Elisabeth Kubler-Ross. It is important to realize, however, that the progression of stages represents a generality of behavioral states rather than an expected or "correct" way of handling grief. In fact, the grief response is affected by many factors, such as the age of the person who has died (or is dying) and the amount of time available to deal with the loss. Some deaths seem likely to increase the intensity of the grief response. The chapter also presents a description of grief in children based on the writings of Earl Grollman. Guidelines for parents and teachers are presented to help identify some ways in which adults can help children cope with death.

This chapter has described the variety of human reactions to death. Recognition that these feelings are shared by others can be comforting and may help to validate one's own feelings. As more and more is learned about the physiological aspects of dying, research on the psychological aspect of dying should be attempted. All must face death, but some will face it with greater ease than others. Open and honest discussion about death can help individuals to understand and accept mortality—their own, as well as that of others they love.

MAJOR CONCEPTS RELATED TO BEREAVEMENT, GRIEF, AND MOURNING

The following concepts can help educators organize the vast body of knowledge related to bereavement, grief, and mourning. These concepts can serve as a basis for the development of instructional programs.

- Bereavement, grief, and mourning are influenced by environmental, physiological, societal, and cultural factors.
- Bereavement and grief are normal responses to death, although the response varies in severity and duration among individuals.
- Qualified help is available for individuals who have difficulty coping with bereavement and grief.
- Grieving is an individual dynamic process characterized by peaks and valleys rather than by distinct stages.

EDUCATIONAL ACTIVITIES RELATED TO BEREAVEMENT, GRIEF, AND MOURNING

Title: *The Tenth Good Thing About Barney*

Age level: Primary grades

Objective: Following reading and discussion of the book, *The Tenth Good Thing About Barney,* students will (1) identify changes in the daily habits of the main character, (2) discuss how they would feel if their cat (or other pet) died, and (3) draw a picture that illustrates "good things" they like about their pet.

Materials: Drawing paper, crayons, *The Tenth Good Thing About Barney,* by Judith Viorst, Hartford, Connecticut, 1971, Atheneum. This book provides an excellent example of a young boy coping with the death of his cat. This text is especially appropriate for this age level for the following reasons:

- The boy shown as a coping model for a situation many youngsters eventually confront.
- The child's questions are answered truthfully.
- The parents discussion sets a framework on which later discussions of death can be based.
- The parents do not deny the child's perceptions or reactions to death.
- The text outlines a life-cycle perspective of death.

Directions: Read the book to the class. Conduct a question and answer discussion session with the students. Some possible questions include the following:

- How did the boy feel about the death of his cat? How did his parents feel? How did his friend feel?
- What happened to make them feel that way?
- Have you ever felt that way? What happened to make you feel that way?
- Were there any changes in the boy's daily habits?
- How would you feel if your cat (pet) died?

After the discussion, ask the students to draw a picture that depicts something good about their pet. Ask all students to explain what they drew.

Variation: *The Tenth Good Thing About Barney* shows a young boy coping with the death of a pet. In addition, the text shows parents coping with the problem of how to explain the death of a pet to their child. As a variation of this activity, read the book to the parents and discuss how the parents explain the death of Barney to the boy.

Title: Mourning customs

Age level: Junior high school

Objective: As a homework assignment, the students will identify unique mourning customs.

Materials: Mourning customs open-ended sentences

Directions: The teacher provides each student with one or more copies of the open-ended sentences worksheet. A sample worksheet with some sample sentences is outlined below. The teacher may wish to add to this list of open-ended sentences after considering special characteristics of the population.

**Mourning customs open-ended
sentences worksheet**

1. The most meaningful custom(s) is (are) . . .
2. A unique mourning custom is . . .
3. The funniest mourning custom is . . .
4. The mourning custom(s) I would like observed at my death is (are) . . .

Ask the students to use the open-ended sentences as a means to interview parents, grandparents, aunts, uncles, neighbors, and so forth concerning the mourning customs these people have observed throughout their life course. The teacher should conduct a follow-up discussion on the results.

Title:	Explaining death to children—case studies
Age level:	High school, adults
Objective:	Given a specific case study related to explaining death to children, the student will be able to identify a psychologically and educationally sound way to handle the situation.
Materials:	Sample case studies
Directions:	There are a variety of life events that provide excellent opportunities to help children understand and cope with death. In addition, 10 principles for explaining death to children have been outlined by Grollman (p. 109). Using these 10 principles, identify the following for each case study: (1) explain why the parent's or teacher's response to the death-related case study is inappropriate, (2) determine the possible reaction and consequence to the child, and (3) identify an appropriate course of action for the parent.

Case study 1

Ms. Jones has been growing plants for her first graders' science fair project. Over Christmas break the plants are not properly watered. The plants lose their color and wither. When the students return from vacation, they ask the teacher what happened to the plants. The teacher explains that everything will be alright when new plants are purchased.

Case study 2

Bobby is 7 years old. His dog, Ruff, is getting old and has not been as active as he once was. When Bobby wakes one morning, his father tells him that Ruff has died. His father also tells Bobby not to be upset because he will get Bobby a new puppy as soon as possible.

Case study 3

Sally is 6 years old. Her grandmother (Mrs. Smith), who lives in the same town as Sally, recently had a stroke and is in the hospital. The doctors believe that there is little hope that Mrs. Smith will regain her speech and mobility and that she will need extensive nursing care when she is discharged from the hospital. Sally's parents have decided to place Mrs. Smith in a nursing home and tell Sally that Grandma went on a long trip.

Title:	How to console friends and relatives—role-playing situations
Age level:	High school, college, adults
Objective:	During the role-playing situations, the students will demonstrate strategies to console friends and relatives.
Materials:	Role-playing story cards

Directions: The teacher develops a variety of role-playing situations appropriate for the age level of the class. Some sample role-playing situations are outlined below.

Role-playing situation 1

While Alyson, your 7-year-old sister, was in school, her cat was struck by a car and was killed. You have to tell Alyson that her cat has been killed and provide consolation. What would you do?

Role-playing situation 2

You and several friends have learned that John, the catcher on your baseball team, has broken his arm and will be unable to participate in the play-offs. How would you console John?

Role-playing situation 3

Your best friend's grandmother has died of a stroke. Your friend is upset and feels guilty because she was out of town and did not get to talk to her grandmother before she died. What would you do to console her?

The teacher breaks the class into small groups. Each group discusses the best way to console the bereaved in the case study. The group then develops a role-playing skit and performs it for the class.

Title: Shared grief experiences

Age level: High school, college, adults

Objective: At the conclusion of the shared grief experiences activity the students will identify situations that cause grief and will outline ways to cope with loss.

Materials: Blank 5 × 8 cards

Directions: Ask the students to select a personal life experience that has caused them grief. Have them write a letter to Dear Abby asking for advice. If they choose to participate in the activity, students should write a brief sketch of their grief experience on the 5 × 8 cards without signing their names on their cards. The teacher then randomly selects the letters to Dear Abby and reads the stories to the class, and the class discusses strategies that could be used to cope with that particular loss situation.

REFERENCES

1. Kastenbaum, R.: Death, society, and human experience, ed. 2, St. Louis, 1981, The C.V. Mosby Co., p. 241.
2. Lindemann, E.: Symptomology and management of acute grief, American Journal of Psychiatry **101:**141-148, 1944.
3. Holmes, T.R., and Rahe, R.H.: The social readjustment rating scale, Journal of Psychosomatic Research **11:**213-218, 1967.
4. Kubler-Ross, E.: On death and dying, New York, 1969, Macmillan Publishing Co., Inc.
5. Degnan, M., Peters, P., Porter, I.,and Gottesman, D.: Genetic counseling, American Family Physician **12:**111-117, 1975.
6. Butler, R., and Lewis, M.: Aging and mental health: positive psychological approaches, ed. 3, St. Louis, 1981, The C.V. Mosby Co.
7. Hutschnecker, A.: Personality factors in the dying patient. In Feifel, Herman, editor: The meaning of death, New York, 1959, McGraw-Hill Book Co., 237-250.
8. Kutscher, A.: Anticipating grief, death and bereavement: a continuum. In Wyschograd, Edith, editor: The phenomenon of death: New York, 1973,Harper & Row, Publishers, Inc., pp. 40-53.
9. Schulz, R., and Aderman, D.: Clinical research and stages of dying, Omega **5:**137-143, 1973.
10. Fulton, R.: Death, grief and social recuperation, Omega **1:**23-28, 1970.
11. Nagy, M.: The child's view of death, Journal of Genetic Psychology **73:**3-27, 1948.
12. Anthony, S.: The discovery of death in childhood and after, New York, 1972, Basic Books, Inc., Publishers.
13. Grollman, E.: Explaining death to children, The Journal of School Health **48:**336-339, 1977.
14. Fredlund, D: Children and death from the school setting viewpoint, The Journal of School Health **48:**533-537, 1977.

Photo by Strix Pix

CHAPTER FIVE

Euthanasia

I do not fear death itself as much as the indignities of deterioration, dependence and hopeless pain.
CONCERN FOR DYING

Euthanasia is a word taken from two Greek words, *eu,* which means easy, happy, or painless, and *thanatos,* which means death. During the 3 centuries in which the word has been part of the English language, its meaning has experienced a gradual transition from a natural death that is painless and easy to a death that is allowed to occur to a terminally ill patient through the withholding of necessary medical treatment. More recently, euthanasia is being used synonymously with mercy killing. The Webster's Third New International Dictionary defines euthanasia as "an easy death or means of inducing one; the act or practice of painlessly putting to death persons suffering from incurable conditions or diseases."

Euthanasia began to take shape as a major social issue in 1935 when the Voluntary Euthanasia Society was formed in England. A bill was brought before the British Parliament in 1936 that called for the legalization of actions to bring about death when certain criteria were met. The criteria stipulated that the individual must be over the age of 21 years, have an incurable and fatal illness, be suffering from severe pain, and sign in the presence of two witnesses a request to be put to death. Although the bill was voted down, the society has remained an active proponent of euthanasia and mercy killing under certain circumstances.

The Euthanasia Society of America was formed in 1938. Although legislation similar to that presented in England has never been brought before Congress, several state legislatures have had to consider euthanasia legislation, and in each case the proposed bill was defeated. Although some physicians and even some clergy favor the legal right to terminate life under specified conditions, no medical society or major religious order in America has endorsed the legalization of mercy killing. Furthermore, there is no country in the world that sanctions the killing of a human being to induce painless, gentle death.

Because of the many ways in which the word *euthanasia* is used, it will be helpful to clarify some of the contemporary interpretations of the word. In decending order of acceptance by society, euthanasia may have the following meanings:

1. *Voluntary indirect (passive) euthanasia:* In voluntary indirect (passive) euthanasia , individuals express their wishes to family members, physicians, lawyers, and others that if they should become comatose or too dysfunctional to live with dignity, they should be allowed to expire without heroic and extraordinary means being applied. This type of euthanasia is also referred to as *negative euthanasia* in that there is no action taken to prolong life. The adjective *negative* has nothing to do with motive. Instead, it is negative euthanasia because failure to act allowed the person to die.

2. *Involuntary indirect (passive) euthanasia:* In involuntary indirect (passive) euthanasia the failure to maintain life-sustaining technology or drugs is a decision made by the family and/or physician on behalf of the patient. This might be done in cases in which patients are comatose and had not previously expressed their feelings about the use of extraordinary measures to prolong life. From an ethical, moral, and religious point of view, there is a substantial difference between an adult giving informed consent and another person giving consent on behalf of one who is unable to make the decision. But the difference between involuntary euthanasia and voluntary euthanasia is not nearly so great as the difference between passive and active euthanasia. While the literature on passive euthanasia seems to indicate that many people can philosophically agree with acts of omission in cases of terminal illness, there is strong vocal support from only a relatively small number of people who advocate active euthanasia.

3. *Voluntary direct (active) euthanasia:* Voluntary direct (active) euthanasia involves the direct action of one person to bring about the death of another. It is commonly referred to as mercy killing and in popular usage has come to mean euthanasia. As an example of this type of action, a patient might request that the physician leave a lethal dose of medication within reach. Although this is done legally in Switzerland, in most cultures the action would be considered as suicide with complicity of the physician. In another example the patient might ask a family member, the attending physician, or nurse to end the suffering mercifully by administering a lethal dose of medicine or by removing an intravenous feeding tube. This type of activity is illegal worldwide although some countries provide a lesser sentence when the motive for homicide is a mercy killing. Occasionally, this type of euthanasia is called positive euthanasia. This may, however, be confusing since in ordinary usage the word *positive* is used to mean beneficial rather than an action taken. This type of euthanasia may be divided in terms of intention. A direct action to cause death to occur more rapidly differs from causing a death in an attempt to alleviate pain.

4. *Involuntary direct (active) euthanasia:* Involuntary direct (active) euthanasia is a the most controverisal form of euthanasia. In this context, death is brought about on behalf of another without the other's consent. On one hand people have equated the practice to the mass executions committed by the Nazis. They refer to Hitler's description of those who made no contribution to society as being "useless eaters." On the other side proponents see little or no difference between voluntary passive euthanasia and involuntary active euthanasia since the outcome is identical. They argue there is no difference between failing to provide extraordinary measures and the application of other measures that are intended to bring about a painless death. For instance, is there a difference between not hooking a person up to a respirator (omission) and pulling the plug (comission)? This type of euthanasia can also be divided according to degrees of intention, similar to voluntary direct (active) euthanasia.

For some readers the idea of euthanasia is repulsive in any form. For others the line of acceptance will be drawn between passive and active euthanasia. For a few each type of euthanasia could be accepted depending on the conditions or situations involved. It is easy to reject involuntary active euthanasia when one uses the Nazi analogy, but it becomes easier to sympathize with the notion when the example of a child with Tay-Sachs disease is used. Tay-Sachs disease is a genetic disorder that is always fatal and brings about a slow suffering death to the victim, usually by the age of 3 or 4 years. Parents are unable to give consent for mercy killing, but the suffering of their infant may be entirely too great a burden. Which is the greater moral wrong: to prolong the suffering until death or to put an end to the suffering by administering a painless but lethal drug? To be sure, the arguments on both sides are powerful, and to feel personally comfortable with one position or another, one will need to give very careful consideration to all of the issues. Several activities at the end of the chapter are intended to help individuals examine their own feelings.

So we have seen the word *euthanasia* has a variety of meanings with considerable importance being attached to the context in which the term is used. As will be seen in the remainder of the chapter, the primary arguments focus on voluntary versus involuntary euthanasia and active versus passive euthanasia. Those who favor voluntary euthanasia, either passive or active, usually invoke the freedom of choice argument. Those who favor involuntary euthanasia, passive or active, base their argument on the notion of death with dignity. Those who favor passive euthanasia, voluntary or involuntary, see it as a process that allows the inevitable to occur without attempting to prolong the dying process. And finally, those who support active euthanasia, voluntary or involuntary, see no difference between a failure to act to prolong the dying process and the direct action taken to shorten the dying process. Furthermore, they defend the right of society to make decisions on behalf of another member of the human species or on behalf of society itself. Proponents at all four levels are sincere in their beliefs, they see their own philosophy as being merciful and compassionate, and their intent is to relieve needless human suffering. In contrast, opponents of euthanasia view the concept as homicide or suicide, and those who take part are seen as murderers and accomplices. For the opponents of euthanasia anything short of best effort to sustain life is morally unacceptable. The following section gives a bit more insight into the issues related to euthanasia.

ARGUMENTS IN FAVOR OF EUTHANASIA

Those who speak in favor of euthanasia usually project a rationale that falls into one of three broad themes. The first of these might be classified as a philosophy of humanism, characterized by respect for human dignity, reverence for quality of life, and compassion in the relief of human suffering. The value of human existence is in the humanness of the being. It is believed that even though the organism is able to sustain life, the meaningfulness of that life and the quality of existence must be weighed when a terminally ill patient suffers from pain or incapacity. A situation in which death is imminent creates an avoidance-avoidance dilemma. In this situation neither alternative (standing by while the person suffers or mercy killing) offers an acceptable course of action. The humanist would invoke the principle of proportionate good. The dilemma would be resolved by considering which of the available negative options renders the least amount of harm. Those who argue for mercy killing believe that human compasion warrants the inducement of a gentle, easy death. Ending a life in this fashion is less reprehensible than nonaction, which simply prolongs the dying process.

The second major theme has to do with personal rights and freedom of choice. It is argued that most people in this country have accepted the notion of individual choice (personal liberty) in matters of conception and birth. By using contraceptive devices and voluntary sterilization, many have disallowed nature taking its course because of an unwillingness to accept the outcome of fertilization. The Supreme Court decision of 1973 on abortion further established the fact that in matters pertaining to the creation of life people have the right to make a choice. The argument continues that to deny this right is to disallow the most fundamental personal liberty, which is individual choice in matters pertaining to one's own body. If the individual has the right to take action so as to not conceive, and also has the right to terminate a pregnancy, shouldn't the individual also have the right to engage in active euthanasia?

120

Each day people make decisions that have an impact on their health and future existence. They say the issue of euthanasia is no more a matter for the courts to decide than is the issue of cigarette smoking, buckling seat belts, or choosing to remain in a job that has pressures that take a daily toll on physiological and emotional well-being. In effect, an individual who decides not to undergo a life-saving surgical operation or not to accept a transfusion of blood is making a decision to die. Persons who resolve not to undergo painful therapy, as in the case of treatment for cancer, are making a choice about how to live their remaining days on earth. If individuals have the right to practice unhealthy behavior or to decide against surgery, transfusion, or therapy, why should they be denied the right to choose a course of treatment that is intended to put an end to life?

A third theme that is used to argue in support of euthanasia falls under the category of societal hypocrisy. Religion, medicine, and law agree with the average person on the street that the withholding of extraordinary measures to prolong the dying process is a legitimate course of action. Hospitals across the country use the so-called *90 stickers* on patient charts to signal "give no intensive care or resuscitation." Passive euthanasia is a fait accompli. It is often considered sanctimonious to believe that acts of omission are proper but acts of comission are improper. Why is it rightful to allow death to happen but wrongful to induce death? The outcomes are identical.

The argument continues that euthanasia is morally the same regardless of form. Voluntary passive euthanasia and involuntary active euthanasia are moral equivalents. Acceptance of one means de facto acceptance of each of the types of euthanasia previously described. Even though the law makes no distinction for motive of a mercy killing, it appears that common sense does account for the motive when actual cases are brought to trial. Few cases of mercy killing have ever been tried in this country, and of those cases that reached the judicial system, most were dismissed on the grounds that the defendant suffered temporary insanity. The thin difference between active euthanasia and passive euthanasia is highlighted by the physician who administers a pain-relieving drug knowing that eventually the dosage required for analgesia is sufficiently strong to bring about death through overdose. Is the physician a murderer or a humanitarian?

Proponents of euthanasia have also sought to quell those in society who speak against euthanasia on the basis of divine righteousness. These people believe that it is sinful to interfere with the intentions of God. Human intervention is perceived as tampering with divine providence. However, those in favor of euthanasia counter that all of medicine would have to be indicted using this logic. Whenever a physician saves a life, it could be interpreted as meddling with the will of God. Stated in a different way,

121

if it is allowable to save a life through medical treatment, isn't it equally right to hasten the inevitable to an early and painless conclusion? If human intervention is contrary to the will of God, why is saving a life considered to be the highest good?

ARGUMENTS AGAINST EUTHANASIA

In its current context, euthanasia has come to mean the inducement of death, or mercy killing. In concept, euthanasia is thought by opponents to be murder. Depending on circumstance, opponents refer to euthanasia as infanticide, homicide, suicide, or genocide. In practice, euthanasia is the debasement of humanity. For this reason euthanasia is an illegal act and no country in the world sanctions its use.

There are an infinite number of problems that arise from proposals to legalize mercy killings. In lieu of a lengthy discussion a few of these problems are described in brief. References at the end of the chapter will direct the reader to sources that provide greater detail. The following information will, however, demonstrate that legalization of euthanasia is an issue that requires considerable contemplation before arriving at a personal philosophy.

1. If euthanasia is to be available only to those who freely and intelligently request it, by what standards shall we judge informed consent? Is it possible for a person suffering intolerably to make a rational decision? Chronic pain can lead to severe depression, personality disorganization, and distortion of reality. What of the patient who has been drugged with a sedative? Can such persons be held responsible for what they utter when their central nervous system has been anesthetized?

2. If involuntary euthanasia is to be made available, whose word serves as the final decision? If parents are to decide, what if they disagree? If spouses are to decide, what if the mate disagrees with the offspring? Having to make a decision to terminate the life of a loved one can produce lifelong psychological disturbance, especially in cases in which the decision was not unanimous.

3. Who would decide about euthanasia when an intelligent, aware minor suffers terminal illness? Do parents have the right to act on behalf of the child when that action is contrary to the child's wishes? Ordinarily, parental consent is required before treatment can be administered. Would euthanasia be an exception?

4. How do you determine for certain that a disease is incurable? Diseases such as tuberculosis and leprosy were once incurable. If euthanasia had been legalized

122

prior to the discovery of antibiotics, how many people would have needlessly been put to death?

5. Diagnosis is an imprecise science. It is quite common for people to be diagnosed as having a particular, even fatal, disease only to discover that the diagnosis is incorrect. This is even true for cancer, a disease that would seem to have a great deal of accuracy when the tissue is examined through biopsy. Upon prognosis of terminal illness, what additional steps would have to be taken to ensure that the diagnosis was accurate?

6. How would one measure intolerable suffering? The threshold of pain is largely subjective. Having the option of painless death or life with pain, some people may opt for an easy death. At what point, and determined by what measurement, would a physician be psychologically prepared to induce death? What if a patient requested death in a moment of pain but later changed his or her mind? Should the physician be required to wait a certain period of time before administering the fatal dose?

7. How would society control for abuses? Legalization of mercy killing makes it difficult to gain a conviction when the intention was not merciful. Currently, a few doctors sell their services without regard to professional ethics or medical responsibility. If mercy killing were made legal, would there be a small cadre of doctors who specialize in such acts in the interest of humanity or profit?

8. Erosion of the law takes place through what some authors have referred to as "the thin edge of the wedge" principle. This technique is popularly called "getting one foot inside the door." If voluntary passive euthanasia were legalized, it would not be too long before involuntary passive legislation would be considered, and so forth. Would euthanasia initially be the domain of physicians and then gradually shift to an acceptance of friends and relatives performing the fatal act? A common plot of television mysteries depicts the wealthy patriarch whose heirs scheme to make the death look natural or accidental. If mercy killings were legal, practically every accused murderer could claim that the deceased pleaded for an easy, gentle death. Since killing is generally wrong, exceptions should be kept to as few as possible.

9. Is it proper to ask physicians to be the instrument of death? By training, personal commitment, and professional philosophy, physicians are obligated to preserve and maintain life. One can imagine the patient who lies in bed while the physician sits on the edge of the bed with a hypodermic in hand. Does the syringe contain the medication or a poison? Does the next capsule before bedtime contain penicillin or cyanide?

10. To protect against error or abuse, it would be necessary to have elaborate steps

in safeguarding the rights of patients. For instance, the British proposal stipulated that the patient would have to provide two certificates of terminal illness, complete a special application, and submit it to an appointed euthanasia referee, who would arrange an interview with the applicant and issue a permit valid for 7 days, unless the nearest relative could persuade the court to rescind the permit.

RELIGIOUS VIEWPOINTS

The three major religions in the United States, Protestant, Catholic, and Jewish, share remarkably similar dogmas pertaining to euthanasia. For each, the deliberate causing of death is morally wrong, sinful, and totally unacceptable. The Catholic Church has made it perfectly clear that active euthanasia is a grave sin. In 1952, the General Convention of the Episcopal Church in America formally objected to the legalization of active euthanasia under any circumstance. The only time a Christian may take a life is when he or she is offering protection against an unjust aggressor. War, self-defense, and capital punishment are permissible exceptions to the Sixth Commandment. Jewish doctrine teaches that every human life has infinite value and that we have a fundamental duty to protect life from assault. Neither motive nor consent of the patient alters the belief that taking a life is murder.

While there are a few theological philosophers who argue on behalf of active euthanasia, both voluntary and involuntary, the overwhelming weight of opinion considers that there is a distinct difference between active and passive euthanasia. Heroic measures to prolong the dying process are not necessary. If the doctor is certain that the patient will not recover, it is acceptable to discontinue extraordinary measures of treatment. Such action is not considered sinful. Generally, extraordinary means of treatment are considered to be those medicines or procedures that cannot be used without excessive expense, pain, or other inconvenience and that would not offer a reasonable hope of benefit.

Consider a patient who is comatose. Mechanical artificial respiration was initiated as a temporary measure in an effort to help the body survive until it could overcome the assault. Eventually, it becomes evident that spontaneous respiration will not occur, but neither will the patient die while hooked up to the machine. If there is no reasonable prospect of recovery, then the resuscitation equipment becomes a permanent substitution for the vital body functions of respiration and circulation. Unplugging the machine is not an act of murder but instead the elimination of an extraordinary means of treatment. It is not only permissible for a physician to discontinue extraordinary methods of treatment when there is certainty that the patient will not recover, but it is also morally allowable for individuals to refuse those treatments that are unable to offer a reasonable hope of recovery.

In 1957 Pope Pius XII addressed three questions on medical ethics related to resuscitation. An international assembly of anesthesiologists sought to determine the value of resuscitation if the damage to the brain is so serious that the patient will very probably not survive. The Pope responded to three specific questions. The following is a synopsis of his response.[1]

Q. Does one have the right or obligation to use modern artificial respiration equipment in all cases, even those that, in the judgment of the physician are completely hopeless?

A. In ordinary cases one has the right to act in this manner, but he or she is not bound to do so. These forms of treatment go beyond ordinary means to which one is bound. The rights and duties of the family depend on the presumed will of the unconscious patient. This does not mean direct disposal of life; that would never be licit. Even when it causes circulatory arrest, the interruption of resuscitation is never more than an indirect cause of death.

Q. Does one have the right or obligation to remove the artificial respiration when, after several days, the state of deep unconsciousness does not improve and when the removal of the artificial respiration will stop blood circulation within a few minutes? What should be done if the family urges the doctor to remove the apparatus?

A. The physician has the right to remove resuscitation before circulation has come to a complete stop. If, in the opinion of the physician, this complete cessation of circulation means a sure separation of the soul from the body, even if particular organs go on functioning, last rights certainly would not be valid, for the recipient would not be a "person" any longer.

Q. Must a patient who is plunged into unconsciousness through central paralysis (maintained through artificial respiration and showing no improvement after several days) be considered dead? Must one not wait for blood circulation to stop, in spite of the artificial respiration, before considering the patient dead?

A. In cases in which the verification of the fact of death is concerned, the answer cannot be deduced from any religious and moral principle and does not fall within the competence of the church. Generally, human life continues for as long as its vital functions—distinguished from the simple life of organs—manifest themselves spontaneously or even with the help of artificial processes.

On May 5, 1980, the Sacred Congregation for the Doctrine of the Faith[2] issued a statement on euthanasia. Pope John Paul II approved its content and ordered its publication. Recognizing the increasing ability of medical science to prolong life, the congregation sought to respond to inquiries about "easy death." It noted that euthanasia refers to medical intervention that lessens the suffering of illness or of the final agony. The congregation defined euthanasia as "an action or omission that by its nature or by interaction causes death with the purpose of putting an end to all suffering."[2]

125

The first part of the document addressed the value of human life. The Congregation wrote that intentional death or suicide is as wrong as homicide, and that no one may attack the life of an innocent person. With this point firmly established, the Congregation reiterated that no one can in any way authorize the killing of an innocent human being. A human being was considered to be a fetus or embryo, a child, an adult, the elderly, someone incurably ill, or someone who is dying. It was further stated that no one may ask for nor may any authority command or permit euthanasia.

The document stated that human and Christian prudence urges the use of pain-killing medications. Echoing the statement made by Pius XII, the congregation felt it was permissible to use analgesics even if it is forseeable that their use may shorten life. In this situation death is neither intended nor sought. The only intention is to alleviate pain.

The final part of the statement raises the question of whether all possible remedies must be applied in every circumstance. The rationale used in answering this question is known as the proportionate use of theraputic agents. The physician must weigh the type of treatment, its degree of danger, its expense, and the possibility of applying it against the results that can be expected. Better than anyone else, expert physicians can judge whether the effort is disproportionate to the forseeable results. With the consent of the sick person, it is permissible to use the most recent medical techniques, even if they have not been fully tested and if they involve some risk to the patient. On the other hand, it is always licit to be content with ordinary treatments. No one may be required to submit to a treatment that poses risk or is excessively burdensome. In this case the rejection of treatment is not to be compared to suicide but rather as a recognition that the application of the treatment is disproportionate to the value of the expected results.

Finally, the congregation indicated that while life is to be regarded as the gift of God, it is also true that death is unavoidable. When death is imminent and cannot be prevented, it is permissible to reject treatments that can only prolong life. In these cases, however, ordinary treatment that is due the patient may not be interrupted.

MEDICAL CONSIDERATIONS

Advancing technology within the field of medicine has created some awkward medical-legal issues that need to be confronted. Specifically, the treatment provided in intensive care for victims of accidents, newborns suffering from severe birth defects, as well as patients afflicted with a terminal illness impose a burdensome responsibility among health professionals. Physicians typically pursue treatment with a sense of optimism. They are tenacious in the belief that death can be conquered. However,

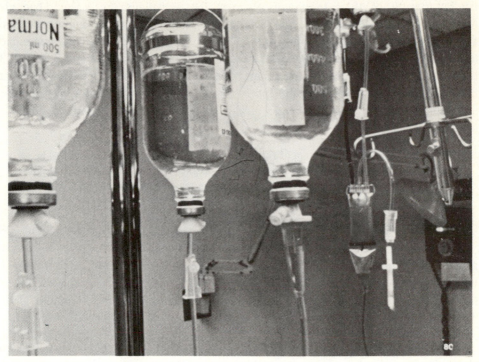

Advancing technology within the field of medicine has created some awkward medical and legal issues related to euthanasia.

Courtesy Guidance Associates, Mt. Kisco, N.Y.

recent developments have somewhat altered the situation. Increasingly, the outcome of medical persistence in intensive care is not the conquest of death but rather the establishment of a situation in which death is denied and life is not fully restored. Ameliorative treatment directed toward the improvement of organic function has replaced the customary treatment for the symptomatic relief of pain and suffering. This type of therapy recognizes the imminence of death and seeks to make the patient as comfortable as possible.

Most people agree that in cases of terminal illness there does come a time when treatment ought to shift from curative to palliative. In fact, there has never been a criminal indictment in this country against a physician who cared for the patient in this fashion. Physicians, nurses, and other related professionsals, however, definitely make a distinction between allowing death to occur and helping to bring about that death. It is certainly accurate to say that the primary deterrent to mercy killing is not a matter of

127

law but a matter of ethics. In the unlikely event that active euthanasia would become legally permissible, it is doubtful that many physicians would actually commit the fatal act. In 1950 the General Assembly of the World Medical Association recommended that all nations condemn the practice of mercy killing under any circumstance. In 1973 the House of Delegates of the American Medical Association[3] adopted a statement that condemned mercy killing but approved the cessation of extraordinary means following discussion with patient or family in cases in which biological death is imminent:

> The cessation of the employment of extraordinary means to prolong the life of the body when there is irrefutable evidence that biological death is imminent is the decision of the patient and/or the immediate family. The advice and judgment of the physician should be freely available to the patient and/or the immediate family.[3]

Some physicians still uphold the ethics of the Hippocratic oath written about 400 years before the birth of Christ. Although some physicians no longer take the oath at graduation, many take a similar pledge that requires the physician to consider the benefit of the patient and abstain from deleterious treatment. Clearly, this section of the oath does not prohibit the removal of extraordinary means to keep the patient alive. The oath may be interpreted that in certain situations it is beneficial to allow death to occur, since treatment intended to prolong the dying process could be deleterious to the patient. The following passage of the oath is clear and leaves no room for interpretation: "I will give no deadly medicine to anyone if asked, nor suggest any such counsel." If active euthanasia were legalized, physicians would have to violate the sacred oath of their profession to perform the mercy killing.

The real dilemma for physicians is not contained in those cases in which an adult patient requests that heroic measures be discontinued. Adults are perfectly free to choose for themselves whether or not to accept treatment. The dilemma is especially pertinent to infants. The neonatal intensive care unit has dramatically reduced the infant mortality rate. Many children born today with birth defects would have died during the decade of the 1960s. Since infants cannot consent to refuse treatment, the physician is both legally and ethically bound to save the life. Generally, even parents do not have the legal right to refuse treatment on behalf of their children. Numerous court decisions have firmly established the obligation of physicians to provide the necessary care even though the treatment may conflict with the wishes of the family.

Most of the cases of this sort focus on severely deformed infants, especially those who suffer mental retardation as well as physical handicaps. A perfect illustration is the disease of spina bifida in which the vertebrae are incompletely formed. Possible complications include paralysis, incontinence, organ dysfunction, and mental retardation. Anencephaly, being born without a functional brain, is another condition that challenges modern medical ethics. The impasse is in being able to determine how vigorously one should pursue the necessary treatment. In both of these cases, spina bifida and anancephaly, there is no curative possibility. Should physicians resort to palliative care without treatment or are they obligated to treat all the conditions and complications regardless of the ultimate quality of life?

A few highly publicized cases will help to illustrate the complexity of the decision-making process. An infant was born with Down's syndrome and a blockage of the intestinal tract. Although the Down's syndrome was not curable, the blockage was, and surgery would probably have enabled the mentally retarded infant to survive for some number of years. In this particular case, the parents refused to consent to surgery and the physician and hospital did not countermand the parental decision. The child died after 15 days of life. In a similar case, the state child abuse laws were used to obtain a court order. The court awarded temporary custody of the child to the hospital and the surgery was performed. In the case of *Maine Medical Center* v. *Houle,* a child was born grossly deformed. The immediate threat to life was a blockage of the trachea, but the parents refused permission to operate. A superior court judge ruled that a human being is entitled to the fullest protection of the law at the moment of birth. The required surgery was not a heroic measure but represented ordinary means of treatment. Being satisfied that the corrective surgery was medically necessary, the court granted the request of the medical center.

Another dilemma is raised when the patient is an incompetent adult. In one case a 67-year-old man named Saikewicz was diagnosed as having acute myeloblastic monocytic leukemia in April of 1976. The patient had been profoundly retarded since birth, having an intelligence quotient of 10 and a mental age of 2 years. His entire life was spent in an institution. The necessary chemotherapy offered little chance of remission. Without treatment, he was expected to survive several weeks and die a relatively painless death. On the other hand, the treatment had serious side effects including pain, bladder irritation, anemia, and possibly even death. In this particular case the judge ruled that chemotherapy was not in the patient's best interest even though the treatment was ordinary in nature. The decision was based on factors related to the age of the patient, relative prognosis, and side effects of the treatment. Saikewicz died on September 4, 1976, with no apparent suffering.

In one of the most widely publicized cases of all time the court had to decide whether the parents of 22-year-old Karen Ann Quinlan should be granted custody of their daughter. The court recognized that once the parents had custody, they would request that the respirator be turned off. The situation was complicated by a number of conditions:

1. The patient was not dead. The electroencephalograph revealed some activity, and this was supported by other neurological tests, including a brain scan and lumbar puncture. The court ruled that her condition did not meet the Harvard criteria. She existed at a primitive reflex level, reacting to light and noxious stimuli. Doctors concluded that removal of the respirator would not conform to medical standards.
2. Allegedly the patient had communicated to others in casual conversation prior to her comatose state that she would not desire extraordinary measures in the event that they needed to be performed to sustain life. The court ruled that these conversations were "remote and impersonal" and therefore did not carry significant weight.
3. Karen experienced sleep-wake cycles, a normal situation among comatose patients. During the wake cycle she blinked, cried out, but was still totally unaware of her surroundings. Her condition was described as a "chronic persistent vegetative state." No form of treatment could cure or improve the condition and she would never be restored to cognitive or "human" life.
4. The New Jersey Catholic Conference (representing Catholic bishops of New Jersey) agreed that she was alive. However, referring to an address by Pope Pius XII to anesthesiologists in 1957, the conference indicated that even if removal of the respirator caused circulatory arrest, it was no more than an indirect cause of death and cited the principle of double effect. Their statement supported the decision of the father, a devout Catholic, that the respirator constituted extraordinary treatment.

The New Jersey State Supreme Court ruled that the father should be granted guardian status. The court stated that it had no doubt that if Karen were able to make the decision herself, she would discontinue the life-support equipment even if it meant her own death. The court saw no compelling interest of the state to force the patient to endure the treatment when the outcome was a sustained vegetative state with no hope of recovery. Furthermore, the court recognized that there comes a time when the rights of the individual are more compelling than the interest of the state.

In recognition of the moral and professional uncertainty created by cases such as Saikewicz and Quinlan, a number of hospitals have developed written standards to serve as a guide to physicians. For instance, the Clinical Care Committee of the Massachusetts General Hospital[4] approved the following patient classification system for critically ill patients:

Class A: Maximal therapeutic effort without reservation.

Class B: Maximal therapeutic effort without reservation but with daily evaluation because the probability of survival is questionable.

Class C: Selective limitation of therapeutic measures (particular attention paid to resuscitation measures).

Class D: All therapy can be discontinued. Any measures that are indicated to ensure maximal comfort may be continued or begun. Class D is ordinarily reserved for patients with brain death or when there is no reasonable probability for return to a "cognitive and sapient life."[4]

The advantage of a classification system is that attending physicians can request an optimum care committee to review the case and recommend the appropriate course of action. Although advisory in nature, the committee can objectively determine the appropriateness of intense therapy for critically ill patients. Unless otherwise stated, full resuscitation efforts would be initiated for all patients. The committee may be used to guide physicians in making difficult decisions and may on occasion also help to ease the conscience of an individual who has in his or her best judgment decided that further therapy should be discontinued.

The rapid technological advances of the past several decades have created a void with respect to social norms of euthanasia. Having no traditional set of values on which to rely, society is forced to determine the parameters of acceptance on a case by case basis until a traditional value has been established. In the matter of medical advances related to critical care social norms did not keep pace with technologic development. This placed the patient, the family or the physician in the uncomfortable position of having to make decisions that had no precedent in law and no guidance from medical doctrine. A committee such as the Optimum Care Committee of the Massachusetts General Hospital helps to distribute the responsibility for decision making.

LIVING WILLS

During the last 10 years it has become increasingly more popular to sign the Living Will. A variety of documents have been prepared with titles such as *Testament Permitting Death, Declaration for Bodily Autonomy,* and *Declaration for Ending Treatment.*[5] They all have the common underlying intent to serve as a personal expression of preference for medical treatment in the event of critical illness or injury. They are signed in advance in the recognition that illness or injury may come suddenly and circumstances may not allow for the preference to be made known, for instance, as in a coma. They are also signed in the hope of being able to relieve family or physician of having to make a difficult decision on behalf of the critically ill patient. A third reason for such an expression is that individuals should be able to retain some control over what happens at the end of their lives.

A LIVING WILL

Prepared by

CONCERN FOR DYING

an educational council

IMPORTANT

Declarants may wish to add specific statements to the Living Will to be inserted in the space provided for that purpose above the signature. Possible additional provisions are suggested below:

1. a) I appoint _____ to make binding decisions concerning my medical treatment.

OR

b) I have discussed my views as to life sustaining measures with the following who understand my wishes

_____,
_____,
_____

2. Measures of artificial life support in the face of impending death that are especially abhorrent to me are:

a) Electrical or mechanical resuscitation of my heart when it has stopped beating.

b) Nasogastric tube feedings when I am paralyzed and no longer able to swallow.

c) Mechanical respiration by machine when my brain can no longer sustain my own breathing.

d) _____

3. If it does not jeopardize the chance of my recovery to a meaningful and sentient life or impose an undue burden on my family, I would like to live out my last days at home rather than in a hospital.

4. If any of my tissues are sound and would be of value as transplants to help other people, I freely give my permission for such donation.

Reprinted with Permission from Concern for Dying, 250 West 57th Street, New York, NY 10107.

For additional copies of the Living Will, or the appropriate document in those states which have passed Living Will legislation, use coupon on reverse side.

Additonal materials available to contributors:

☐ Questions and Answers About the Living Will
☐ Selected articles and case histories
☐ A bibliography
☐ Information on films

The Concern for Dying newsletter is a quarterly publication reporting the most recent developments in the field of death and dying. It contains announcements of upcoming educational conferences, workshops and symposia, as well as reviews of current literature. The Newsletter is sent to anyone who contributes $5.00 or more annually to the CONCERN FOR DYING.

☐ I would like to receive the Newsletter.

A mini-will, a condensed version of the Living Will which can be carried in a wallet in case of accident or emergency, will be sent upon receipt of a contribution.

To obtain additional materials check above and fill in name and address on reverse side.

For information, call: (212) 246-6962

Reprinted with Permission from Concern for Dying, 250 West 57th Street, New York, NY 10107.

To My Family, My Physician, My Lawyer and All Others Whom It May Concern

Death is as much a reality as birth, growth, maturity and old age—it is the one certainty of life. If the time comes when I can no longer take part in decisions for my own future, let this statement stand as an expression of my wishes and directions, while I am still of sound mind.

If at such a time the situation should arise in which there is no reasonable expectation of my recovery from extreme physical or mental disability, I direct that I be allowed to die and not be kept alive by medications, artificial means or "heroic measures". I do, however, ask that medication be mercifully administered to me to alleviate suffering even though this may shorten my remaining life.

This statement is made after careful consideration and is in accordance with my strong convictions and beliefs. I want the wishes and directions here expressed carried out to the extent permitted by law. Insofar as they are not legally enforceable, I hope that those to whom this Will is addressed will regard themselves as morally bound by these provisions.

Signed _____

Date _____

Witness _____

Witness _____

Copies of this request have been given to _____

_____

_____

_____

Reprinted with Permission from Concern for Dying, 250 West 57th Street, New York, NY 10107.

To secure extra copies for your own use and to give to friends, tear off this portion and mail to:

CONCERN FOR DYING
250 West 57th Street, New York, N.Y. 10019

Please send me _____ copies of a Living Will

Enclosed is my contribution of $ _____ (tax deductible)

NAME _____
please print

ADDRESS _____

CITY _____ STATE _____ ZIP _____

See additional information on reverse side.

To make best use of your LIVING WILL

1. Sign and date before two witnesses. (This is to insure that you signed of your own free will and not under any pressure.)

2. If you have a doctor, give him a copy for your medical file and discuss it with him to make sure he is in agreement.

   Give copies to those most likely to be concerned "if the time comes when you can no longer take part in decisions for your own future". Enter their names on bottom line of the Living Will. Keep the original nearby, easily and readily available.

3. Above all discuss your intentions with those closest to you, NOW.

4. It is a good idea to look over your Living Will once a year and redate it and initial the new date to make it clear that your wishes are unchanged.

35th printing
Revised May, 1978

Reprinted with Permission from Concern for Dying, 250 West 57th Street, New York, NY 10107.

The legal status of these documents is unclear. Although they appear to carry substantial weight with relatives and the attending physician, living wills have not been accepted by the courts as binding. In the absence of legislation that demands that the Living Will be honored, the statement at least expresses the wishes of the patient and increases the likelihood that extraordinary measures will desist without guilt or legal liability.

The Concern for Dying organization (formerly known as the Euthanasia Educational Council) recommends that the individual sign and date the Living Will in front of two witnesses to show that it was signed freely and without coercion. Further, it is recommended that individuals give a copy to their physicians to be discussed and placed into their medical files. Copies should also be given to those most likely to be concerned "if the time comes when you can no longer take part in the decisions of your own future." These same names are written on the bottom line of the Living Will. Since these people are made aware of the individual's intentions when they receive a copy of the document, discussion with them is advisable. A requisite for any such document is that the individual has the right to cancel the will at any time. For this reason, it is a good idea to review the Living Will on a regular basis and to initial a new date on the paper to make it clear that the individual's wishes are unchanged.

The key words of the Living Will are " . . . no reasonable expectation of my recovery from physical or mental disability." Interpretation of the words *reasonable expectation* may need to be more clearly defined. The individual may wish to add a paragraph that specifies the conditions under which treatment would be discontinued. It may also be desirable to request that certain individual(s) be fully informed of the situation and that they be consulted on any decision pertaining to life-supportive techniques. Obviously, this requires a clear understanding by the named individual of the intent of the signer of the Living Will.

A document known as the Christian Affirmation of Life, approved by the Catholic Hospital Association in 1974, offers an alternative to the Living Will. Addressed to family, friends, physician, lawyer, and clergy, the first part issues a statement of beliefs pertaining to God, human dignity, and death. This is followed by a series of requests. The most important sentence in the context of this discussion reads, "If I can no longer take part in decisions concerning my future and if there is no reasonable expectation of my recovery from physical and mental disability, I request that no extraordinary means be used to prolong my life." Quite apparently, the Christian Affirmation of Life intends to achieve the same objective as the Living Will.

Both of these documents differ from the Voluntary Euthanasia Act, which states:

> If I should at any time suffer from a serious physical illness or impairment reasonably thought in my case to be incurable and expected to cause me severe distress or render

Christian affirmation of life

To my family, friends, physician, lawyer, and clergyman:

I believe that each individual person is created by God our Father in love and that God retains a loving relationship to each person throughout human life and eternity.

I believe that Jesus Christ, lived, suffered, and died for me and that his suffering, death, and resurrection prefigure and make possible the death-resurrection process which I now anticipate.

I believe that each person's worth and dignity derives from the relationship of love in Christ that God has for each individual person and not from one's usefulness or effectiveness in society.

I believe that God our Father has entrusted to me a shared dominion with him over my earthly existence so that I am bound to use ordinary means to preserve my life but I am free to refuse extraordinary means to prolong my life.

I believe that through death life is not taken away but merely changed, and though I may experience fear, suffering, and sorrow, by the grace of the Holy Spirit, I hope to accept death as a free human act which enables me to surrender this life and to be united with God for eternity.

Because of my belief:

I request that I be informed as death approaches so that I may continue to prepare for the full encounter with Christ through the help of the sacraments and the consolation and prayers of my family and friends.

I request that, if possible, I be consulted concerning the medical procedures which might be used to prolong my life as death approaches. If I can no longer take part in decisions concerning my own future and if there is no reasonable expectation of my recovery from physical and mental disability, I request that no extraordinary means be used to prolong my life.

I request, though I wish to join my suffering to the suffering of Jesus so I may be united fully with him in the act of death-resurrection, that my pain, if unbearable, be alleviated. However, no means should be used with the intention of shortening my life.

I request, because I am a sinner and in need of reconciliation and because my faith, hope, and love may not overcome all fear and doubt, that my family, friends, and the whole Christian community join me in prayer and mortification as I prepare for the great personal act of dying.

Finally, I request that after death, my family, my friends, and the whole Christian community pray for me, and rejoice with me because of the mercy and love of the Trinity, with whom I hope to be united for all eternity.

Signed: _____ Date: _____

This document was approved by the Board of Trustees of the Catholic Health Association of the United States, June 1974.

me incapable of rational existence, I request the administration of euthanasia at a time or in circumstances to be indicated or specified by me or, if it is apparent that I have become incapable of giving directions, at the discretion of the physician in charge of my case.

The Voluntary Euthanasia Act then goes on to request that no resuscitation techniques be used to prolong life. This latter statement is similar to the expression contained in other documents; however, the sentence in quotes calls for active euthanasia, an expression not shared by either the Christian Affirmation of Life or the Living Will.

In 1976 California became the first state to legalize the Living Will. Since then, legislative bills have been introduced in 38 states, with eight states having created the statutory right to expect that the provisions of the document will be honored. Written into the Health and Safety Code, the Natural Death Act is designed to make the will of the patient binding on the physician in cases of terminal illness. If the physician is unable to oblige the request, the patient is to be transferred to the care of another physician. The New Mexico and Arkansas bills go one step beyond the California law in permitting the execution of a Living Will by relatives on behalf of a minor or incompetent adult. Idaho, Nevada, Oregon, North Carolina, and Texas have also enacted variations of the Natural Death Act (Appendix F).

SUMMARY

For many people, the word *euthanasia* creates an immediate and negative reaction. Chapter 5 attempts to provide the reader with an accurate conceptualization of the term and an explanation of the issues voiced by proponents and opponents of this controversial topic. The chapter neither endorses nor rejects euthanasia. Instead, we expect that the reader will be able to perceive the legitimacy of the various agruments and conclude that decision making in specific cases is never a comfortable thing, regardless of the general attitude of the individual toward euthanasia. The three major issues seem to focus on reverence for the quality of life, respect for personal rights and freedom, and hyprocrisy of life and death matters, which is especially observable with regard to war, abortion, and capital punishment. Case studies at the end of the chapter offer stimulating challenge for the reader.

The chapter presents religious viewpoints, concerns by the medical community, and complications raised by the legal experts with regard to application of law in matter of personal preference. This section of the chapter enables the reader to see the complications created by advances in medical technology. One illustration of a current dilemma is the question of whether and when palliative care should replace curative treatment. Many hospitals have appointed optimum care committees to establish position statements and protocols for care. This has helped to relieve the burden placed on physicians and nurses who must often make difficult decisions under considerable emotional strain.

The final section of the chapter deals with the Living Will, an *a priori* statement of personal preference in the event that a critical illness should render the individual unable to communicate his or her wishes. The Christian Affirmation of Life, an alternative document written in a religious context, is also presented. California was the first state to officially endorse the legality of the Living Will. Other states have more recently taken similar action.

CONCEPTS RELATED TO EUTHANASIA EDUCATION

- Knowledge and understanding of the medical and social aspects of euthanasia are the basis for effective values formation and decision making.

- The concept and definition of euthanasia is influenced by the interrelationship of social and cultural factors.

- Adequate knowledge of euthanasia, the ability to adjust to various situations, and respect and understanding for the feelings of others tend to produce healthy attitudes toward euthanasia.

- Clarification of individual values regarding euthanasia may help improve subsequent decision making.

- Society needs to accept responsibility for making sound decisions regarding euthanasia and preventing abuse of those decisions.

EDUCATIONAL ACTIVITIES RELATED TO EUTHANASIA EDUCATION

Title: *Death with Dignity: Model Bill*

Age level: College, adults

Objective: Using *Death with Dignity: Model Bill,* students will develop a death with dignity legislative proposal to send to their elected representatives.

Materials: *Death with Dignity: Model Bill.* Copies of the Model Bill along with a legislative manual can be obtained from Society for the Right to Die, Inc., 250 West 57th St., New York, NY 10019.

Directions: Provide each student with a model bill. As a class discuss any additions, corrections, or clarifications to the model bill (you may need to divide the class into groups for this task). Arrive at a class consensus. Provide students with information and appropriate practice for writing letters to elected representatives.

NOTE: You may want to provide students with copies of related legislation in Appendix H.

Title: Definitions of euthanasia

Age level: High school, college, adults

Objective: Given a euthanasia case study, students will classify the euthanasia situation as one of the following classifications or descriptions of euthanasia:
Voluntary indirect (passive) euthanasia
Involuntary indirect (passive) euthanasia
Voluntary direct (active) euthanasia
Involuntary direct (active) euthanasia

Material: Case study worksheet

Directions: Provide students with a presentation of the contemporary interpretations of euthanasia. Develop a student worksheet of sample euthanasia situations (a sample worksheet is provided below). Ask students to classify the situation as one of the four types of euthanasia cited above. Conduct a classroom discussion on each of the situations.

Definition of euthanasia worksheet

Directions: For each of the euthanasia situations described below, identify how you believe this situation would be classified. Use the following symbols:
VIE–Voluntary indirect euthanasia
IIE–Involuntary indirect euthanasia
VDE–Voluntary direct euthanasia
IDE–Involuntary direct euthanasia

_____ Stanley Kowalski, 27, was in a motorcycle accident and he is paralyzed from the neck down. He is in severe pain. Every day when his close friend visits he pleads that he be shot. Finally, the friend consents.

_____ Naomi Johnson, 62, has completed a Living Will. When she has a severe stroke, the family decides that no heroic measures should be taken to prolong Naomi's life.

_____ Myrna Goldman, 56, has been diagnosed as having terminal lung cancer. Repulsed by the thought of proceeding through a long and painful treatment process, Myrna takes an overdose of sleeping pills.

_____ John Deluca, 43, is in a serious auto accident. There are definite indications that if John survives, he will live in a vegetative condition

140

for the remainder of his life. The Deluca family decides to remove John from all forms of life-support systems.

_____ Basil Worthington, 72, believes he has lived a useful and productive life. When he has a heart attack, Mr. Worthington opts not to sign the consent form for the required surgical procedures.

Title: Euthanasia decision-making situations

Age level: College, health professionals, adult

Objective: In a small group decision-making situation the students will outline three alternatives and identify a personal position for one of the euthanasia decision-making situations. At the conclusion of the euthanasia decision-making situation the student will develop an awareness of the complexity of the euthanasia issue.

Materials: Euthanasia decision-making situations

Directions: Divide the class into four groups. Provide each group one of the four situations listed below. Ask the groups to answer the following questions:
- What is the dilemma or problem?
- What relevant information is needed?
- What are the alternatives to the problem?
- What are the pros and cons of each alternative?
- Which alternative is the most feasible?

Have each group present their situation and answers to the questions to the class.

Situation 1

Mr. A. suffered from a malignancy of the bladder and underwent surgery. A year later a painful kidney infection developed, and the left kidney and ureter were removed. Two years after that further blockage developed. Mr. A. was unable to void and suffered excruciating pain.

He then contracted pneumonia. His wife asked that everything be done to cure his pneumonia, so that his bladder and urethra could be removed; then he could live a few more months, or years, with artificial provision for urinary elimination.

Mr. A. knew further malignancies were likely. He believed that his meaningful life was over, and he did not wish to face the loss of his bladder.

Should he be given pain-killing medication and allowed to die of pneumonia—or should he be given antibiotics to face another major surgery and probable death later from toxemia?

Situation 2

Mr. G., 69, was a widower. He and his wife had worked and saved to help provide for their children and the education of their grandchildren. Mr. G. had to retire 4 years ago at a time when his wife had terminal cancer. Much of what they had saved for their family went into her hospital and medical expenses.

141

Then Mr. G. became critically ill with nephritis and cardiac complications. He had been living frugally, to help rebuild his savings. Since the death of his wife, he had no desire to prolong his own life, and he was concerned about the cost of his own care. He became obsessed with the thought that his own hospital expenses now were eating away the rest of the education fund he had saved for his grandchildren.

Mr. G. told his family and his children that he wanted to be allowed to die. One night after being given routine care, he pulled the life-giving intravenous needle from his arm and scrawled a note asking that he be allowed to die in peace. Unconscious but still alive, he was found about an hour later by a nurse. She called the resident, who also knew about Mr. G.'s wishes.

What should the resident have done?

Situation 3

Mr. E. was to be 30 in less than a month. He had recently suffered irreparable brain damage in an automobile accident and had a flat electro-encephalogram.

Before his own death and before his son's marriage, Mr. E.'s father had set up a trust fund giving his son the income until he was 30, at which time Mr. E. would receive the principal. If Mr. E. had no children and died before he was 30, the principal was to be divided among Mr. E.'s brothers and sisters. Mr. E.'s wife, then, would receive nothing.

Would it be justifiable to take extraordinary measures, which might not otherwise have been taken, to "keep the body warm" until Mr. E.'s thirtieth birthday?

Situation 4

Mrs. H. was a brilliant woman and a well-known activist. She came from a family of considerable wealth and was married to a physician who was highly regarded in medical circles and taught at a leading medical school.

Mrs. H. suddenly, at the age of 50, suffered a massive but not lethal cerebral hemorrhage. Dr. H. knew the prognosis was hopeless. He knew also that his wife would have hated more than anything the indignity of a helpless vegetative existence.

Because he was a distinguished member of the medical school faculty, the staff of the university hospital would go all out to keep Mrs. H. alive. There would be no financial problem. Dr. H. prayed for his wife's release, but the weight of his traditional medical attitudes and his own sense of guilt made it impossible for him to ask that the plugs and tubes be pulled.

Should his friends and colleagues have given him support in making the decision that Dr. H. knew would be in line with his wife's wishes?

Title: The Living Will

Age level: High school, college, adults

Objective: After weighing the pros and cons, the students will develop a personal course of action with regard to the Living Will.

Materials: Newsprint, felt markers, individual copies of the Living Will. A copy of this document is included in this chapter. Additional copies may be obtained by writing to Concern for Dying, 250 West 57th St., New York, NY 10019.

Directions: Divide the class into small groups. Provide each student with a copy of the Living Will. Ask each group to brainstorm all the possible arguments for and against completing such a document and list them on the newsprint. Hang the newsprint with the responses around the classroom. Conduct a class discussion to clarify each response. Ask each student to arrive at a personal decision concerning the Living Will.

Title: Euthanasia role playing

Age level: High school, adult

Objective: Following the role-playing situation, the student will develop a personal position statement related to the dilemma presented in the role-playing situation.

Materials: Role-playing situation cards

Directions: Assign students to one of the four roles outlined below. Allow the role-playing participants time to rehearse their roles. Read the introduction to the class. Present the role-playing dramatization. Allow time for students to develop a personal position statement outlining how they would resolve the role-playing dilemma.

Introduction: Death is an indisputable fact of life. Humans have questioned and examined their view regarding death throughout the ages. However, today modern techniques for prolonging life have forced a reexamination of traditional attitudes and values toward life and death. Countless families are faced with the responsibility of having to make an urgent decision concerning the life of a dying loved one. In fact, there is the distinct possibility that all may have to make such a decision at sometime during the course of life. Therefore it is important to establish personal values and attitudes from which we can make subsequent decisions.

To begin establishing these attitudes, it becomes necessary to answer some basic questions:

- Do the means for prolonging life artificially add to the quality of life of the patient?
- Is it desirable to prolong life when death is near?
- What influence do moral, legal, and religious responsibilities play in this decision?

The following is a dramatization that will help to clarify values. Sara Smith, a 76-year-old widow, has just suffered a severe stroke. Her two sons and one daughter have just arrived at the hospital. The doctor informs them that they have to make a decision concerning whether to implant a pace-maker to regulate Mrs. Smith's heart function.

Role 1

Dennis Smith believes that his mother would not want to live the remainder of her life dependent on others. He feels that the operation to implant the pace-maker should not be performed and that his mother should be allowed to die a "dignified death."

Role 2

Sue Ann Smith believes that it is selfish not to do everything possible to keep her mother alive. She feels that God gave us the technology to prolong life and we should take advantage of it.

Role 3

Sam Smith does not want to make such a complex decision concerning life and death. He feels that the family should consult with their minister and family physician and let them decide which is the best course of action in this situation.

Role 4

Dr. Fernandez believes that the family should sign the consent forms for the operation as soon as possible. He cannot predict Mrs. Smith will even partially recover from the stroke, but he believes that every effort should be taken to keep Mrs. Smith alive.

REFERENCES

1. Louisell, David: Euthanasia and biathanasia: on dying and killing, In Horan, Dennis, and Mall, David, editors: Death, dying, and euthanasia, 1977, Washington, D.C., University Publications of America, Inc., p. 394.
2. Sacred Congregation for the Doctrine of the Faith: Euthanasia, The Pope Speaks **25**(4): 289-296, 1980.
3. American Medical Association, House of Delegates, 1973. Cited by Rachels, James: Active and passive euthanasia, New England Journal of Medicine **292:**78-80, 1975.
4. Clinical Care Committee of the Massachusetts General Hospital: Optimum care for hopelessly ill patients, New England Journal of Medicine **295:**362-364, 1976.
5. Elliott, Neil: The gods of life, New York, 1974, New York, Macmillan Publishing Co., p.41.

Photo by Pfister Photographic

CHAPTER SIX

Suicide

Most people who commit acts of self-damage
with more or less conscious self-destructive intent
do not want either to live or die,
*but to do both at the same time—usually, one more than the other.**
ERWIN STENGEL

Suicide has been an option exercised by humans ever since people began to interact, to become interdependent, and to form societies. On the surface, it is an action that is seemingly easy to understand. However, it is a tremendously complex issue that has until recently remained unstudied. The first notable scientific investigation was conducted by the French sociologist, Emile Durkheim, at the turn of the century. For at least 50 years the further study of suicide remained virtually dormant. This is evidenced by the fact that two of the leading journals in public health (American Journal of Public Health and Public Health Reports) published no articles on suicide prior to 1950.

Before offering a conceptualization of suicide, it would be interesting to have individuals place a check mark next to the following situations that they believe should be recorded as suicide and reevaluate their decisions after they have read the chapter.

_____ A person who consumes an overdose of barbiturates

_____ A person who mixes barbiturates and alcohol

_____ A diabetic individual who carelessly follows the prescribed diet

_____ A person suffering from intractable pain shoots himself or herself

_____ A person who so strongly believes in a cause that he or she goes on a hunger strike

_____ A person who commits a capital offense despite knowing the penalty if he or she is caught

_____ A person who provokes another to attack himself or herself

_____ A person who chooses a high-risk form of recreation, such as sky diving, hang gliding, or Grand Prix racing

---

*From Stengel, Erwin: A matter of communication. In Schneidman, Edwin S., editor: On the nature of suicide, San Francisco, 1969, Jossey-Bass, Inc., Publishers, p. 78.

DEFINING SUICIDE

The word suicide is derived from two Latin words: *suus,* meaning self, and *caedere,* meaning to hurt or kill. Literally translated, suicide means to hurt or kill oneself. It is probable that most people would define suicide in this way, but the definition is woefully inadequate in that it does not account for the dynamics of the event, only the outcome. Many suicidologists have carefully considered these dynamics, and we will use their definitions to build a more holistic concept of self-destruction. Given the variety of personal motives and desired outcomes, one can only understand suicide after considering the circumstances that lead to the self-destructive event.

Durkheim[1] defined suicide as those cases of death resulting directly or indirectly from positive or negative acts of the victims themselves; the victims know the result that will be produced by their actions. Examples of negative acts that result in death include intentional starvation, refusal of blood transfusion or surgery, and failure to heed the warnings of an impending disaster such as a hurricane or tornado. Thus suicide may occur as the result of action or inaction. The last part of Durkheim's definition, however, seems inappropriate. Should a death be classified as suicide only when the individual knows for certain that death will result? This would exclude those people who die as the result of an activity euphemistically called Russian roulette. It would also seemingly include those people who bravely volunteer for a military mission that has a high probability of the volunteer being killed by the enemy. Among the general public the former would more likely be classified as a suicide than the latter even though the latter carries a greater certainty of death.

Suicide has also been conceptualized as death resulting from a nonsacrificial act undertaken by the victim with the intention of killing himself or herself. This definition raises another issue. In many cultures it is considered a privilege to die in sacrificial fashion. Obviously, such a death is not considered by that society as being suicide. Is sacrificial death (sacrifice of one's life for a person or cause) always to be considered a nonsuicide, or is there some flexibility in principle so that it may be possible to classify some acts of altruism as suicide? A police officer who comes to the aid of a citizen who is being assaulted would probably not be recorded as a suicidal death. Similarly, a parent who reenters a burning house to save a child would not be demonstrating suicidal behavior. In contrast, a monk who self-immolates for a just cause or an individual who consumes poison rather than suffer indignation would be considered to have committed suicide. In each of these illustrations the cause is just. For the police officer and the parent the just cause is tangible, whereas for the monk or the person swallowing poison the just cause is philosophic but no less understandable than the

148

human who is sacrificed to please the spirits. The predicament is whether sacrifical death should always, sometimes, or never be considered as suicide.

Another significant dimension is raised by the concept of suicide as the act by which a fully competent person kills himself or herself. The person is able to live but chooses to die. This concept identifies suicide as the voluntary action of a rational person. Would alcoholic or drug-addicted individuals who inflict fatal injuries on themselves therefore be ruled out as suicides? Would those suffering from severe depression or schizophrenia be excluded because they are not fully competent? It has been argued that people who attempt to kill themselves are mentally ill. If this were true, there would be no suicides because according to the previous definition, the "fully competent" person would not commit suicide.

Stengel[2] defined suicide as the fatal act of self-injury undertaken with conscious self-destructive intent, however vague and ambiguous. This definition recognizes the fact that suicidal intent may be subconscious. The decision may have been achieved only after careful contemplation, and a weighing of pros and cons, or it may result from subconscious drives that are unknown to the individual. The focus is on intent rather than outcome. Whether motivated by conscious or subconscious drives, it is the intent of the action that causes it to be classified as suicide. This concept would accept those people who by volunteering for a military mission intend to die (whether or not their intent is recognized). In contrast, another person who joins this same mission but without the intent to die would not meet the criteria. Even though both soldiers may die, the former would be a suicide and the latter a casualty of war. The difficulty here of course is that if the drives are unrecognized by the victims themselves, there is no way that an observer could actually determine the intent of the victim.

Baechler[3] introduces another facet of the issue. He defines suicide as "all behavior which seeks and finds the solution to an existential problem by making an attempt on the life of the subject."[3] In this definition suicide is not an end in itself but a means to an end. Furthermore, the attempt itself whether death results or not is considered suicide. This issue is slightly different from the one just presented that deals with intent. According to this definition, a person may intend to die as a result of the action taken, but because of chance or method selected, the person does not die. Baechler would classify this event as a suicide. Another person may attempt suicide as a means of communicating a message to a loved one. The prospect of death may never have occurred to the individual. Nevertheless, the solution to the existential problem is found in the self-destructive attempt the individual makes. This is why it is inappropriate to classify suicides as being either successful or unsuccessful on the basis of whether or not death results. This implies that death is the goal of every suicide attempt. For the person who wants to communicate a message by way of a suicide attempt, the success or failure of the action is in whether or not the message was received. If death should result from the attempt of one who does not intend to die, then the attempt and subsequent fatality is an unsuccessful suicide. As pointed out by Freeman and others,[4] it is reasonable to attach the concept of "attempt to kill oneself" only to those who have a high intention of dying.

Stengel elaborated on this point. He indicated that human behavior has multiple motivations, not all of which are obvious, and some of which are antagonistic to each other. It is inappropriate to say that people either want to live or want to die. Individuals who attempt suicide want both to live and to die at the same time. Conscious and subconscious drives seek opposing outcomes. Life or death may be determined by the relative strength of these conflicting motivations. The World Health Organization[5] defined a suicidal act as self-injury with varying degrees of lethal intent and a suicide as a suicidal act with fatal outcome.

Recognizing that the outcome of the suicidal act depends on intentionality, Freeman and others[4] developed a grid that is useful in attempting to characterize the lethal intent of the person involved. He reasoned that intentionality is inversely proportional to the degree of reversibility and the likelihood of intervention. The outcome of lethal behavior is determined by the method chosen and by the timing and location of the event, with chance factors having a potentially significant role in the outcome. Some methods of self-destructive behavior are less subject to reversibility than others. For instance, jumping from a tall building is irreversible once the leap has begun, whereas the effects of barbiturates can be neutralized if the person should have a change of mind or be found in the early stage of unconsciousness. Intervention is more a function of timing and location than of method. If a person decides to put a gun to his or her chest at a family gathering, the likelihood of the trigger being pulled is less than if the person chooses a remote location or a time when others are not expected to be around. If the method chosen has a low reversibility and was carried out in a private setting, it can be inferred that the intentionality of death was high. On the other hand, if the act was likely to be discovered and if it offered the potential for remediation, it can be inferred that intentionality of death was low. Figure 3 is an adaptation of Freeman's model.[4]

Although self-destructive behavior of all types is properly classified as suicidal behavior, it cannot be assumed that the intended purpose of every attempt is death. The greatest amount of intentionality and the greatest likelihood of a fatal suicide are found in the lower left quadrant of the model, while the lowest intentionality and risk of death are found in the upper right quadrant. With low reversibility and unlikely intervention, the person probably does not want to be talked out of the life-threatening

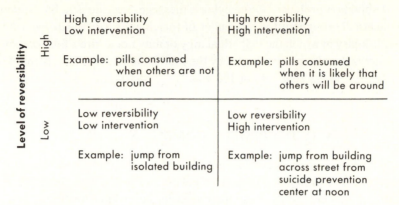

Figure 3. Adaptation of Freeman model of intentionality.

Modified from Freeman, Douglas J., and others: Assessing intention to die in self-injury behavior. In Neuringer, Charles, editor: Psychological assessment of suicidal risk, Springfield, Ill., 1974, Charles C Thomas, Publisher.

behavior. For this individual the wish to die is greater than the wish to live. If the person has a low degree of intentionality, the circumstances of the action would seem to indicate that the wish to live is greater than the wish to die. However, chance can play a role in the outcome. Instead of a suicide prevention center volunteer seeing the person and responding with humanistic compassion, an onlooker may anger or humiliate the person into carrying out the threat by yelling, "You don't have any guts. Go ahead and jump."

Generally, the more violent mechanisms of self-destructive behavior have the lowest degree of reversibility. This can help to explain why adolescent suicide attempts, especially female attempts, are less successful than attempts made by the elderly. Choosing a less violent method probably indicates a low level of intention and a greater desire to live than to die. Ambivalent feelings, both conscious and unconscious, probably lead to the selection of a method that is potentially fatal but offers the possibility of being saved. The availability of method does not determine which type of self-destructive behavior will be chosen. Tall buildings and ropes are easily accessible; barbiturates, poisons, and guns are less so. It should be apparent then that when someone engages in a suicide attempt that is not fatal, survival is not the result of a botched effort. For those who intend to die, the act is carefully planned and calculated to leave little to chance.

Our definition of suicide combines the concepts of the World Health Organization and Jean Baechler. A suicidal act is self-injury with varying degrees of lethal intent as a means of solving a problem or conveying a message. Suicide is lethal behavior that results in death. Throughout the remainder of the chapter, *suicide attempt* is used to describe self-injury in which the individual may or may not desire a fatal outcome. The attempt or act is the alternative chosen by the individual to solve a problem. A suicide attempt does not mean that loss of life was the motive that led to the action.

WHY DO PEOPLE COMMIT SUICIDE?

Like all forms of human behavior, suicide is difficult to understand because it is an event motivated by a complex, interrelated network of psychosocial variables. A person who attempts suicide on three different occasions may have a different reason each time. To discover the true meaning of suicide, though, it is necessary to dig beneath the surface of what appears to be the proximate cause of the self-destructive behavior. There is no circumstance in life for which suicide is the only possible mode of behavior. As observed by Stengel, "If people killed themselves only because they were tired of life, or if they endangered their life only to get empathy, the problem would not be why there are so many but why there are so few suicide attempts."[2]

Observers of suicide rarely determine the true significance of the act, for its meaning is not to be found in the behavior itself or in the events immediately preceding the suicide. Instead, suicide is the culmination of experiences and thought derived from interactions of the self with the religious, political, and cultural milieu. The condition of poverty can be used to illustrate this point. It is probably found in every civilization on Earth. If several societies were identified in which the relative proportions of the population suffering from poverty were nearly equal, similar rates of suicide would not be expected. Even though all of these people would suffer from the same deprivations, the rate of suicide would vary. Within these civilizations suicide may be forbidden, permitted, or condoned. Within any of these contexts some individuals will decide to commit suicide and others will not. If poverty alone were the cause of suicide, there would certainly be no poverty in the world since all impoverished people would have committed suicide. If suicide is caused by poverty, how can we explain the cases of suicide that occur among the wealthy? Given identical conditions, one person may choose suicide while his neighbor may choose alcohol, schizophrenia, violence, or dogmatic acceptance of the conditions. Suicide is a means to an end. However, it is only one means among many that can be used to achieve the same end. Furthermore, the same means can be used to achieve different ends, as is shown in the following examples:

For the Vikings, the only way to enter Valhalla was through a violent death. Battle and suicide were encouraged as a way of gaining honor and immortality.

In certain nomadic tribes it is customary for the elderly to leave the group and go to an isolated place to die. This prevents the elderly from becoming a burden on the rest of the group.

The early Christians, emphasizing faith in God, nonviolence, humility, and the belief in a better afterlife, often provoked the Romans into killing them. Death was welcomed as an act of martyrdom and a display of faith.

For the ancient Greeks the concept of honor was pervasive. If an individual suffered a dishonor, it was considered appropriate to petition the magistrate for a lethal dose of poison. Socrates was one of many who found honor in the drink of hemlock.

In AD 73 the Romans were about to conquer a Jewish settlement. Rather than be enslaved, 960 people committed suicide.

Social aspects

The social theory of suicide began with Emile Durkheim, the French sociologist who wrote *Le Suicide* in 1897. Until this time suicides were explained on a case by case basis. Inductive logic was used to account for the action taken. Freud was just beginning his work, so psychological explanations were weak and superficial. Durkheim reasoned that it was impossible to understand suicide by analyzing case studies. Suicide was a phenomenon that had to be studied within the context of the society in which the person lived. Suicide could not be understood until the entire ecosystem was observed.

Durkheim believed that suicide was a function of social malaise. If the nature of the malaise could be identified, and if appropriate steps were taken, the incidence of suicide could be reduced. His study began by analyzing the accumulated data. He calculated rates of suicide according to a host of demographic variables in the belief that there was a social explanation for the variation in suicide rates. He used these data and inferences from them to develop a theory in which four types of suicide were identified: egoistic, altruistic, anomic, and fatalistic.[1]

Egoistic suicides. Egoistic suicide exists because the person is not properly integrated into society. For this individual, collective life is of little importance and traditions and values of society are meaningless. Therefore personal goals and private rules supercede the sanctioned conduct of the group. Private interests outweigh social good. Durkheim observed that during periods of social crises such as war the suicide rate drops. He reasoned that this is so because during a crisis, society becomes more strongly integrated. When the crisis is over, individualism is no longer subordinate to the ethics of the group, and the rates begin to rise. It is believed that suicides that occur among celebrities and professionals may fall under this classification. Because of their occupational goals and expectations, these individuals are not properly integrated into the society, and therefore in a time of crisis they have difficulty finding appropriate support systems.

Altruistic suicides. Altruistic suicide also results from improper integration of the individual into society. This time, however, the person becomes so completely absorbed in the group that its goals become the individual's goals. Members are willing to sacrifice their own lives for the sake of the social whole. Individuality is forsaken and is replaced by loyalty to the group that has nurtured the person in time of need. The determination of personal conduct lies outside the individual. It is dictated by society. In certain situations self-sacrifice is necessary and suicide represents a demonstration of loyalty to the group. Death is taken with enthusiasm, optimism, and a deep sense of satisfaction for having done the right thing. The kamikaze pilots of Japan provide an example of altruistic suicide. They sacrificed their lives for the perceived good of the nation.

Anomic suicides. Rather than from integration, anomic suicide results from too little social regulation placed on the individual. Being free from social control and social restraint, the individual is free to exercise personal judgment in matters of morality. Without social controls behavior is determined solely by individual constraints. Attempting to balance right and wrong without a social standard of conduct is frustrating and leads to aggressive behavior. Anomic suicides are less a function of the individual's ability to integrate into society and more a function of the ability of society to function appropriately. Suicides triggered by severe economic depressions may fall under this classification.

Fatalistic suicide. Although not reported by many people who have studied Durkheim, there is actually a fourth type of suicide, which he called *fatalism*. Its mention is limited to a footnote because Durkheim felt that it had little contemporary importance and examples were hard to find. Fatalistic suicide is opposite anomic suicide on the social regulation continuum. It occurs when society applies excessive regulations that become oppressive. There is excessive disciplinary action with no mechanism for appeal. When the individual's needs are not being met, a "what's the use" philosophy appears. The individual sees no benefit in living a life in which behavior is so strictly regulated that personal choice is absent. Slavery is an example of a societal condition that may trigger a fatalistic suicide. This societal structure offers little opportunity for self-esteem or satisfaction, and individuals see their avenues of advancement blocked.

■ ■ ■

According to Durkheim then, suicide results from excess or deficiencies of integration and regulation. Each society has a fairly stable collective inclination toward these two factors that predispose a potential number of suicides. The suicide rate will remain constant as long as the basic conditions of personal existence remain the same. It is impossible to predict which person will commit suicide, but it is possible to predict a rate of suicide based on the prevailing degree of integration and regulation. In effect, society forms the individual in its own image. Being a product of that society determines to a greater or lesser extent one's propensity to commit suicide.

Figure 4 is presented to help the reader conceptualize the typology of suicide developed by Durkheim. It demonstrates that moderate amounts of integration and regulation are protective against suicide, but in extreme levels these characteristics

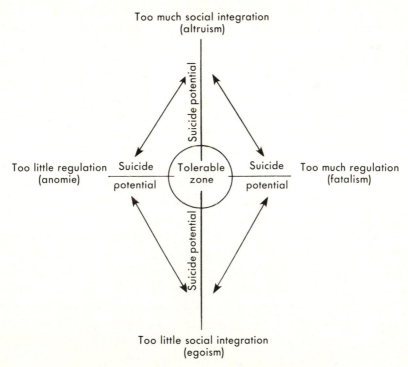

Figure 4. Model to illustrate Durkheim's theory.

Data from Durkheim, Emile: Suicide: a study in sociology, 1951, Glencoe, Ill., The Free Press of Glencoe. (Translated by John A. Spaulding and George Simpson.)

155

create an increasing potential for suicide. In addition to the pure types of suicide, it is possible to have combinations of types such as egoistic-fatalistic suicide. Altruism can be described as, "Society is everything," while egoism is, "I am everything." Fatalism can be described as, "Everything I do is society's business," whereas anomie is "Nothing I do is society's business."

Several contemporary studies offer credibility to Durkheim's theory. Wenz[6] administered a scale that measured anomie in three groups of people. One group had made a serious attempt at suicide. The second group had made a less serious attempt, and the control group had never made a suicide attempt. He found that anomie is positively related to the degree of lethality and concluded that people who make serious attempts at self-destruction are more alienated, isolated, disorganized, and demoralized than people who do not make serious attempts on their own life. In another study Wenz[7] evaluated the relationship between lethality and powerlessness. He hypothesized that powerlessness scores would be higher among those who attempted than among a control group of nonattempters and found that the data supported his belief.

French and Brice[8] studied the relationship between female assertiveness associated with the women's rights movement and female suicides. They reasoned that changes brought about by the movement would lead to conflict and that social disorganization of this type creates alienation. They hypothesized that whereas women traditionally used passive methods of suicide, the disorganization would lead to more aggressive methods, and this change would alter the completion-to-attempt ratio. The results showed that among the 131 female suicides studied in the years of 1966 to 1972 the aggressive modes for women showed a dramatic increase. In 1966 only 33% of the women used aggressive methods, such as gunshot, hanging, stabbing, drowning, or jumping, but in 1972 the rate was 77%, only slightly below the rate of men. This probably accounts for the fact that in 1966 the completion-to-attempt ratio among females was 19%, and in 1972 it was 24%. It would appear that social disorganization during these 7 years was not associated with an overall increase in the number of female suicides but was associated with the use of more aggressive modes of self-destruction. It should be pointed out that the proportion of male-to-female completed suicides did not change substantially during these years and that nationwide the female suicide rate did not evidence a dramatic increase during the height of the women's rights movement.

Psychological aspects

Psychological explanations of suicide focus on the individual and attempt to create a theoretical basis on which treatment and prevention modalities can be based. The writings of Freud contain two themes. The first is that suicide is aggression turned inward. Rather than attack someone else, individuals direct hostility toward themselves. Some authors have referred to this as 180-degree homicide. The second theme describes a battle between eros, the wish to live, and thanatos, the wish to die. As a person grows older, the thanatos drive becomes stronger. Whenever the death wish exceeds the will to live, suicide becomes a viable option.

Suicide has been attributed to many psychological states, including hostility, shame, guilt, anxiety, inferiority, dependency, and disorganization. Krauss[9] believed that suicide results when an individual is deprived of a cherished goal or relationship and destroys the representation of the goal or object within the self. Farber[10] thought that the variable most intimately related to suicide is hopelessness. Hope is the confident expectation that a desired outcome will occur, and hopelessness is the despair that results from a loss of hope. Hopelessness is characterized by a depreciated self-image and loss of gratification from significant relationships or roles in life.[11] The perception of inescapable suffering leads to fatigue, loss of willpower, and symptoms of physical, mental, and emotional illness.

In their study of self-destructive behavior among alcoholic and nonalcoholic individuals, Beck, Weissman, and Kovacs[12] found that alcoholic individuals have a high risk of suicide, and further, the key determinant in both groups was hopelessness. The investigators reported that as many as 10% to 20% of alcoholics die by suicide compared to 1% of the general population. The confusing issue is whether hopelessness led to the alcoholism or whether alcoholism contributed to the onset of despair. Is chronic intoxication caused by chronic depression, or is it the other way around? Some people believe that alcoholism may represent a subconscious death wish, yet others think the death wish is a consequence of the intoxication that was caused by hopelessness.

The message to parents and teachers seems clear. People need to have a sense of optimism to fight off the disappointments of life. A wholesome future orientation is largely based on an individual's sense of personal worth. Having an ample supply of self-esteem serves as protection against the loss of hope. Having the willingness to apply knowledge or skill to the solution of a problem helps to protect a person from frustration. Being able and having confidence in one's ability offers considerable protection against the seemingly relentless assaults on the ego.

Baechler used a psychological context to describe four types of suicide.

1. Escapist
   a. Flight—to escape from an intolerable situation
   b. Grief—following the loss of a significant other
   c. Punishment—to expiate a real or imagined fault

2. Aggressive
   a. Vengeance—to provoke remorse or inflict opprobrium
   b. Crime—involving another in one's own death, for example, an individual who commits homicide and then commits suicide
   c. Blackmail—resulting from manipulative pressure
   d. Appeal—to inform others of one's predicament
3. Oblative
   a. Sacrifice—to gain value greater than life
   b. Transfiguration—to attain a state of delight
4. Ludic
   a. Ordeal—risking one's life to prove oneself
   b. Game—to take a chance or a gamble with death

It is a misconception to believe that a person must be mentally ill to engage in self-destructive behavior. To be sure, mental illness places a person at a higher risk than those with a healthy psyche. However, among the population who attempt suicide are those whose motives are understandable if not altogether acceptable. Honor, freedom from pain, reunion with a loved one, attempts to make restitution, and martydom are not synonyms for psychosis. Among the mentally ill, some choose suicide and others do not. The same is true for those among the general population who are assumed to be in good mental health. It is easy to understand that a psychotic may attempt suicide to escape an imaginary fear or hallucination. Likewise, the exaggerated sadness and extreme depression of melancholy is accepted because one can see the problem and relate to it. When an apparently healthy person commits an act of self-injury or suicide, it is somewhat natural to assume that mental illness must exist at a subclinical level because the motives are unclear. Even though suicide is the means chosen to solve a variety of problems or to satisfy a multitude of social or personal needs, the hidden mental illness—the proverbial skeleton in the closet—is persistently sought. This myth that only mentally ill persons commit suicide relates closely to the notion that America is a death-denying society. For if it is consciously or subconsciously believed that only mentally ill people commit suicide and that the rest of society is sane, then the rest of society is secure in their notion that they would never commit suicide.

Religion views suicide as sinful. By helping people to maintain faith, religion seeks to prevent suicide. A person who commits suicide has lost faith, and the path to recovery is to restore the spirit of the sinner. The law views suicide as illegal. By establishing penalties for violation of statute, the law seeks to prevent suicide. A person who commits suicide has lost respect for the laws of humanity and the path to recovery is to punish the criminal. Medicine views suicide as an illness. By keeping people healthy, medicine seeks to prevent suicide. A person who commits suicide has become mentally ill, and the path to recovery is through psychotherapy, surgery, or medication. Obviously, these paradigms are too simplistic to explain the phenomenon of self destructive behavior. The suicidal person may be a sinner, a criminal, and a psychotic or may be none of these.

If mental illness raises the risk of suicide, so too does physical illness. Dorpat, Anderson, and Ripley[13] studied 80 cases of completed suicide and found that 56 of the individuals had at least one sickness at the time of the suicide. It is interesting to observe that the illnesses of the people studied are quite prominent in the stress literature. Peptic ulcers, rheumatoid arthritis, hypertension, asthma, colitis, and cardiospasm were among the diseases listed in the study. In the stress literature they have been referred to as diseases of adaptation. They result from failure of the body to adapt adequately to the environment and psychosocial pressures of modern society. Like the physical illnesses listed above, suicide is an adaptive mechanism, an adjustment that can lead to physical harm and even death. Failure of an organ or system to adjust to stress can lead to damage of the organ or system. Similarly, failure of an organism to adjust to stress can lead to damage of the person. Ulcers and colitis are no less self-inflicted than suicide, yet most people would not call the predisposing behavior of these diseases mental illness.

The psychological study of suicide has several difficulties that must be mentioned. Foremost among these difficulties is that they are based on retrospective research technique. Interviews are conducted with people who have attempted suicide to determine the individuals' motives. There is a self-selection factor present in this situation. Since it is impossible to interview those who killed themselves, information is restricted to a segment of population who have committed self-destructive behavior. It is incorrect to generalize the findings and apply them to those who have killed themselves. The psychodynamics may be considerably different from those whose lethal intent led to death. Another problem is determining whether the individual who attempted suicide can accurately recall the events, feelings, and drives prior to the attempt or whether subconscious activity takes advantage of ego defense mechanisms to insulate the self after the attempt. Finally, psychological theories are based on case studies which are singular events. It is questionable whether two people who attempt suicide because of a broken romance can be placed neatly and easily into the same category. A broken romance may have contributed to the event but was not the cause of the event. As mentioned earlier in the chapter, suicide is only one possible way to handle a problem, and there is no human problem for which suicide is the only solution.

159

Developmental considerations

Many authors have written that suicide may be related to events that take place during the growth and developmental years of infancy and childhood. For instance, many adolescents who committed suicide grew up in disruptive home environments. Death of a parent also seems to increase the potential for suicide later in life. Apparently, these events have an impact on ego development, which is not identical with the breakdown of ego discussed under psychological aspects. As a consequence of their developmental history certain individuals are more vulnerable to frustration than others.

Patterns of behavior form as personality develops. People develop a modus operandi for dealing with problems that could be called a propensity to act. When a problem occurs, the individual depends on behavior that has worked successfully in the past to solve a problem or satisfy a need. Some people have a large repertoire of possible solutions yet others have only a few. Diekstra[14] indicates that when an individual does not have an act in his or her repertoire for which the expected outcome is the preferred outcome, the person is said to have entered a crisis situation. Children who are encouraged to be independent and to try to handle childhood problems on their own will probably have a greater number of alternative solutions available to handle adult problems. One possible solution to an adult problem is to say, "I can't." This precludes the searching of the repertoire to find an adequate solution. High school teachers are well aware of this concept because they see it all too often in their students. However, kindergarten teachers also see this type of defeatist attitude in very young children who cannot (will not) tie their shoes or cannot (will not) button their shirts. It is quite probable that the high school students who way, "I can't," are the same children who "couldn't" in junior high and elementary school. This limited repertoire probably developed early in life. Although the schools cannot be blamed for its occurrence, some teachers can be chastised for weak attempts at changing the situation. Children and adolescents who have a large repertoire of problem-solving alternatives are less likely to experience frustration. As they succeed in solving problem after problem, an "I can" personality evolves, and this helps to prevent anxiety, despair, and hopelessness. A person with an "I can" approach to life would seem to be an unlikely candidate for lethal behavior.

Another developmental theory that may account for some suicides is the notion that children raised in violent environments tend to view violence as a possible solution to their problems. An analogy can be drawn between suicide and child abuse. The common theme that appears to run through generations of child abusers is that people who abuse their children were subject to child abuse when they were children. In essence, they learn that violence is one way to deal with a problem. If a personal crisis develops, the individual with this type of family background may again believe that violence will solve the problem. Suicide is a violent act. Therefore people with a history of violence in their families may be more prone to view suicide as an option.

Another facet of developmental psychology involves a concept known as locus of control. Some individuals believe that everything that happens to them is outside of their control. People succeed because others helped them. People fail because others did not help them or because of bad luck. This attitude is extremely frustrating since it places one's own life in the hands of others. Not being in control is a terribly frustrating situation. Success or failure, love or rejection, joy or sorrow—to all come from outside of the self. Internal locus of control is a healthier way of life. Choice resides within the person and what happens in life is perceived as having a direct relationship to the choices made. External locus of control encourages statements such as, "I can't do anything about this problem," whereas internal locus of control facilitates statements such as, "I have to do something about this problem."

Toolan[15] presented five categories of suicide attempts among youth. It is interesting to note that for each of these categories, other alternatives might have been selected instead of suicide:

1. Anger at another, which is internalized as guilt and depression
2. Attempts to manipulate another to gain affection or to punish
3. A signal of distress in the hope that someone will help
4. Reactions to feelings of inner disintegration
5. A desire to join a dead relative

The other interesting thing about this categorization is that it tells us nothing about the reasons that led to the suicide attempt. In an effort to understand more about why children and adolescents engage in lethal behavior, Paulson, Stone, and Sposto[16] conducted case study research. They found that the children's disorders were symptomatic of acute family breakdown, marital disharmony, and domestic violence. Only 32% of the youth were living with both biological parents. Divorce apparently plays a significant role because 38% of the children were living with a divorced parent, 24% were living with a divorced parent and a stepparent, and 6% were living in foster homes.

This same study found that self-esteem, anomie, and the search for love and affection play a definite role in suicide and lethal behavior. This is evidenced by the statements the children made during the interviews.[16]

A 4-year-old child found hanging from a fourth floor window wanted to escape a poor home life and fly away to join Santa Claus.

A 6-year-old child said, "I want to die because nobody loves me."

An 8-year-old child said, "I want to see what it's like in heaven. They want me dead."

An 11-year-old child said, "It will not matter if I'm dead. I don't get much attention from my mother."

A 12-year-old child said, "I would be better off dead. No one would ever have to look at my ugly face again."

This research points to the important role that can be played by teachers, school nurses, and other members of the helping professions who interact with children. Having knowledge of a family situation that is chaotic or violent should encourage some extra attention being paid to the child and the child's statements. A first grade teacher who has a student who wants to die "because nobody loves me" has a moral and professional obligation to find out more about what prompted that statement. A fifth grade teacher whose student says, "It will not matter if I'm dead," has to take the comment seriously. When statements such as these are offered by students and especially when the home life is known to be disruptive, teachers, nurses, and other responsible adults should seek clarification of the statement and make referrals to appropriate authorities when it is necessary.

■　　■　　■

To summarize this section of the chapter it is fair to say that suicide is a complex event related to social, psychological, and developmental issues. It is an endeavor that is not caused by any single event. A broken romance will only lead to suicide when suicide is a possibility within the repetoire of problem-solving behavior. It may contribute to suicide when social forces permit or encourage this type of behavior, but in societies in which suicide is prohibited, the likelihood of death caused by one's own hand is greatly reduced. Suicide takes place in an ecosystem that includes the self and the physical and social environment. An understanding of suicide requires that each of these elements be studied. Prevention of suicide requires action be taken in multiple directions. A suicide prevention center can deal with immediate psychosocial problems, but true prevention lies in effective parenting, teaching, and social activities aimed at self-development, psychological integrity, and effective interpersonal relationships.

Demographic aspects

Every 20 minutes in the United States someone dies from a suicidal action. On a daily basis there are about 73 fatalities, which means that by the end of the year 27,-000 people have ended their own lives. Suicide is the ninth leading cause of death in this country and accounts for substantially more fatalities than homicide. For people between the ages of 15 and 24 years, suicide is the second leading cause of death, behind accidents. These findings portray only the tip of the iceberg since many suicidologists believe that for every completed suicide there are at least 10 suicide attempts. If three people commit a fatal act of suicide per hour, then 30 people make a suicide attempt in the same period. On any given day in this country 67 whites, 4 blacks, and 1 person of another race will die by suicide. Men will account for 53 of these deaths and women 20.

Demographic data describe certain characteristics of the person involved in a recordable event. These data are then studied to demonstrate comparisons. For instance, suicide data reveal the following:

Men commit suicide more often than women.

Women have a greater number of incompleted suicides than men.

Older people commit suicide more often than younger people.

Younger people have a greater number of incompleted suicides than older people.

City dwellers commit suicide more often than rural residents.

Protestants commit suicide more often than Catholics or Jews.

Wealthy people commit suicide more often than poor people.

Professionals commit suicide more often than nonprofessionals.

Alcoholics commit suicide more often than social drinkers.

Table 6-1 portrays the U.S. suicide rate by age and sex. Men have a higher suicide rate in each age group, with the male:female ratio being lowest in the 30 to 50 year age group and highest in young adulthood and during the postretirement years.

Table 6-1. Death rates for suicide by age and sex in United States (rate per 100,000 in specified group)

Age	Both sexes	Male	Female	Male:female ratio
Under 1 year	—	—	—	—
1-4 years	—	—	—	—
5-14 years	0.4	0.7	0.2	3.5 to 1
15-24 years	11.7	18.5	4.8	3.9 to 1
25-34 years	15.9	23.6	8.4	2.8 to 1
35-44 years	16.3	22.8	10.2	2.2 to 1
45-54 years	19.2	26.2	12.7	2.1 to 1
55-64 years	20.0	29.8	11.1	2.7 to 1
65 years and over	19.5	34.0	8.4	4.0 to 1

From U.S. Department of Health, Education, and Welfare, Office of the Assistant Secretary for Health, the National Center for Health Statistics: Facts of life and death, 1978, U.S. Department of Health, Education, and Welfare, p. 46.

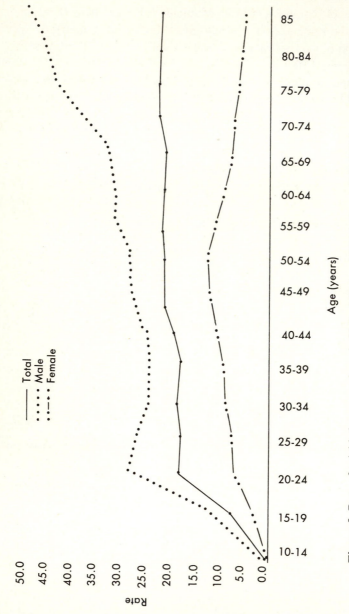

Figure 5. Rate of suicide by age and sex in United States, 1976 (rate per 100,000 in specified group).

Modified from National Center for Health Statistics: Vital statistics of the U.S., 1976, vol. 2, Part A, Hyattsville, MD, 1980, U.S. Department of Health and Human Services.

Figure 5 shows a graphic impression of these rates. Generally speaking, suicide rates increase with advancing age. For women, however, the suicide rate peaks at age 45 and then falls off fairly sharply. In contrast, men begin an upward trend at age 65 that continues with a dramatic rise into the eighth decade of life. It is reasonable to presume that retirement plays a role in this observation. It will be interesting to see whether the women's pattern begins to change as more women take on a career. Currently a substantial portion of the population of women aged 65 and over spent a lifetime as homemakers and wives. Apparently, retirement does not require the same degree of adjustment for them as it does for a population of men who spent 45 years or more in the labor force building an identity around their jobs. We will say more about suicide and aging later in this section of the chapter.

Table 6-2 shows the rate of suicide for a 27-year period. The rates for white men and women have risen less than 20%, while the increase for black men and women has nearly doubled. Even with this increase, white men still have twice the rate of suicide of black men, and white women have three times the suicide rate of black women.

Table 6-3 presents a comparison of suicide rates among selected countries as reported by the World Health Organization. The United States seems to fall somewhere near the middle. Denmark has the highest rate (of those presented), and Greece has the lowest rate. The male:female ratio shows a fairly narrow range with a variance between 1.7 to 1 and 2.9 to 1. The country with the greatest male:female differential is the United States.

A comparison of methods used in fatal suicides is offered in Table 6-4. Both men and women most often use firearms to kill themselves, but the men who die by this

Table 6-2. Suicides by race and sex in United States, 1950 to 1977 (rates per 100,000 resident population in specified group)

Year	Total	White		Black	
		Male	Female	Male	Female
1950	11.3	19.0	5.5	6.8	1.6
1955	10.2	17.1	4.9	6.0	1.5
1960	10.6	17.6	5.3	7.1	1.9
1965	11.1	17.5	6.6	7.8	2.5
1970	11.5	17.9	7.1	8.6	2.9
1975	12.7	20.1	7.4	10.6	3.3
1977	13.3	21.4	7.3	11.4	3.5

From U.S. Bureau of Census: Statistical abstracts of the United States, ed. 100, Washington, D.C., 1979, U.S. Bureau of Census, p. 181.

Table 6-3. Suicide rates for selected countries
(rates per 100,000, population aged 15 years and over)

Country	Total	Male	Female	Male:female ratio
Australia	14.8	21.7	7.9	2.7 to 1
Austria	29.2	43.6	17.0	2.6 to 1
Denmark	30.7	39.2	22.6	1.7 to 1
Greece	3.6	5.0	2.3	2.2 to 1
Israel	11.8	14.9	8.8	1.7 to 1
Japan	23.1	28.2	18.3	1.7 to 1
Sweden	23.8	33.6	14.1	2.4 to 1
Switzerland	28.1	41.4	15.9	2.6 to 1
United States	16.4	24.9	8.6	2.9 to 1

From U.S. Bureau of Census: Statistical Abstracts of the United States, ed. 100, Washington, D.C., 1979, U.S. Bureau of Census, p. 182.

Table 6-4. Suicides by method and sex in United States

Method of suicide	Both sexes		Male		Female	
	Number	Percent	Number	Percent	Number	Percent
Poisoning (solid or liquid)	3,676	14	1,425	7	2,251	31
Poisoning by gas	2,424	9	1,617	8	807	11
Drowning	494	2	270	1	224	3
Firearm and explosives	14,728	55	12,128	62	2,600	35
Cutting and piercing	437	2	317	2	120	2
Jumping	861	3	548	3	313	4
Hanging, strangulation, and suffocation	3,689	14	2,834	15	855	12
Other	523	2	355	2	169	2
TOTALS	26,832	100*	19,493	100*	7,339	100*

From Office of Health Research, Statistics and Technology, National Center for Health Statistics: Vital statistics of the U.S., 1976, Hyattsville, MD, 1980, U.S. Department of Health and Human Services.
*Totals do not equal 100% because percentages are in round numbers.

method represent 65% of the total suicide deaths, whereas among women slightly more than one third use firearms. Poisoning accounts for 31% of the women's fatalities but only 7% of the men's fatalities. Drowning, cutting, and jumping are uncommon causes of death in both sexes.

Figure 6 shows considerable variability among regions of the United States. The Mountain and Pacific regions have rates of suicide nearly double the rate found in the

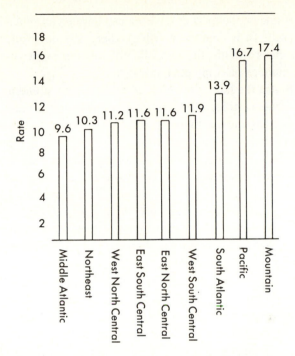

Figure 6. Suicide rates by geographic region of United States, 1976 (rate per 100,000 population).

From National Center for Health Statistics: Vital statistics of the U.S., 1976: American statistical index, Hyattsville, MD, 1980, U.S. Department of Health and Human Services, pp. 1-164.

middle-Atlantic region. The Central region from north to south shows little variation.

As interesting as these statistics are, it is important to point out that they portray an approximation of fact. Statistics are always subject to scrutiny, but when the factor being measured carries a social stigma, accuracy cannot be assumed. First of all, the very definition of the factor being measured may create a problem. This is obviously true when an attempt to compare the data from several countries is made. On a national basis an officially adopted definition will determine, for instance, which deaths are classified as suicide and which are to be recorded as an accident. In a study conducted by the World Health Organization, coroners from Great Britain and Denmark were given information about the death of individuals. Using the same information, the Danes were more likely to record the death as a suicide. Interpretation of the facts is apparently colored by the cultural factors operating within the society. In a country that rejects suicide the facts of the case can be seen as evidence in support of accidental occurrence. In a country in which there are no legal, civil, or social penalties for taking one's own life, the data will probably represent a closer approximation of the actual number of completed suicides.

In the United States the fact of death is certified by the attending physician who also completes the death certificate and records the cause of death. Recording is fairly exact since all physicians use the International Classification of Diseases to identify the specific cause of death. When there is doubt as to the exact cause of death, a postmortem examination, or autopsy, may be performed. In those cases in which the deceased was not under a physician's care or in which death was sudden, unexpected, or violent, each state has enacted its own regulations for certifying and recording the cause of death. These data, which serve as official records, are sent to the state capital for processing and eventually to the National Center for Health Statistics. This is why the data presented in Tables 6-1 to 6-4 and Figures 5 and 6 are reported in 1978 and 1979 publications but include suicides only up to 1976 or 1977. Most political subdivisions depend on the services of a coroner. After examining the evidence of each case, the coroner determines whether the death was a result of natural causes. If not, was the death caused by someone else or by the victim? If death was caused by the victim, was it an accident or a suicide? When there is doubt, a coroner's inquest may be convened to gather additional information. Postmortem evidence may be presented to clarify the cause of death. This would seem to indicate that judgments are fairly accurate and that the suicide data are therefore accurate.

The qualifications of the coroner vary tremendously. While the person filling this medical-legal position may be a forensic pathologist, this is not the ordinary situation. There are no formal educational requirements to serve as coroner, although coroners usually receive in-service education or on the job training to develop a degree of competence. Three California researchers studying the qualifications of coroners in 11 western states found that it was an elected position in 62% of the counties and an appointed position in 38% of the counties[17]. Six percent of the coroners did not graduate from high school, while 37% had a medical degree. Before becoming coroner, one third of the people were physicians, 23% were morticians, 16% were police officers, and the remainder had a variety of occupations. The vast majority of the coroners were serving this function on a part-time basis. In California the elected sheriff assumes the duty of coroner, although in larger cities a medical examiner (physician) is used instead of a coroner. The researchers concluded that the function of the coroner's office has a significant impact on the recorded suicide rates. For example, the determination of death by accident or death by suicide of a person who dies on election evening could depend on whether the examination of the body occurred before or after midnight. Atkinson[18] gives an account of a conversation with a coroner who regularly completed death certificates. When Atkinson asked the coroner for the legal definition of suicide, the coroner reached for his handbook and said,"It will be in here." Unable to find it, the coroner was unable to define it.

Studies have shown that even physicians make mistakes when they determine the cause of death. Whereas autopsy examinations reveal conclusive evidence, a physician must rely on knowledge of the situation, intuition, and educated hunches based on medical experience. When the cause of death is established by a person who does not have a medical degree, substantial room for error exists. There are overt political pressures and social considerations in addition to subtle persuasions such as status of the victim within the community and personal feelings of the coroner toward suicide. The research of Allen[19] demonstrates this concept in his interviews with coroners. He found that some would only record death as a suicide when a note was found with the body. Generally, coroners believed their primary responsibility was to analyze the evidence and rule out foul play. But quite often, the family would intentionally hide evidence of a suicide, such as throwing a suicide note in the trash to make the death appear as an accident. Coroners reported that frequently the family would not tell the truth in answering questions about the deceased. This could mean that when asked whether there had been a previous attempt at suicide, the family would say no to avoid creating suspicion that the death was not accidental.

The data show that deaths below the age of 10 years are not recorded as suicide. For the most part, suicide will not be assigned as the cause of death unless the victim was aware of the consequences of the fatal act, and generally, it is believed that children below the age of 10 years do not comprehend the irreversibility of death. Adolescents and young adults do commit suicide fairly often. In fact, suicide is a leading cause of death for those aged 15 to 24. Adolescent suicides are characterized as being impulsive. The ratio of completed to incompleted suicide is low because the intentionality is low and the plan is not fully worked out. Baechler[3] describes suicides in this age group as being conducted for appeal, revenge, or blackmail. Adolescence is often a time of inner conflict and having to deal with issues such as independence versus dependence, peer pressure, insecurity, answering the question, "Who am I?" and finding a place in the world. Wenz[20] found eight variables to be associated with adolescent suicide. In descending order, they are the following:

1. Low social contact with peers in the neighborhood
2. Conflict with parents
3. Broken romance
4. Low socioeconomic status of parents
5. Blocked communication with parents

6. Poor school performance, that is, grades or truancy
7. Living with stepparent
8. Broken home, separation, divorce, death of parent, or institutionalization of parent

This list demonstrates that high-risk adolescents are alienated. Inner strife results from inadequate supporting relationships among family, peers, and school personnel. The suicide attempt may signal a cry for help, but quite often it compounds the problem by adding momentum to a cycle of conflict, alienation, isolation, lack of support, lethal behavior, and alienation. Parents, teachers, and friends need to be observant of attitudes and severe changes in mood or personality. Statements that raise the issue of lethal intent should not be ignored.

Most often the suicide attempt of an adolescent comes as a shock to parents, relatives, and friends. On reflection of the situation, however, it is quite often found that the individual has communicated his or her lethal thoughts and that suicide might have been predicted. Communication might have been offered to one person only or to several people in the hope that someone would respond to the message. Being aware of the common indicators that signal lethal intent can possibly save a life. Intervention and referral depend on a recognition of the potentially dangerous state of mind. Some people have raised the issue of whether asking another person about suicidal intent will place an idea into the head of another who was not contemplating suicide. The literature seems to be unanimous in its denial of this possibility. Experts believe there is little if any danger in asking a person about lethal intent. Certainly, sharing one's concern with family and friends of the person in question is a feasible first step in confirming suspicion. Talking about suicide with the individual or with others who know the person may be embarrassing, but the consequences of not taking action should also be considered.

Indicators of suicidal risk for adolescents and adults include the following:
Previous suicide attempt
Intense and constant unhappiness (melancholy)
Hopelessness regarding change of circumstance
Giving away prized possessions
The absence or breakdown of support systems
Isolation
Belittling of self
Putting affairs in order, such as preparing a will or buying a burial plot
Direct statements, such as "I'm going to kill myself," "You'd be better off without me," or "I don't feel like I'm in my own body"

Indirect statements, such as "I'm not afraid to die" or "I can't go on any
   longer"
Decline in academic or job performance
Poor communication with peers or relatives
Psychosomatic complaints
Rebellious behavior
Neglect of responsibilities
Excessive use of alcohol or drugs
Anorexia nervosa
Neglect of personal appearance
Sudden or severe personality changes

The cause of suicide among the elderly is quite different than the circumstances
that characterize adolescent suicide. For the elderly, lethal behavior is not often a cry
for help or an impulsive moment motivated by anger, revenge, or appeal. Fewer than
average leave notes to explain their behavior, possibly feeling that no explanation is
necessary or that the decision is a private matter not open for discussion. The action is
ordinarily well planned so as to leave little doubt of the intended outcome.

In some cases physiologic factors contribute to the situation. Senility, terminal illness, organic brain syndrome, the effects of medicine on body, mind and spirit, and
chronic disease with its pain and debilitation enhance the likelihood of suicide. Social
factors also play a role since old age is dominated by exits and losses rather than
entries and gains. Retirement signifies loss of a job and exit from the work force. Moving to a warm sunny climate and observing the death of friends create additional losses
and exits. Loss of income except for a pension or Social Security may bring an end to
hobbies and usual modes of recreation. There are psychological forces, too. With so
many physical and social changes it is possible to lose one's perspective on life.
Independence, self-esteem, optimism, internal locus of control, and ability to control
the future may not seem possible. If one could pretend that he or she were born in
1914, the changes that have occurred since one's birth and the changes that remain
ahead could be considered. The problems of life are different than they used to be. The
old ways of coping are no longer viable. The future brings anxiety, frustration, and
despair. A lifetime of change has taken its toll on the ability of the body to adapt and
adjust, so the person becomes weary. The concepts of Toffler and the predictions of
Orwell, once considered abstract works of fiction, are brought into sharp focus as we
enter the *Future Shock* of *1984*.

Like other topics that are not entirely open for discussion, suicide is surrounded by
many fallacies and myths, such as the following:

Myth: Bad weather increases the likelihood of suicide.

Truth: There is no evidence to support this statement. Many suicides occur on sunny, warm, and beautiful days.

Myth: Those who threaten suicide will not carry out the threat.

Truth: Most people who attempt suicide have communicated their intention to at least one person beforehand. Threats must be taken seriously.

Myth: Suicide happens without warning.

Truth: Retrospectively, people can recognize warning signs. Knowledge of these signs can be detected in advance of a suicide so that intervention can save a life.

Myth: Those who have attempted suicide once will not try it again.

Truth: Having attempted suicide once indicates that lethal action is a possible mode of behavior. This population is at greater than average risk of future lethal behavior.

Myth: Suicide and attempted suicide are the same class of behavior.

Truth: There are many motives that lead to lethal behavior. Some motives demand a fatal outcome to achieve the intended purpose, while other motives require an incompleted suicide to achieve the intended purpose.

Myth: Suicide is more common among the poor, the jobless, and blue-collar workers.

Truth: In fact, the opposite is true. There is a higher rate of suicide among the wealthy, the professional class, and the white-collar workers. However, suicide is a complex issue, and an attempt is never made just because an individual is employed or unemployed, rich or poor, or white collar or blue collar.

Myth: Suicide is inherited.

Truth: Suicide results from a complex ecologic interaction of the individual and his or her environment. There is no gene or chromosome that increases or decreases the risk of suicide. If there is a tendency for suicide to run in families, it is a result of the learned repetoire of behavior and the effectiveness or ineffectiveness of coping skills taught from parent to child. It is also probable that the individual who lives in a home in which violence such as child abuse is normal will accept violence as a way of life.

Myth: You have to be insane to commit suicide.

Truth: Some people who take lethal action are insane, but most are not. There are many motives that lead to suicide, some of which are perfectly understandable even among those of us who would not consider suicide under similar circumstances. Depression and melancholy increase the risk of suicide, but often the person who considers committing suicide is outwardly happy and secure.

Myth: Suicide is related to phases of the moon.

Truth: This kind of relationship creates popular appeal when reported in the mass media. Garth and Lester[21] reported finding a study that concluded that there is a relationship between the incidence of suicide and the full moon. They also found four studies that reported an association did not exist. Their research used the same procedures as were employed in the study that found a relationship, but they did not find one. For the 3 days of a full moon and the three days of a new moon their 12-month study found no significant difference between the number of suicides during either phase and the number of suicides throughout the remainder of the year.

Myth: Only a professional can help a person deal with a crisis.

Truth: There are hundreds of suicide prevention centers worldwide that depend on lay volunteers to help individuals during crisis situations. With proper guidance and support from professionals, these volunteers have saved thousands of lives. In fact, some suicidal people utilize the services of the center precisely because they know the person at the other end of the line is not a psychologist, minister, or physician.

Myth: People who commit suicide want to die.

Truth: Some people who commit suicide do want to die. This is especially true for the elderly. Many people do not want to die but use the suicidal act as a cry for help or a warning that they are having trouble coping with the problems of life. It is especially true that adolescents use a suicide attempt in this fashion. It is probably safe to say that all people who commit suicide have mixed feelings about living and dying.

Myth: Improvement following a crisis means the crisis is over.

Truth: People who make a suicide attempt are at greater risk of making a subsequent attempt. If the attempt was a manipulative action that had positive effects, the behavior might repeat itself. If the circumstances that led to the crisis do not improve, the crisis may reappear. If the coping skills are not improved, the problem of inadequate alternatives may lead to future attempts. For the suicide attempt that was a gamble with death and provided some type of psychological gratification, the behavior could become addictive with each pull of the trigger.

PUNISHMENT FOR SUICIDE

Throughout recorded history penalties have been attached to the act of suicide. A primary function of legal regulation or religious doctrine is to serve as a controlling agent for behavior that threatens the well-being of society. By analyzing the punishment assigned to the crime, it is possible to detect the feelings of a society toward that offense. One set of beliefs holds that each person is a valuable asset of the state and that suicide deprives the government (or monarchy) of that individual's productivity and strength. The appropriate punishment therefore would be to confiscate the personal property and wealth of the offender.

Christianity and Judaism view suicide as morally wrong. The message of the Sixth Commandment does not make exception for death by one's own hand. Since God alone has the power to decide life or death suicide is an indignity to the ethereal as well as the physical entity. Obviously, such a violation would require the severest punishment. Desecration of the body was a common penalty. The offending hand might be severed and buried separately from the body. Hanging the corpse in a public place or dragging it through the streets might discourage others from similar behavior. In some societies it was customery to throw the remains into the public garbage heap. If the suicide attempt was not fatal, the authorities might inflict torture or crucify the body and leave it to rot on the cross. It is paradoxical that in many cultures the attempt to take one's life was considered a capital offense. More compassionate societies defamed the individual, demanded a prison sentence, banished the person from the group, or denied the rite of a religious burial.

Over the years the punishment imposed against suicide became increasingly less severe. Until 1961 suicide was considered a felony in Great Britain. Much of the law in the United States is derived from British common law, and although a number of states never enacted legislation against suicide, it was nevertheless illegal in common law. Although not published anywhere, criminal and civil penalties against the person or the person's possessions have been eliminated by most if not all states. Religious views have also changed. The focus has shifted from sinfulness to tragedy and from punishment to prevention. Intervention and humanistic understanding are preferable to rehabilitation and recrimination.

The attitude has so changed that life and health insurance benefits are no longer canceled in the event of suicide. Most policies do contain a clause that repeals the benefits if the lethal behavior occurs within a given amount of time after the contract was put into effect. This is done to prevent someone from taking out a policy for a large amount of money and then collecting on the policy by commiting suicide. If it can be proven that suicide was the motive for purchasing the policy (within the time limit stated in the contract), the benefits may be declared null and void.

INTERVENTION

An interesting concept known as befriending has proven itself as an effective intervention technique. The prototype was begun in New York City in 1906. Known as the National Save A Life League, the group was staffed by ministers who volunteered to serve as crisis counselors. The concept had limited success. In 1953 Great Britain improved on the concept by using lay volunteers to handle crisis calls over the telephone. This ensured anonymity to the caller and prompted a willingness to take the initiative to place the call because the person at the other end of line was not a mental health professional. Known as the Samaritans, the organization still provides 24-hour service in more than 100 locations with an average of 130 volunteers per center. The volunteers are carefully screened and appropriately trained and have access to specialized consultation from a mental health team. The organization has been so successful that the concept has spread to countries around the world. In France the S.O.S. Amitie receives more than 38,000 calls annually.

The Los Angeles Suicide Prevention Center was established in 1958 with a grant from the National Institute of Mental Health. Four distinct types of responsibility have been identified by the center. The first of these involves clinical activities. People may walk into the center for help or use the phone. Not only the person in crisis, but friends, clergy, and employers as well, are welcome to ask questions and seek advice about how to handle a particular crisis situation. The center teaches its volunteers to follow these five steps when dealing with a caller[22]:

1. Establish a relationship, maintain contact, and obtain information.
2. Identify and focus on problems.
3. Evaluate lethality of threat (level of stress, character of the individual, and existence of a suicidal plan).
4. Assess the person's resources for mobilizing support.
5. Formulate and initiate therapeutic or rehabilitation plans.

The second function of a suicide prevention center is research. Professionals are constantly seeking better techniques of intervention and rehabilitation. The third type of activity is education and training. Volunteers receive intensive training, and the center serves as a professional practicum for students studying in the helping professions. Additionally, many communities looking to organize a similar service have sent representatives to examine the operations of the Los Angeles Suicide Prevention Center. The fourth purpose of the agency is to serve as a catalyst to coordinate services within the community and to make referrals to the appropriate source of help.

Many communities have followed the Los Angeles model in establishing crisis intervention services. Friends, an organization in Miami, and Rescue, in Boston, were begun in 1959. All across the country centers such as Life Line, Help, and We Care have been established. Volunteers are dedicated, well-adjusted, outgoing people who possess psychological health and are willing to share themselves with another human being. The American Association of Suicidology has published criteria for certification of these centers. The criteria define standards for administration, operating procedures, training of volunteers, delivery of services, and record keeping. The center must offer 24-hour telephone service and provide professional consultation to support the work of the volunteers.

Suicide prevention centers handle a variety of types of calls. Some people call to dictate a suicide note or to unburden themselves by confessing to a real or imagined behavior. A common question asked of the volunteer is, "Am I crazy?" This type of caller is testing his or her sanity and perhaps is determining whether professional help is needed. Sometimes callers belittle themselves with expressions of low self-esteem. Others seek pity from the person at the other end of the line. It is a frequent occurrence for callers to use the service as a listening post while they sort things out. Some volunteers have been on the line for hours just listening. Talking with someone can frequently vent frustrations and dissipate worry and anxiety. Talking also helps to cool off the individual who is prone to impulsive acts of violence. For those who see no other solution to their problems, the volunteer can suggest alternatives and make referrals to available mental health services. While it is impossible to say how many lives have been saved by suicide prevention centers, the cumulative effect of their work on the health of the nation cannot be denied.

SCHOOLS AND TEACHERS

For 10 months of the year children spend about one fourth of their time in school. As a socializing institution, a school can play a significant role in the development of adults who are virtually immune to self-destructive behaviors, including suicide. The educational literature is replete with principles and philosophy of what has come to be known as humanistic education. Schools have an opportunity to build the self-esteem of individuals who are in their formative years and to help young people learn how to solve problems, how to cope, and how to use their abilities to full advantage. Together with the family and the church these institutions have the potential to create strong human beings who are optimistic, self-sufficient, and physically, mentally, and emotionally durable. The educational film entitled *Cypher in the Snow,* produced by Brigham Young University, is a brilliant illustration of the consequences of neglect. Although a young boy exhibits all of the warning signs (distruptive home life, poor school work, no friends among his peers, lack of interest in life, and pervasive sense of hopelessness and despair), his family and school remain blind to his needs. The burden for the blame of his death must be shared by teachers and counselors as well as his family.

Teachers are in an excellent position to be able to recognize symptoms and to intervene, but naturally they are frightened by the prospect of doing the wrong thing. It might be comforting to know that suicide is frightening even for psychotherapists. Taking no action at all is probably the most ineffective way of dealing with a child who is suspected of being suicidal. The literature points out that asking someone if he or she is considering suicide *does not* put lethal ideas in the individual's head. If suicide has not been contemplated, this question will have little impact on the individual's state of mind. If suicide is a viable and present option, the question will not provoke thought into action. Instead, it may open up a channel of communication and positive dialogue.

The following list is given in the hope that teachers, counselors and administrators will incorporate these suggestions into their relationships with children and adolescents:

Close personal contact among faculty and students should be encouraged.

Teachers should know students as individuals.

Teachers can look for dramatic changes in mood, personality, or interactions with peer group.

An atmosphere of mutual trust and respect among faculty and students should be encouraged.

The students should know they can depend on their teacher to help them—if it is possible, the students should be allowed to call the teacher at home for a good reason.

School failure should be examined for the underlying reasons—failure is the symptom, not the cause of the problem.

Students should be encouraged to get along with one another, to respect differences, and to offer support for a peer who needs help.

Youngsters should be helped to become strong, able, and confident of themselves.

Referrals to a guidance counselor, school nurse, or outside mental health professional can be made.

Students can be encouraged to become involved in school activities, such as sports, band, government, clubs, and newspaper.

School administrators can follow these suggestions:

Teachers who genuinely enjoy working with youth should be hired.

In-service education of faculty to help them recognize warning signs of potential suicide should be arranged.

An atmosphere of empathetic presence among faculty, staff, and administration should be encouraged.

The efforts of community agencies and the use of their services as necessary should be coordinated.

The establishment of a crisis center in the community can be supported.

Adult education classes on parenting skills should be arranged.

Policies that facilitate mental health among students and faculty should be established.

Teachers who are trusted and respected by students should be rewarded.

SUMMARY

This chapter begins with an activity designed to challenge the reader to consider which of several situations represents suicide. This activity demonstrates that suicide is a complex issue and that behavior is open to a variety of interpretations. The first section of the chapter offers a conceptualization of the meaning of suicide. We defined a suicidal act as self-injury with varying degrees of intent as a means of solving a problem or conveying a message. Suicide is lethal behavior that results in death.

People commit suicide for a multitude of different reasons. Human behavior is complicated. It is therefore simplistic and inappropriate to say that a person committed suicide for this reason or for that reason. In fact, the action was taken as the result of a blending of many reasons. Some of the reasons reinforce the others, while others may actually conflict with one another. Suicide is the culminating act of an individual who chooses from among the available alternatives a lethal behavior that causes death.

The social theories of suicide attribute lethal behavior of an individual to the dysfuntion found in society. If the nature of the social malaise can be identified, appropriate steps to remedy the problem will prevent future suicides. The psychological theories of suicide focus on the psyche of the person. Prevention is achieved through activities that engender mental health. Some authors believe that suicide is caused by events that take place during the early years of growth and development. Rather than believing that suicide is a breakdown of ego, these theorists believe the ego was not properly developed.

Demographic data are presented to characterize the incidence of suicide. Useful as these statistics are, it must be pointed out that they portray only completed suicides and cannot be used to explain the reasons why a person chooses suicide as the method to solve a problem or to convey a message. The statistics themselves are probably underrepresentations of fact since many suicides are not officially recorded that way. The section ends with a description of the myths and truths about suicide.

The final portion of the chapter is concerned with intervention. Since this textbook is written for those people who intend to teach death education, the material deals with lay support and crisis intervention centers rather than professional counseling strategies. A special section deals with teachers and schools. The reader is furnished with a list of suicide prevention concepts appropriate for school personnel.

MAJOR CONCEPTS RELATED TO SUICIDE

The following concepts can help educators organize the vast body of knowledge related to suicide and suicidal behavior. These concepts can serve as a basis for the development of instructional programs related to suicide:

- Suicidal behavior is influenced by cultural, societal, enrivonmental, and individual factors.
- Suicidal individuals often provide behavioral indicators of their suicidal intentions.
- Suicidal tendency is not inherited and does not occur only in the mentally ill.
- Qualified help is available for suicidal individuals.

EDUCATIONAL ACTIVITIES RELATED TO SUICIDE

Title: Behavioral indicators of suicide

Age level: High school, college, adults

179

Objective: At the completion of the activity the students will identify behavioral indicators of suicide behavior.

Materials: *But Jack Was a Good Driver*, CRM Films

Directions: The teacher or facilitator outlines some of the behavioral indicators of suicide. The following are included in this list of possible indicators:

> Intense and constant unhappiness
> Hopelessness regarding change of circumstances
> Giving away prized possessions
> The absence of breakdown of support systems
> Isolation
> Poor self-concept
> Decline in job or academic performance
> Poor communication with peers or relatives
> Verbal attitude
> Substance abuse
> Prior acts of suicide
> Neglect of personal appearance

Then the film is viewed. The film shows two teenagers at the funeral of a mutual friend, Jack. As they discuss the events surrounding Jack's death, they begin to piece together clues that clearly show Jack's subtle plea for help. The film clearly reinforces the occurrence of the behavioral indicators listed above. The teacher or facilitator should guide the students through a discussion of the behavioral indicators of suicide identified in the film and how they can apply to real-life situations.

Title: Who is suicidal?

Age level: High school, college, adults

Objective: Following the completion of the Who Is Suicidal Worksheet, the students will develop a personal definition of suicide.

Materials: Who Is Suicidal Worksheet

Directions: The teacher or facilitator discusses with the students the controversy surrounding the determination of what constitutes suicidal behavior. The class is asked to complete the Who Is Suicidal Worksheet. Following the completion of the worksheet, the teacher or facilitator guides the students through a discussion of personal opinions concerning which of those acts listed on the worksheet are acts of a suicidal person.

Title: Personal suicide thoughts (guided discussion)

Age level: High school, college, adults

Who is suicidal worksheet

Rank each of the following situations on a scale of 1 to 5 with 1 indicating that the person in the situation was not suicidal and 5 indicating that the person was suicidal. You may also rank the situation somewhere between 1 and 5.

	Not suicidal			Suicidal	
1. A person who consumes an overdose of barbiturates	1	2	3	4	5
2. A person who mixes barbiturates and alcohol	1	2	3	4	5
3. A diabetic who carelessly follows the prescribed diet	1	2	3	4	5
4. A person suffering from intractable pain shoots himself	1	2	3	4	5
5. A person who goes on a long hunger strike to support a cause	1	2	3	4	5
6. A person who commits a capital offense despite knowing the death penalty will be administered if the individual is caught	1	2	3	4	5
7. A person who smokes three packs of cigarettes a day	1	2	3	4	5
8. A person who constantly drinks and drives	1	2	3	4	5
9. A person who skydives or hang glides	1	2	3	4	5
10. A person who is a professional Grand Prix racer or bullfighter	1	2	3	4	5
11. An alcoholic who continues to drink	1	2	3	4	5

Objective: 1. Following the activity, the student will arrive at a personal position statement regarding suicide.

2. Following the suicide thoughts discussion, the students will have an increased awareness of personal feelings regarding suicide (affective).

Directions: The purpose of this activity is for the teacher or facilitator to guide the students through a discussion of personal thoughts and feelings related to suicide. First, the teacher asks the students to indicate which of the following statements best describes themselves:

I have never had a suicidal thought.

I rarely (no more than once a year) think of suicide.

I occasionally think about suicide.

I often think about suicide when I'm depressed.

I frequently have suicidal thoughts.

I have attempted suicide.

The teacher or facilitator should discuss with the class the notion that many people think about suicide and that a significant minority actually decide to take their own life.

181

Then the students are asked to complete the following checklist designed to help students clarify when they might consider suicide.

I would consider committing suicide
To get even with someone
If I had a terminal illness
If I was about to go insane
If I was experiencing severe pain
If I was quadriplegic
If I was bored with life
If I felt lonely and abandoned
If I disgraced my family or myself
If my spouse died
If I could no longer work and support myself
To support a government or cause
If I felt all avenues for advancement were blocked

The teacher or facilitator then discusses with the class the various motivations for committing suicide and some of the societal implications.

REFERENCES

1. Durkheim, Emile: Suicide: a study in sociology, 1951, The Free Press of Glencoe, p. 44. (Translated by John A. Spaulding and George Simpson.)
2. Stengel, Erwin: Suicide and attempted suicide, Baltimore, 1964, Penguin Books, p. 12.
3. Baechler, Jean: Suicides, New York, 1979, Basic Books, Inc., Publishers, p. 11.
4. Freeman, Douglas J., and others: Assessing intention to die in self-injury behavior. In Neuringer, Charles, editor: Psychological assessment of suicidal risk, Springfield, IL, 1974, Charles C Thomas, Publisher, p. 38.
5. World Health Organization: Prevention of suicide, Public Health Paper No. 35, 1968.
6. Wenz, Fredrich V.: Anomie and level of suicidality in individuals, Psychological Reports **36:** 817-818, 1975.
7. Wenz, Fredrich V.: Subjective powerlessness, sex, and suicide potential, Psychological Reports **40:**927-928, 1977.
8. French, Laurence, and Brice, Forbes O.: Suicide and female aggression: a contemporary analysis of anomic suicide, Journal of Clinical Psychiatry **39:**761-765, 1978.
9. Krauss, Herbert H.: Suicide: a psychosocial phenomenon. In Wolman, Benjamin B., editor: Between survival and suicide, New York, 1976, Gardner Press, Inc., p. 32.
10. Farber, M.L.: The prediction of suicidal risk: the quest for optimal variables. In Speyer, Nico, Diekstra, Rene F. W., and Van De Loo, Karel J.M.: Proceedings of the 7th International Conference for Suicide Prevention, Amsterdam, 1974, Swets en Zeitlinger BV, pp. 68-69.
11. Engle, George L.: A life setting conducive to illness: the giving up–given up complex, Annals of Internal Medicine **69:**293-300, 1968.
12. Beck, Aaron T., Weissman, Arlene, and Kovacs, Maria: Alcoholism, hopelessness and suicidal behavior, Journal of Studies on Alcohol **37:**66-75, 1976.
13. Dorpat, Theodore L., Anderson, William F., and Ripley, Herbert S.: The relationship of physical illness to suicide. In Resnik, H.L.P., editor: Suicidal behaviors, Boston, 1968, Little, Brown & Co., pp. 209-219.
14. Diekstra, Rene F.W.: A social learning theory

approach to the prediction of suicidal behaviors. In Speyer, Nico, Diekstra, Rene F.W., and Van De Loo, Karel J.M.: Proceedings of the 7th International Conference for Suicide Prevention, Amsterdam, 1974, Swets en Zeitlinger BV, p. 56.

15. Toolan, James M.: Suicide in childhood and adolescence. In Resnik, H.L.P., editor: Suicidal behaviors, Boston, 1968, Little, Brown & Co., pp. 220-227.

16. Paulson, Morris J., Stone, Dorothy, and Sposto, Richard: Suicide potential and behavior in children ages 4 to 12, Suicide and Life Threatening Behavior 8:225-242, 1978.

17. Nelson, Franklyn L., Farberow, Norman L., and MacKinnon, Douglas R.: The certification of suicide in eleven western states: an inquiry into the validity of reported suicide rates, Suicide and Life Threatening Behavior 8:75-88, 1978.

18. Atkinson, J. Maxwell: Discovering suicide, Pittsburgh, 1978 University of Pittsburgh Press, pp. 90-91.

19. Allen, N.H.: Suicide in California, 1960-1970. In Speyer, Nico, Diekstra, Rene F.W., and Van De Loo, Karel J.M.: Proceedings of the 7th International Conference for Suicide Prevention, Amsterdam, 1974, Swets en Zeitlinger BV, pp. 202-217.

20. Wenz, Fredrich V.: Sociological correlates of alienation among adolescent suicide attempts, Adolescence 14:19-29, 1979.

21. Garth, Jerald M., and Lester, David: The moon and suicide, Psychological Reports 43:678, 1978.

22. Shneidman, Edwin S., and Farberow, Norman L.: The Suicide Prevention Center of Los Angeles. In Resnik, H.L.P.: Suicidal behaviors, Boston, 1968, Little, Brown & Co., pp.367-380.

43

CHAPTER SEVEN

Consumer aspects of death and dying

The bereaved are often less in need of a clergyman or a social worker
than they are of the services of a good tax accountant,
a forceful insurance agent, or someone to do hardheaded bargaining
*with the mortician.**

YAFFA DRAZNIN

The goals of death education outlined in Chapter 2 stress the need to include consumer aspects of death and dying in a comprehensive death education course. In a popular book entitled *The Business of Dying,* Draznin[1] reported that much of the trauma surrounding death may have a pragmatic base. In our civilization death is an event that has significant economic and legal implications in addition to the medical and emotional dimensions. Draznin's approach to death education is steeped in consumerism with an emphasis on personal decision-making skills and planning for the future. But Americans tend to know little of what to do when there is a death in the family. Additionally, many are unaware of the procedures that should be taken care of to plan for their own death or the death of a significant other. This lack of general information in the various consumer related areas of death and dying emphasizes the need for more instruction.

THE FUNERAL SERVICE INDUSTRY

The disposal of a corpse has always been a concern of human civilization. It is a necessity that offers few alternatives. Traditional modes included ground burial, sea burial, and cremation. Body donation is a more recent alternative. While the options related to body disposal are limited, the ceremony attached to the death offers many possibilities. The funeral ceremony varies from culture to culture, and ordinarily the differences are attributable to religious beliefs and customs. The funeral of a culture that believes that death symbolizes entry into the next life in physical form will not be

*From Draznin, Yaffa: The business of dying, New York, 1976, Hawthorn Books, Inc., p. viii.

the same as for a culture that believes that life after death is a spiritual resurrection. Although economic considerations, laws, and social pressures are capable of influencing the mode of body disposal, it is religion that exerts the greatest impact on the funeral ceremony. In early American culture most people were buried in the ground. The ceremony may have been simple or elaborate, but in either case burial occurred within a day of the death. Some parts of the ceremony took place in the home and some took place in the church. The dead always received a brief celebration at graveside if nowhere else. One aspect of the funeral was to honor the dead, and another was to offer community support to the bereaved family. The role of the undertaker was to provide a coffin, to prepare the grave site, and to place the tombstone.

The funeral industry in the United States began to blossom during the 1800s as carpenters, cabinetmakers, and the furniture retail industry found the sale of coffins to be profitable. Gradually other services were included in the undertakers' area of service. Transportation and preservation of the remains increased in popularity. The Civil War played a major role in enhancing the popularity of embalming, especially in the North and East. Soldiers from the North who died in battle in the South were generally returned to northern soil for burial. This practice necessitated embalming. Obviously, the technical skills related to embalming were improved, and the preservation of the remains through embalming gained public acceptance.

The process of embalming was initially developed by the physicians and chemists so that the remains could be preserved long enough for the family to gather for the wake and funeral. As the popularity of embalming increased, these physicians and chemists began to conduct training sessions on embalming techniques. The obvious trainees for such a program were the cabinetmakers who were providing coffins and transportation services. The funeral service industry emerged from two occupational groups, the cabinetmakers and the embalmers. By the middle of the nineteenth century, the cabinetmaking guild was recognized as the group of tradesmen who not only provided burial merchandise but were also trained in the preservation of the human remains. Since then the funeral industry has been constantly attempting to improve its status from identity as a guild or trade to that of a profession.

Gradually the events that take place when a person dies have become more and more complicated. The state requires specific information about the mode of death, body disposal, and survivors. Insurance companies also need this information. Because of the tremendous mobility of people, paperwork may be required to send a corpse from one jurisdiction to another. Since relatives often live far away and want to be part of the ceremony, disposal may not occur for several days, necessitating the preservation of the body with embalming fluids. Most houses are not large enough to accommodate the family and friends who mourn the loss of the deceased. Whereas the funeral used to be a religious function, it has slowly become a secularized ceremony. Because of these changes, and many others, a demand was created for a specialist, a professional who could attend to the necessary details thereby enabling the family to mourn the death without having to deal with legal and social worries.

This is the role performed by the funeral director, and this is why consumer aspects of death and dying mostly focus on the relationship between the consumer (bereaved) and the provider of services. It is a difficult situation. First of all, the bereaved are not prepared with the information necessary for making important decisions, and their ability to reach decisions is hindered by their emotional condition. Second, there are many psychological dynamics involved in the decision-making process. Decisions may be prompted by guilt, pride, anger, or other subconscious motivations. Third, decisions must be made quickly. This usually means that the decisions are called for during the height of the grief response. Ignorance and emotional turmoil are the two major issues with which the funeral director is faced when providing services for the clients. It is a fine line that distinguishes between serving the best interest of the clients and using marketing techniques to achieve greater profit.

It is easy to see that the potential for abuse within the funeral industry is great. By what means should consumers be protected? In their efforts to raise the industry from a semiskilled guild to a recognized profession, funeral directors have fought against legislation to regulate the industry, believing instead that as in other professions, regulation should come from within. Abuses would be limited because of (1) entry requirements into the profession, (2) adherence to a professional code of ethics, and (3) specified measures to deal with unethical behavior. Whereas the undertaker was trained as an apprentice, the funeral director (mortician) must receive preparatory education and is licensed by the state only when the required formal education is completed.

Funeral directors and embalmers

According to the Bureau of Labor Statistics, few occupations require the tact, discretion, and compassion called for in the work of funeral directors. Since the family of the deceased is under considerable mental and emotional stress and they may not be aware of the many details that need to be handled, the funeral director helps to make the arrangements necessary for the funeral service and body disposal.

The director's duties begin when a call is received from a family requesting services. After arranging for the deceased to be removed to the funeral home, the director obtains the information needed for the death certificate, such as date and place of birth and cause of death. The director makes an appointment with the family to discuss the details of the funeral. These include time and place of service, clergy and organist,

187

selection of casket and clothing, and provision for burial or cremation. Directors also make arrangements with the cemetery, place obituary notices in newspapers, and take care of other details as necessary. Directors must be familiar with the funeral and burial customs of various religious faiths and fraternal organizations.

Embalming is a sanitary, preservative, and cosmetic measure. Embalmers, perhaps with the help of resident trainees (apprentices), first wash the body with germicidal soap. The embalming process itself entails the replacement of blood with a preservative fluid. Embalmers apply cosmetics to give the body a natural appearance and if necessary restore disfigured features. Finally, they dress the body and place it in the casket selected by the family.

On the day of the funeral, directors provide cars for the family and casket bearers, receive and usher guests to their seats, and organize the funeral procession. After the service they may help the family file claims for Social Security, insurance, and other benefits. Directors may serve a family for several months following the funeral until such matters are satisfactorily completed.

About 45,000 persons were licensed as funeral directors and embalmers in 1978. A substantial number of the directors were funeral home owners. Most of the 22,000 funeral homes in 1978 had one to three directors and embalmers, including the owner. Many large homes, however, had 20 or more. Besides the embalmers employed by funeral homes, several hundred worked for morgues and hospitals.

A license is needed to practice embalming. State licensing standards vary, but generally an embalmer must be 21 years old, have a high school diploma or its equivalent, graduate from a funeral service college, serve a 1- or 2-year resident traineeship, and pass a state board examination. One half of the states require a year or more of college in addition to training in mortuary science. All but six states also require funeral directors to be licensed. Qualifications are similar to those for embalmers, but directors may have to take special apprenticeship training and board examinations. Most people entering the field obtain both licenses; however, some states issue a single license to embalmer/funeral directors. Information on licensing requirements is available from the state office of occupational licensing.

In 1978, 35 schools had mortuary science programs accredited by the American Board of Funeral Service Education. About one half were private vocational schools that offer 1-year programs emphasizing basic subjects such as anatomy and physiology as well as practical skills such as embalming techniques and restorative art. Community colleges offer 2-year programs, and a small number of colleges and universities offer 2- and 4-year programs in funeral service. These programs include liberal arts and management courses as well as mortuary science. All programs offered courses in psychology, accounting, and funeral law.

State board examinations consist of written and oral tests and actual demonstration of skill. After passing the examination and meeting other requirements, resident trainees receive a license to practice. If licensed residents want to work in another state, they may have to pass its examination, although many states have mutual agreements that make this unnecessary.[2]

To demonstrate the educational changes required by the funeral industry, the mortuary science curriculum of the University of Minnesota will be used as an example. Established in 1908, it was the first program to be organized as part of a state university. From its inception until 1951 the program grew from a 6-week session to a 36-week course of study. In 1951 a 2-year curriculum leading to an associate degree was approved. Four years later the associate degree was expanded to 3 years. The baccalaureate degree, conferred after completion of a 4-year curriculum, was adopted in 1968. Implications for changes in program length and academic credentials resulted from changes in the philosophy and needs of the funeral service profession:

> While funeral service provides care for the dead that shows the dignity of human life, it is best characterized by direct care for the living. Bereavement and guilt are part of the continuum of life experiences. The faculty believes that helping individuals to adapt to these changes is a principal aim of the funeral service.[3]

Students enrolling in the University of Minnesota program usually enter the Department of Mortuary Service at the beginning of their junior year. The first 2 years of study focus on liberal arts education, that is, communications, physical, biological, and behavioral science, and the arts and humanities. The junior and senior years focus on mortuary science and satisfy the requirements of the American Board of Funeral Service Education. Required courses include orientation in funeral service, mortuary law, embalming chemistry, psychology of funeral service, restorative art, gross human anatomy, funeral management, pathology for mortuary science, and a 10-credit practicum.

Since the funeral service is becoming more secularized, it is likely that grief counseling will become a shared responsibility of the clergy and the funeral director. Currently little course work is devoted to the behavioral sciences and specifically to the counseling process. If funeral directors see their emerging role as a helping profession, it is probable that the preparatory and in-service educational requirements will reflect this concern. More information about the funeral service profession can be obtained from the following associations:

189

American Certified Morticians Association
35 North Arroyo Parkway
Pasadena, CA 91109

Center for Death Education and Research
1167 Social Science Building
University of Minnesota
Minneapolis, MN 55455

Continental Association for Funeral and
  Memorial Societies, Inc.
Suite 1100
1828 L St., N.W.
Washington, DC 20036

Guild of American Funeral Directors
30112 Silver Spur Road
San Juan Capistrano, CA 92675

Jewish Funeral Directors of America, Inc.
3501 14th St., N.W.
Washington, DC 20010

National Association of Coroners and Medical
  Examiners
2121 Adelbert Road
Cleveland, OH 44106

The National Funeral Directors Association
  of the United States, Inc.
135 North Wells St.
Milwaukee, WI 53203

National Selected Morticians
1616 Central St.
Evanston, IL 60201

A list of accredited schools of mortuary science can be obtained from:

The American Board of Funeral Service
  Education, Inc.
201 Columbia St.
Fairmont, WV 26554

Criticisms of the American funeral industry

No nationality spends as much money on funerals as Americans. The traditional American funeral provides a whole range of goods and services to a population that typically does not know what merchandise, prices, and procedures are appropriate or even required by law. Probably the worst time to learn about this information is during the emotional crisis brought about by the death of a loved one. Yet many people experience their first decision-making encounter in exactly this way. The potential problems created by consumer ignorance and grief are compounded by the dual role of the funeral director who provides the goods and services while at the same time offering guidance and counseling to the bereaved. Morticians are put in the awkward position of wanting to help the consumer make appropriate decisions while their profit to a greater or lesser extent is based on the decisions reached. On occasion some morticians have used their position to influence consumers to purchase goods and services beyond what is required by law, custom, or sense of personal duty. The following is an example of the type of promotional material that has encouraged some members of the funeral industry to persuade customers to purchase an expensive casket. These statements are taken from a pamphlet entitled "Why the Explanation of Caskets to the Family in the Selection Room?" (author unknown).

190

The average person selecting a casket has an opportunity to do so only once every ten years. Because of the lack of education on caskets, it must be assumed that all persons entering the selection room have something in common. They know little, if anything, about caskets.

There are two additional items common with every selecting party. They have *desires* as well as *needs*. The need is obvious to them and to you. Because of the circumstances, they *need* a casket. This *need* can be filled by the most inexpensive casket you offer.

Desire is what we want to concern ourselves with because desire is what may cause them to select above the minimum unit. Because they know nothing about caskets, desire on their part is largely unknown, even to themselves, and must be stimulated by us. The desire is stimulated by giving them reasons to buy better.

In essence, what this document is saying is that the ignornace of the American people regarding the selection of a casket coupled with conscious and unconscious desires can be exploited to encourage the bereaved to purchase a more expensive casket than is necessary. Obviously, not all funeral directors are motivated by excessive profits, but this statement does support the notion that grief-stricken consumers are not only ignorant but also vulnerable. The document cited above continues by saying that there are three factors that can stimulate desire on the part of a customer to buy an elaborate casket:

Beauty

It is obvious that people will pay more for something that is pleasing to the eye. . . . Whatever it is they like about that particular casket, to obtain it, they are willing to pay additional money. Beauty, however, is totally in the eyes of the beholder.

There is little control which can be exercised other than offering the best choice of caskets, in a profitable bracket, so that most people can find something from this group that appeals to them. You are automatically giving the people this reason to buy simply by offering a wide variety of designs and colors.

Prestige

. . . The desire for prestige and recognition is inherent in all of us and it manifests itself in many ways. For the person selecting a casket, it might go something like this: "Father lived by certain standards and therefore deserves to be buried by these same standards" or "How I bury Dad will show the community what I thought of him." However, as mentioned, this is an area over which you do not have absolute control. What is prestigious to one person may not be prestigious to another. . . .

As with beauty, the desire for prestige is given an opportunity to manifest itself almost automatically, simply because of the wide range of casket values you are offering.

Protection

In life, the desire for protection of the ones we love is instinctive. . . . It is a major motivating force, pervading all human life. Protection against harm, protection against disease, protection against the elements and protection of life itself, is instinctive and inherent in man.

This powerful protective instinct has prevailed since the beginning of time. Witness the prehistoric burial mounds, the tombs of the Pharaohs and even the practice of burning the dead, to prevent desecration of their remains.

Before a child is born, the mother and child are protected against harm in every possible way. This powerful urge to provide protection for those we love continues throughout life. It is inconceivable that this inherent instinct, so powerful during life, could cease abruptly when a death occurs. On the contrary, doesn't it reach its utmost intensity at the end of life, as a final act of protection?

Although the innate desire for protection may not always be expressed in words, we should not permit our natural proximity to the conditions surrounding death to lead us to believe that the desire does not exist, or that it is a subordinate one.

Because most Americans choose to wait until someone has died before they make decisions about body disposal, the funeral director ordinarily comes face-to-face with the grief-stricken person seeking advice. Difficult decisions must be reached during extremely difficult circumstances. For this reason, the funeral director not only provides advice about body disposal but often serves as an agent of support for the bereaved. Some morticians have used this dependence for their own financial gain. Consumers should be aware that the funeral director has little or no training as a professional counselor, and this role obviously conflicts with the funeral director's role as a salesperson. The California Department of Consumer Affairs publication entitled *The Compleat Consumer Catalogue* stated:

> A large contributing factor to the con job put over on the consumer is the funeral director's self-proclaimed role as a "professional counselor." He sets himself up giving advice to the family on what is right and what kind of funeral they need. He conveniently forgets that he is also a salesman who stands to make hundreds of dollars in profit if his advice is accepted.[4]

The notion that the funeral director is a professional counselor tends to ignore the fact that the primary purpose of the funeral industry is to provide the necessary services related to body disposal. Nevertheless, the idea that the funeral director should serve as a professional counselor is supported by the National Funeral Directors Association. A handbook entitled *The Funeral Director and His Role as a Counselor,* available to association members, highlights the conflict between the role of funeral directors as counselors and their role as business persons:

> There is a feeling on the part of some funeral directors that to call on the family immediately is not ethical or shows poor professional judgment. We cannot agree with this. The family has called you, and by virtue of their request for your service, you

should feel free to go to them at anytime in any place including the hospital or home. Many times the nature of certain requests (no embalming, no funeral, a private funeral or body donation) are indications of the need for immediate and individual counseling.[5]

Federal Trade Commission report on the funeral industry

In 1978 The Federal Trade Commission Bureau of Consumer Protection completed a comprehensive study of the American funeral industry. Although this report states that the results are not intended to slur the majority of ethical funeral directors, it does highlight a variety of unethical funeral practices and suggests legislative remedies. The report found that one feature of the funeral industry that has had a significant impact on the buying practices of the public has been the efforts of the funeral industry to elevate itself to the status of a profession. These efforts have af-

Funeral directors sometimes perform two confusing roles as counselors and as business persons.

Courtesy Guidance Associates, Mt. Kisco, NY.

193

fected funeral services in three significant ways. First, the funeral industry has attempted to deemphasize the commerical (profit-making) aspects of the business. The report concluded:

> This posture which has been espoused and advanced by the dominant trade association, the National Funeral Directors Association, has meant that funeral directors do not advertise prices, do not provide price information over the telephone, do not encourage the preplanning of funerals and do not otherwise make basic information on prices and offerings available to the public.[6]

Second, the professional aspirations of the funeral industry are largely responsible for the nature of funeral regulations. Historically, health and sanitation issues were the major focus of most funeral regulations. In many states the funeral industry has continued to stress the need for such regulations that serve to protect the funeral industry from competitive challenges. Currently many of the regulatory agencies are composed almost entirely of funeral directors. Therefore the regulations they suggest have done little to protect the consumer from abuses or to encourage competition within the profession.

Third, the aspirations of the funeral industry to be elevated to a professional status has resulted in the belief that the funeral director is not just a merchant of goods and services but rather a professional counselor who can assist the bereaved through the grieving process by helping them to make satisfactory funeral arrangements. This practice is based on the notion that the traditional American funeral has a therapeutic effect for the bereaved. While the traditional and expensive American funeral may have a soothing effect on some people, its widespread advocacy by the funeral industry has served to limit the choices available to consumers for less costly alternative modes of body disposal.

In addition to the general problems of the funeral industry, the report highlighted some common problems identified by consumers. Again, it should be noted that not all funeral directors engage in these unethical practices; nevertheless, these problems have occurred with sufficient frequency to warrant concern. The following problems were cited in the report.

Unauthorized removal of remains. Generally, the authorization to remove the remains is granted to the funeral home by the family of the deceased. The funeral industry condemns what has been termed body snatching or body grabbing; nevertheless, the report found that his practice does exist. The report cited numerous case studies in which consumers found that a funeral director had picked up the remains without authorization. It was discovered that funeral directors often had contacts in hospitals, nursing homes, and morgues who directed business to their homes. Obviously, custody of a body often creates a substantial obstacle to the consumer's selec-

194

tion of another mortician and to alternative forms of body disposal. Once a funeral home has possession of the remains, it is difficult to effect a change of funeral directors or to negotiate a price. Obviously in a bereaved state the family is not likely to argue over possession of a body or to request that it be moved to another funeral home, especially without knowledge of pertinent laws and consumer rights.

Embalming without permission. Embalming is generally the first step performed in the traditional funeral. Many of the goods and services that the funeral director offers depend on the body being embalmed to delay the onset of decay. The report stated that by embalming the body "the funeral director provides incentives for the family to purchase a full, traditional funeral, thus increasing the likelihood that he will sell more expensive merchandise and services."[6] The report added that embalming without authorization has gained widespread acceptance in the funeral industry. Numerous funeral directors stated they often do not obtain appropriate authorization prior to embalming. The funeral industry position is that embalming is a negative option. In other words, it is the family's responsibility to request specifically that the body not be embalmed. This philosophy creates an especially difficult consumer problem since it is difficult to determine after the fact whether the family would have requested the embalming if they had been asked to give appropriate authorization.

Refusal to release the remains. Obviously, the family of the deceased has the legal right to make arrangements for the disposal of the remains. The report found instances in which an unscrupulous funeral director interfered with the family's right to make appropriate arrangements for disposition by refusing to release the remains. Although it is not the norm for funeral directors, this practice exists for obvious economic reasons and is illegal.

Casket for cremation. If the family chooses immediate cremation as the method of disposal, there is no need to purchase a casket or to have the body embalmed. However, funeral directors may be opposed to cremation for obvious reasons. The report states, "Funeral directors and crematories can discourage selection of cremation by requiring purchase of a casket in situations where its principal—if not sole—function is to transport the body to the crematory."[6] The purpose of this rule is to reduce the price differential between cremation and the traditional arrangements. The report cited cases in which funeral directors simply told families that a casket was required to transport the remains to the crematory. Again, the bereaved are often emotionally unprepared to argue with the funeral director. In addition, they are often not aware of the state laws related to this issue and consequently believe that the funeral director must be knowledgeable in this area. In fact, there is only one state that requires a casket for cremation, Massachusetts. Other states require that the body be placed in a suitable container for the cremation. A Rochester, New York, memorial society testified that in a random survey of 15 local funeral directors, 8 stated they required a casket for cremation. Although state law does not require a casket, the policy established by the funeral director makes it difficult for the consumer to freely choose whether or not a casket will be purchased.

Overcharges on cash advance items. In the typical funeral arrangement, the consumer must pay for a variety of other services in addition to those offered by the funeral director. Goods and services, such as flowers, obituary notices, clergy honoraria, cemetery fees, and limousine rentals, often fall into this category. Usually the funeral director will advance the money for these goods and services to the third party and adjust the final bill accordingly. In other words, the family is simply reimbursing the funeral director for previous cash outlays. However, the Federal Trade Commission investigation found that some funeral directors generated extra revenue by charging more for the cash item than the funeral director actually paid. In other cases the funeral director received a rebate or kickback from the third party for referring business to that company.[6]

Merchandising techniques. Merchandising techniques are used in almost all sales transactions. However, the report found that the funeral industry used sales tactics that fall outside the boundaries of acceptable salesmanship. Again, this problem was compounded by consumer ignorance and by the bereaved state of the consumer. These factors along with a desire to escape quickly from the emotional pain of the casket room facilitated consumer vulnerability to the ethical and unethical merchandising techniques. The report found that some funeral directors manipulated consumers into buying more expensive items by displaying lower-priced merchandise in inaccessible places (narrow aisles) or by using less attractive colors or defaced merchandise. The report found that one merchandising strategy utilized two principles called the avenue of approach and the resistance lane. This technique placed the more expensive casket to the right of the entrance along a wide aisle, whereas the inexpensive caskets were placed to the left of the entrance along a narrow aisle. Funeral industry research had revealed that most people naturally turn to their right, especially in times of emotional distress, and that there is a natural inclination to avoid a narrow aisle. Therefore by employing these two strategies, the funeral director could manipulate people away from the inexpensive merchandise and toward the expensive merchandise.[6]

■　　■　　■

The concern with using subtle or subconscious merchandising to influence choice is not so much the profit incentive as it is the unethical manipulation of a vulnerable population. Certainly, the funeral director, no less than other merchants, is entitled to make a reasonable profit. What is disturbing is that consumers are deprived of their ability to freely choose which goods and services they desire for a ceremony of such human importance. The matter is further complicated because the bereaved are actually making choices for the deceased, and even with absolute freedom to choose, the decision is based on an educated guess of what the deceased would want. It seems reasonable to speculate that more often than not the consumer will choose a more elaborate and expensive funeral than the deceased would choose for himself or herself. The core of the issue is whether funeral directors should take advantage of the circumstances and encourage or manipulate the bereaved into purchasing unnecessary but available goods and services.

The best way to deal with this situation is to inform consumers about the laws, customs, traditions, and alternative modes of body disposal. The goal of the educational process is to encourage more people to preplan their funerals and to make known their wishes related to ceremony and body disposal. This ensures that the wishes of the individual will be carried out, and more importantly it removes the burden of decision making from a grief-stricken family. If the funeral industry has been partly at fault for taking advantage of clients, consumers must bear part of the fault for being so vulnerable. Ignorance and emotional distress offer a poor foundation for consumerism. Knowledge and preplanning can be the best security against manipulation and fraud.

Existing regulations for funeral homes

The basis of funeral home regulations in the United States is generally derived from two sources, state laws and self-regulatory policies imposed by trade associations. There is no federal policy that uniformly regulates the funeral industry. The Federal Trade Commission study of the funeral industry found that many of the regulations and licensing requirements were "drafted and sponsored by funeral director associations and are directed toward enhancing the image of the funeral director as a professional and guardian of the health of the community."[6] Therefore many of the state laws regarding the funeral industry insulate the funeral director from competition rather than provide consumer information or sanction unscrupulous funeral directors.

It is interesting to note that many of the state regulatory boards that govern the funeral industry are composed primarily or exclusively of funeral directors. This policy creates an obvious conflict of interest. The Federal Trade Commission conducted a careful examination of state laws, rules, and regulations governing the funeral

Table 7-1. Licensure requirements of various states related to the funeral industry

	Require's embalmer's license	Requires funeral director's license	Issues joint director's embalmer's or mortician's license	Requires licenses for funeral establishments
Alabama	X	X		X
Alaska	X			
Arizona	X	X		X
Arkansas	X	X		X
California	X	X		X
Colorado			X	
Connecticut	X	X		
Delaware			X	X
District of Columbia	X	X		
Florida	X	X		X
Georgia	X	X		X
Hawaii	X			X
Idaho		X	X	
Illinois	X	X		
Indiana	X	X		X
Iowa	X	X		
Kansas	X	X		X
Kentucky	X	X		
Louisiana		X	X	X
Maine			X	X
Maryland			X	X
Massachusetts	X	X		X
Michigan		X		X
Minnesota		X	X	X
Mississippi				
Missouri	X	X		X
Montana		X		X
Nebraska	X	X		X
Nevada		X		X
New Hampshire	X	X		X
New Jersey	X	X	X	X
New Mexico	X			X
New York	X	X	X	X
North Carolina	X	X	X	X
North Dakota	X			X
Ohio	X	X		X
Oklahoma	X	X		
Oregon	X	X		X
Pennsylvania			X	
Rhode Island	X	X		X

Table 7-1. Licensure requirements of various states related
to the funeral industry—cont'd

	Require's embalmer's license	Requires funeral director's license	Issues joint director's embalmer's or mortician's license	Requires licenses for funeral establishments
South Carolina	X	X		X
South Dakota	X	X	X	X
Tennessee	X	X		X
Texas	X	X		X
Utah	X	X		
Vermont	X	X		X
Virginia	X	X	X	X
Washington	X	X		X
West Virginia	X	X		X
Wisconsin	X	X		X
Wyoming	X	X		

industry in various states. This examination classified statutes into five broad categories:

1. Procedures and standards relating to licensure
2. Provisions relating to public health
3. Provisions relating to the operation of funeral establishments
4. Provisions regulating competitive behavior among licensees
5. Provisions defining standards of conduct and consumer protection, including disclosure requirements

The bulk of the rules and regulations governing the funeral industry consist of procedures and standards related to licensure. Table 7-1 identifies the states that require a license for embalmers and funeral directors. In addition, state law may regulate the age, education, apprenticeship, and licensure requirements for funeral directors.

Many of the early state regulations of the funeral industry concerned the need to ensure that public health provisions were being met. Today there is really no serious threat to human health that justifies the need for embalming other than those dictated by common sense. As a result, "This exaggerated concern for public health and sanitation has resulted in funeral directors obtaining a virtual monopoly over the disposition of the body."[6]

Along with health-related provisions and licensure for funeral home personnel, many states have regulatory codes for funeral homes. Most of the regulations relate to

Text continued on p. 204.

Code of Ethics, National Funeral Directors' Association of the United States, Inc.

I

As funeral directors, we herewith fully acknowledge our individual and collective obligations to the public, especially to those we serve, and our mutual responsibilities for the proper welfare of the funeral service profession.

II

To the public we pledge: vigilant support of public health laws; proper legal regulations for the members of our profession; devotion to high moral and service standards; conduct befitting good citizens; honesty in all offerings of service and merchandise, and in all business transactions.

III

To those we serve we pledge: confidential business and professional relationships; cooperation with the customs of all religions and creeds; observance of all respect due the deceased; high standards of competence and dignity in the conduct of all services; truthful representation of all services and merchandise.

IV

To our profession we pledge: support of high educational standards and proper licensing laws; encouragement of scientific research; adherence to sound business practices; adoption of improved techniques; observance of all rules of fair competition; maintenance of favorable personnel relations.

Code of Professional Practices for Funeral Directors, NFDA (originally adopted Nov. 1965; revised in 1969 and in 1972)

When a death occurs a survivor in the immediate family or the person or persons who will be responsible for the funeral of the deceased should be advised to contact their family funeral director or should direct that said funeral director be notified. This should be done regardless of where or when death takes place. The funeral director then becomes the representative of the family for the purpose of the funeral arrangements.

When once a funeral director is called by the family or their representative and as a result of such call removes the body, he shall provide the necessary services and merchandise in keeping with the wishes and finances of the family or their representative.

Before any funeral arrangements are made the funeral director should determine, if he does not know, who is the minister, priest or rabbi of the deceased and/or of the family. The funeral director should ascertain if such clergyman has been notified of the death. If this has not been done the funeral director should suggest it be done and should offer to do so for the family.

Before the specifics as to any and all aspects of the religious part of the funeral are decided, they should be discussed and cleared with the clergyman. This can be done either by the family or the funeral director as their representative or by both.

Before the family selects the funeral service, the funeral director should explain the various aspects of the funeral and the costs thereof as to the services and the merchandise he provides and as to that obtained from others such as cemeteries, florists and so forth. This should be done before the family goes into the casket selection room. In such explanation the funeral director should make clear the range of prices of funerals he has available. Also the funeral director should welcome any questions or discussions as to that which is or is not required by laws and/or regulations to such laws.

The funeral director should review for the family the various death benefits and/or burial allowances that may be available to them such as those involving Social Security, the Veterans Administration, labor unions, fraternal and other organizations. He will assist in the preparation and filing of the necessary forms to secure these benefits and allowances for the family. Where further professional assistance is required he should suggest that the families seek the advice of other professionals.

Because the price of the funeral as to the funeral director is related to the casked selection, there should be a card or brochure in each casket in the selection room. Such card or brochure should outline the services offered by the funeral home. Services and merchandise not included where a unit price method is used should be listed on the card or brochure as separate items.

Representations of the funeral director with respect to caskets should be as to material, construction, design, hardware, mattressing and interior. The use of an outside receptacle in which the casketed body is placed should be fully explained. Facts should be given regarding the requirements of cemeteries as to such receptacles where they exist. The various kinds of receptacles and their materials, construction and design should be reviewed.

When a family decides on the kind of service desired the funeral director should provide a memorandum or agreement for the family to approve or sign showing (1) the price of the service that the family has selected and what is included therein; (2) the price of each of the supplemental items of service and/or merchandise requested; (3) the amount involved for each of the items for which the funeral director will advance monies as an accommodation to the family; and (4) the method of payment agreed upon by the family and the funeral director.

When death occurs in a place other than where the funeral and/or burial are to take place, most times the services of two funeral directors are necessary. Under such circumstances the family should not pay for a complete service both where death occurred and also where the burial or cremation is held.

The forwarding funeral director should make an allowance or adjustment for those of his services not required and should notify the receiving funeral director thereof. Likewise the receiving funeral director should not charge the family for the services already provided by the forwarding funeral director unless there is a duplication thereof desired by the family.

Continued.

Code of Professional Practices for Funeral Directors, NFDA (originally adopted Nov. 1965; revised in 1969 and in 1972)—cont'd

The family should pay for only one complete service plus any additional charges incurred because the place of death and the place of final disposition require the services of two funeral firms.

As soon as the details and schedule in the transporting of remains are known to the forwarding funeral director, he shall immediately notify the receiving funeral director thereof.

It is suggested that when a body is transported a report made out by the person who did the embalming should accompany the remains. Such a report could be of assistance to the receiving funeral director in the event additional professional work is required on the body.

Where burial is at a point distant from where the funeral service is to be conducted and a concrete or metal burial vault is to be used, the funeral director called for the service should suggest the funeral director who will be responsible for the interment provide said vault for a number of reasons including the saving to the family of the added cost of handling and transporting the vault to the place of burial.

When a funeral service is conducted in a place other than the church of the clergyman, his wishes and desires should be considered to whatever extent possible.

In the matter of the honorarium or the stipend the personal wishes of the clergyman should be respected. If the family is a member of the clergyman's church or parish it is a personal matter between the family and the clergyman. When the funeral director assumes the responsibility for the honorarium at the direction of the family, it is desirable to use a check for the transaction for record keeping purposes. If the clergyman does not accept honoraria, the family should be so informed in order that they may express their appreciation in other ways. When the family has no choice of a clergyman and the funeral director makes arrangements for one, the matter of the honorarium becomes the responsibility of the funeral director and a cash advance for the family.

When conducting a funeral in a church the polity, rules and regulations of that church must serve as the guide to the conduct of the service. Any exceptions to such procedures requested by the family should be cleared with the clergyman or proper authority well in advance of the time of their actual performance.

The funeral director should remain alert to the needs of the families he serves and when the need for religious or pastoral counseling is indicated he should make proper referrals whenever possible.

Funeral directors should be available to discuss with anyone all matters relative to the conduct of a funeral. Whenever possible the funeral director should assume active leadership in seminars or discussions which will bring a deeper understanding to all concerned about death, the funeral and bereavement.

The Code of Good Funeral Practice, National Selected Morticians

As funeral directors, our calling imposes upon us special responsibilities to those we serve and to the public at large. Chief among them is the obligation to inform the public so that everyone can make knowledgeable decisions about funerals and funeral directors.

In acceptance of our responsibilities, and as a condition of our membership in National Selected Morticians, we affirm the following standards of good funeral practice and hereby pledge:

1. To provide the public with information about funerals, including prices, and about the functions, services and responsibilities of funeral directors.
2. To afford a continuing opportunity to all persons to discuss or arrange funerals in advance.
3. To make funerals available in as wide a range of price categories as necessary to meet the need of all segments of the community, and affirmatively to extend to everyone the right of inspecting and freely considering all of them.
4. To quote conspicuously in writing the charges for every funeral offered; to identify clearly the services, facilities, equipment and merchandise included in such quotations; and to follow a policy of reasonable adjustment when less than the quoted offering is utilized.
5. To furnish to each family at the time funeral arrangements are made, a written memorandum of charges and to make no additional charge without the approval of the purchaser.
6. To make no representation, written or oral, which may be false or misleading, and to apply a standard of total honesty in all dealings.
7. To respect all faiths, creeds and customs, and to give full effect to the role of the clergy.
8. To maintain a qualified and competent staff, complete facilities and suitable equipment required for comprehensive funeral service.
9. To assure those we serve the right of personal choice and decision in making funeral arrangements.
10. To be responsive to the needs of the poor, serving them within their means.

We pledge to conduct ourselves in every way and at all times in such a manner as to deserve the public trust, and to place a copy of this Code of Good Funeral Practice in the possession of a representative of all parties with whom we arrange funerals.

the physical characteristics of building. For example, the state of Minnesota has stringent requirements regarding the equipment in the preparation room, waste disposal and other plumbing, lighting, ventilation, and furnishing. Other states have regulations requiring minimum floor space, utensils on the premises, casket display rooms, a minimum number of caskets, and the availability of an on-site chapel. The funeral home regulatory boards often write and administer rules with regard to competitive practices. Most of the rules and regulations in this regard prohibit defamation of competitors, prohibit unlicensed funeral directing, and restrict advertising of goods and services.

Some states have provisions defining standards of conduct and consumer protection. These regulations vary from state to state and range from prohibiting the serving of food, drink, and alcoholic beverages to general standards for fraud or incompetence. These laws include prohibition of casket reuse, protection from embalming without permission, requirements for providing the consumers with an itemized price list prior to the funeral service, and providing the consumer with a choice of inexpensive caskets that have a variety of interior lining colors.

Funeral directors are also governed by their own professional associations. See the Code of Ethics for the National Funeral Director's Association of the United States, Inc., and for the National Selected Morticians (pp. 200-203). It is interesting to note that many of the practices identified by the Federal Trade commission are specifically addressed in the two documents. Obviously, funeral directors who engage in fraudulent practices are in violation of industry ethics as well as in violation of the law. Choosing a funeral director who subscribes to the principles contained in these codes can decrease the likelihood that consumers will experience unethical behavior.

The funeral consumer

The controversy between the funeral industry and consumer groups concerns the ability of the typical consumer in the United States. Most consumer groups believe that the death of a close friend or relative brings about profound emotional and psychological trauma that hinders the rational decision-making process. In contrast, the funeral industry states that the consumer can and does make rational decisions at this time. In testimony given at the Federal Trade Commission hearings on the funeral industry, funeral directors testified that they believed the individual making funeral arrangements was no more vulnerable than the consumer who buys a motorboat or arranges for hotel accommodations.

1. *Emotional trauma:* Research related to the emotional status of the bereaved indicates that they are generally in a state of shock characterized by confusion

and disorganization. It is during this time of increased vulnerability that they must make appropriate funeral arrangements.

2. *Guilt:* The bereaved often experience self-accusation and feelings that they have been negligent with regard to the deceased. There is the notion that the bereaved often feel that they could have done something to prevent the death. Also feelings of guilt arise when the bereaved believe they did not adequately express their personal feelings toward the deceased. As a result the bereaved may purchase an expensive funeral in an attempt to make restitution. The funeral director who indicates that this gesture represents "the last thing you can do for the deceased" is subtly increasing the guilt of the bereaved.

3. *Dependency and suggestibility:* The vulnerability of the bereaved increases their dependency on others. During this period the bereaved generally have feelings of hopelessness and helplessness. This hypersuggestibility causes the bereaved to look to others for help and guidance.

4. *Ignorance:* In ordinary transactions the consumer generally has a plethora of information regarding funerals for a variety of reasons. First, because death tends to be considered a taboo subject, there is not a great deal of information shared between friends and relatives prior to death. Second, because of the fact that people tend not to preplan funerals, they have little information concerning funeral arrangements when there is a death. And third, because funeral directors tend not to advertise prices or services, the bereaved often have a vague notion of what products and services must be purchased along with their own responsibilities in the funeral process.

5. *Time pressures:* Because they are not likely to preplan or investigate funeral options, consumers are put at a distinct disadvantage when there is a death in the family because funeral decisions must be made quickly. Since institutions (nursing homes and hospitals) do not have the facilities to store bodies, the bereaved are forced to make rather sudden decisions related to funeral arrangements. This feeling on the part of the bereaved that they must act quickly tends to increase the consumer's dependency on the funeral director.

Obviously, the emotional trauma, guilt, dependency, ignorance, and time constraints of the funeral places the consumer at a definite disadvantage in the marketplace. One goal of death education should be to help individuals become wise consumers of funeral goods and services. A death education course should help students identify their responsibilities as funeral consumers along with funeral-related costs and options. There is a definite need to help students recognize the value of preplanning funeral arrangements.

THE FUNERAL

The funeral is an important aspect of any death. It is an opportunity to celebrate the life of the deceased and it offers support for the bereaved by way of the compassion displayed among family and friends. For those with a religious orientation the funeral helps to soothe the loss by supporting the belief that the deceased now exists in a spiritual form—the deceased is in heaven. Regardless of the means of body disposal or the type of funeral selected, the essential purpose of the funeral is to help reconcile the loss. Irion[7] identified the following benefits of a funeral:

1. It can provide an opportunity to share the loss.
2. It can express social understanding of the relationship that existed between the living and the deceased.
3. It can strengthen the relational patterns among the living.
4. It can reinforce among the bereaved the reality of death.
5. It can help the living begin to establish a new psychological relationship with the deceased.
6. It can force the living to establish new relational patterns without violating the integrity of the previous relationship with the deceased.
7. It can encourage the release of authentic feelings.
8. It can facilitate a religious understanding and acceptance of suffering.
9. It can develop perspective on the meaning of life and death.
10. It can assist the mourners in comprehending the nature of humanity as a unity of body and spirit.

Rituals and ceremonies ordinarily take root from religious beliefs and cultural traditions. To an extent they may be influenced by community norms and practices. It is important to note that considerations other than cost should be a part of the decision-making process with regard to funeral type and mode of body disposal. Based on the potential benefits just listed, one might assume that a majority of funerals are pre-planned to guarantee that the benefits will be maximized. As it is necessary in a wedding, a baptism, or a golden wedding anniversary, good planning can ensure that everything occurs just as the participants have envisioned. Although cost is a factor that needs to be considered, it is not the only factor of importance when an individual purchases a funeral.

The funeral should effectively serve the needs of the people involved. Decisions reached before the fact are more likely to accomplish this goal. For instance, visitations to several funeral homes in the community may reveal that one home is more appealing, that a particular director is more cooperative, that a particular service is offered by one mortician but not another, or that a larger choice of caskets is offered in one home but the availability of a preferred ceremony is offered in another. Many factors need to be considered. The following checklist demonstrates the importance of preplanning the funeral. Observe that each consideration is stated in the first person. This is done to emphasize the importance of preplanning one's own funeral.

Since the method of body disposal has some influence on the services that are offered or necessary, the following should be the first consideration:

Method of body disposal

1. Do I want to be buried? _____
   Which cemetery? _____
   _____ In a family plot with spouse
   _____ In a crypt
   _____ At sea

2. Do I want to be cremated? _____
   _____ Remains placed in a mausoleum
   _____ Ashes scattered
   _____ Ashes placed in an urn

3. Do I want to donate my body or parts? _____

These decisions do have implications for the type of funeral selected, however, many of the considerations below apply well to any of the three methods of body disposal.

Funeral

4. What type of funeral do I want?
   _____ Secular (humanist)
   _____ Sectarian (religious)
   _____ A combination of the two

5. Where do I want the service(s) to be held?
   _____ In the home
   _____ In the funeral home
   _____ In the church
   _____ At the graveside or mausoleum
   _____ A combination of these

6. Will there be a viewing? _____
   _____ Open casket
   _____ Closed casket
   _____ Public viewing
   _____ Family viewing
   _____ Viewing the day before the final disposal
   _____ Viewing only during the funeral ceremony

7. What type of casket do I want?

_____ Wood
_____ Metal
_____ Sealed
_____ Lined
Liner material and color _____
Maximum cost _____

8. Do I want flowers? _____

_____ Sent to the home
_____ Sent to the funeral home
_____ Sent to the church
_____ Sent to the cemetery or crematory

9. Do I want memorials in lieu of flowers? _____ If so, to which agency or institution? _____

10. Who do I want to serve as pallbearers (6)? _____

_____
_____

11. Do I want music? _____

_____ Organ
_____ Choir
_____ Solo
_____ Hymns

12. Do I want a sermon or eulogy delivered? _____

_____ By a member of the family
_____ By a friend
_____ By my pastor, priest, or rabbi
_____ By the funeral director

13. Do I want prayers to be a part of the ceremony? _____
14. How do I want my obituary to read? _____

_____
_____

15. Do I want a memorial service held after the burial, cremation, or body disposal?

_____

16. Do I want my fraternal group to take part in the funeral? _____

17. Do I want the mourners to celebrate my life's passing with a gathering of family and friends? _____

One alternative that has been gaining popularity is known as the memorial service. A service of this type is held after the body has been disposed of and may occur regardless of the method of body disposal and whether or not a funeral ceremony was conducted. The service can be either secular or religious. Since the body is not present, the focus of the service is in the spiritual domain rather than the physical domain. The life of the deceased is celebrated to honor and memorialize the person who has lived and is now dead. If the service has religious qualities, the purpose is often to communicate transcendence from physical form to spiritual form and from temporary earthly existence to eternal existence in heaven.

Some people have chosen to have a memorial service instead of a funeral service strictly on the basis of economics. Since a service does not have to be held prior to disposal of the body, this may take place immediately. The need for body preparation and embalming, body storage, public viewing, an expensive casket, and a funeral ceremony is eliminated. This helps to reduce the overall financial expense of the death. What should be weighed against the financial savings, which may not be substantial, is the issue of whether a service that is motivated strictly by cost is able to achieve the benefits previously outlined.

In contrast, other people have opted for extravagant funerals. The motivation for this extravagance may have been based on an extension of standards during the lifetime of the deceased. A stereophonic casket may seem appropriate for some people who are accustomed to every luxury in life. For some people the motivating factor is the issue of social status gained when mourners take part in the funeral ceremony. Some individuals no doubt believe that an expensive funeral shows a greater love for the deceased, as if the more things cost, the more worthwhile they are. Other people perhaps are motivated by guilt to purchase an expensive funeral.

In our judgment it seems more important to maximize the benefits of the funeral rather than to minimize its cost. Similarly, the desired qualities of a funeral are more appropriate criteria for selection than are subconscious motivations that promote extravagance. Once again the essential question remains, "What kind of funeral do you want?"

Although there are no standardized legal requirements mandated for funeral arrangements, there are some common procedures for body disposition. Once a death has occurred, the first step is to contact a funeral home to remove the body. Although this is usually done by the family, an employee of the institution in which the death has occurred sometimes contacts the mortuary, thereby initiating the funeral process. The decision of which funeral home to select is based on a variety of factors, including location, religious and ethnic background, previous experience, social status, recommendations of friends and relatives, and affiliation with a memorial society.

The funeral director, after being called by the family or institutional employee, generally transports the body. The remains are cleaned and the process of embalming is begun unless there are specific instructions to the contrary. Embalming basically involves replacing the blood with chemical fluids to retard decomposition for a short period of time. Although this process can delay the decomposition, it is inaccurate to believe that embalming keeps the body lifelike forever. The purpose of embalming, which requires the use of substances such as alcohol, formaldehyde, and glycerin, is to preserve the body until the viewing is over.

The next step in the traditional funeral process is for the family to visit the funeral home. During this visit the funeral director and the family will make appropriate arrangements for disposition of the body and complete appropriate financial and legal paperwork. Prior to this meeting, or the first task of this meeting, is to gather the appropriate information for the death certificate. The death certificate is needed to complete a variety of financial and legal transactions. For example, a death certificate is needed to notify insurance companies, change titles on checking and saving accounts, change titles on stocks and bonds, and provide proof of ownership. Multiple copies of the death certificate are needed to complete the business transactions related to the death of a relative. The bereaved should plan to obtain at least five copies of the death certificate to avoid any problems.

Also during the family visit the funeral director will help the bereaved fill out appropriate applications for burial benefits of the deceased. The funeral director should be aware of these benefits. The California Department of Consumer Affairs provides the following list of financial assistance that may be available to the family of the deceased:

Social Security death payment (a simple payment of about $255) is available in practically all cases in which the deceased was covered by Social Security. Also monthly Social Security benefits may be payable to certain dependents and survivors of the deceased. These benefits may range from $100 to several hundred dollars per month.

Medicare benefits are frequently available to help pay final medical bills if the deceased qualified under this insurance coverage.

Veterans Administration benefits may provide up to $400 for burial costs, depending on the service record of the deceased. If the death occurs in a Veterans Administration hospital, certain additional travel costs usually are allowable. A U.S. flag for the casket and a government headstone, if the regulations of the cemetery permit one, may also be obtained. Interment without cost in the U.S. National Cemetery can be arranged if certain requirements are met. In some circumstances the widow or survivors may also receive further benefits.

Union or employer pension funds sometimes help defray funeral costs. They also may allow a survivor's pension.

Insurance policies (life, health, and accident) may have benefits. Sometimes medical payments from automobile insurance benefits can be applied to funeral expenses if death resulted from a car accident.

Fraternal orders and professional groups may have funds available for members.

Workmen's compensation insurance may allow certain benefits if the cause of death is related to the deceased's employment.

During the family visit the type of funeral that will be held and the final disposition of the body are discussed. Usually in the traditional funeral there is a public viewing of the body along with a graveside service. A private family viewing, a service at the funeral home, and transportation to a church for a brief service are also possible. If the family does choose to have the traditional funeral with viewing, there are other body preparations that are necessary. The mouth and face must be given a realistic appearance. Cotton may be used to fill out the cheeks, or the mouth may be permanently closed. The deceased may be dressed, shaved, given a haircut, and placed in the casket of the family's choice. Cosmetic procedures are often used by the funeral director to make the body look as lifelike as possible.

The entire process of preparing the body for viewing and final disposition is a long and detailed process. It is estimated that the funeral director spends an average of 10 hours to prepare the body for viewing and up to 60 hours for the total funeral process. Simpson[8] provides the following checklist for funeral arrangements:

_____ Obtain death certificate from physician.
_____ Register death; obtain burial permit.
_____ Decide on time and place of funeral or memorial service.
_____ Make a list of family, friends, and colleagues or employers to be informed, and inform each of them by phone.
_____ Notify memorial society or funeral home, and give clear instructions in terms of plan.
_____ If flowers are to be omitted, choose charity (or institution, such as hospital, church, or school) to which gifts may be sent instead.
_____ Write death notice, funeral notice or obituary and deliver it in person or by phone, to appropriate newspaper(s).
_____ Notify insurance companies and union.
_____ Notify lawyer and executor(s).
_____ Arrange special household needs—answering callers, taking phone messages, caring for children, food, and housework.
_____ Select pallbearers, where appropriate, and notify them.
_____ Where more distant family or friends should be notified by letter, list them and write appropriately.
_____ Check life insurance and other relevant insurance and benefits, such as Social Security, unions, and veterans' organization.
_____ Arrange wake or reception, if planned, to follow funeral.
_____ Arrange transportation.

It is interesting to note that many of these can be either preplanned or completed by the family of the deceased. However, because of the emotional trauma surrounding death, more often the funeral director is asked to handle many of these responsibilities. As a result the cost of funeral and body disposition is increased to compensate the funeral director for his or her time and services.

Funeral costs

The cost of funerals varies greatly in different sections of the country and from one funeral director to another. However, there are generally two ways to bill the consumer for services rendered. The first and most common is the single-unit pricing method. In this method of pricing the cost of the standard adult funeral is displayed on the top or inside the caskets in the display room. The single-unit price can be considered a package deal in that all services of the funeral director are included in one price. Therefore under the single-unit pricing method the cost of a funeral package is linked to the cost of the casket. The funeral consumer who buys a $1,500 package may get the same services as the consumer who buys a package worth $1,000, the only difference being the cost of the casket. The single-unit price generally does not include the costs related to the grave itself or to grave markers.

The second method of funeral pricing is the itemized list method. With this method the funeral consumer is given a listing of costs for all the funeral services offered. Table 7-2 provides a sample outline of these expenses.

The funeral industry is generally in favor of the single-unit pricing method for several reasons. First, it simplifies the accounting procedures and the consultation time needed during the family visit. Second, it perpetuates the traditional American funeral, rather than selection of services on an a la carte (itemized) basis. Single-unit pricing also permits the funeral director to offer the same services to all clients with only the cost of the casket changing the total cost of the funeral. As such, the consumer would be paying a fee for professional services rendered plus the cost of the casket. Third, if the funeral home offers the consumer an itemized list of expenses, it implies that the consumer has the option to shop around for services and may choose their funeral director on the basis of cost rather than on the quality of services rendered.

Currently in most states funeral directors have the option to price funeral merchandise in the manner most feasible to their business interests. The Consumer Survival Kit reported that only three states required the funeral director to provide an itemized listing of expenses: Minnesota, New Jersey, and New York. With the funeral directors comprising the majority of membership on the regulatory boards in most states, it is unlikely that these laws will be modified to favor the consumer.

Table 7-2. Funeral costs cited by various authors

Itemized expenses	Simpson (1979)	Consumer Service Kit (1977)	Hardt (1979): inexpensive rural funeral in 1979	Hardt (1979): inexpensive urban funeral in 1976	Draznin (1976)
Casket	$800	$600+	$125	$400	$450-2000+(*)
Body removal from site of death	20	40	35	45	
Embalming and preparation	100+	150+	100	125	415
Use of funeral home facility	200-500(*)	200-300(*)	150	240	Included above(*)
Professional services of director	Included above(*)	Included above(*)	50	180	
Use of hearse	50+	60	65	65	25-85
Burial garments	Included above(*)	Included above(*)	50	30	
Carnations	Included above(*)	Included above(*)	25	10	
Clergy honorarium	Included above(*)	Included above(*)	30-75	25	
Death notice	20	20-60	3	18	15
Grave site	215	100-400	200	275	300
Opening and closing grave	140-160+	120-250	125	200	
Vault	160	300	170	100	122
Simple grave marker	250+	75-275	150	245	
Burial permit	15	40			
Limousines	45 each	12 each			
Pallbearers					
Flowers	Included above(*)	Included above(*)	100-150		35
TOTAL	$1815-2135+	$1627-2397+	$1258	$1958	$1362-2912+

213

Table 7-2 provides a brief synopsis of the average costs of various funeral expenses. Obviously, these figures are subject to change and will vary according to funeral director and geographic regions of the country. The purpose of Table 7-2 is to provide the consumer with a notion of the goods and services available along with their approximate price ranges. The following is a closer look at some of these goods and services and their approximate costs.

Casket or coffin. The casket or coffin is usually the most expensive item on the funeral bill. Whether a casket (the lozenge-shaped box) or a rectangular coffin is purchased, the price can vary drastically according to the material, quality of lining, and sealer. The price of the casket or coffin can range from $125 for a plain, cloth-lined pine box to $5,000 for a copper-coated, velvet-interior casket with adjustable couches and stereophonic sound. Most families choose a casket somewhere between these two extremes. Usually a walnut, mahogany, or steel casket would retail for about $650 to $750 if not purchased as part of a package.

Transportation. There are a variety of livery services performed by the funeral director. For example, the funeral director removes the body from the site of the death and provides a hearse and limousine for transporting close friends and family to the cemetery. In addition, there may be a charge for delivery of flowers and for the services of nonvolunteer pallbearers. If the body needs to be transported a long distance, the funeral director will often charge a flat rate per mile. With the rising cost of gasoline and maintenance and the cost of vehicles, the amount of money needed to cover transportation costs is likely to increase.

Use of funeral home facility. Depending on the type of funeral arrangements, there will be varying costs for the use of the funeral home. This cost can be reduced or eliminated if the family elects to use their church for the services. Churches generally do not charge congregation members for the use of their facilities for funeral services.

Professional services of the funeral director. As stated previously, the funeral director spends up to 60 hours for body preparation and other funeral-related activities. There are a variety of responsibilities the funeral director is generally called on to do that could be easily assumed by friends and relatives. In addition, preplanning of funeral arrangements could eliminate the need for the funeral director to perform some of these services.

Honorarium. Whether or not there is an honorarium paid to the officiating clergyman is often a function of procedures set by the participating church. Generally, the honorarium ranges from $10 to $30 up to $50 to $75.

Flowers. It has been estimated that approximately $1 billion are spent annually on funeral flowers. This averages out to about $450 per funeral. The family's share is about $100 to $150. The popularity of flowers for funeral services seems to be waning. This may relate to the high cost of floral arrangements but more importantly may be a result of the funeral directors' desire not to be responsible for removing flowers from the funeral home and the church. Currently in some states the floral industry is seeking to prohibit the funeral director from writing obituary notices that request that no flowers be sent.[4]

Grave site. The grave site generally ranges from $100 to $300, although the funeral consumer can spend much more on a funeral plot, especially in congested urban areas.

Vault. Some state laws and some cemetery contracts insist that a durable casting surround the casket or coffin. This vault serves two purposes: it eliminates problems during an extreme flood situation and it prevents the grave from collapsing when the casket and remains decay. The vault is usually made of metal or concrete and can cost from $100 to $300.

Grave marker. Many cemeteries have restrictions on the type of grave marker they allow. Many modern cemeteries allow only grave markers that are flush with the ground to simplify maintenance of the grounds. Again, the cost of the grave marker varies. The average cost of a grave marker is $250 although the families of the deceased can spend thousands of dollars for an elaborate headstone marker.

Alternatives to traditional funerals

There are a variety of alternatives to the traditional American funeral, consisting of ceremony and earth burial. This section will discuss the three alternatives selected most often in the United States: cremation, memorial services, and body donation.

Cremation. Today, cremation is an orderly and clean way to return the remains to the elements. The actual process of cremation is fairly simple. The body is delivered to the crematory usually in a plain container. Inexpensive fiberboard containers are manufactured for this purpose. The remains and the container are placed under tremendous heat that reduces the remains to ashes. The cremation can take place immediately after death without ceremony or may follow a traditional American funeral ceremony. Therefore the cost of cremation as a means of body disposal can vary tremendously depending on the other services added.

The cost of cremation and the disposition of the body is generally less expensive than the cost of a traditional funeral. The crematory charge for the actual cremation ranges from $50 to $150. The cost of final disposition of the remains varies according to type of disposition chosen. A niche in a columbarium (a building or wall for aboveground storage of cremated remains) costs from $50 to $750, while burial in a cemetery may cost $50 to $150. This is less than for casket burial because there is no need to buy a full-sized plot. Urns (containers for cremated remains) can be purchased for as little as $50, but they range in price according to material and workmanship. Of course, the ashes can be scattered. A few states have laws that prohibit or limit the scattering of ashes. The Federal Trade Commission report found that commercial services that scatter ashes can charge up to $250. Obviously, when compared to the traditional funeral, cremation costs significantly less if done immediately following the death and if the ceremony is small. In the United States approximately 60% of the cremations are performed immediately with no prior ceremony.

It has been estimated that cremation accounts for 8% to 10% of the body disposals in the United States. Although the percentage of people who are opting for cremation is not as high as in other nations (well over 50% in Great Britain and West Germany and approaching 75% in Japan), the percentage of people selecting cremation as a means of body disposal is increasing. There are several reasons for this increase. First, cremation is supported by individuals and groups because it stresses simplicity and dignity. Another reason is that the traditional funeral process with all its trimmings often detracts from the primary purpose of the body disposal, which is to return the human remains to the elements. Cremation is viewed as a means to return the human remains to the elements uncluttered by expensive trappings, such as caskets, flowers, embalming, and hearse rentals. Third, there is an ecological argument for cremation. Cremation provides a more frugal use of land than does burial. With the population rising and the cost of land increasing, cremation may gain popularity from a land-use standpoint. Perhaps the major reason for the widespread use of cremation in Great Britain and Japan relates to the shortage of property available for cemetery plots. Fourth, religious groups in countries in which cremation is the norm view cremation as an acceptable means of body disposal. While cremation is discouraged by the Mormon, Islamic, Jewish, and Roman Catholic religions, it is viewed as acceptable or identified as an individual decision by the Methodist, Presbyterian, Lutheran, Hindu, Episcopal, Baptist, Jehovah's Witness, and Quaker religions. Fifth, the cost of cremation is often cited as an argument in support of this form of body disposal: about $250 for cremation versus $2,000 or more for traditional burial procedures.

Funeral and memorial societies. Funeral and memorial societies are nonprofit, volunteer organizations designed to help plan a simple, dignified, and personally meaningful form of body disposal at a reasonable cost. The basic purpose of the funeral and memorial society is to help members preplan their funerals to obtain the type of funeral service desired and to estimate the cost. The reaction of the funeral industry toward funeral and memorial societies has been generally hostile. Nevertheless, these societies usually know of funeral directors in the area who will provide the necessary services at a preset price. (See pp. 218-221 for some answers to the most commonly asked questions about funeral and memorial societies. In addition, Appendix G provides a listing of memorial societies in the United States and Canada.)

Body donation or donation of body parts. The donation of the human remains, in part or whole, is a mode of body disposal that does not appeal to all people. But those who are interested in this form of body disposal generally have a desire to serve the needs of humanity after they die. The Uniform Anatomical Gift Act of 1968 has helped to facilitate the donation of the human remains (see Appendix H for further information):

1. Persons 18 years of age or older can donate all or part of their bodies after death for transplantation, research, or placement in a tissue bank.
2. A donor's valid statement of gift supercedes the rights of anyone else unless a state autopsy law prevails and has conflicting requirements.
3. If a donor has not acted in his lifetime to specify a wish to donate, his survivors may do so, in specified order of priority (spouse, adult son or daughter, either parent, adult brother or sister, guardian, or any other person authorized or under obligation to dispose of the body).
4. Physicians who accept anatomical gifts and rely in good faith on documents provided to them in such cases are protected from legal action.
5. When a transplant is planned, the fact and time of death must be determined by a physician *not* involved in the transplant.
6. The donor has the right to revoke the gift, and it may be rejected by those for whom it is intended.

When donating a body to science, there are some important points that the donor should keep in mind. For example, the need for bodies varies in different sections of the country. There is generally an ample supply of bodies in the Far West and a greater need for bodies in other sections of the country. Also, if body donation is chosen as the means of disposition, appropriate arrangements should be made with the next of kin. In many states the next of kin must comply with the wishes of the deceased before the body can be donated. In addition, a medical school that does not have an urgent need for bodies may be reluctant to accept an anatomical gift when there is an objection by the next of kin. Another point for the donor to remember is that many medical schools will not accept a body that has been embalmed or on which an autopsy has been performed. These two procedures are often performed as a matter of course when someone dies, so it is important that the donor educate the next of kin on the need to omit these procedures if possible and to decide on a second alternative when necessary. Also, many medical schools will not accept a body that has had organs removed. It is difficult to donate certain body parts to one organization and then to donate the remains to a medical school. *Text continued on p. 224.*

Funeral and memorial societies

There are now Memorial Societies in 170 cities in Canada and the U.S., representing some half a million members. Most Canadian societies are united in the Memorial Society Association of Canada, Box 96, Weston, Ontario M9N 3M6. Most U.S. Societies belong to the Continental Association of Funeral and Memorial Societies, 1828 L Street, N.W., Washington, DC 20036. The two groups work closely and membership is reciprocal between them.

How funeral and memorial societies work

Q. What is a memorial society?
A. A memorial society is a voluntary group of people who have joined together to obtain dignity, simplicity and economy in funeral arrangements through advance planning.

Q. Is it run by funeral directors?
A. No. It is an organization of consumers that helps its members to make dignified funeral arrangements at reasonable costs.

Q. How is it controlled?
A. It is a democratic organization managed by an unpaid board of directors elected from its membership.

Q. Who organizes memorial societies?
A. Usually they have been started by a church or ministerial association; occasionally by labor, civic or educational groups; sometimes by a few concerned individuals.

Q. Is membership limited?
A. No. Membership is open to all regardless of creed, color, occupation or nationality, even though a society may be organized by a church or other group.

Q. How are memorial societies supported?
A. Most have a single modest membership fee for individual or family memberships. A few have annual dues. Some receive gifts or bequests. Some make a small charge which is remitted to them by the funeral director at time of death.

Q. Who does the work?
A. The members. Most societies are run by unpaid officers and committees, some by church staffs. A few larger ones have part- or full-time paid secretaries.

Q. What happens when you join?
A. The society lets you know what kind of funeral services are available and at what cost. You talk it over with your family and decide on your preference, then fill out forms provided by the society.

From A Manual of Death Education and Simple Burial, by Ernest Morgan. ($2.50 plus 50 cents postage from Celo Press, Route 5, Burnsville, NC 28714.)

Q. Can these plans be cancelled or changed?
A. Certainly. Any time.

Q. How does preplanning help at time of death?
A. In several ways:
1. You know what you want, how to get it and what it will cost. You don't have to choose a casket or negotiate for a funeral.
2. Your family understands what is being done. Simplicity will reflect dignity rather than lack of respect.
3. By accepting in advance the reality of death, and by discussing it frankly, you and your family are better able to meet it when it comes.

Q. Does planning really save money?
A. The amounts vary greatly, but memorial society members usually save several hundred dollars on a funeral. One large society estimates that its members save upwards of a million dollars a year by belonging to the organization.

Q. What is the basis of these savings?
A. Simplicity. A dignified and satisfying funeral need not be costly if you are not trying to demonstrate social status or compete with the neighbors. There is also the element of collective bargaining in your favor, and the advantage of knowing where to go to get the desired services at moderate cost.

Q. Can these savings be made without a memorial society?
A. Theoretically, yes. But it rarely happens. One has to search carefully and inquire widely to discover all the possibilities, something few families are prepared to do, especially at a time of death.

Q. How do I join a memorial society?
A. Phone or write the nearest society and ask for their literature. They will send you information about the membership fee.

Q. What if there is no society nearby?
A. Write the Continental Association or the Canadian Association to find out if there is a society that serves your area or if one is being formed. If you are interested in helping start a society, the Association will supply information and frequently local contacts as well.

Q. What if I move to another place?
A. There are memorial societies in 170 cities in the U.S. and Canada, affiliated with the Continental or Canadian Association. They accept transfers of membership with little or no charge.

Q. Are all societies alike?
A. Memorial societies vary in their arrangements and mode of operation. Their common characteristic is that they are democratic and non-profit. Occasionally pseudomemorial societies have been set up as "fronts" for funeral directions.

Continued.

Funeral and memorial societies—cont'd

Q. How can I tell the real thing from the imitation?

A. In two ways:

1. Virtually all genuine memorial societies are members of one of the two Associations. The Associations screen their members with care.
2. The bona fide society has no commercial interests. Membership rarely costs over $20. If an organization calling itself a memorial society tries to sell you a cemetery lot or if it asks a large membership fee, you had better investigate it carefully.

Q. What does a memorial society have to do with funeral directors?

A. Some societies serve only in an advisory capacity, informing their members where specific services may be had at specific costs. Most societies, however, have contracts or agreements on behalf of their members with one or more funeral directors.

Q. Does the society handle the business details of a funeral?

A. Not ordinarily. The society commonly brings the family and the funeral director together on a prearranged understanding of services and terms. The family itself deals directly with the funeral director.

Q. Are funerals necessary?

A. Survivors have important social and emotional need which should not be ignored. A funeral is one way of meeting some of these needs.

Q. Are there other ways?

A. Yes. Disposition of the body can be made immediately after death and a memorial service held later.

Q. What is the difference?

A. In a funeral the center of attention is the dead body; the emphasis is on death. In a memorial service the center of concern is the personality of the individual who has died, and the emphasis is on life. In addition, a memorial service generally involves less expense and can be held in a greater variety of locations.

Q. What are memorial services like?

A. They vary, taking into account the religious customs of the family and the personal relationships of the one who has died. The distinctive thing is that they stress the ongoing qualities of the person's life rather than his death. Each service can be worked out to meet the need and circumstances of the particular family.

Q. Is there any essential difference between funeral societies and memorial societies?

A. No. Both types of services are arranged by most societies. In every case, however, the family is encouraged to make the type of arrangements most congenial to its background and religious beliefs.

Q. Is embalming mandatory?

A. If the body is to be kept several days for a funeral service or, in some cases when it is to be transported by common carrier, yes. Otherwise embalming serves no useful purpose and except in one or two states is not legally required.

Q. Why then is embalming usually practiced in this country?

A. Funeral directors assume that unless otherwise advised, there will be viewing of the body and a service in its presence, and that embalming and "restoration" are desired. If this is not the case, the funeral director can be instructed to omit embalming.

Q. What appropriate disposition can be made of a body?

A. There are three alternatives:

1. Earth burial was once the simplest and most economical arrangement. With increasing population, rising land values, cost of caskets, vaults and other items usually required, it is becoming more and more costly.
2. Cremation, a clean orderly method of returning the body to the elements, is economical and is rapidly increasing in use.
3. Bequeathal to a medical school performs a valuable service and saves expense. In many areas there is a shortage of bodies for the proper training of doctors. Many public-spirited people leave their bodies for this purpose. A number of body parts can now be transplanted or otherwise used to promote medical research, restore sight or save a life. To facilitate the gift of body parts at the time of death, a "Uniform Anatomical Gift Act" has recently been passed by most states and provinces. Everyone is encouraged to cooperate.

The Ultimate Gift . . .

How to Help Others After Your Death by Donating Your Body

'The Ultimate Gift'

The greatest potential for serving others comes with the unrestricted gift of the entire body. With such gifts, medical science is given the opportunity to serve the greatest need at the time of the donor's death by using any or all body organs or body parts that may be needed to save or enhance the lives of others and to use the entire body for medical research and medical education.

HOW DOES ONE MAKE SUCH A GIFT?

The procedure is a simple one since the Uniform Anatomical Gift Act became law in Pennsylvania is 1970.

All the donor needs to do is to fill out Uniform Donor cards attached to this brochure. The Uniform Donor Identification Card and Uniform Donor Registration Card must be signed by the donor in the presence of two witnesses who also sign the cards. The greatest potential for good occurs when the donor checks item (a) and (c) and does not list any limitations. The Identification Card is kept by the donor, and the Registration Card is mailed to the Humanity Gifts Registry. If a person wishes to make a gift of only parts and organs, it is suggested that the appropriate agencies be contacted.

WHO MAY DONATE?

Anyone aged 18 or over may be a donor. If you are under the age of 18, either parent or - if you are married - your spouse may donate your body and body parts immediately prior to or after your death. If a person fails to fill out a donor card, he or she may still be a donor. The next of kin may donate the body and parts immediately after or immediately prior to death. The order in which legal authority is granted for this purpose is as follows: (1) Spouse; (2) An adult son or daughter; (3) Either parent; (4) An adult brother or sister; (5) Legal guardian.

PROCEDURE AT THE TIME OF DEATH

A phone call to the Humanity Gifts Registry is all that is necessary upon death of the donor. A funeral director will be notified who will transport the body from the place of death to the nearest medical or dental school in Pennsylvania.

COSTS

The Humanity Gifts Registry assumes the responsibility for the first fifty dollars ($50.00) of expense involved in taking the body from the place of death to the nearest appropriate institution in Pennsylvania. The Registry also assumes the cost of cremation, burial of the ashes and memorial services arranged by the Registry.

Memorial services are held twice a year by the Humanity Gifts Registry conducted by ministers of various faiths.

Plots are maintained by the Registry in established cemeteries in Philadelphia, Hershey and Pittsburgh. A record of the names of all bodies and the number of the grave in which the ashes are interred is kept by the registry.

The Uniform Donor Card is a legal document in all fifty (50) states. If death occurs outside the Commonwealth of Pennsylvania, contact the nearest medical school or health department.

HUMANITY GIFTS REGISTRY RESERVES THE RIGHT TO REFUSE A DONATION

Examples of bodies which may be refused include those which are recently operated on, autopsied, decomposed, obese, emaciated, amputated, infectious, mutilated or otherwise unfit for medical studies. Also long range changes in needs may preclude acceptance.

A DONOR MAY CHANGE HIS MIND

If a donor wishes to rescind his donation, he simply destroys his card, and notifies this office. Upon notification, his card will be removed from our files.

RUMORS

Rumors persist that one may sell one's body to a medical school or the Humanity Gifts Registry. Under no circumstances will payment be made for a body or body parts.

DEATH CERTIFICATES

The family may obtain copies of Death Certificates from the local registrar or Bureau of Vital Statistics. Humanity Gifts Registry is not legally empowered to distribute copies of Death Certificates.

For further information consult
HUMANITY GIFTS REGISTRY
130 South 9th Street
Philadelphia, Pennsylvania 19107
Telephone: 215-922-4440

Rev. 7-80

When donating their bodies to a medical school, individuals need to read the fine print. Some medical schools will accept a body only from within the state or local region. Other medical schools may require that transportation costs be paid by the estate of the deceased. Occasionally the institution will charge the full amount of Social Security entitlement for transportation. Appendix I provides a list of medical schools in the United States and Canada that accept body donations.

There is a distinct difference between body donation to a medical school and donation of body parts. Prior to death, the individual can arrange to donate a variety of organs and tissues for transplantation or research. The next of kin will still have to make arrangements for body disposition after these parts have been removed. The Uniform Donor Card is readily available and provides the physician and next of kin with information concerning one's wishes. It is important to stress that wishes and intentions should be made clear to physicians, friends, and relatives so that the manner of disposal and the nature of the ceremony are carried out as planned.

The need for donor organs has increased over the past decade. The increase in media and public attention given to this need has motivated more than 30 states to pass legislation that allocates space on drivers' licenses for those who desire to donate body organs. The following are some commonly donated organs:

Eyes: In the United States, it is estimated that there are 30,000 blind persons whose sight could be restored if a sufficient number of corneas were available. Although all vision problems cannot be alleviated by transplants, approximately 90% of corneal transplants are successful. The eyes have to be removed within 2 to 4 hours of death, so it is important that the physician and family know of the person's wishes, and Uniform Donor Card should be carried as well. Appendix J provides a list of eye banks in Canada and the United States. One of these organizations can be contacted by individuals interested in donating their eyes.

Ear bones: Accelerated research into the causes and cures of deafness has increased the need for people to bequeath their inner-ear structures. The removal of these inner-ear structures is a complex task that requires special procedures to be arranged. For further information one may contact the Deafness Research Foundation, 342 Madison Ave., New York, NY 10002.

Body tissue: A variety of body tissues are needed for transplantation. If interested in donating tissue, the individual should contact the American Association of Tissue Banks, 12111 Parkinson Drive, Rockville, MD 20852. This group is a nongovernment organization of health professionals whose primary goal is setting up standard tissue banking and establishing regional tissue banks.

Kidneys: Kidneys for transplanting are urgently needed. Many kidney patients who are currently on dialysis are waiting for kidneys for transplantation. The success rate for these operations is about 60% and has been improving each year. More information on kidney donation can be obtained from the national Kidney Foundation, 116 East 27th St., New York, NY 10016.

Pituitary glands: In the United States it is estimated that 5,000 to 10,000 children are suffering from severe pituitary deficiency. The extract from approximately 200 to 300 pituitary glands is needed to maintain the normal growth of a child for 1 year. Obviously, there is a need for pituitary glands. For more information one may contact the National Pituitary Agency, Suite 503-7, 210 West Fayette St., Baltimore, MD 21201.

WILLS

The reasons for not drawing up a will can only be hypothesized. If America is a admit they should prepare a will, but a relatively small percentage complete the process of writing one. Yaffa Draznin in his book, *The Business of Dying,* states, "Less than one-fourth of all Americans get around to making a will before they die, even though many admit they should."[1]

The reasons for not drawing up a will can only be hypothesized. If American is a death-denying society as many thanatologists suggest, then writing and witnessing a will would not be a social imperative. The act of writing or witnessing a will is an open admission that the individual or a close friend or relative is going to die. In essence, it is a declaration of the intent to die, a notion that is not compatible with the denial of death. Another reason for not writing a will is the often-held misconception by an individual that he or she does not own enough property to warrant the preparation of a will. Even people with an extremely modest estate should consider writing a will if for no other reason than to arrange to give their belongings to their survivors. A third reason may relate to the notion that people need to employ a lawyer to write a will. Although a lawyer is strongly recommended, a will can be written without a lawyer present. Simpson[8] outlines 10 items to consider when an individual writes a will:

1. Write it clearly and specifically enough to make your intentions clear and unambiguous.
2. Let the opening paragraph identify clearly who you (the "testator" or willmaker) are, with your address and the statement that you are knowingly making your will. Generally, you should include a clear statement that you are revoking any and all previous wills you may have made. Otherwise, there could be contradictory versions of your will that lead to costly confusion and delay.

3. It is common to state that burial expenses and legal debts, taxes, and costs of administering the estate are to be promptly paid as a first claim against your estate.

4. Specify the way you want your assets distributed. You may decide on a series of specific bequests of money or property to individual people or charities, and leave the rest, what is called your "residuary estate," to your main heir. Remember that such specific legacies you make will usually take precedence, so if you give large amounts to others, and especially if the value of your estate falls, there may be little left for your main heirs. You may help to avoid this by specifying general legacies as a percentage of the total value of your estate.

5. As has been mentioned, you should appoint an executor to manage and settle your affairs.

6. You may wish to set up a trust, especially if you feel your heirs are too financially in-experienced to manage your estate; this may achieve some tax savings. Trusts are governed by so many laws and regulations that you will certainly need legal help to establish one.

7. Remember to make allowance for the possibility that the person(s) to whom you wish to leave your estate may die before you or, as in the death by accident of a married couple, your spouse may die at the same time as you. So include alternative instructions to deal with these possibilities. Remember, too, that subsequent events such as marriages, divorces, and changes in the financial status of those to whom you intend to leave your estate may require you to revise your will at a later date.

8. Type the will. Your handwriting may not be clearly deciphered, and such wills are often not accepted. Don't mix typing and handwriting. Fasten the pages of a lengthy will firmly together and initial and number every page and any corrections. The will may be voided if a page is lost, misplaced, or replaced. Any changes, additions, or deletions that are not initialed to show they were made before you signed your will may make the provision or even the whole will void.

9. At the end of the will you must add your signature (don't add any provisions *after* this point), the date, and a clause that contains the signatures and addresses of your witnesses and a statement certifying that they saw you sign the will. Your witnesses must sign in the presence of each other and you. Generally, you will need two wit-nesses, though some states require three; three is thus the safest number if you have property in several states. *Never* use as a witness a person who will benefit in any way from your will.

10. Every married woman should have her own will. Even if she believes she has no pro-perty of her own, she will probably inherit at least some of her husband's estate and will need to decide how she wishes to dispose of that. Wives usually outlive their husbands, but they cannot rely on this. Also a wife may need a will to name the guar-dian or trustee to care for her minor children in order to avoid later custody battles.*

---

*From the book The Facts of Death by Michael A. Simpson. ©1979 by Prentice-Hall, Inc., Englewood Cliffs, New Jersey 07632.

Again, it should be stressed that it is advisable to consult a lawyer when a will is being written. The average legal fee for writing a will ranges from $35 to $150. Obviously, if the will is more complex, the fee will increase. The fee should be discussed with the lawyer prior to writing the document.

Probate

Probate is the process of proving the validity of a will. The laws regarding probate vary from state to state. The probate court has developed a reputation for delay and expense, which has forced many people to look for ways to avoid probate. Joint ownership of property, life insurance plans, pension benefits, U.S. Savings Bonds, and inter vivos trusts have been used to avoid probate. Because of the wide variations in state laws, it is advisable to consult a lawyer to identify the state laws regarding wills and estates.

In an attempt to simplify, hasten, and reduce the cost of passing possessions to friends and relatives, many states are adopting the Uniform Probate Code. This code simplifies laws with regard to dying intestate and allows for small estates to be administered without constant supervision by the courts. The primary purpose of the Uniform Probate Code is to obtain essential uniformity rather than to obtain laws of identical language in each of the states of the United States. The basic argument for a uniform probate code is based on the tendency of Americans to migrate and invest money without regard to state boundaries. The major objectives of the code are divided into three categories: estate planning and settlement, guardianship and other arrangements, and courts. These major objectives are summarized below.[9]

Estate planning and settlement. The following are objectives of the Uniform Probate Code in regard to estate planning and settlement:

To relieve married persons with children of the necessity to make wills to prevent unwanted inheritance by children of fractions of property and savings that most prefer to pass to the surviving spouse and to provide a satisfactory, statutory estate plan for these persons.

To reduce procedural requirements relating to all inheritances to shorten the time that heirs must wait to receive assets and to lower the expense of probate in small and trouble-free estates.

To strengthen the institution of individual control of wealth and savings by making transmission of wealth at death by will or intestacy more safe and efficient. Thus ordinary persons would be relieved of existing pressure to entangle their affairs with complex arrangements that appear to involve present commitments but are selected simply to avoid probate.

227

To enable efficient planning and unified administration of the decedent's estate consisting of land or savings located in two or more states.

Guardianship and other arrangements. The following are objectives of the Uniform Probate Code in regard to guardianship and other arrangements:

To modernize the law of guardianship by reducing the need for court-appointed guardians of minors and by simplifying procedures relating to the appointment of guardians when appointments are necessary or desirable.

To provide modern and efficient proceedings, possibly leading to court appointment of conservators who may function as private trustees, for the necessary care of substantial estates of minors and protection of dependents of disabled (including disappeared) adults.

To strengthen agency arrangements commonly known as powers of attorney so that elderly persons can arrange for private management of their affairs by simple documents that will remain effective in spite of later incompetency.

To achieve interstate uniformity and predictability regarding multiple-party accounts in forms widely used as will substitutes by depositors in banks, savings and loans, credit unions, and other financial institutions.

Courts. The following are objectives of the Uniform Probate Code in regard to courts:

To establish efficient judicial proceedings available on an optional basis to trustees and beneficiaries of inter vivos and testamentary trusts.

To clarify the role of local probate officials in regard to decedent's estates, guardianship (not involving juvenile jurisdiction), and trusts by separating nonjudicial from judicial functions, permitting the former to be handled by nonlawyers, and encouraging law-training judges to handle only serious problems. In this connection the code encourages elimination of jurisdictional and procedural differences between courts of general jurisdiction and courts handling estates and guardianship matters, insofar as judicial activities are concerned.

The major objectives of the Uniform Probate Code serve to highlight some of the major concerns regarding the laws of wills and estates throughout the United States. The adoption of a uniform probate code by all states would help to provide a consistent and simplified set of probate laws that the general population could more easily understand and apply to their own particular situation.

The complete Uniform Probate Code is organized into eight articles and 301 sections. The official text is available from the office of Richard Wellman, Educational

Director for the Joint Editorial Board for the UPC, School of Law, University of Georgia, Athens, 30602. Unlike many legal documents, the official text of the Uniform Probate Code contains extensive textual comments designed to aid in the comprehension of the material.

Storage of will

Even the best written, most up-to-date is worthless if it cannot be found. A will should be stored in a place where it can be easily found when needed. A will should not be stored in a safety deposit box at a bank. In many states safety deposit boxes are sealed at death and an executor may need the sanction of the court to obtain the will. It is generally advisable to have several duplicated copies of the will and to ask a lawyer to retain one copy of the will for his or her files.

Revision or revocation of will

When only minor modifications of a will are needed, a codicil may be added to the will. The codicil is an attached statement that adds to or modifies the will. If an individual changes residences, acquires new assets, has any additions or deletions in family members, or wants to disinherit someone, a will revision may be in order. (A child cannot be disinherited automatically by omitting his or her name from the will. A clear, concise statement of disinheritance must be included in the document.)

If the will needs to be revoked, it should be remembered that the provisions for revocation will vary from state to state. If a lawyer draws up the new will, he or she will generally include an opening statement that indicates the revocation of all previous wills.

Role of executor

The naming of an executor for a will is an important task. This is a complicated job with a myriad of responsibilities. Therefore it is important to discuss with the prospective executor the roles, responsibilities, and compensation that are included in the position. Neither institutions (for example, banks or trust companies), nor individuals are under any legal obligation to administer an estate simply because they are named in the will. The general responsibilities of an executor are to see that the terms of the will are carried out, submit the will to the probate court, collect monies due the estate, pay debts owed by the estate, catalog and appraise all assets, arrange for family living expenses, manage the estate and assets, and file appropriate estate, income, and inheritance tax forms. It is obvious that the executor must have both an understanding of legal and financial aspects of wills and estate planning as well as a sensitivity to the unique problems and needs of the family. For this reason many estates need to name coexecutors. This is most often done by naming a family member and a lawyer, bank, or trust company to administer the estate.

SUMMARY

Consumerism is an important and practical content area of death education. The selection of goods and services will depend in part on the cultural beliefs and customs of the individual, taking into consideration factors such as beliefs in afterlife and spiritual dimensions of life and death. The funeral as it is known today emerged from gradual changes that have taken place in society. The multimillion dollar funeral industry grew in response to these changes. Funeral directors, once a guild of tradesmen, have continued to upgrade their training and educational requirements in an attempt to provide the necessary services to the public. The event of death brings about a host of sanitary, health, religious, medical, legal, and personal and family concerns. The funeral director may be asked to provide a variety of services that require specialized knowledge and skill.

One section of the chapter focuses on criticisms of the funeral industry. Examples taken mostly from the Federal Trade Commission report present fraud and unethical behavior. Although these abuses apply to a small number of funeral directors, they point to the need for consumer education and funeral preplanning. The most vulnerable consumer is one who is ignorant and one who must make quick decisions while suffering from the emotional strain of grief, guilt, or depression. One of the essential messages of the chapter is that preplanning can be a personally satisfying experience and can help to guarantee individuals the type of funeral they want. The funeral should be a celebration of the life of the deceased and should help the bereaved mourners to accept the loss of someone close to them. A checklist of funeral considerations is presented to maximize the potential benefits of a funeral ceremony. In completing the checklist individuals may find it helpful to consult with their families, clergy, physicians, lawyers, and close friends. A current estimate of funeral expenses is also provided.

Glossary of terms related to wills and estate planning

administrator Person appointed by the court to administer the estate of a person who dies without a will. Or an administrator may be appointed by a court to carry out the terms of a will in lieu of an executor.

attestation Witnessing the signing of a will and verification of such by signing as a witness.

beneficiary Person for whom a trust is created or for whom a bequest is made.

codicil Statement attached to the will that modifies the provisions of the will.

corpus Assets of an estate or trust.

execution Signing of the will and the fulfillment of the terms of the will.

executor Person or institution appointed by the person who draws up a will to carry out the terms of the will.

fiduciary Person entrusted with the rights and powers to handle the assets of others.

inter vivos Trust that is made while the grantor is alive.

intestate Dying without executing a valid will.

legacy Bequest, usually of personal property, made by a will.

probate Legal process of proving a will is valid. This process takes place after the person dies.

remainder Assets of an estate or trust after the estate or trust is terminated.

surrogate General term meaning a person designated to act for another. In a will it often refers to the person who handles the guardianship of children.

testamentary Trust created in the will of the deceased that becomes effective on the death of the grantor.

testate Dying after the writing of a valid will.

trust Process of holding property and assets for the benefit of those for whom the trust was created.

trustee Person or institution who manages a trust for the beneficiaries of a trust.

CONCEPTS RELATED TO CONSUMER ASPECTS
OF DEATH AND DYING

- The proper preplanning of funeral arrangements takes time, planning, and motivation.

- Knowledge and understanding of the funeral process and alternatives is the basis for the selection of body disposal methods and services.

- Decisions related to body disposal techniques are influenced by social and cultural factors.

- The family and its constituent members exert a significant influence on funeral decisions.

- Utilization of community, state, and national resources can assist the individual and family to effectively plan for body disposal.

- A variety of techniques to dispose of body remains are available to the individual and the family.

- Preplanning of body disposal helps to ensure that the individual and family will view the process favorably.

EDUCATIONAL ACTIVITIES RELATED TO CONSUMER
ASPECTS OF DEATH AND DYING

Title:	Wills
Age level:	High school, adults
Objective:	Given a case example, the students assemble in small groups and will draw up an appropriate will for the case example using the 10 criteria to consider when writing a will.
Materials:	Case examples, a copy of Simpson's 10 criteria that should be considered when writing a will. (See Chapter 7.)
Directions:	Provide each group with a case example. Ask the group to devise a last will and testament for their particular case. Have each group appoint a spokesperson to read their will to the class. Discuss the wills. Be sure to highlight the strengths and weaknesses of each will. Listed below is a sample case example. The teacher should develop other case examples in accordance with the nature of the audience.
Case example:	Mr. Jackson, 43, has a wife who is a successful real estate broker and two children: Joel, age 13, and Sally, age 9. The Jacksons own a house and two cars. Mr. Jackson has investments and savings that he would like used for the education of his two children if he should die before they reach college age. If the children choose not to attend college, Mr. Jackson would like the balance of the investments and savings to go to his wife.

Title:	How to dispose of a pet
Age level:	Primary
Objective:	1. Following the activity, the student will describe the life cycle of a cat.
	2. During the class discussion of *The Tenth Good Thing About Barney,* the students will discuss the need to dispose of dead animals.
Materials:	*The Tenth Good Thing About Barney* by Judith Viorst (New York, 1971, Antheneum). The text describes the process a family goes through to help a young boy deal with the death of his cat Barney. The text depicts the family burying the cat and discusses life-cycle concepts.
Directions:	Arrange students into reading groups or into a small circle around the teacher. Read the text and conduct a follow-up discussion. Some sample questions might include:

- Do all living things have a life cycle?
- Why did the father want to bury Barney the next day?
- Why was Barney buried under a tree?
- How was Barney helping to make things grow?
- What are some reasons Barney was buried?

Title:	Donation of body or body parts
Age level:	High school, adults
Objective:	At the completion of the activity, the students will make a personal decision on whether or not to complete the Uniform Donor Card.
Materials:	Felt markers, large newsprint pad, a copy of "The Ultimate Gift" (from the Humanities Gift Registry) and the Uniform Donor Card for each student. A replica of the Uniform Donor Card is shown on p. 234.
	For further information on the Uniform Donor Card write to the Humanity Gift Registry, 130 South 9th St., Philadelphia, PA 19107, Telephone: 215-922-4440.
Directions:	Break the class or seminar participants into small groups. Provide each group with a copy of the Uniform Anatomical Gift Act of 1968. Provide each student with a copy of "The Ultimate Gift . . . How to Help Others After Your Death By Donating Your Body or Body Parts" and a copy of the Uniform Donor Card. Using the materials provided, ask each group to outline the perceived pros and cons of the donation of the body for anatomical study on one piece of newsprint and the perceived pros and cons of donating body parts for transplantation on another. Then ask each group to tape their pros and cons on the walls around the room. Conduct a follow-up discussion on the students' thoughts. Allow time for individual students to decide whether or not to complete their Uniform Donor Card.

-KEEP THIS CARD-
UNIFORM DONOR IDENTIFICATION CARD
OF
_____
Print or Type name of donor
In the hope that I may help others, I hereby make this anatomical gift, if medically acceptable, to take effect upon my death. *'* The words and marks below indicate my desires.

I give (a) _____ any needed organs or parts.

(b) _____ only the following organs or parts
_____
Specify the organ(s) or part(s)
for the purpose of transplantation, therapy, medical research or education.

(c) ___ my body for anatomical study if needed.
Limitations or special wishes, if any _____

Signed by the donor and the following two witnesses in the presence of each other.

_____   _____
Signature of Donor   *Date of Birth of Donor*

_____   _____
Date Signed   *City & State*

_____   _____
Witness   *Witness*
This is a legal document under the Uniform Anatomical Gift Act or similar laws.
Rev. 7-80

CALL HUMANITY GIFTS REGISTRY — (215) 922-4440

* CALL HUMANITY GIFTS REGISTRY — (215) 922-4440

RETURN THIS CARD
UNIFORM DONOR REGISTRATION CARD
OF_____
Print or Type name of donor
Social Security No. _____

In the hope that I may help others, I hereby make this anatomical gift, if medically acceptable, to take effect upon my death.   The words and marks below indicate my desires.

I give (a) _____ any needed organs or parts.

(b) _____ only the following organs or parts
_____
Specify the organ(s) or part(s)
for the purpose of transplantation, therapy, medical research or education.

(c) ___ my body for anatomical study if needed.
Limitations or special wishes, if any _____
Signed by the donor and the following two witnesses in the presence of each other.

_____   _____
Signature of Donor   *Date of Birth of Donor*

_____   _____
Date Signed   *City & State*

_____   _____
Witness   *Witness*

_____
Donor's Address

_____
City   *State*   *Zip Code*
This is a legal document under the Uniform Anatomical Gift Act or similar laws.
Rev. 7-80

Body disposal questionnaire

Directions: Please respond to each of the items listed below according to the following scale.

SA–Strongly agree A–Agree U–Undecided
D–Disagree SD–Strongly disagree

_____ Funerals in the United States are overpriced.
_____ Cremation is an attractive alternative to traditional burial.
_____ Donation of the body for anatomical study is an attractive alternative to traditional burial.
_____ The funeral director is a qualified grief counselor.
_____ Every adult should draw up a last will and testament.
_____ Public viewing of the body (a wake) is distasteful.
_____ A memorial service (without the body present) is undesirable.
_____ It is important to preplan your funeral arrangements.
_____ The funeral industry should be regulated by the Federal Trade Commission.

Title:	Body disposal questionnaire
Age level:	High school, adults
Objectives:	At the completion of the body disposal questionnaire, the students will have formulated position statements on issues related to funerals and body disposal.
Materials:	One questionnaire for each student.
Directions:	Distribute copies of the questionnaire to all students. Ask students to rate each item on a Likert scale. Discuss the results of the questionnaire. This questionnaire could serve as a basis for further discussion in the area.

Title:	Position paper: Burial vs. Cremation
Age level:	High school, adults
Objective:	At the completion of the burial vs. cremation debate the students will be able to outline the commonly expressed reasons for traditional burial and cremation.
Materials:	Sources of information on cremation and traditional burial.
Directions:	Ask students to select a position in favor of either traditional burial or cremation. Have the student research these two methods of body disposal and identify information in support of their positions. Make sure such

issues as environmental impact, cost, benefit to society, and opportunity for bereavement are covered. Sample pros and cons are listed below.

Reasons for burial

1. It is a more socially accepted means of body disposal.
2. It has the endorsement of many dominant religious groups.
3. It provides an eternal monument for the deceased.
4. The viewing of the body and graveside service may have a therapeutic value.

Reasons for cremation

1. This mode of body disposal can cost significantly less than traditional burial.
2. This is a simple and dignified means of body disposal.
3. Cremation is a clean and orderly way to return human remains to the elements.
4. Cremation is a more ecologically sound and frugal use of land.

Title:	Funeral role-playing
Age level:	High school, adults
Objective:	Following the funeral role-playing situation, the student will identify the procedures and costs involved in the traditional funeral process.
Materials:	Role playing cards, itemized funeral cost list.
Directions:	Assign the roles as listed below to students. It is important that the funeral director knows more about the funeral process than the bereaved, so it is advisable to give this role player ample time to study the funeral cost list and funeral directors' check list.
	Conduct the role-playing situation. During the follow-up discussion outline procedures the bereaved could have taken to deal with this emotionally trying situation more effectively.
Roles:	Mr. (or Mrs.) Jones, funeral director. Mr. Jones owns and operates a medium-sized funeral home in a suburban area. Mr. Jones believes there is a therapeutic benefit from having a complete funeral with embalming, a public viewing, and a graveside service.
	Mrs. Smith, the widow of the deceased. Mrs. Smith does not know what procedures or services to expect when she goes to the family visit with the funeral director. She asked Mr. Jones what she should do to give her deceased husband a dignified funeral.
	Mrs. Johnson, the sister of the widow. Mrs. Johnson has recently had to plan a funeral for her husband and has some preconceived notions regarding how to give the late Mr. Smith a proper burial.

Itemized funeral list

Casket	$400-$1,100
Embalming	$175
Use of funeral home	$225
Professional services	$150
Hearse	$ 65
Burial garments	$ 50
Clergy honorarium	$ 35
Removal from site	$ 45
Flowers	$ 75
Death notice	$ 40
	$ 50
Limousine	$ 45 each
Death certificate	$ 2 each
Tent rental	$ 50
Opening and closing the grave	$180
Vault	$195
Gravemarker	$475

REFERENCES

1. Draznin, Yaffa: The business of dying, New York, 1976, Hawthorn Books, Inc., p. viii.
2. U.S. Department of Labor, Bureau of Labor Statistics: Occupational outlook handbook, Bulletin No. 2075, Washington, D.C., 1980, U.S. Government Printing Office, p. 151.
3. University of Minnesota Department of Mortuary Science Bulletin, Minneapolis, 1978, University of Minnesota Office of Admissions and Records.
4. California Department of Consumer Affairs: The last rights: benefits to which you may be entitled. In Compleat consumer catalogue, Sacramento, 1978, The Department, p. 94.
5. Raether, Howard, and Slater, Robert: The funeral director and his role as a counselor, Milwaukee, 1975, The National Funeral Director's Association.
6. Federal Trade Commission: Funeral Industry Practices, Washington, D.C., 1978, U.S. Government Printing Office, pp. 2-3.
7. Irion, Paul E.: The funeral: vestige or value, Nashville, Tenn., 1966, Abingdon Press, pp. 117-119.
8. Simpson, Michael: The facts of death: a complete guide for being prepared, Englewood Cliffs, N.J., 1979, Prentice-Hall, Inc.
9. Joint Editorial Board for the Uniform Probate Code: U.P.C. highlights, Chicago, The Board.

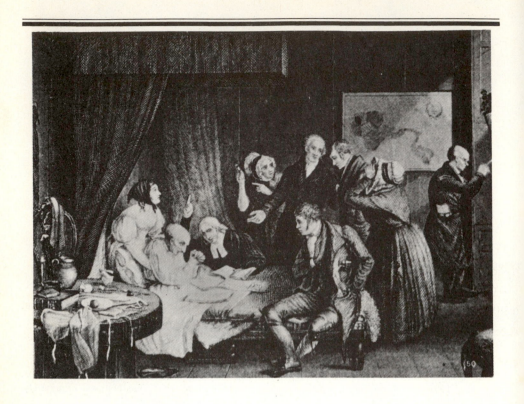

CHAPTER EIGHT

Dying and death in the United States

*I do not consider myself dying of cancer, but living despite it. I do not look upon each day as another day as another day close to death, but as another day of life to be appreciated and enjoyed.**

ORVILLE KELLY

Death is a fact of life. Every day in this country about 6,000 people will die. That amounts to about 300 deaths every hour and nearly 2 million deaths annually. Everyone has to face death—the death of others close to us and inescapably our own death. The way in which death is viewed is shaped by factors such as education, religious faith, cultural heritage, and past experiences related to living and dying. Since death is an inevitability for every human being, this chapter is devoted to a few of the current issues in the hope that the problems that arise from death will be considered and resolved. Discussion is focused on terminal illness and the implications for the patient, the family, and the professionals who care for them.

DEATH IN AMERICAN SOCIETY

Throughout most of the history of this country death was distributed fairly evenly across the life span. The population was composed of many young people and few elderly so that even though a small proportion of youth died, their actual numbers were many. During this century there has been a gradual shift in the population pyramid. Today there are a great many people living beyond middle age. In fact, about 10% of our total population now exceeds age 65. In 1900 about 16% of the deaths occurred to people over the age of 65, while more recently the elderly account for nearly two thirds

---

*From Kelly, Orville: Make today count, Death Education 1:159-164, 1977.

of the total deaths. The field of gerontology has begun to emerge and will play a significant role in shaping our attitudes and clarifying the issues surrounding dying and death.

The leading causes of death at the turn of the century were infectious diseases such as influenza, tuberculosis, and gastritis. The communicable childhood diseases of measles, mumps, diphtheria, and pertussis also caused a significant number of deaths. Immunizations and antibiotics for these diseases had not yet been discovered. Treatment was limited to those activities that reduced the intensity of symptoms while the body utilized its natural autoimmune response to fight the infection. The diseases were classified as acute, which means they were of rapid onset. Not only were the symptoms quick to appear, but ordinarily the person either recuperated or succumbed to the illness within a relatively brief time. Because of the nature of the disease and the unsophisticated medical equipment available at this time, many deaths occurred in the home instead of the hospital.

After World War II a tremendous profusion of medical technology was begun. During the 1960s there was an explosion of technology and miracle cures that drastically changed the causes of death and the nature of treatment. Each new piece of medical equipment seemed to establish the need for a new allied health professional who would become an essential member of the health care team. Simultaneously research was accelerating at such a rapid pace that physicians were unable to keep up with the advances. Gradually serious illness was handled by a specialist in the hospital setting where the machinery and the technicians were located. Treatment in the home by the family physician was limited to conditions that were not life threatening. Consequently the hospital became a complex organization of specialists, each being responsible for a designated portion of the patient's overall treatment.

Along with these changes in the health care delivery system were changes related to the nature of critical illness. Whereas patient care and hospitalization once consisted of the treatment of acute diseases of brief duration, eventually chronic diseases and trauma became the major causes of hospitalization and death. Trauma centers, intensive care and cardiac care units, renal dialysis systems, and cancer research and treatment facilities are recent developments in the delivery of health care services. Because of the nature of life-threatening conditions and the availability of specialized services, the time between the onset of illness or injury and the actual death of the person has grown longer and longer. In some instances a person is made aware of the terminal prognosis years in advance of death. This means that prolonged hospital stays and repeated visits for treatment may be required. Contact with care givers is extensive and may create for the patient an intense emotional dependence on the health care professionals.

THE HOSPITAL WAY OF DYING

Responsibility for patient care had previously been limited to physician and registered nurse. In most instances the family physician coordinated patient care. This was advantageous because physicians knew as much about the patient being treated as they did about the disease being treated. Established during the course of many years, the relationship was based on mutual trust and respect. Communication between physician and patient reflected this mutual respect. However, as specialists replaced the family physician and as technicians began to assume some of the bedside responsibilities for patient care, the human aspects of the patient's hospitalization began to diminish. Instead of a physician and nurse being responsible for the total care of perhaps 10 patients, the larger team of specialists became responsible for a small portion of the care of many patients. Although this is definitely a medical advantage for dealing with the illness, it has often conflicted with the human aspects of care. In a case in which the patient is terminally ill adequate psychological support from the health care team may not be present. This creates the need for a still larger team trained in the social sciences. Thus the patient must interact with a great number of professionals, each of whom contributes a fraction of the total care. For the patient this can be frustrating and dehumanizing. To live the remaining days of one's life in this fashion may be unacceptable to the patient and the family, especially if institutional rules and regulations limit independence and family contact with the patient.

According to Heller and Schneider, "The fascinating aspect of the hospital setting as the locus of dying is that the medical profession, in whose hands we place ourselves to die, is not trained to deal with the personal needs of dying persons, and in fact, seems to be characterized by a marked fear of death."[1] When an individual is diagnosed as having a terminal condition and is placed into a technological institution, the potential for conflict is great. The system sees the patient as a medical challenge. It does the best it can to keep the patient alive for as long as possible. It is difficult to see the patient as a unique person who holds certain values, who respects certain ideologies, who formerly held a particular job, who is a father or mother, brother or sister, or aunt or uncle. Individuality is lost in favor of medical efficiency.

Conflict may also arise when the providers who are working to extend life regardless of the humanistic or financial cost see the patient as obstructing or sabotaging their efforts. For the patient the extension of life for a few extra days or weeks may not be an equitable trade-off for the loss of privacy, dignity, and independence. Such a case is a person with a diagnosis of cancer who is given 6 months to live provided that chemotherapy and radiation treatments are maintained. The situation is of greater scope than the medical diagnosis. The crisis has a profound

241

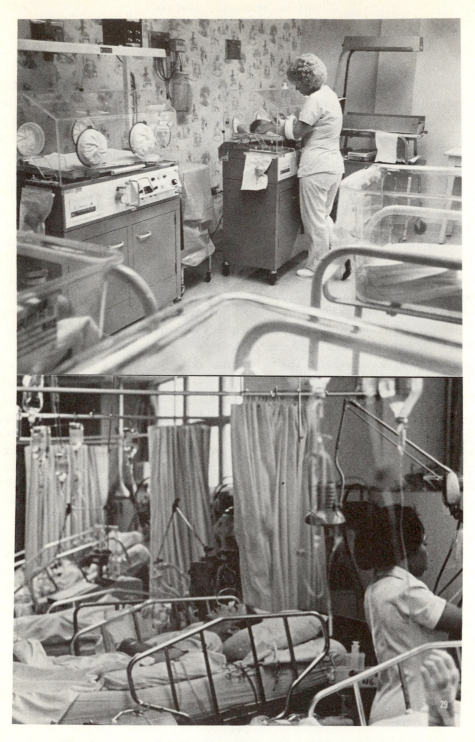

Top photo courtesy Strix Pix. Above photo courtesy Guidance Associates.

impact on the total state of affairs of the person. Diet and exercise may need to be altered. Interactions with family and friends may take on new meaning. Regular therapy with an occasional inpatient stay may bring about the loss of career and the subsequent loss of identity as John Doe, chemist, or Jane Doe, school principal. The pain created by the disease and the side effects of the treatment can precipitate psychological distress. Feelings of anxiety, guilt, fear, resentment, and anger may disintegrate self-esteem. Worry over financial obligations created by the sickness, especially if health insurance benefits are inadequate, may compound the problems. Long-time friendships may be challenged as the give-and-take of friendship becomes a one-way flow of energy. While the health care team is searching for a way to extend life, the individual is searching for a way to live the remainder of life with as much quality and peace of mind as possible. The provider and the patient have different objectives, and the means for attaining them will most certainly be different.

The diagnosis of a terminal illness has an impact that extends beyond the medical condition of the patient. Such a diagnosis has been known to cause the deterioration of family relationships. Psychiatric care has been necessary for family and close friends unable to cope with the situation. Somatic conditions such as hypertension, asthma, and ulcers have appeared. The psychosocial aspects of the medical condition have implications for the treatment being offered. It is well known that individuals do not respond similarily to medication. Similarly, not everyone will respond in like manner to a terminal illness. For health care providers knowledge of the patient is as important in deciding the nature of treatment as is knowledge of the disease. Decisions about treatment should not be based on physiology alone but on the emotional, psychological treatment should not be based on physiology alone but on the emotional, psychological, and spiritual needs of the patient as well. The impact of hospitalization is a relevant variable that must be considered in determining the course of treatment. As Sherizen and Paul concluded, "The critical aspect of the patient's situation for the family, is not the illness and death, per se, but rather, the family involvement with the dying patient."[2]

Changes related to the nature of sickness and treatment have created the need for changes within the hospital itself. Visitation is a prime example. In some instances it may be useful to limit the number of visitors, the hours of visitation, or the age of visitors. However, terminal illness would seem to be a different matter; after all, health care facilities are established to serve the needs of people, not vice versa. The most important concern of the dying patient may be close contact with family and friends regardless of institutional policy or convenience of hospital personnel.

The physical aspects of the facility are important considerations related to the quality of care. The long corridor of semiprivate rooms is probably less comforting than an arrangement more similar to the home environment. Rooms with lounging chairs, pictures on the walls, carpeting, and privacy would help to achieve this effect. A chapel in close proximity that is accessible to the patient as well as to the family would offer spiritual support. Color and texture of surfaces could help to bring about emotional calm and psychological peace. Medical equipment necessary for palliative care could be stored out of sight and reserved for use only as requested by the patient.

Health care facilities that deal with the terminally ill will need to employ nonmedical personnel. A team available to the patient might include a psychologist, a social worker, and a chaplain. Outpatient care while clients are living at home could also be coordinated. Visiting nurses could be assigned to a regular schedule of therapy offered in the home instead of the hospital. Health educators could inform clients about the nature of the sickness; treatment; implications for changes in diet or the use of alcohol, tobacco, over-the-counter drugs, or prescribed medicines for other conditions; and consumer and preparatory concerns.

According to Hine,[3] 80% of the population indicate they would like to die at home, but in practice the reverse is true. Despite the fact that health care facilities have been responsive to change in terms of patient services and procedures, some dying people still indicate a desire to spend as much time in the home as possible. Recognizing that at some point in their illness they will be forced to move to the hospital, individuals choose to prolong the time they remain at home. For some the prospect of hypodermic injections, catheters, implants, and machinery that is connected to their bodies is abhorrent. Nash[4] pointed out that patients who are in their last phase of life are not just dying; they are also living. The comforting support of family and friends in the home environment and the proper medication used only for the relief of pain may be preferable to an extension of life that is dependent on drugs, machinery, or physical modes of therapy.

In addition to the options of living at home or in the hospital, a couple of alternative facilities have begun to gain public popularity. So-called nursing homes actually exist at a variety of levels. One type is a resident facility without medical care. However, there are extended care facilities that provide complete medical care. These facilities are not hospitals in that they do not provide as wide a range of services as might be found in a community hospital. Predominantly, they serve the residence and medical needs of the elderly, some of whom are close to death and others who are fully expected to live.

Oncologic hospitals represent another alternative. Established for the treatment of cancer patients, these hospitals take advantage of many of the recommended changes mentioned earlier in the chapter. Counseling services are available, and the medical staff is prepared to deal with the psychosocial dimensions of health care. Patients are permitted to use the facility as necessary. At times they may be outpatients in need of a private room for several hours during recovery from therapy, and at times they may need to spend several days as inpatients. Ultimately, patients will live their last few days in the hospital while they receive expert palliative care.

Sanders[5] compared the reactions of people whose relative died within 7 days of the onset of illness with those whose relative died from a chronic illness. A statistically significant difference was not found. She inferred that while there may be individual differences in the reaction of these two kinds of death, the differences averaged out among participants. It would appear that hospital personnel who work in emergency rooms and intensive care units need to be as competent in dealing with the surviving family as the specialist who works in a cancer, renal dialysis, burn, or coronary care unit. Emergency room personnel should be taught how to meet the family and how to explain the condition of the patient. They should also be able to help complete the necessary paperwork. Periodic updating of patient status and comforting of relatives would help to relieve needless anxiety. Families who rush to the emergency room in response to a telephone call are deserving of the same considerations given to families who must deal with the terminal effects of a chronic disease. While the emotional climate of the emergency room may be more frantic, the human issues remain consistent despite the cause of the critical illness.

THE HOSPICE MOVEMENT

Probably the most talked-about innovation in terminal care is the evolution of a facility and a philosophy known as the hospice. The health care system in the United States has historically reinforced the notion that we are a death-denying society. As a consequence, until recently the terminally ill patient received little attention and support from health care providers, except for relief or minimization of pain. Traditionally, the goal of the medical profession has been to cure the patient. The health care delivery system is based on this premise. Generally, hospitals are designed to relate to patients in terms of a cure for their illness. However, what the terminally ill patient needs is care rather than cure. The hospice is designed to provide such care.

In medieval times, the term *hospice* referred to a way station for the traveler on a long and difficult journey. Today the term represents a movement that aims to provide terminally ill persons with a way station on their long and difficult journey through the end of the life course. The hospice is not a particular facility or building but rather a program that is designed to provide care, support services, and educational programs for the terminally ill and their families.

The hospice movement has been an outgrowth of the general dissatisfaction with the ability of the hospital to provide appropriate care for the terminally ill. For example, as stated previously the hospital is geared to cure, but the terminally ill patient needs care. The hospice is greared to provide such care for the terminally ill as well as their families. In addition, a basic tenet of the hospice philosophy is that terminally ill patients be allowed to exercise some degree of control over the remainder of their lives. In a hospital the patient has little such control. Terminally ill patients must follow a strict regimen designed to ensure that the hospital functions smoothly, which does not necessarily meet the need of the terminally ill patient.

The first modern hospice was organized in London in 1967 by Cicely Saunders. St. Christopher's Hospice has served as a model for the hospice movement that spread throughout northern Europe and the United States. Originally trained in the nursing profession, Saunders earned a medical degree to influence the way in which the health care delivery system in England cared for the dying. She believed that it was inappropriate for terminally ill patients to have to spend their last day in sterile hospital surroundings, heavily sedated, and separated from the people and life-styles that had given their lives meaning. From this first hospice, a variety of similar programs were developed in the United States. A comprehensive listing of hospices in the United States is provided below.

Directory of hospices in the United States

Arizona

Hillhaven Hospice
5504 E. Pima
Tucson, AZ   85712

California

Community Support Group—Hospice
   Concept
21 Willow Road
Menlo Park, CA   94025

Hospice of Marin
P.O. Box 72
Kentfield, CA   94904

Hospice of Santa Barbara, Inc.
Suite 11
1525 State St.
Santa Barbara, CA   93101

Kaiser-Permanente Medical Care
   Program
Southern California Permanente Medical
   Group
1505 Edgemont
Los Angeles, CA   90027

Parkwood Community Hospital
7011 Shoup Ave.
Conoga Park, CA   91304

Colorado

Penrose Hospital
2215 North Cascade Ave.
Colorado Springs, CO   80907

Connecticut

Hospice, Inc.
765 Prospect St.
New Haven, CT   06511

District of Columbia

Washington Hospice Society
1511 K St., N.W.
Washington, DC   20005

Florida

Hospice Orlando
P.O. Box 8581
Orlando, FL   32806

Georgia

Hospice Atlanta, Inc.
1055 McLynn Ave., N.E.
Atlanta, GA   30306

Illinois

Highland Park Hospital
718 Glenview Ave.
Highland Park, IL   60035

St. John's Hospital
Southern Illinois University
    School of Medicine
Department of Family Practice
P.O. Box 3926
Springfield, IL   62708

Maine

Hospice of Maine, Inc.
32 Thomas St.
Portland, ME   04102

New Hampshire

The Salemhaven, Inc.
8 Pleasant St.
Salem, NH   03079

New York

Burke Rehabilitation Center
785 Mamaroneck Ave.
White Plains, NY   10605

Haven of Schenectady
2217 Niskayuna Dr.
Schenectady, NY   12309

Hospice of Rockland, Inc.
4 Union Rd.
Spring Valley, NY   10977

Hospice at St. Luke's
114th St. and Amsterdam Ave.
New York, NY   10025

Our Lady of Lourdes Memorial Hospital
169 Riverside Dr.
Binghamton, NY   13905

North Carolina

Hospice of North Carolina, Inc.
P.O. Box 11452
Winston-Salem, NC   27106

Texas

Hospice of Southeast Texas
312 Pine St.
Orange, TX   77630

Virginia

Haven of Northern Virginia, Inc.
7300 McWhorter Pl.
Annandale, VA   22003

Wisconsin

Bellin Memorial Hospital
P.O. Box 1700
744 South Webster Ave.
Green Bay, WI   54305

The hospice program can be administered in a variety of ways. It can be a home care program, a separate autonomous facility, a department in a hospital, or a combination of the above. Regardless of the type of program, the overall goal of the hospice is to ensure that what time remains of the patient's life is free from pain, comfortable, and satisfying to the patient and family whether care is provided at a special hospice facility or at home.

Goals of hospices

The goals of the hospice will obviously vary depending on the type of program offered, the facilities available, and the nature of the staff. The St. John's Hospice, which is affiliated with the Southern Illinois University School of Medicine, divides the objectives of their hospice program into four major categories: (1) care of the terminally ill patient, (2) family support and family care, (3) staff care and development and consultation services, and (4) education.[6]

Care for the terminally ill patient. A major thrust of the hospice is the successful management of pain and suffering. The primary objective in pain control is to provide rational and realistic relief of pain, which increases the patient's quality of life rather than the length of life. (In a hospice, drugs are used for pain control, not sedation.) The hospice tries to provide a pleasant environment that gives the patient some measure of death with dignity. Care in this sense does not refer solely to the relief of physical symptoms. Care needs to be provided for the psychological, sociological, spiritual, and economic concerns of the terminally ill patient. The hospice generally provides counseling that promotes meaningful dialogue between patients and staff to help them realistically confront their death-related feelings, problems, and concerns. Such assistance is often unavailable in the traditional hospital setting.

Because of the complex nature of the hospice and terminally ill patient, it is important for services and staff to be available on a round-the-clock basis. The success of the hospice may hinge on its ability to provide appropriate medical, psychological, and nursing services when the need arises. Therefore it is important that the hospice provide day and night services for those patients who would otherwise have to be admitted to the traditional hospital inpatient facilities because of a lack of support services in the home. Care of the terminally ill patient is obviously a multidisciplinary concern. The hospice needs to blend the expertise and skills of professionals, such as nurses, doctors, social workers, and clergy, as well as volunteers to provide meaningful and realistic care.

Family support and family care. The hospice differs from the traditional hospital in that it encourages the family to become actively involved in the care of the patient.

Through a family-centered approach to care, the hospice hopes to foster a maintenance and strengthening of family ties. Hackley, Farr, and McIntier believe that "it is a unique experience to be emotionally and intellectually aware of the death process and at the same time to hear joyful laughter and delighted voices of children ring through the corridors."[7] Our attitudes toward death are learned. Therefore if children or family members are permitted to visit the terminally ill patient and observe the interaction of the hospice staff and the other family members with the patient, they may formulate a healthy attitude toward death and loss.

A second goal of the hospice in this area is to provide support services for the family. The hospice should provide bereavement care and counseling for the family. In addition, however, the hospice should educate the family concerning how to meet the physical, social, psychological, and spiritual needs of the patient and the family. The major focus here is to preserve the integrity of the family and to provide support for their needs and concerns.

Staff care, development, and consultation services. The staff of a hospice faces a problem somewhat unique in the health care field. The staff must form close human relationships with terminally ill patients and their families. This is the foundation of the hospice concept. Because of the nature of their work, hospice personnel often need support services that are not usually found in other health care agencies. Therefore the hospice needs to provide consultation and support services for its staff, as well as to provide a mechanism to maintain the morale and mental health of the hospice team. The death of a patient causes grief among the staff. Unless these grief experiences are properly verbalized, the staff may suffer from the burnout syndrome.

This is an area in which further study needs to be done. Research needs to be conducted concerning the types of support services needed by the hospice staff, the types of work loads that increase the level of efficiency of the staff, and the types of programs that increase staff morale.

Education. The educational component of the hospice has two focuses: the inservice education of the staff and the education of the community with regard to the goals and services of the hospice. Because the hospice concept is a relatively recent concern, there is still a great deal that the staff can learn with regard to the social, psychological, and spiritual aspects of death as well as new techniques for the control of pain and other symptoms.

The hospice can also serve as a vehicle to educate the medical community on new modalities that emphasize a holistic approach in the care of the terminally ill. Exposing medical students and concerned professionals to the hospice model of care is an important first step to enhancing the status of the hospice.

The second educational function of the hospice is to educate the community concerning the nature, role, and function of the hospice concept in the health care delivery system. Through the development and coordination of community-based educational activities, such as courses, speeches, news releases, and talks with visitors, the hospice can inform the community of its mission, and it is hoped, enhance its stature in the community.

Team concept. The hospice concept of patient care advocates and necessitates a team approach. For a hospice to function smoothly it has to blend the expertise and skills of professionals from a wide range of disciplines as well as volunteers and family members. The members of an ideal health care team and a brief description of their function is outlined below[7a]:

Nurses: The nursing staff is a vital component to the successful operation of the hospice. They provide much of the immediate and consistent care. The nurse must have an affection for people and be able to work as a member of a team. A major function of the nurse is to enhance patients; ability for self-care and to allow patients to gain some measure of control over the remainder of their lives. In essence the nurse tries to help create an atmosphere that allows patients to live out their lives and die with dignity.

Physicians: The major role of the physician is to ensure that patients receive the appropriate treatment modalities for their conditions and to provide for the relief of pain and symptoms. In addition, the physician can be involved in patient support, education, and research aspects of the hospice and administrative concerns.

Volunteers: The volunteers generally work under the supervision of the hospice staff. The volunteer may work with the patient or families in the hospice or the home to provide home care, consultation, educational services and bereavement follow-up. The volunteers should come from a wide range of ethnic and professional backgrounds and have a diversity of talents, interests, and skills. The best volunteers seem to be able to communicate in a calm, unobtrusive manner with the patient and the families.

Social workers: The social worker helps the family deal with bereavement concerns and financial and legal problems, such as wills, estates, and pensions. The social worker should have a strong background in counseling and be able to work as a member of the support team.

Chaplain: The chaplain should allow for religious dialogue and expression but be neither a provider nor a promoter of a specific religion. The chaplain must be a skilled listener who helps the patient identify and deal with spiritual problems.

Physiotherapist: The major purpose of the physiotherapist is to plan a regimen of acitivty to enhance the patient's ability to function in light of diminishing skills.

The physiotherapist trains volunteers and family members to perform appropriate skills in the home.

Dietitian: The dietitian, obviously, provides for the nutritive care of the patient. However, the dietitian should provide tasty and attractive meals that help to enhance the patient's quality of life. This is one area in which the care team should be sensitive to patients' needs to have some control over their lives.

Hospice director or administrator: The function of the administrator is to coordinate the services of the hospice and develop appropriate research and evaluative activities. In addition, the hospice director should perform public relations and educational activities necessary to enhance the image and public support of the hospice.

Educational coordinator: The education coordinator needs to monitor the educational activities of the team members to ensure that the educational goals of the hospice are being met and to avoid the duplication of services. Also the educational director provides training courses for the staff, coordinates inservice training of volunteers, and organizes educational materials.

Pharmacist: The pharmacist develops, coordinates, and supervises all pharmaceutical services. The pharmacist keeps records on the patients and consults with the educational coordinator on appropriate home care procedures.

CONCERNS OF DYING PATIENTS AND THEIR FAMILIES

The dying and their families have a variety of concerns, fears, and questions. Many of these concerns deal with interpersonal issues, for example, "How should I interact with my terminally ill mother?" or, "When should I tell my wife she has a terminal illness?" Others deal with religious concerns, for example, "Is there life after death?" Some of the more salient of these concerns will be discussed in the remainder of this chapter.

Life after life

In 1975 Raymond Moody[8] wrote a book entitled *Life After Life.* The book told of the experiences of people who had come to the edge of death and described a peaceful altered state of consciousness. The book was immensely popular and received the attention of television, newspaper, and magazines. The following experiences were commonly reported[8]:

1. A panoramic flashback of life events.
2. Hearing a strange noise—sometimes a ringing and sometimes a buzzing.

251

3. Moving through a long dark tunnel, often described as being part of another dimension—this experience is known as transcendence.
4. Perceiving the situation from outside the body as an onlooker and occasionally witnessing the efforts to revive the body—this phenomenon has been called autoscopy.
5. Approaching a border that separates earthly life from the next life.
6. Being met by dead relatives, friends, or strangers who were present to assist them through the dying process or to indicate it was not yet their time to die.
7. Feeling the presence of a warm spirit—sometimes a bright light—with whom the individual communicated nonverbally.
8. Being apart from the frantic situation, the subjects experienced serenity, peace, and calm.
9. The person realized it was not yet time to relinquish earthly form and returned to the body.

Sabom and Kreutziger[9] reported similar findings. In their study 50 patients ranging in age from 19 to 76 years who had suffered from a documented near-fatal crisis resulting in unconsciousness were interviewed. Sabom and Kreutziger found that only 11 patients had definite recollections of the near-death experience, and their experiences were limited to autoscopy and transcendence. They also observed that during autoscopy patients reported clear details of events in the operating room (or emergency room), with accuracy substantiated by those present in the room. Although it may seem strange, the patients reported they were not in pain. Rather, they experienced a feeling of well-being that was described as a state of harmony with the universe. Consciousness became a mystical extension of the body to which they were no longer attached. Obviously, these findings differ both qualitatively and quantitatively from Moody's work.

These reports stimulated tremendous fascination among the general public. They created a tangible spark of hope about life after death. The religious community also took keen interest in the material. Frederick Holck,[10] a religious historian, examined the secular literature for previous reports of these experiences. He reasoned that if these events were true happenings, their presence in the literature would not be limited to current writings. Holck found previous information to substantiate the recent reports. Notably, out-of-body experiences, the awareness of a spiritual body, a reunion with ancestors, and recognition of a border between earthly existence and some other existence appeared in religious writings.

The phenomenon known as panoramic memory is interesting because of the many people who have reported its occurrence. In the face of life-threatening danger, such as in drowning or accidents, the individual experiences a vivid recall of significant past events both pleasant and unpleasant.[11] In some instances the events occur in chronological or reverse chronological order, yet in other instances the events seem to occur in a random sequence. Interestingly, the flashback seems to bring forth the same emotions that were present when the event took place. The events pass in review in rapid succession and people have likened the situation to watching a slide presentation of their own life. The characteristics that distinguish the flashback from mere recollections of life that take place during daydreaming are the high speed and the vividness or clarity of detail of the experience. Even remote memories produce recent familiarity. The images appear without conscious effort or control, and although the experience is pleasurable, persons feel a sadness associated with the loss of the life they are reviewing.

Several possible physiological and psychological explanations for the near-death phenomena have been advanced in recent years. The lack of oxygen to the brain may be responsible for some experiences outlined by Moody and others. Also, the notion of self-fulfilling prophecy may influence near-death experiences. If the person believes in an afterlife or that everyone experiences a panoramic review of their life, then these experiences may occur.

Because of experiences related to life after life and panoramic flashback, new organizations have been created. The Second Attempt at Living is a nonprofit group dedicated to the conviction that human life is eternal. Lumena was established to provide opportunities for those who have experienced near-death phenomena to share their feelings with others and to promote public awareness of these occurrences.

The right to be told about a terminal illness

Prior to 1970 the majority of physicians did not favor telling a patient about a terminal condition. In a recent study researchers found that more than 80% of the study population would want to be told about their condition if they had a terminal disease.[12] This was true regardless of age, sex, race, level of education completed, or socioeconomic status. In another study Carey and Posavac[13] conducted four parallel surveys to compare the attitudes of physicians, nurses, hospital chaplains, and college students with regard to patients being told about their terminal prognosis. They found that the attitudes of physicians were not significantly different from the attitudes of the other three groups. All groups were in agreement that patients who request information have the unqualified right to know the truth about their condition. Additionally, they found that the vast majority of all participants would want to be told this information by a physician and believed that the physician should tell a patient regardless of the wishes of the patient's spouse.

Patients who are not told of their terminal prognosis will not be adequately prepared, both psychologically and financially. Also not informing the patient or family of the patient's prognosis may create a mutual game of pretense in which both the patient and the family are aware of the prognosis but neither wants to inform the other for fear of causing unnecessary emotional stress. Obviously, for all parties concerned a clear, sensitive explanation of the patient's condition can be a positive step toward death with dignity.

EMOTIONAL SUPPORT SYSTEMS

As previously mentioned, terminal illness affects the entire family. It is not simply a medical conditon of a single human being. Rather, it represents a traumatic event, perhaps the most horrendous event a family will ever face. Terminal illness has been responsible for marital disharmony, divorce, suicide, emotional crises popularly known as nervous breakdowns, and somatic distress. The health care system will need to offer support services to all those people affected by critical illness. Carey[14] asked a population of widows and widowers to describe the support given by providers within the hospital setting. Physicians were considered to be of great help by 47% of the widowers and 40% of the widows. They were considered to be of great help when they were honest, compassionate, not hurried, and comforting to the family. Meanwhile 27% of the widowers and 33% of the widows expressed disappointment in physicians and alleged that the physician failed to be honest, avoided the family, and was unconcerned.

In this same study nurses fared somewhat better. They were considered to be of great help by about 53% of the people while complaints were registered by only about 15% of the population. It is curious that 71% of the widows found hospital chaplains to be of great help, but only 44% of the widowers responded this way. Nevertheless, only about 6% of both populations expressed disappointment in the support provided by clergy. The majority of people had no contact with a social worker, and some did not even know they were available.

Carey also studied the sources of support outside the hospital personnel. More than 80% of the widows and widowers considered the family to be of great help. Neighbors also proved to be an excellent resource with very few individuals expressing disappointment with their neighbors' support during bereavement. Visits by clergy after the death of a spouse were found to be rare, but greatly appreciated. In view of information presented in Chapter 7 about the funeral industry, it is interesting to see that about 75% of both groups found the funeral directors to be of great help. Specifically, people mentioned the following as positive attributes of the funeral director: their assistance in providing information about Social Security benefits, helping with insurance papers, being courteous and professional, and not pressuring them.

A number of groups have emerged to offer volunteer support for the bereaved. Sometimes these groups center around a specific disease like cancer or are established to serve a particular population of survivors such as widows, parents, and siblings. Some organizations have evolved for the terminally ill to share their fears and to legitimize their feelings of guilt, frustration, or anger. The best known organization of this type is called Make Today Count, founded by the late Orville Kelly.[15] More than 100 chapters are in existence throughout the United States, Canada, and Germany. By promoting openness and honesty about dying, the organization seeks to help the patient and family cope with the situation. Make Today Count hopes to improve the quality of life for all people who are faced with a serious illness. Its members also offer help to professionals who must communicate with the terminally ill. Mr. Kelly's belief is that having a terminal illness is an advantage in that everyone is going to die, but most do not know when they will die. Often this precludes adequate preparation for death. However, those who know when they are going to die are able to focus on the meaningful things in life and to live each day as fully as possible.

The Shanti Project is a community support model located in Berkeley, California. It is a voluntary counseling service for terminally ill patients and their families. It was organized in response to the emotional alienation experienced by those who face terminal illness. In concept it is similar to the suicide prevention centers. When people call and ask for help, a volunteer worker is assigned. Volunteers come from all walks of life and combine a willingness to help with emotional strength and sensitivity.[16]

It appears that the death of a child is especially hard to handle. Sanders concluded, "Thus, it can be safely said that those who experience the death of a child revealed more intense grief reactions of somatic types, greater depression, as well as anger and guilt with accompanying feelings of despair, than did those bereaved who had experienced the death of either a spouse or parent."[5] In Great Britain the Society of Compassionate Friends was organized by Simon Stevens. It is an organization composed of bereaved parents who help others deal with the loss of a child. There are currently more than 20 chapters located in the United States. The Candlelighters Foundation was similarly established to help parents of children who suffer from cancer or who have died from cancer to cope with the loss of a child.

Much of this chapter has focused on the needs of those who are dying and on their families. Providers are also in danger of suffering physical and mental consequences when interacting with critically ill patients. Even though the specialist may not be as familiar with the sick person as is the primary care physician, the constant battle with death and the persistent emotional environment takes its toll in a phenomenon known as burnout. Burnout affects people in all of the helping professions. It manifests itself as chronic physiological and psychological fatigue related to the job. Burnout is characterized by somatic conditions such as lower back pain, insomnia, headaches, shortness of breath, dizziness, tightness in the chest, and abdominal pain. The individual finds it difficult to get out of bed in the morning. While at work individuals may begin to avoid situations for which they are responsible. They become apathetic and see the job as closing in on them. Dissatisfaction with the work environment and professional relationships lead to low morale, loss of a sense of purpose, and feelings of cynicism. The appearance of a quick temper and irritability as well as being easily startled and being suspicious of colleagues are additional symptoms of burnout.

Research has begun to examine the causes of burnout, especially among nurses who work in a critical care unit of the hospital. Recently three researchers found that the staff on a palliative care unit experienced only slightly less stress related to death than a group of newly widowed women.[17] Apparently, one of the major contributors to burnout is the inability of the professional to be in control of the situation. The outcome of any critical case is dependent on many factors that are outside the control of the care giver, such as previous medical history of the patient. In some cases the patient will die no matter how proficiently knowledge and skills are applied. It is difficult to keep in mind that the care giver is not responsible for the illness or the circumstance, and it may be impossible to avoid feeling partly responsible when death occurs.

Most health care providers are empathetic, compassionate, and sensitive to the feelings of others. The death of a patient not only has significance in their professional lives but also serves as a reminder of their own mortality. Before the health care provider has a chance to recuperate from the death of one patient, another patient dies. Over the course of a prolonged period of time the individual may cross a threshold of tolerance and succumb to chronic bereavement and professional burnout.

It is likely that some physicians and nurses cope with death by removing it from the human context. Health care professionals may subconsciously build a defense against empathy to protect themselves from the emotional trauma of another person's death. Minimizing the emotional ties between patient and professional may help to insulate the spirit of the care giver. Unfortunately, this type of person tends to come across as being unconcerned and apathetic toward the patient. It appears that a delicate balance exists between emotional involvement that creates trust and maintaining an emotional distance that generates suspicion about the quality of care being offered.

Another thin edge of palliative care is the dilemma of doing too much to keep the patient alive, which produces needless suffering, versus giving up too soon. It is better to keep the patient alive and ignore the aspects of dignity, suffering, and quality of life, or is it better to treat the symptoms and allow the person to die as comfortably as possible? Is there a point when the physician or nurse knows for certain that one or the other is the correct decision?

Hoggatt and Spilka[18] found that nearly 80% of a nursing population felt that the profession places more emphasis on preservation of life than on symptomatic care of the dying. Yet many nurses reported feeling a sense of relief when the suffering was over. Thus an avoidance-avoidance dilemma has been constructed. In their efforts to prolong life nurses are fulfilling a professional ethic but contributing to suffering that is morally objectionable. On the other hand, palliative care violates a professional ethic. It would appear that both sets of principles cannot be satisfied. Once again, physical, psychological, and emotional difficulties may arise from the critical illness of another.

Most nurses feel their training does not prepare them adequately to deal with these issues. Perhaps baccalaureate course work or inservice seminars can help to ease the anxiety of critical care. However, it is unlikely that education can train nurses to control their emotions. It is likely that the hospital will need to sponsor group sessions among staff to legitimize feelings of frustration and guilt. Traditionally, people tend to deal with problems individually in the mistaken belief that asking for consultation is a sign of weakness. The hospital can facilitate communication by encouraging group discussion. Perhaps it will become necessary to alter the scheduling patterns or the staffing patterns in an effort to reduce burnout. A reward system might be established that helps to build self-esteem. Personnel can be taught the symptoms of burnout and be encouraged to offer help to others before the problem gets out of hand. Time off from work might be necessary to rebuild a supply of adaptive energy. Since burnout tends to isolate the person from colleagues, a strong unit or team approach might be successful. It is clear that hospitals must take steps to protect their personnel. The shortage of nurses and physicians is aggravated when professionals leave the field prematurely as a result of burnout.

SUMMARY

Quite often in America the death of a friend or relative does not occur until adulthood. The majority of people who die are beyond the age of 65; their children and lifelong friends have in most instances lived many years as adults. It is ironic that medical science has contributed heavily to increased longevity while at the same time it has contributed to some of the major problems associated with terminal illness. When a person is diagnosed as having a terminal condition, and this happens more and more each year, the best medical care in the world is available. However, it is offered in large institutions by specialists who are strangers to terminally ill patients and their families.

While the disease itself is being treated expertly, the human aspects of the situation are often neglected. Meaningfulness of the final days of life and the culmination of relationships may be sacrificed on behalf of the medical treatments necessary to prolong life. Death with dignity may yield to technological advances that are capable of prolonging life at the expense of privacy, independence, and freedom from pain. The current state of affairs also takes a toll on the specialists who deal with critically ill patients day after day. The family physician would have experienced an occasional death but this was balanced with recovery by other patients. The physician and other providers of care had time to adjust before they faced another death. Bereavement was an occasional event. For the specialist, though, bereavement tends to be chronic. Everyday of the week a patient may die or be diagnosed as critically or terminally ill. The physician or nurse has to deal with grieving families on a continual basis. Eventually the human psyche may no longer be able to tolerate this situation and the body responds with somatic or emotional symptoms that have come to be known as burnout. New ways are needed to help the providers cope with the constant stress of death and dying.

It is likely that some of the techniques that have begun to emerge for handling terminal illness will continue to evolve. Support groups for the patient, the family, and the provider of care will gain popularity. So too will alternative centers for care such as the hospice and the oncologic center. Palliative care will need to face issues related to the type of medications offered to patients and the determination of when palliative care should replace the idealistic goal of restoration and healing. As the major causes of death gradually shift and as the ability to predict the time of death increases, the mode of handling the terminally ill population will also need to adjust to meet the situation and to offer death with dignity to everyone who suffers from a terminal ilness.

MAJOR CONCEPTS RELATED TO DYING AND DEATH IN THE UNITED STATES

- The ways in which Americans respond to death have changed over the past century.
- A terminally ill patient's environment, including clinical surroundings and emotional support, influences his or her mental health.
- The patient's reaction to a terminal prognosis is influenced by a variety of factors.
- Quality care for the terminally ill includes both physical and emotional support.
- The changes in the causes of death in the United States over the past 75 years have influenced the ways in which the health care delivery system responds to terminal illness and death.

EDUCATIONAL ACTIVITIES RELATED TO DYING AND DEATH IN THE UNITED STATES

Title: Terminal prognosis: attitude survey

Age level: High school, college, adults

Objective: Following the completion of the attitude survey, the student will form a personal position statement concerning how and when to inform a family member of a terminal prognosis.

Materials: Attitude survey

Directions: Ask students to complete the attitude survey outlined below. After the students complete the survey, discuss each of the items. Ask the students to formulate a personal position statement on whether or when they would inform a family member of a terminal prognosis.

Terminal prognosis: attitude survey

Please respond to the following questions according to criteria outlined below:

SA=Strongly agree   A=Agree   U=Undecided
D=Disagree   SD=Strongly disagree

_____ If I had a terminal illness, I would want to be informed.

_____ It is important for the family members to be informed of a terminal prognosis.

_____ The physician is the best person to inform a patient of a terminal illness.

_____ If patients are informed of a terminal prognosis too soon, they will lose the will to live.

_____ I would feel uncomfortable informing a family member that he or she had a terminal illness.

_____ Telling family members about a terminal prognosis of another relative would be a personally difficult responsibility.

_____ I would prefer to die suddenly.

_____ Patients who are informed of a terminal prognosis are better able to prepare for their own death.

_____ Knowing that their illness is terminal can improve communications between patients and their families.

_____ The decision to inform the patient of a terminal illness should be made on a case-by-case basis.

Title: The cemetery as a death education resource

Age level: Elementary grades

Objective: At the completion of the activity the students will be able to (1) identify the change in life expectancy in the past century, (2) write their epitaph, and (3) identify the change in childhood death rate during the past century.

Materials: Cemetery, appropriate worksheets

Directions: There are a variety of activities that can be developed using the cemetery as a resource. Most of these activities can be integrated into other subject area or included as part of the death education program.

Activity 1

After having students look at headstones in a cemetery, ask them to record the ages at death for 10 men and 10 women from the following time periods: (1) before 1900, (2) 1900 to 1950, and (3) after 1950. Ask students to calculate an average age for men and women for each time period. Once the students have completed the tasks, the following questions may help to facilitate a follow-up discussion:

- Is there any difference in the average ages of men and women?
- Is there any difference in the average ages of men and women in various times?
- If there are differences, why do you think one group lived longer?
- What do you think is the average age of people dying today?

Activity 2

Ask students to cite 10 epitaphs they find in the cemetery. Have them identify their favorite and funniest epitaph. As a follow-up activity, ask the students to write their epitaphs.

Activity 3

Ask students to identify children who have died prior to the age of 10 for each of the following time periods: (1) before 1900, (2) 1900 to 1950, and (3) 1950 to present. Is there a difference in the number of deaths for each period? What are some possible reasons for these differences?

Title: Debate: hospice versus hospital care versus dying at home

Age level: High school, college, adults

Objective: Following the debate the students will be able to (1) list five pros and five cons of each position and (2) select a personal course of action related to this issue.

Materials: Large newsprint, felt markers

Directions: Break the class into three groups. Group 1 will favor the hospice concept. Group 2 will favor traditional hospital care for the terminally ill. Group 3 will favor dying at home. Group 4 will comprise the panel of judges who will prepare sets of questions to ask and score the debate.

Provide all groups with adequate time to prepare for their group tasks. In addition, appropriate print materials need to be provided depending on the resources available and the age level of the group.

Ask groups 1, 2, and 3 to outline their major points on the newsprint. Review the rules of debating and then begin the debate process.

Title:	Brainstorm: support for the terminally ill
Age level:	Junior high school, high school
Objective:	Following the brainstorming activity, the students will identify the support needs of the terminally ill.
Materials:	Large newsprint, felt markers
Directions:	Divide the class into small groups. Ask each group to brainstorm their perception of the needs of the terminally ill patient. Ask each group to list their ideas on the newsprint and display them around the room. Conduct a follow-up discussion. You may want to divide the needs of the terminally ill into the following categories to facilitate discussion:

Emotional support	Financial support
Legal support	Medical support
Family support	Social support
Educational support	Religious support

Title:	Death image: trigger activity
Age level:	Elementary grades
Objective:	During the trigger activity students will draw pictures depicting their concept of death.
Materials:	Drawing paper, crayons, or felt markers
Directions:	Provide each student with the materials suggested. On side A of the drawing paper ask the children to draw a picture of their concept of death. On side B ask them to provide an explanation of their drawings. You may ask the students to describe their pictures or choose several to discuss.

Title:	A community support system for the terminally ill
Age level:	College, adults
Objective:	During the activity the students will identify a community support system for the terminally ill.
Materials:	None
Directions:	Break the class into small groups. Ask each group to research their community and identify resources that will help to meet the support needs of the terminally ill. The following needs of the terminally ill can be addressed:

Legal support	Medical support
Emotional support	Religious support
Family support	Social support
Financial support	Educational support

REFERENCES

1. Heller, D. Brian, and Schneider, Carl D.: Interpersonal methods for coping with stress: helping families of dying children, Omega **8**:323, 1977-1978.
2. Sherizen, Sanford, and Paul, Lester: Dying in a hospital intensive care unit: the social significance for the family of the patient, Omega **8**:29, 1977.
3. Hine, Virginia H.: Dying at home: can families cope? Omega **10**:175-187, 1979-1980.
4. Nash, Mary Louise: Dignity of person in the final phase of life: an explanatory story, Omega **8**:72, 1977.
5. Sanders, Catherine M.: A comparison of adult bereavement in the death of a spouse, child, and parent, Omega **10**:311-312, 1979-1980.
6. Cox, J.: Springfield (1978): St. John's Hospice, Death Education **2**:83-95, 1979.
7. Hackley, J., Farr, W., and McIntier, J.: Tucson (1977): Hillhaven Hospice, Death Education **2**:63-82, 1979.
7a. Wilson, D., Ajemian, I., and Mount, B.: Montreal (1975): the Royal Victoria Hospital palliative care service, Death Education **2**:3-18, 1979.
8. Moody, Raymond A., Jr.: Life after life, New York, 1975, Bantam Books, Inc.
9. Sabom, Michael B., and Kreutziger, S.: The experience of near death, Death Education **1**:195-203, 1978.
10. Holck, Frederick H.: Life revisited: parallels in death experiences, Omega **9**:1-11, 1978-1979.
11. Noyes, Russell, Jr., and Kletti, Roy: Panoramic memory: a response to the threat of death, Omega **8**:181-193, 1977.
12. Blumenfield, Michael, Leny, Norman G., and Kaufman, Diane: The wish to be informed of a fatal illness, Omega **9**:323:325, 1978-1979.
13. Carey, Raymond G., and Posavac, Emil J.: Attitudes of physicians on disclosing information to and maintaining life for terminal patients, Omega **9**:67-76, 1978-1979.
14. Carey, Raymond G.: Weathering widowhood: problems and adjustment of the widowed during the first year, Omega **10**:163:174, 1979-1980.
15. Kelly, Orville: Make today count, Death Education **1**:159-164, 1978.
16. Garfield, Charles A., and Clark, Rachel Ogren: The Shanti Project: a community model, Death Education **1**:397-408, 1978.
17. Vachon, M. L. S., Lyall, W. A. L., and Freeman, S. J. J.: Measurement and management of stress in health professionals working with cancer patients, Death Education **1**:365-375, 1978.
18. Hoggatt, Loretta and Spilka, Bernard: The nurse and the terminally ill patient: some perspectives and projected actions, Omega **9**:255-266, 1978-1979.

APPENDIX A

Educational activities

The following activities represent examples of general death education activities. These activities could be modified for use with a particular aspect of death education, such as euthanasia, suicide, or bereavement.

Title: Poetry, prose, and death

Age level: High school, adults

Objective: During the poetry, prose, and death activity the students will identify the poetic passage that most resembles their personal beliefs concerning death.

Materials: A variety of poems or literary thoughts regarding death

Directions: Present the students with a variety of poems or literary thoughts related to death. Ask the students to identify which one closely resembles their personal thoughts or feelings concerning death. Some sample passages are listed below*:

- A man is falling out of the sky. For just one instant more, he is a living person, a super-executive whose success one might envy. But in the next instant there will be no life in this body, nor will the body itself resemble a human being.

- The bed: not her own. The room: somebody else's. The smell of the place: certainly not home. Nothing of home is here. The other people? They do not really know her. The showy rhododendron in the lobby receives more affectionate care. What a place to be. What a place to die.

- "I felt so-o good. Really peaceful with myself and everything. Maybe this is death, I was thinking, but then what have I been afraid of all this time? If this is what it is, then I could (smiling) stay dead forever! But that figure, that person, that one-man light show I was telling you about: he just wouldn't let me stay dead. I don't know whether he said anything or not, but he blocked

*From Kastenbaum, Robert: Death, society and human experience, ed. 2, St. Louis, 1981, The C. V. Mosby Co.

263

my way and made it clear I had to go back. And I didn't want to get back into that body and get back into that life. I was just getting to enjoy myself!"

Title:	Photo essay: the life cycle
Age level:	Primary grades
Objective:	During the photo essay activity, the students will develop a photo essay that depicts various stages of the life cycle.
Materials:	Scissors, construction paper, paste, magazines, and other materials with photos of people of various ages
Directions:	Ask the students to cut out photos of people of different ages and prepare a collage or photo essay that would depict a life cycle. You may want to ask the students to identify and discuss the basic characteristics of people of different ages.

Title:	Causes of death scrapbook
Age level:	Third, fourth, and fifth grades
Objective:	As a class, the students will develop a scrapbook of newspaper clippings that classifies the causes of death.
Materials:	Newspapers, magazines, scissors, construction paper, paste
Directions:	Provide the students with information on the leading causes of death in the United States. Then ask the students to cut out newspaper and magazine clippings to include in the scrapbook. Some categories of death that may be included in the scrapbook are heart disease, cancer, accidents, communicable diseases, and childhood disorders. After the scrapbook is completed, conduct a follow-up discussion on the causes of death that are most likely to occur to people of various ages, with special attention to those that occur in elementary school–aged populations.

Title:	Your personal death inventory
Age level:	High school, college, adults
Objective:	At the completion of the inventory, the students will have assessed their personal reactions and level of preparedness for death.
Materials:	Your personal death inventory
Directions:	Provide each student with a copy of the inventory. Ask students to complete the inventory and conduct a follow-up discussion on the various points the inventory highlights.

Title:	The life cycle

Your personal death inventory

Listed below are some questions that reflect your personal interaction and beliefs concerning dying and death–related issues. Please answer yes or no to the following questions and provide appropriate clarification for each question in the space provided.

1. Would your personal life-style change drastically if you were diagnosed as having a terminal illness? If yes, explain what the changes would be.

   _____

2. Are you afraid of death? If yes, what do you think is causing this fear of death?

   _____

3. Do your family, friends, and relatives discuss death openly? If no, why do you think such discussions are taboo?

   _____

4. Have you made plans for your final days? If yes, what do such plans include?

   _____

5. Do you feel that there are some things you would like to complete before your death? If yes, what are these undone things?

   _____

6. Do you feel that there are some legal and consumer matters that you need to complete prior to your death? If yes, what are these?

   _____

7. Do you believe that there are people to whom you wish to make peace, express gratitude, praise, thank, or express love prior to your death? If yes, who are they?

   _____

Age level: Primary grades

Objective: During the activity the students will identify characteristics of living and nonliving things.

Materials: A variety of both living and nonliving plant materials, such as seeds, buds, live plants, dried leaves, twigs, vegetables, and leaves

Directions: Place all the plant materials on a table. Then ask the students to identify those that are living versus those that are not living. Ask the student to state the difference between living and nonliving things.

Depending on the developmental level of the students, use the materials to discuss the complete life cycle of a plant. You may wish to plant the seeds and the nonliving materials and compare the results.

Title: Euphemistic death language

Age level: Junior high and high school

Objective: During the euphemistic language activity, the students will brainstorm as many euphemisms as they can.

Materials: Chalkboard or easel paper

Directions: On a poster, chalkboard, or a large poster, list the following euphemisms for dying and death:

Kicked the bucket	Scared to death
Went to their reward	Never say die
Passed on	Dead center
Dead tired	Kill the ump
I wish I could die	Deadbeat
Dead wrong	Deadly sin
Killing time	

After the teacher puts the list on the chalkboard, brainstorm reasons why these euphemisms are used, and consider how they reflect our attitude toward death. Conduct a discussion on the meaning of these euphemisms. Be sure to point out that some of these sayings reflect the notion that as a society we tend not to say that someone died and that we use the words dead, die, and kill to describe ideas that may not be appropriate. Conduct a discussion focusing on how euphemistic language reflects the attitude of society toward death.

Title: Gravestone rubbings

Age level: Junior high and senior high school

Objective: Following the gravestone rubbing activity, the students will compare and contrast characteristics of various grave markers.

Materials: Newsprint, charcoal or crayons, cemetery with a variety of gravestones. It would be good to locate an old cemetery with gravestones from several eras.

Directions: Take the class on a field trip to a cemetery. Be sure to obtain permission from the cemetery proprietor or manager before taking the class there. For this activity, have individual students select a gravestone of interest. Then ask students to place a piece of newsprint over the gravestone and rub the entire surface of the newsprint with a piece of charcoal. Ask the students to hang the newsprint gravestone rubbings around the room. Conduct a discussion on the rubbings. Some possible questions may include:

What was the deceased remembered for?

What would you want to be remembered for?

Do you want a gravestone if you are buried?

    If yes, what inscription would you want on it?

What inferences can be drawn about American burial customs from different eras?

Title: Death customs around the world

Age level: Elementary, junior high and senior high school

Objective: At the completion of the death customs activity, the students will have analyzed the customs in various parts of the world.

Materials: Each class will need a sample wall chart similar to Table A-1. Students will also need a list of questions and a felt marker.

Directions: Divide the class into small groups. Allow each group to select a country from the list on the wall chart. Provide each group with a list of questions. Give each group a set period of time to find the answers to the specific questions. In some cases, you may need to supply appropriate information to each group if such information is not otherwise available.

After the wall chart is complete, conduct an appropriate follow-up discussion. Sample questions include:
How were burial customs in various countries similar?
How do burial customs in various countries differ?
Is there any custom that is consistent in all countries?
Which burial custom was unique?
Which burial customs would you want observed when you die?

Title: Death notices

Age level: Junior high and high school

Objective: At the completion of the death notices activity, the students will be able to list reasons for including death notices in newspapers and compare death notices from various regions of the United States.

Materials: Newsprint, felt markers, copies of death notices and obituaries from various parts of the country. The teacher will have to locate the death notices or have the students in the class write to friends and relatives to obtain these. If there is a college or university nearby, the periodical section may subscribe to a variety of out-of-state newspapers.

Directions: Break the students into small groups. Provide each group with newsprint and felt markers. Ask them to respond to the following questions:
What are some reasons for including death notices in the paper?
What are some similar components of death notices in different regions?
What are some different components of death notices in different regions?
Which was the most unusual death notice?
Which death notice contained the most information?
You may want to conduct a follow-up discussion on these questions. As a follow-up activity, ask students to identify the components they believe should

Table A-1. Death customs

Questions	United States	Great Britain	Japan	China	Mexico	Australia
Where are the funeral services generally held?						
Who usually attends to funeral ceremony?						
Are there any legal requirements for funerals in this country?						
What is the most common method of transporting the body?						
Are there any customs peculiar to this country?						
How does the community express their condolences in this country?						
What are the mourning customs in this country?						
What is the most common method of body disposal?						
What are the most common beliefs concerning life after death?						
What procedures are taken to prepare the body for burial?						
List any other findings of interest.						
List what you feel is the most unusual custom.						

be included in a death notice. Using this list, ask students to write their own obituaries on newsprint. Hang the newsprint around the room as examples.

Title:	Fear inventory: implications for death and dying
Age level:	Junior high and high school
Objective:	During the activity the students will examine personal fears and discuss how the non-death-related fears have death and dying implications.
Materials:	Each student will need a fear inventory form.
Directions:	Give each student a copy of the fear inventory. Ask them to complete the inventory following the directions provided. Conduct a follow-up discussion that highlights the different fears students have and which of those fears relate directly to death. Also discuss with students the emotions that may be of a similar nature for death and non-death-related fears.

Fear inventory

Rank each of the following events, objects, or animals according to your personal level of fear. Please use the definitions for levels of fear listed below.

HF = High fear, something that you avoid in all cases.

MF = Moderate fear, something that causes fear that you avoid if possible.

LF = Low fear, something that causes a little fear, but something you would not avoid.

NF = No fear, something that does not cause fear and you would freely approach.

_____ Loaded guns
_____ Sudden noises
_____ Sick people
_____ Insects
_____ Shots
_____ Vampire bats
_____ Falling down a set of stairs
_____ Amusement rides
_____ Strange dogs
_____ Fire
_____ Walking in cemeteries
_____ Public speaking
_____ Being alone at night
_____ Deep water
_____ The sight of blood
_____ Total darkness
_____ Death
_____ Moving to a new home
_____ Pregnancy
_____ Seeing rodents (rats or mice)
_____ Arguments with friends

_____ Automobile accidents
_____ Going to the dentist
_____ Seeing dead people
_____ Heights
_____ Visiting a friend in a hospital
_____ Death of a loved one
_____ Going to funerals
_____ Flying in an airplane
_____ Watching spiders
_____ Going to the doctor for a physical exam
_____ Being in enclosed spaces
_____ Failing a test at school
_____ Other, specify

_____

_____ Other, specify

_____

_____ Other, specify

_____

Title:	Questionnaire about death
Age level:	Junior high and high school, college, adults
Objective:	During and following the activity, the students will identify and discuss fears, attitudes, and opinions related to dying and death.
Materials:	Death attitudes and opinions survey. (Excerpted from the full questionnaire in Schneidman, Edwin: You and death, Psychology Today, pp. 43-80, June 1971.
Directions:	Provide each student with a copy of the questionnaire and ask them to complete it as honestly as possible. Be sure to inform the students that there are no correct or incorrect answers to the questions. The purpose of the activity is to share opinions, thoughts, beliefs, fears, and attitudes related to dying and death. Some sample discussion questions include the following:

What has influenced your thoughts and opinions about death?
Which question was the most difficult to answer?
What are some different concepts your classmates have regarding death?
Why did you choose a particular method of burial?
What question would you want to know how the other students answer?

Death attitudes and opinions survey

Please answer the following items. Keep in mind there are no correct or incorrect responses. The purpose of the items is to allow students to share opinions, beliefs, and attitudes related to death.

1. Which of the following most closely relates to your personal concept of the meaning of death?
   a. The beginning of a spiritual afterlife
   b. The beginning of a nonspiritual afterlife
   c. The termination of all life processes
   d. The end of existence as we know it but the survival of the spirit
   e. I have not formulated a personal concept
   f. Other (specify) _____

2. How frequently do you think about your own death?
   a. Often (once a day)
   b. Frequently
   c. Occasionally
   d. Rarely
   e. Never

3. How frequently do you think about the death of a close friend or relative?
   a. Often (once a day)
   b. Frequently
   c. Occasionally
   d. Rarely
   e. Never

---

4. A variety of factors influence personal attitudes about death. Of the following, which most influenced your present attitude about death?

   a. Personal experience
   b. Mourning rituals, for example, wakes, funerals, and memorial services
   c. Religious beliefs
   d. Readings on thanatology
   e. Death-related presentations in the popular media

5. Which of the following aspects of death do you find most distasteful?

   a. I could no longer perform family roles.
   b. I could no longer perform social roles.
   c. I could no longer have any experiences.
   d. The uncertainty of what will happen to me.
   e. The grief I will cause for my friends and relatives.
   f. The pain sometimes associated with dying.
   g. Other (please specify) _____.

6. When you think about your own death or are confronted by situations that require you to assess your own mortality, how do you feel? (Circle all that apply.)

   a. Anxious
   b. Fearful
   c. Without purpose
   d. Sad
   e. Depressed
   f. Happy to be alive
   g. Other (specify) _____.

7. If you were diagnosed as having a terminal illness, how would you want this information processed?

   a. I would want the physician to inform me so I could tell my family.
   b. I would want the physician to explain the terminal prognosis to me and my family separately.
   c. I would not want to know that I had a terminal illness.
   d. I would not want my family to know that I had a terminal illness.

8. If a person is seriously ill, what efforts should be taken to keep the person alive?

   a. The amount of effort given should be appropriate for the person's age, mental status, physical condition, and chances of resuming a normal lifestyle.
   b. Every effort should be made to keep the person alive regardless of the situation.
   c. The person should be allowed to die a natural death after reasonable care is given.

9. How important do you believe that a traditional funeral, including practices such as embalming and providing a wake and graveside service, is for the survivors?
   a. Very important, has therapeutic value for the community
   b. Only has significance for close family and friends
   c. Undecided
   d. Has little importance
   e. Has no importance

10. How do you want your remains disposed of when you die?
    a. Traditional burial
    b. Cremated
    c. Donated to science
    d. I would let my survivors decide

11. How much money would you spend on your own funeral or body disposal?
    a. Less than $500
    b. Between $500 and $1,000
    c. Between $1,000 and $1,500
    d. Between $1,500 and $2,000
    e. Between $2,000 and $3,000
    f. More than $3,000

Modified from Schneidman, Edwin: You and death, Psychology Today **4:**67-72, August, 1970.

Title: Plants are living things

Age level: Elementary grades

Objective: During the activity, the students will (1) grow two plants in the classroom, (2) observe and discuss the changes that occur over a 3-month period, (3) write a progress report on each plant, and (4) devise a list of differences between living and dead plants.

Materials: Planting, potting soil, pots

Directions: Ask each student to plant and observe the growth and development of plants over a 3-month period. To mark the progress, the teacher may wish to conduct weekly discussions on living things. Some sample questions include the following:
What does it mean to be alive?
How do we know our plants are alive?
What do plants use for food?
How does water help keep the plants alive?
What would happen to the plants if they had no water or food?
A week before discussing death, ask each student to mark their plants *A* and *B*.

The students will be instructed to properly water plant *A* and give plant *B* no water. Ask the students to watch each plant and record the changes.

On the first day of the death education unit, conduct a discussion related to what happened to the plants that received no water. Suggested discussion questions might include the following:

Why did the plants die?

What happened to the plant as it was dying?

Can the plant come alive again?

What is the difference between the living and the dead plant?

Ask students to write a progress report on their plants. End the report with a class discussion of living versus nonliving things.

Title:	Death of animals
Age level:	Elementary grades
Objective:	Following the death of animals activity, the students will (1) have listened to the reading of the book *The Dead Bird*, (2) discuss their feelings and reactions to the book, (3) discuss what it means to die, (4) list emotions people have when their pet dies, and (5) draw a picture of themselves and their possible reaction to the death of a pet.
Materials:	Drawing paper, crayons, *The Dead Bird*, by Margaret Brown, New York, 1958, Young Scott Books.
Directions:	Read the book or any book of a similar nature to the class. Discuss with the children how they reacted to the death of a bird. Suggested questions include the following:

How did the children know the bird was dead?

What did they do with the bird when it died?

How did they feel, what emotion did they display when the bird died?

Will the bird every fly again? Why not?

Conduct a class discussion about what it means to die and the emotions people show when a pet dies. Ask the students to share personal experiences on the death of a pet. Ask the students to draw pictures that express how they would feel if their pets died. Ask the children to share their drawings and discuss the emotions in the drawings.

Title:	Memories are really, really me
Age level:	Elementary grades
Objective:	During the activity, the students will (1) develop a collage of pictures that remind them of someone, (2) discuss their collages and explain what some of the pictures mean, (3) watch the film *In My Memory* and discuss how the family dealth with the death of the grandmother, and (4) discuss how they think they would like to be remembered.

Poster paper, paste, pictures, scissors, film: *In My Memory,* Bloomington, Ind., 1973, National Instructional Television Center.

Directions: Ask the students to develop a collage that reminds them of people they know. Ask each student to present their collage to the class and discuss the thoughts or memories associated with it.

Show the film *In My Memory*. Discuss how the family dealt with the death of the grandmother. The following are some sample questions:

What did Linda remember most about her grandmother?

Was Linda able to have a good time again after her grandmother died?

Were Linda's memories happy or sad?

Why did Linda play with her old lady doll?

Ask students to sit in a circle and discuss the memory they have about a pet or person that they knew who had died. Ask the following questions:

What kind of special memories do you have?

How do these memories make you feel?

How do people support each other with feelings?

Title: Death-related crossword puzzle

Age level: Junior high and senior high school

Objective: While completing the crossword puzzle, the students will define various death-related terms.

Materials: Crossword puzzle

Across

1. A building or room for storage of cremation urns
2. Exemption of death through everlasting life
3. Treatment of a body to preserve it for the viewing
4. A legal declaration that makes known the final wishes of the deceased
5. A method of body disposal that reduces the body to ashes
6. Public notification of a person's death, usually having a short biography
7. A dead person
8. Removing an organ from one person and giving it to another
9. Literally, means a good death
10. State of being brought about by the death (loss) of another
11. Customs and rituals related to death

Down

1. A public official who decides whether the cause of death is natural, accidental, suicide, or homicide
2. The person who prepares bodies for disposal and makes arrangements related to the funeral ceremony
3. The assets and liabilities left by a person at death
4. Physiologic changes among survivors of the deceased

274

5. An underground chamber used as a burial place
6. An official record of death that indicates cause(s) of death, place of death, and time of death
7. A vehicle used to transport the corpse for the final disposal
8. A speech praising the life of the deceased
9. Examination performed on the deceased to determine cause of death
10. Person who carries the coffin at a funeral

Title: Values and death: a position paper

Age level: High school

Objective: At the completion of the activity, the students will have formulated a personal position statement on values and death-related issues.

275

Materials:	None
Directions:	Have students prepare a position paper on one of the following topics:

        Capital punishment
        Abortion
        Euthanasia
        Television violence
        Gun control
        Nuclear power

Make sure students consider both sides of the issue and then take a stand that describes their personal feelings. Students might be required to make an oral presentation to describe the issues or their viewpoint.

Title:	Cryogenics
Age level:	High school
Objective:	Following the cryogenics activity, the student will (1) develop a definition of cryogenics, (2) outline the future implications of cryogenics, and (3) discuss the implications of life change on health and happiness.
Materials:	None
Directions:	After a discussion on cryogenics, have students consider the following questions:

1. Project into the future 50 years. What will life be like in the twenty-first century?
2. What new skills or knowledge will the time traveler need to function effectively?
3. What new values do you think will require adjustment?
4. What was life like 50 years ago compared with today?
5. What were the most difficult issues for people born 50 years ago to cope with during the recent past?
6. Ask a few senior citizens to describe their feelings about changes that occur throughout a lifetime. What techniques have they used to adapt successfully?
7. What are the implications of life change on health and happiness?

Title:	*Run For Your Life*
Age level:	Junior high school
Objective:	During the activity, the students will identify what they would do if they had a limited time to live.
Materials:	None
Directions:	Several years ago, there was a television program entitled *Run For Your Life.* Each week consisted of an exciting episode of a man who had been told he had 1 year to live. Rather than focusing on the eventual death, the leading character

chose to maximize his daily living with adventure and fulfillment of lifelong dreams. He decided that the someday he had looked forward to was now.

Have students complete the following:
1. What are the three major objectives you would like to accomplish in life?
2. Name the people you would most want to spend time with.
3. Prepare a list of unfinished business.
4. How would you take care of these unfinished needs?
5. What arrangements would you make for your funeral?
6. As a healthy person who is not likely to die within the year, consider the information you have provided yourself. Are there any implications for living or changes that you might want to implement?

Title:	*Future Shock*
Age level:	High school
Objective:	Following the viewing of the film *Future Shock,* New York, 1972, McGraw-Hill Text Films, the students will develop a personal plan of action to live each day to the fullest.
Materials:	None
Directions:	Show the film (or have students read the book) *Future Shock* by Alvin Toffler, New York, 1971, Random House, Inc. In small group format have students consider the following questions.

1. What is the primary meaning of future shock?
2. What are the physiological and psychological consequences?
3. What can individuals do to minimize these consequences?
4. What can individuals do to help other people see the value of living each day to the fullest?

Title:	Religious aspects of death
Age level:	High school
Objective:	After listening to the guest speakers, the students will compare and contrast various religious views on death.
Materials:	None
Directions:	Invite several members of the clergy into class to discuss a variety of religious concepts related to death. Topics for discussion may include:

Historical perspective
Mourning rituals and customs, including the funeral
Concepts related to after life
The role of pastoral counseling
Organ transplantation and body donation

Following the class, assign students to prepare a reaction paper on the topics presented.

Title:	The life cycle through pictures
Age level:	Junior high school
Objective:	After the activities, the student will have (1) discussed the life cycle process and (2) developed a personal life cycle time line.
Materials:	Poster paper, scissors, photos, paste
Directions:	As an assignment, have students bring to class their early childhood pictures. Pictures of grandparents and parents when they were children would also be appropriate.

Discuss the life cycle, pointing out major events that occur during various phases. Have students create a time line using their own birth as the starting point and death as the ending point on the continuum. Ask students to place

Example of life cycle time line

Possible life cycle events	Age (years)	Life cycle events
	Birth	
	1	
	2	
	3	
	4	
	5	
	6	
	7	Moved to Cleveland
	8	
	9	Broke arm
	10	
	11	
	12	
	13	
	14	Started high school
	15	
	16	Sixteenth birthday
	17	
Graduation, start college	18	
	19	
	20	
	21	
Graduate from college, start new job	22	
	23	
	24	
Marry	25	
	26	
	27	
	28	
First child born	29	

278

major events along the time line. Points of interest might include graduation, marriage, birth of children, major events in the lives of their children, occupational promotions, retirement, and death. Have the students discuss their time line with other students in small groups. Identify trends or patterns of the life cycle in our culture.

APPENDIX B

Annotated bibliography

Appendix B presents an annotated bibliography of selected works. We believe that the articles, books, and other materials referenced in this chapter are germane to the death educator. As such this appendix provides an overview of the materials available in the field and is not intended to be comprehensive in scope.

We would like to thank David G. Bower II, School Health Educator, Area High School, Williamsport, Pennsylvania, for his assistance in the development and organization of the annotated bibliography.

Ames, L.B.: Death, Instructor **78**:59-118, January 1978.

Ames discusses the need to include death education in the curriculum but that the topic is often avoided. All too often when confronted with death, teachers do little because they fear they will add to the child's distress. Or they are unwilling to contradict something taught at home or having problems in resolving personal conflicts or feelings about death. Ames believes that death education should not be avoided to spare the child grief and that the child should be allowed a forum to express thoughts and feelings about death.

Bailis, Lawrence A.: Death in children's literature: a conceptual analysis, Omega **8**:295-303, 1979.

Bailis provides an analysis of the concept of death portrayed in children's literature. He analyzed 40 books and found that each could be classified under one of the following conceptions of death: immortality, inevitability, and the inherent effects of death. Bailis found that there was a tendency for these books to display death in the context of ongoing existence. The article provides interesting and useful reading for the educators who want to incorporate such literature into the death education curriculum.

Balkin, Ester, Epstein, Carole, and Bush, David: Attitudes toward classroom discussions of death and dying among urban and suburban children, Omega **7**:183-189, 1976.

Balkin, Epstein, and Bush asked 50 black inner-city children and 50 white suburban children what their views were of discussing death in the classroom. The results were that suburban upper middle-class children were more likely to believe that issues related to dying and death should be included in the classroom discussions. Also urban children did not want to discuss death because they had a fear that bad things would happen or that they would experience unwanted emotions while suburban children generally did not want to discuss death because of a fear of unwanted emotions. The authors discuss some related implications for death education.

Barton, David, and Crowder, Miles: The use of role playing techniques as an instructional aid in teaching about dying, death and bereavement, Omega **6**:243-250, 1975.

    Barton and Crowder believe that role-playing activities are useful educational tools to teach health care professionals about dying and death. Role-playing activities are especially useful for reevaluating stereotypes, observing behaviors, and working through role conflicts. This article provides examples of useful role-playing vignettes.

Barton, David, Crowder, Miles, and Flexner, John: Teaching about dying in a multidisciplinary student group, Omega **10**:265-270, 1979.

    Barton, Crowder, and Flexner discuss a number of dimensions that emerged in the course of their dying and death class to students from various academic disciplines. They found that the group process proved to be the most important aspect of the course, and accordingly, more time was devoted to that experience. The authors believed that the course provided a vehicle for students to examine their roles and transactions with death and to devise a personal plan of action for coping with the death of a patient or client. In the development of such a plan students came to the realization that caring for the dying was an interdisciplinary and mutual support effort.

Berg, D.W., and Daugherty, G.W.: Teaching about death, Today's Education **62**:47, March 1973.

    Berg and Daugherty highlight the need for death education and discuss historical precedents for this need. They believe that not too many years ago dying and death were a natural part of the total family life cycle. Because there were more extended families and the dying process usually took place in the home, young people were able to view the process of dying, death, grief, and bereavement as a natural part of the total life cycle. Today the dying process is generally removed from the family experience. This void must be filled through death education if society is to retain a proper perspective toward the value of life.

Bernstein, B.E.: Lawyer and counselor as an interdisciplinary team: interfacing for the terminally ill, Death Education **1**:277-291, 1977.

    When a person dies without a will, the difficulties are enormous. This study examines the need for mental health professionals to consult and prepare the client and family for interviews with lawyers. Also discussed is the need for assessing how the lawyer ensures that the family's emotional needs and legal problems are both considered.

Bernstein, Joanne: Loss and how to cope with it, New York, 1977, The Seabury Press, Inc., 151 pages.

Bernstein's book is written for a variety of professions and age groups. She expresses personal feelings about her experience with loss and bereavement. The book also has much factual information and definitions of terms with which most people are not familiar. Chapters that deal with particular feelings that people may express when a death occurs are included as well as a concise appendix with references that would appeal to all age levels. In the bibliography are listed films on death, resources, and service agencies. The book presents a sensitive, informative, and realistic picture of coping with loss.

Bertman, Sandra L.: Workshops in caring: a first module, Death Education **3**:271-281, 1979.

Bertman explores attitudes and concerns of nursing staff members regarding the elderly, illness, and death. *Workshops in Caring* introduces techniques and materials that enhance participants to share feelings. Direction is also given to what facilitates and inhibits open relationships between staff members and the elderly or terminally ill.

Birx, C.R.: Concept of death presented in contemporary realistics children's literature: a content analysis, doctoral dissertation, Flagstaff, 1979, Northern Arizona University.

Birx selected 42 books that deal with death and children's literature to determine the concepts of death presented to various age groups. The readability of the books was also evaluated. This study sought to gauge the appropriateness of the concepts presented to various age levels. The results indicated that in general the basic concepts of death for the various age groups were not adequately covered in the selected sample of books. Birx concluded that books on death and dying are available for various interest and readability levels.

Black, P.: Criteria for brain death, Postgraduate Medicine **57**(2):69-74, 1975.

Black discusses criteria for determining brain death. Special attention is given to the recommendations of the Harvard Medical School's Ad Hoc Committee to Examine the Definition of Brain Death. Some of the problems associated with the determination of death and appropriate case study examples are provided.

Bodine, George, E.: Hospice concept: a health care program to improve the quality of life for the dying and their families, Pub. No. ERIC #ED 200-842, Washington, D.C., 1980, Resources In Education.

This nine-page pamphlet describes the hospice as an alternative method of caring for the terminally ill. The article describes the delivery of care, finality of life, and holistic approach to death. A chart portrays the differences between hospital, nursing home, and hospice care.

Bohart, J.B., and Bergland, B.W.: The impact of death and dying counseling groups on death anxiety in college students, Death Education 2:381-391, 1979.

In this study Bohart and Bergland examine in vivo systematic desensitization and systematic desensitization with symbolic modeling on college students who participated in counseling groups on death and dying. All subjects were pretested and posttested on a variety of measures designed to assess death anxiety. The pretest-treatment-posttest cycle, was completed in a 6-month period. Analysis of covariance was performed on two immediate posttest questionnaires and on the follow-up questionnaire. Pretests were used as covariants. Treatment groups and control groups showed no significant differences when measured by immediate posttests or the follow-up posttest.

Brantner, J.: Positive approaches to dying, Death Education 1:293-304, 1977.

Brantner indicates that all relationships end in parting and separation; there are no exceptions to the rule, and people must first admit their own mortality if they are going to learn to cope with death positively. This paper directs the reader to look at death as a positive, healthy occurance and not as a rare and unwelcome event that has no benefits.

Breindel, Charles L., and Acree-Charis, Lee: Estimates of need for hospice services, Death Education 4:215:221, 1980.

Identifying alternative estimates of the need for hospice care service was done because of the growing interest in this country. The estimates should serve as a useful device in helping health care administrators plan implementation of hospice beds and services.

Bugen, Larry A.: Coping: effects of death education, Omega 11:175-183, 1980.

Bugen sought to evaluate the effects of one death education seminar on the coping capacities of students. Experimental (N = 24) and control (N = 30) groups were identified and given the Coping with Death Scale at a 3-week interval. For the experimental group, the results showed a significant change in the coping capacity on 23 of the 30 scale items while the control group showed significant improvement on one item only.

Bugen, Larry A.: Death and dying: theory, research, practice, Dubuque, IA, 1979, Wm. C. Brown Co., Publishers, 488 pages.

Bugen provides a comprehensive selection of readings on the psychological and sociological aspects of dying and death in America. The text is divided into three parts: individual dynamics, family, group and organizational dynamics, and community and societal dynamics. Each of these three parts includes readings on theory, research, and practice. The list of contributors includes a variety of well-respected thanatologists, including Aderman, Kalish, Kelly, Kubler-Ross, Lindemann, Schulz, and Susman. The chapter entitled "Death Education: Perspectives for Schools and Communities," by Bugen includes an instructional model for death education, goals of death education, the effects of death education, a coping with death scale, death education for the community, and emerging standards for death education. The appendixes contain a variety of excellent educational activities.

Butler, Robert N.: Need for quality hospice care, Death Education 3:215-225, 1979.

In an address delivered to the National Hospice Organization, the importance of the hospice movement in North America is stressed. Butler indicated that when people die, it should be in a supportive environment if possible. The hospice movement should also be directed to younger people as well as the elderly.

Campo, D.R.: Attitudes toward death and dying: a comparison of senior nursing students and seniors from other academic disciplines, doctoral dissertation, Hattiesburg, 1980, University of Southern Mississippi.

Campo used the Collett-Lester Fear of Death Scale to compare the death attitudes of nurses to those of students from six other disciplines. Overall, or general, fears and four components of fear, death of self, death of others, dying of self, and dying of others, were analyzed. The results showed that the nursing students had lower death fear scores, but there was no significant difference between nursing students and students from other disciplines.

The author suggested that nursing research concerning dying and death move in several directions in the future. Included among these suggestions were that studies need to consider the multidimensionality of death anxiety, studies need to determine if death fear and death anxiety are separate phenomena, experimental studies of approaches to death education need to be conducted, studies that determine the functional or behavioral consequences of death anxiety need to be conducted, and since nursing educators serve as role models, the attitudes and behaviors of faculty toward dying patients need to be explored.

Carr, Robin L.: Death, children and books, Pub. No. ERIC #ED 168-024, Washington, D.C., 1977, Resources In Education.

This 25-page annotated bibliography is intended to identify materials that may help children understand the reality of death and the emotions that accompany it. Each entry evaluates the appropriate reading level (grades K to 12) and offers a brief description of the content. The selections are subdivided into fables, fantasy, poetry, humor, realistic fiction, historical fiction, mystery, and picture books. An appendix includes a list of articles, essays, and books on children's reactions to death.

Carse, James P., and Dallery, Arlene B.: Death and soiety: a book of readings and sources, New York, 1977, Harcourt Brace Jovanovich, Inc., 472 pages.

This text provides an overview of dying and death–related issues from a sociological perspective. The readings are grouped into six sections: abortion, euthanasia, suicide, death and the law, death and dying, and death and the caring institution. The articles included are well written and would provide a valid source of reference for the death educator.

Childers, P., and Wimmer, M.: The concept of death in early childhood, Child Development **42:**1299-1301, 1971.

Childers and Wimmer believe that many researchers have studied the child's approach to life, but few have tried to assess the perpetual awareness of death that a child might have regardless of his or her emotional reaction. A study was conducted to assess the awareness of children (N = 75) aged 4 to 10 years of the universality and irrevocability of death. It was found that there were wide individual variations among the various age groups regarding the universality of death and that there was no systematic understanding on the part of the subjects that death was a function of age and the process was irrevocable.

Colton, Arthur, Gearhart, Darwin, and Janaro, Richard: A faculty workshop on death attitudes and life affirmation, Omega **4:**51-56, 1973.

The article reports on a faculty workshop devoted to the analysis of death attitudes and life affirmation as a part of faculty development program at Miami-Dade Junior College. A team approach that incorporated faculty from three disciplines (mortuary science, social science, and philosophy) was utilized in the workshop. The goals of the workshop, the pretest used, sample educational strategies and evaluation procedures, and results of the workshop were reported. The article provides interesting information for death educators who want to design a similar course.

Crase, Darrell: The making of a death educator, Pub. No. ERIC #ED 196-370, Washington, D.C., 1980, Resources In Education.

This 15-page pamphlet offers suggestions to aid teachers in the preparation of death education courses. Major headings consist of the following: Where to begin, opportunities for professional development, support organizations, goals and objectives, content and methodology, resources, what should be expected of students, assessment tools, and what will the new teacher experience.

Crase, Darrell, and Crase, Dixier: Helping children understand death, Young Children **32:**20-25, November 1976.

Crase and Crase believe that the "challenge of providing developmentally appropriate death education experiences is an immediate concern of many educators." The following are five principles of communication educators should consider when a death education course for children is being developed:

Children's questions should be answered truthfully. One should not try to protect the child from this sensitive area.

It is necessary to understand what the child is asking. The needs of the child should be met.

Confusing explanations of death should be avoided. Children need a framework on which they can build.

Denying a child's perception or reaction to death should be avoided.

When a child is specifically searching for a direct answer that lies within the domain of philosophical and religious beliefs, a teacher may choose to suggest that different points of view exist.

Crase, Darrell, and Crase, Dixier: Live issues surrounding death education, The Journal of School Health **44**(2):70-73, 1974.

Crase and Crase believe that children are growing up in a death-denying society and that real experience with death is taken out of the home and replaced by violent death portrayed on television. Therefore the authors believe that death education should occur throughout the child's development whenever relevant issues arise. In addition, death education should be part of the formal curriculum in public and parochial schools and universities. Death education courses should be interdisciplinary in nature, drawing information from law, medicine, science, health, psychology, sociology, and religion. The authors also believe that because of the nature of health education as a discipline, the coordination and development of a formal course in death education is a legitimate function of the health educator. The following are a variety of points to consider when a death education course is being implemented:

Determination of the interest, knowledge, and attitudes of the students

Appropriate written resource materials

Ensurance of an interdisciplinary approach

Enlistment of the assistance of appropriate resource persons, for example, ministers, former soldiers, terminally ill individuals, and psychologists

Attempting a comparative approach of different death practices across cultures

Inclusion of current issues, such as abortion, suicide, and euthanasia

Adherence to sound principles of group discussion or individual counseling

Delisle, Robert G., and Woods McNamee, Abigail S.: Children's perceptions of death: a look at the appropriateness of selected picture books, Pub. No. ERIC #ED 173-786, Washington, D.C., 1977, Resources In Education.

This 20-page pamphlet analyzes six children's picture books and indicates that the suggested age level for these books does not always correspond to the developmental stage of the child. Following a brief description of the perception of death in children aged 3 to 12 years, the authors review *Across the Meadow* (ages 6 to 8), *First Snow* (ages 6 to 8), *Annie and the Old One* (ages 7 to 9), *The Tenth Good Thing About Barney* (ages 5 to 11), *My Grandson, Lew* (ages 6 to 8), and *The Dead Bird* (ages 5 to 7).

Delisle, Robert G., and Woods, Abigail S.: Children and death: coping models in literature, Pub. No. ERIC #ED 173-788, Washington, D.C., 1977, Resources In Education.

This 18-page pamphlet discusses the use of "bibliotherapy" as a tool for helping children cope with death experiences. Through the use of literature, readers identify with others who have shared a similar experience, and an emotional release may result. Bibliotherapy is seen as being able to help children gain independence and strength when they must cope with death. Five books are analyzed: *Nora Upstairs and Nora Downstairs* (ages 4 to 6), *The Dead Bird* (ages 5 to 7), *My Grandson, Lew* (ages 6 to 8), *A Taste of Blackberries* (ages 8 to 10), and *By the Highway Home* (ages 9 to 12).

Dobbelaere, C.J.: A teaching strategy on tragedy, Health Education **8**(6):11-12, 1977.

The author believes that a death education unit needs to be implemented for the benefit of each student. If death is accepted as a natural and inevitable life event, then educators can be better able to stress the importance of living life to the utmost today. A teaching strategy on tragedy is discussed.

Dorval, J.H.: A comparison of selected authors' intended ideas and the actual under-standings by young children of selected primary grade books in which death is the main theme, doctoral dissertation, Philadelphia, 1981, Temple University.

The purpose of the study was to assess why authors of children's books selected death as a theme, what concepts the authors were trying to convey to children, and what concepts children developed as a result of reading the book. A questionnaire was sent to the five authors used in the study. The conclusions indicated that these authors tended to write about death as a result of a personal life event. Also children tended not to understand the concept of death presented by two of the five authors.

Draznin, Yaffa: The business of dying, New York, 1976, Hawthorn Books, Inc., 228 pages.

Draznin believes that as a result of the changes in the way people interact with death in America, the trauma surrounding death may have a much more pragmatic base than many thanatologists realize. He believes that the bereaved may need the services of a good tax accountant or knowledgeable lawyer to do the hardheaded bargaining with the mortician. In essence, Draznin believes there is a need for increased consumer awareness related to dying and death. He has written a thorough text on the consumer aspects of dying and death. The manuscript pro-vides practical suggestions for preparing for one's own death and coping with a death in the family. Chapters include subjects such as mortuary estate planning, insurance, and steps to take when someone dies unexpectedly. Draznin has pro-vided much useful information. The text is a valuable resource for death educators, especially those dealing with adult populations.

Duncan, C.C.: Teaching children about death: a rationale and curriculum guide to grades K-12, doctoral dissertation, Chestnut Hill, MA, 1979, Boston College.

Duncan examined developmental theory to determine the factors that might account for the child's concepts of death. Psychoanalytic, cognitive, and behavioral theory were discussed and used as rationale for developing a curriculum guide for grades K to 12 for teaching about dying and death. The curriculum includes concepts, behavioral objectives, and sample lessons for the grade groups K to 2, 3 to 6, and 7 to 12.

Eldredge, L.E.: Attitudes toward death, doctoral dissertation, Fayetteville, 1975, University of Arkansas.

This study investigated the attitudes toward death of a nursing group, a college group, and a non-college-bound group. The analysis of the data revealed the following:

Persons have ambivalent feelings toward death

Persons want to know if they have a terminal condition but do not want to know the exact date of their death.

The thought of elimination as a result of a massive nuclear war was no longer a threat.

Transplantations and autopsy were generally felt to be acceptable.

Individuals generally believe they could not commit suicide under any condition.

Society continues to favor traditional means of body disposal.

Nursing education curricula prepare the student to deal with the care and support of the patient but psychological understanding is lacking.

Eldredge believes that further research needs to be done on public attitudes toward death-related issues.

Engel, George: A group dynamic approach to teaching and learning about grief, Omega **11**:45-49, 1980.

Engel believes that both didactic instruction and group dynamics of personal involvement are needed for effective classroom instruction of grief and mourning. This article describes the exercises conducted in a workshop designed to help the bereaved.

Fallon, M.T.: Fear of death in young adolescents: a study of the relationship between fear of death and selected anxiety, personality and intelligence variables, doctoral dissertation, Notre Dame, IN, 1976, University of Notre Dame.

This study sought to determine the nature of fear of death in adolescence. Eighth grade students from public schools and Catholic parochial schools were used as subjects. The results showed a significant relationship between death fear scores and general anxiety measures. General anxiety and age had an interactive effect on fear of death scores. The author highlights the need for careful delineation of fear of death terms and further refinement of measuring instruments.

Feifel, Herman, editor: New meanings of death, New York, 1977, McGraw-Hill Book Co., 366 pages.

This book provides an excellent selection of readings. The text does not attempt to cover the total field of thanatology but concentrates on a variety of topics, including clinical and empirical findings; lifespan perspectives of death; clinical management of death, bereavement, grief, and mourning; and death education. The list of contributors includes numerous well-known and respected thanatologists, such as Kastenbaum, Weisman, Kalish, Leviton, Lifton, and Simpson. The chapter entitled "Death Education," by Dan Leviton, includes information on the historical development of death education, goals of death education, the death educator, and sample death education courses.

Fish, William C., and Letzel-Waldhart,Edith.: Suicide and children, Death Education **5**:215-222, 1981.

    This is a description of children and suicide. Fish and Letzel-Waldhart explore the extent of the problem, symptoms, and causes, which include ego weakness, child rearing, and influence of society. The question of the ethics of suicide is also raised. Emphasis is placed on reinforcing a positive self-image in the suicidal child.

Fontenot, C.: The subject nobody teaches, English Journal **63**:62-63, February 1976.

    Fontenot believes that we are bombarded with a wide range of views on a myriad of issues, including sex, drugs, counterculture, and abortion. However, until recently death has been an untouchable subject. It is believed that death themes are prevalent in children's literature, and teachers should be able to use these resources. Also discusses is the need to integrate death education into the curriculum. However, the topic has been systematically neglected by education.

Fredlund, Delphie: Children and death from the school setting viewpoint, Journal of School Health **47**:533-537, 1977.

    Fredlund states that children are interested in the subject of death, and at an early age they begin to ask questions. However, as they grow older children soon learn that death is a taboo subject. Fredlund found that even though parents were uncomfortable discussing death with children, they thought it was their responsibility. But some assistance from churches and schools would be appropriate. In this article Fredlund also synthesized research on the child's development of a concept of death and found the following:

    Most children younger than 3 years old do not comprehend anything regarding death although they may experience grief as a reaction to the loss or separation.

    Children 3 to 5 years old begin to accept that there is a powerful force controlling events. Toward age 5, children see death as a departure, but at the same time they view death as reversible.

    As they near age 6, children begin to believe that death is permanent. At this age children become anxious about death and demonstrate great concern about death. By the time they are 8 or 9 years old, children begin to realize that death is universal.

Children 10 to 12 years old are ready to deal with the reality of death. At this
stage they learn death can occur to anyone at any time.

Adolescents continue to joke about death. However, at the same time adolescents may try to prove they are immune to death. This may be one explanation for their risk-taking behavior.

Freitag, Carl B., and Hassler, Shawn David: The effects of death education, Publ. No.
ERIC #ED 200-878, Washington, D.C., 1980, Resources In Education.

This 14-page paper reports the results of a study conducted at Middle Tennessee State University on the effects of participation in a death education course.
The Pondly Death Anxiety Scale and the topics of thanatology scale were
employed as pretests and posttests.

Fulton, Robert: Death, grief and social recuperation, Omega **1**:23-28, 1970.

Fulton distinguishes between high-grief deaths and low-grief deaths. A high-
grief death is one that is accidental or sudden or affects a younger person. A low-
grief death involves an older person or a prolonged illness. This is based on the
degree of anticipatory grief prior to death. The author identified four stages of
anticipatory grief: depression, heightened concern for the terminally ill, rehearsal of
death, and an attempt to adjust to the consequences of death.

Galen, H.: A matter of life and death, Young Children **27**:351-356, 1972.

Galen believes that educators display ambivalent feelings concerning the inclusion of death into the curriculum of young children. Three broad guidelines to help
teachers deal with the subject of death were developed:

Assumption of the proper perspective. The teacher must accept the preschoolers' curiosity about death as an essential part of their desire to understand their environment.

Encouragement of children's comprehension. The teacher has to take into consideration the child's cognitive and affective level of development.

Fostering of children's expression and awareness of death. The teacher has to
help children identify their emotions and also help them find satisfactory
forms of expression.

Gamm, Cindy: Books on death, divorce and handicaps for primary grades: an
annotated bibliography, Pub. No. ERIC #ED 198-928, Washington, D.C., 1981,

This 13-page annotated bibliography presents books written to help children
cope with death, divorce, and handicaps. For each reference the appropriate grade
level is given. Thirty-one books on death, 28 books on divorce, and 25 books on
handicaps are listed. All references are for preschool-aged to elementary school-
aged children.

Gideon, Marianne D., and Taylor, Phyllis B.: A sexual bill of rights for dying persons, Death Education **4:**303-314, 1981.

In this article Gideon and Taylor identify the rights of dying people. Fifteen rights of the dying person are distinguished. Emphasis is placed on the fact that dying individuals can continue to grow and be life asserting while expressing their sexuality.

Goldsmith, Malcolm C.: Future health educators and death education, doctoral dissertation, Carbondale, 1978, Southern Illinois University.

The purpose of this study was to clarify the future relationship between health education and death education. The study also sought to identify how comfortable the health educator would be teaching about dying and death. Perceptions as to whether personal beliefs about dying and death should be a major concern when a philosophy of life is developed are discussed. Also the personal opinions of future health educators with regard to the importance of death education as a part of health education were analyzed.

The results indicate 87% of the future health educators would feel somewhat or fully comfortable teaching a course on dying and death, 84% believed that one's beliefs about death should be a determinant in evolving a philosophy of life, and 92% believed death education should be a component in the professional preparation of health educators. Also 96% of those surveyed indicated that they would be somewhat or fully willing to implement a unit on dying and death in the health education instructional programs. In light of these findings Goldsmith believes that future research should look at the professional preparation of health educators with regard to death education.

Gordon, Audrey, and Klass, Dennis: They need to know: how to teach children about death, Englewood Cliffs, NJ, 1979, Prentice-Hall, Inc., 274 pages.

Gordon and Klass have provided an excellent reference book for the death educator or elementary educator. The title is misleading in that the manuscript discusses a variety of timely topics besides those germane to children. Part I of the text includes chapters on death and children from a historical perspective, the child's response to death, helping children handle death, and coping with dying and death–related subjects in the schools. Part II concentrates on teaching about death. Chapters on personal awareness of death, goals of death education, curricular suggestions by grade level, consumer aspects of dying and death, and politics and pedagogy are included in this section of the text. The appendixes provide much useful information for the death educator. Overall, the text provides a variety of good learning strategies, a workable curricular outline, and much useful information. the text is an excellent resource for any educator seeking to develop a death education curriculum.

Grof, S., and Halifax, J.: The human encounter with death, New York, 1977, E.P. Dutton, 240 pages.

The focus of this book is on what happens to a person on an LSD trip who hallucinates an encounter with death. The clinical information is brought out in detail, and superb descriptions of the use of LSD with terminally ill patients are provided.

Guthman, Robert F., and Womack, Sharon K.: Death, dying and grief: a bibliography, Lincoln, NE, 1978, Pied Publications, 154 pages.

This text provides a fairly extensive collection of titles related to dying and death. The text primarily catalogs books, journal articles, printed documents, theses, dissertations, and a number of unpublished manuscripts.

Hafen, Brent Q.: Death and dying, Health Education 8(6):4-7, 1977.

Hafen provides an extensive overview of many of the issues related to death education. He believes that the reluctance to face and understand death leaves families and terminally ill individuals unprepared to cope with these crises. The physical changes that occur during the last hour of life and the needs of the dying are also discussed.

Hair, J.M.: What shall we teach about death in science classes? The Elementary School Journal 65:414-418, 1965.

Hair says that death is everywhere, but children are shielded from the topic. Hair gives four reasons why death is an important topic in the school curriculum:

An understanding of the life cycle is not complete without an understanding of the characteristics, role, and necessity of death.

An understanding of the nature and the significance of death is important to conservation, ecology, and health concepts.

An understanding of the scientific facts is needed to eliminate or prevent debilitating superstitions and fears in situations involving death.

Understanding and appreciation of life and living are increased and sharpened by conscious contrast and comparisons to death and dying.

Hankoff, L.D.: Adolescence and the crisis of dying, Adolescence 10:373-389, 1975.

Hankoff believes that adolescents' emerging neuropsychological organization and abilities for conceptual and systematic thinking provide them with the necessary cognitive abilities to fully grasp the meaning of death. Therefore death education should be integrated into the curriculum at this level.

Hardt, Dale V.: Death: the final frontier, Englewood Cliffs, NJ, 1979, Prentice-Hall, Inc., 194 pages.

This book provides a brief overview of a broad spectrum of issues related to dying and death. The text includes chapters on origins of death attitudes, attitudes and education, definition of death, euthanasia, burial customs, funerals, bereavement, grief and mourning, and wills and estate planning. This text could be used in death and dying courses of the high school or college level.

Hardt, Dale V.: A measurement of the improvement of attitudes toward death, The Journal of School Health **46**:269-270, 1976.

Hardt believes there has been a dearth of reported evidence that indicates the success of death education to support the growth of this topic. To meet the need for research, Hardt conducted a study of 86 university students to assess the changes of attitudes as a result of death education courses. The subjects were given the same pretest and posttest designed to assess attitudes toward death, the dying process, the terminally ill, euthanasia, suicide, bereavement, grief, and funerals. The results showed that 61% of the students showed improvement in their attitudes toward death, 23% showed a decline, and 10% stayed the same.

Hart, Edward J.: Philosophical views of death, Health Education **8**(6):2-3, 1977.

Hart believes that a central issue in death education is human loss, especially loss that effects personal security. Therefore even in the absence of an actual death there are a variety of social and psychological life events, such as loss of a job, divorce, economic failure, and relocation, that are capable of eliciting behaviors similar to ordinary bereavement.

Hart, Edward J.: Death education and mental health, The Journal of School Health **46**:407-412, 1976.

Hart believes that death education is a subject area that should be of immediate concern to all health educators. Hart also thinks the health problems in schools have changed over the years from an approach stressing physical health to an approach stressing mental and emotional concerns. Death education falls into this latter category, and therefore schools should integrate a multidisciplinary approach to death education.

The real issue in death education is enhancing individuals' abilities to cope with loss situations. The feelings that arise in death situations are similar to other mental health problems. Therefore death education must help students deal effectively with these mental health concerns.

Hilker, Christine and others: A bibliography on euthanasia, 1958-1978, Pub. No. ERIC #ED 177-458, Washington, D.C., 1978, Resources In Education.

This 75-page pamphlet identifies the references on euthanasia across a 20-year span. The contents consist of more than 650 periodicals and 26 books with citations listed alphabetically by author.

Hine, Virginia: The last letter to the pebble people: *Aldie Soars,* Miami, 1977, St. Alden's in the Weeds, 138 pages.

In this book Hine describes a number of personal experiences she and her husband encountered following a diagnosis of lung cancer. The experiences involved many people focusing on a search for life and continued health and finally accepting and coping with the process of dying.

Kass, L.R.: Problems in the meaning of death, Science **170:**1235-1236, 1970.

A conflict of values is developing between the value of human life and the value of a worthy or socially useful existence. Kass believes that sophisticated machinery used for resuscitation and maintenance of human life only makes the physician's task of tending to the human needs of the dying patient more difficult. In addition, Kass believes these gadgets cloud the definition of when death actually occurs. Therefore perhaps a valid definition of death should include a certain degree of consciousness as a criterion.

Kastenbaum, Robert J.: Death, society and human experience, ed. 2, St. Louis, 1981, The C.V. Mosby Co., 350 pages.

Kastenbaum provides a complete overview of the sociological aspects of dying and death in the American culture. Excellent chapters are provided related to death systems, the child's concept of death, the hospice concepts, and suicide.

Kastenbaum, a pioneer in the study of thanatology, provides an especially good discussion of bereavement, grief, and mourning. This text provides an excellent resource for death educators.

Kelly, Orville†: Make today count, Providence, UT, 1975, Media Marketing, Brigham Young University. (Film.)

The film uses a flashback technique to expose the world of Orville Kelly, a man in his mid-40s who has lymphoma. He had been given 3 years to live and had survived 2 years when the film was made. The viewer observes the check-up Kelly must go through as well as the speaking engagements at high schools and health professional groups. Mr. Kelly speaks about his family and his concern over communication gaps with them. The film produces a clear picture of a man facing death and gives the audience a passive, realistic awareness of Orville Kelly's life-threatening disease and how he is helping others to cope and open up about death.

Kerr, Lucille E., and Kaplan, Mimi: A bibliography of resources on the subject of death for children, junior high and younger, Pub. No. ERIC #ED 179876, Washington, D.C., 1979, Resources In Education.

---

†Deceased.

This 45-page bibliography on death contains resources for children aged 14 and younger. The following categories are presented: literature (listing books and media separately), age of readers, relationship of the deceased, reactions to death and dying, and coping techniques (conceptual and practical). More than 150 resources for children are listed. The book section of the literature classification is subdivided into seven categories: biographical, fantasy, fiction, folk and fairy tales, informational books, legends, and poetry. The media section is subdivided into three categories: films, filmstrips, and records. Materials are also presented according to the relationshp between the child and the deceased: grandparents, parents, siblings and children, friends, famous persons, oneself, and pets and living things. Kerr and Kaplan list materials dealing with coping techniques under the following headings: death is permanent, death is inevitable, death is a necessary part of the cycle of life, immortality, funerals and other rituals, memories, replacement of the loved one, affirmation and appreciation of life, support groups, and combinations of coping techniques.

Klingman, Avigdor: Death education through literature: a preventive approach, Death Education **4**:271-279, 1980.

In this article Klingman introduces the use of children's stories in the classroom to help deal with death and topics associated with death. The affective and cognitive reactions to the literature are discussed. It is expressed that children's readers are beneficial in helping children and teachers deal in a comfortable and anxiety free atmosphere with death and topics concerning death.

Knott, J. Eugene, and Prull, Richard: Death education: accountable to whom? for what? Omega **7**:177-181, 1976.

The article focuses on establishing and evaluating some learning outcomes for a death education course. Knott and Prull believe that in this age of accountability death educators discern ways to make the teaching of dying and death more meaningful and accountable.

Krahn, J.H.: Pervasive death: an avoided concept, Educational Leadership **31**:18-20, October 1973.

Krahn believes that children approach death with curiosity and that they are open and ready to explore death. However, the subject of death is not considered an integral part of the child's elementary education. Krahn believes that death education can be integrated into a variety of curricular areas, including health and safety, science, reading, and language.

Kutscher, Austin H.: Anticipatory grief, death and bereavement: a continuum. In Wyschograd, E., editor: The phenomenon of death: faces of mortality, New York, 1973, Harper and Row, Publishers, Inc., pp. 40-53.

Kutscher believes that life is full of major and minor preparations for death that all too few of us realize. He states, "There are constant and superficial losses whose value in the process of this preparation should not be underestimated." Such losses include the loss of a job, loss of social status, divorce, and loss of financial security. All of these losses can be accompanied and complicated by evidences of grief and anticipatory grief. Kutscher believes that these losses help to prepare human beings for greater losses in their lives, such as the death of a loved one or the individual's own death. The symptoms of grief and stages of anticipatory grief are also discussed.

LaGrand, Louis E.: Loss reactions of college students: a descriptive analysis, Death Education **5:**235-247, 1981.

Over a 2-year period 1,139 college and university students were observed, and an analysis of their reaction to death and loss was recorded. Types of loss, various ways of coping, and both psychological and physiological reactions were examined. Systems for resolving the loss, such as communicating with friends and social support, were supplied by the students. Based on information from the students, many suggestions were given on understanding and dealing with loss.

LaGrand, Louis E.: Reducing burnout in the hospice and the death education movement, Death Education **4:**61-75, 1980.

The subject of stress and stress management is of concern to those working in the helping professions and the death education movement. LaGrand introduces four possibilities in reducing stress: (1) cognitive modification, (2) exercise outlets, (3) relaxation techniques, and (4) stimulus control. When a stress-management program is being developed, professional input should be utilized.

Leviton, Dan.: Education for death or death becomes less a stranger, Omega **6:**1830191, 1975.

Leviton describes a death education course taught to a large section of students. Leviton found that the course had improved the conscious thinking about death on the part of the students and improved their communications with others about death. He includes sections on history of death education courses, goals and syllabus, and student response of a dying and death course. The article is useful reading for educators planning to develop and implement a college level death education course.

Leviton, Dan: Education for death, Journal of Health, Physical Education and Recreation **40:**46-47, September 1969.

Leviton believes that death education should be an integral component of a comprehensive health education course of instruction. Leviton also provides the following suggested course outline:

The nature of death
    Western philosophy of death and dying
    Great religions and their view of death
Theoretical views of death
Medical-legal aspects of death
Attitudinal and emotional correlates of death and dying
    Attitudes of children and adolescents toward dying and death
    Adult attitudes toward death and dying
    Attitudes of death-defying athletes and soldiers and of war-torn populations toward death
Coping with death and dying
    Communicating with the terminally ill loved one
    The effects of the death of a loved one on the living
    The relationship between style of life and style of death
    Explaining death to children
    The American funeral
    Coming to terms with the inevitability of personal death
    The role of language in reducing fear of death

Lippit-Graham, J.E.: The attitudes and life experiences of university death education students, Death Education **4:**355-367, 1981.

In this investigation Lippit-Graham identifies some correlation and differences between college students who enroll in a death education course and students who do not. Three groups of students were used; a group enrolled in a death-education course (N = 33), a group that completed a course in death education (N = 38), and a control group (N = 65) were all compared. The overall findings indicated that students involved in death education had been exposed during their childhood to a more open atmosphere concerning death; therefore they were less denying of death.

Liston, Edward H.: Education on death and dying: a neglected area in the medical curriculum, Omega **6:**193-198, 1975.

Liston states that there is evidence that the instruction of medical students on the psychosocial aspects of life-threatening illness is a neglected component of the medical student's curriculum. Liston also states that the number of structured courses and educational experiences in this area are increasing. Liston believes that there is a need to determine the optimal teaching methods for such a course and to improve communications among death educators in this area.

Lobsenz, N.: How postmortems help the living, Today's Health, pp. 40-43, May 1972.

Lobsenz believes that the postmortem examination serves a variety of useful purposes:

It reveals pathological problems and changes in disease patterns.

It reveals how chemicals, food additives, pesticides, radiation, and environmental pollution affect the body.

It reveals how effective prescribed medicines have been.

It helps check the efficiency of surgical techniques.

It aids in the detection of inheritable or communicable disease.

It acts as a double check on the diagnosis.

It helps solve legal problems.

Miles, Margaret Shandor: The effects of a course on death and grief on nurses' attitudes toward dying patients and death, Death Education **4**:245-260, 1980.

This study was done to determine or measure the attitudes of nurses after they had a course on death and grief. The nurses in the study worked with dying patients. There were four groups of subjects: treatment group, waiting list control group who then experienced the treatment, and two control groups. The course length was 6 weeks. The results point out the education experience did have an impact on attitudes.

Mills, Gretchen, Reisler, Raymond, Robinson, Alice, and Vermilye, Gretchen: Discussing death: a guide to death education, Homewood, IL, 1976, ETC Publications, 140 pages.

This text provides a rationale, a curricular framework, and a series of excellent learning strategies. The concepts and activities are divided by age levels. The book is an excellent resource for death educators.

Mueller, M. L.: Death education and death fear reduction, Education **97**:145-148, 1976.

Mueller examined the fear reduction of eighth grade students. Experimental and control groups were formed. The experimental group received a 12-lesson death education unit that included both cognitive and affective components. The control group received no instruction. Two forms of a fear reduction inventory were developed by the investigator. The result showed no significant difference on the fear reduction inventory between the two groups.

Nannis, Ellen D., and others: The adolescent with a life threatening illness: cultural myths and social realities, Pub. No. ERIC #ED 175-530, Washington, D.C., 1978, Resources In Education.

This 15-page paper discusses the attitudes of terminally ill adolescent patients toward their illness and their behaviors during treatment. Information is based on interviews with patients and parents, daily systematic observations, and daily ratings of the patients by nurses and parents.

National Institute of Mental Health: Caring about kids: talking to children about death, Pub. No. ERIC #ED 190-917, Washington, D.C., 1979, Resources In Education.

This 20-page pamphlet is designed for parents and others who play an important role in the lives of children to help care for their children in ways that nurture good mental health. Major headings include children are aware, communication barriers, not having all the answers, overcoming the taboos, developmental stages, the individual experience, the challenge of talking to a young child, religion and death, the unemotional opportunity, death in the family, should children visit the dying, should children attend funerals, sending children away from home, and children also mourn.

Nelson, R.C., and Peterson, W.: Challenging the last great taboo: death, The School Counselor **22**:353-359, 1975.

Nelson and Peterson believe that death education, like sex education, is still looked on negatively in American culture. The lack of death education leads to misunderstanding and fear of death. It also leads to a lack of preparation for reality of life and the inevitability of death.

Noland, Melody: The systematic development and efficacy of a death education unit for ninth grade girls, Death Education **4**:43-59, 1980.

Noland utilized two experiments in trying to determine the responsiveness of a planned death education unit for ninth grade girls. Cognitive, affective, and behavioral tools were used to determine or assess findings. These instruments were administered before, after, and 6 weeks following the completion of the unit. During the first experiment (experiment I) both the experimental group and control group attended the same high school and were exposed to the same teachers. The result of experiment I showed both the experimental and control groups demonstrated improvement on the cognitive scores. Cognitive and attitude scores were improved for the experimental group in experiment II, but the control group showed no improvement. The experimental group demonstrated more behaviors associated to the death education unit. Overall, it is indicated that a death education unit should be a part of any comprehensive health education curriculum.

Death as a reality of life, expressing grief, ages of understanding, explaining death to children, and the importance of funerals are topics covered in the filmstrip. The purpose of this filmstrip is to inform adults about children who have experienced a death of a family member or close friend and some of the questions that may be asked. The material is best suited for parents and teachers. The filmstrip is brief and to the point with much repetition of material. The series is not in depth because of the broad area that is covered. Interested buyers should preview before ordering.

O'Connell, W.E., Kopel, K., Paris, J., Girardin, P., and Batsel, W.: Thanatology for everyone: developmental labs and workshops, Death Education **1**:305-313, 1977.

    Many hospital medical staffs are expressing concerns about the need to help professionals and the general public cope with death. This paper examines how death and dying laboratories and workshops function to desensitize death fears. The workshops are structured for a number of small groups within the institution. Groups outside the hospital setting may have fewer people because of the death-denying attitude of our society. This would make the testing of the laboratories extremely difficult.

Ordal, Carol C.: Death as seen in books for young children, Death Education **4**:223-236, 1980.

    Identified are children's books and books dealing with death. The books are directed to children aged 3 to 9 years. Twenty-two books are evaluated; twelve deal with the death of animals and reactions of children to the death of a pet, and the other ten refer to the death of people. The purpose of these books and evaluations is to help parents, teachers, and children become more secure and comfortable talking about death.

Periles, C.A., and Schildt, R.: Death-related attitudes of adolescent males and females, Death Education Volume **2**:359-369, 1979.

    In this study Periles and Schildt attempt to measure death-related attitudes among 152 seventh, eighth, and ninth grade males ($N = 71$) and females ($N = 81$). Using a Likert-type instrument and Chi-square statistic, Periles and Schildt found the males and females differed significantly on 11 of the 22 items on the survey. Generally, females agreed with abortion, saw the need for funerals, and expressed concern about their bodies after death. Also the issues of capital punishment and life after death brought out attitude differences. The study concluded that traditional sex roles may influence adolescent attitudes toward death.

Pine, Vanderlyn R.: A socio-historical portrait of death education, Death Education **1**:57-58, 1977

    Pine believes that the concern for death education has increased dramatically since the early 1960s. This article focuses on the sociological and historical development of death education with an emphasis on problems that will be faced in the next few years. Pine provides an excellent discussion of the genesis and development of death education. This discussion is divided into three sections: the era of exploration (1928-1957), the decade of development (1958-1967), and the period of popularity (1968-1977).

Reck, A.J.: A contextualist thanatology: a pragmatic approach to death and dying, Death Education **1:**315-323, 1977.

In this study Reck discusses the pragmatic approach to death and dying. In modern society the thanatologist's problem is to make people aware of the value of death. The focus of the paper is on the dying individual but also recognized is the medical, religious, and family context. Reck indicates that dying contains an opportunity for growth not only for the dying person but for friends and relatives as well. The grief that is expressed must not be denied or suppressed, and these feelings should make the living sensitive to how much value is placed on life.

Rodabough, Tillman: Alternatives to the stages model of the dying process, Death Education **4:**1-20, 1980.

Rodabough reviews the models of the dying process. The death trajectory phases model, the personality repetitive alternation model, and the interpersonal reactions model are compared to Kubler-Ross' five sequential stages through which the dying individual passes. Rodabough hopes to point out the contribution these models have made to those who interact with the terminally ill and how the interactant's expectations can have an impact on the dying person. Rodabough indicates it is best for the interactant to have an open mind, a good ear for listening, and patience in making a judgment.

Rudolph, Marguerita: Should the children know: encounters with death in the lives of children, New York, 1978, Schocken Books, Inc., 113 pages.

Rudolph has been most involved in preschool and day-care programs. The book deals specifically with children and their experiences with death, whether it be the death of an animal, classmate, or family member. She speaks briefly about books that have helped children to learn about death. One of the chapters explains the concept that children have formulated about death and how it compares to the adults' concept. She uses a variety of poems and folk songs to help clarify her points.

Russell, Robert D.: Educating about death, Health Education **8**(6):8-10, 1977.

Russell believes that death education is a relatively new topic for health educators and one that has a large factual base because many people experience the death of others before their own death. Russell believes that death education should enhance the students' ability to function when someone else dies. In addition, by studying dying and death, students can become aware of the value of life and may actually live life more fully.

Sadwith, J.A.: An interdisciplinary approach to death education, The Journal of School Health **44**:455-458, 1974.

·Sadwith discusses a week-by-week format for structuring a death education course at the postsecondary school level. Suggestions for structuring a death education course are also provided:

The course must provide adequate time for student-oriented discussion.

The course should be flexible to meet student needs and interests.

The course should use local personnel, such as physicians and religious leaders.

A sense of humor in an appropriate manner must be maintained.

The instructor must be able to discuss potential problems that might develop.

Sanders, Catherine: Houses for the dead, New York, 1976, David McKay Co., Inc., 144 pages.

The book takes a cross-cultural view of the problem of death and bereavement. Included are 10 different cultures from the Neanderthal times to the early twentieth century. Brief descriptions of mourning rituals and burial customs are given along with major themes and beliefs that give the reader a better understanding of the ritual. The last two chapters summarize two basic cross-cultural questions: what is the relationship between the living and the dead? and Why do human beings die? This book does not direct itself to important questions facing our culture nor does it recognize most of the functional customs in the book as being obsolete.

Schulz, Richard: The psychology of death, dying and bereavement, Reading, MA, 1978, Addison-Wesley Publishing Company, Inc., 197 pages.

Schulz presents a clear, concise, and well-written overview of the psychology of dying and death. The text is approached from a research orientation and appropriate documentation is provided. Chapters on the demography of death, the terminal phase of death, the lengthening of life, the concepts of bereavement and grief, and the status of death education are included. The chapter on death education discussed the need for death education across the life span. Schulz has written a good reference text for death educators.

Schulz, Richard, and Aderman, D.: How the medical staff copes with dying patients: a critical review, Omega **7**:11-21, 1976.

The article examines the relationship and attitudes between medical practitioners and dying patients. Schulz and Aderman state that physicians often avoid patients once they begin to die. A variety of psychological speculations for this occurrence are given. Schulz and Aderman also believe that the patients' desire to be informed about their condition is typically ignored even though research data suggest that terminally ill patients suffer no psychological damage if tactfully informed about the true nature of their condition.

Schwartz, S.: Death education: suggested readings and audiovisuals, The Journal of School Health **47:**607-609, 1977.

Schwartz provides a brief discussion of the need to incorporate death education concepts in the curriculum and provides an extensive list of readings and audiovisual materials.

Shanfield, Stephen B.: The mourning of the health care professional: an important element in education about death and loss, Death Education **4:**385-395, 1981.

This article acknowledges the need for health professionals to explore the mourning process. A seminar was held for senior medical students and graduate nurses. Shanfield indicates that death and dying courses are necessary and important for health professionals, but clinical teachers must also recognize the students' needs to learn about their response to loss and provide an atmosphere that deals with these issues.

Silverman, A.S.: Development of content areas and objectives for a curriculum in death and dying education and junior high school students, doctoral dissertation, New York, 1981, Columbia University.

The Tyler rationale was used to develop appropriate content and objectives for a junior high school curriculum on death and dying. A modified three-round delphi technique was used to gather the data from a panel of 50 experts. The results indicated that the highest-ranked content areas were influences on attitudes toward death, bereavement, and grief and the meaning of death. Society and death and funeral customs and practices were the next-highest ranked. Legal and economic and religious and spiritual beliefs received the lowest ratings.

Simpson, Michael: The facts of death: a complete guide for being prepared, Englewood Cliffs, NJ, 1979, Prentice-Hall, Inc. 276 pages.

Simpson provides a well-written, concise, and thorough text on dying and death. Chapters include the definition of death, living with your own death, living with the dying, planning for death, children and death, euthanasia, suicide and grief, and loss and bereavement. The appendix provides useful information related to resources and support groups. The chapter on death is especially useful for death educators. Included in this chapter is information on funeral arrangements and costs, guidelines to follow when a will is written, and a family information register and planning guide. Overall this text provides a useful resource for death educators.

Spinetta, John J., and others: Talking with children with a life threatening illness: a handbook for health care professionals, Pub. No. ERIC #ED 178-213, Washington, D.C., 1979, Resources In Education.

This 35-page handbook was written for health care professionals who work with children who have a life-threatening illness. The five sections of the report include laying the groundwork for communication with the child, communication with family members, communication between health care professionals and the child's school, and objectives to consider when a seriously ill child is talked to about death.

Swain, H. L.: Childhood views of death, Death Education **2:**341-358, 1979.

This study examined children aged 2 to 16 years and the relationship between their concepts of death and their age, sex, level of parents' education, and degree of religious influence within the family. Swain interviewed 120 children. The interview responses were rated by two judges on a 5-point rating scale, and a four-way analysis of variance was used to analyze the data. The result of the analysis of the data found that age was the only significant variable and that the greatest change in death concept appears to occur in children aged 5 to 7 years.

Swetland, Sandra, and Calhoun, Nancy: Helping children cope with death: a guide for school personnel, Pub. No. ERIC #ED 190-977, Washington, D.C., 1980, Resources In Education.

This 18-page guide was developed to enable school support personnel to help children cope with death. Five seminar sessions on death and dying are discussed. Chapter titles include self awareness, stages of acceptance, grief reactions to death, children's special needs, educational development preparation, and managing the stress-building school supports.

Terhune, J.: About aging and death, Health Education **8**(6):13-16, 1977.

This article presents a scope and sequence for a program in aging, death, and grief education for grades K to 12.

Wass, H., and Shaak, J.: Helping children understand death through literature, Childhood Education **53:**80-85, November 1976.

Wass and Shaak believe that at the beginning of the twentieth century death became an avoided topic, but recently death has become a topic of increased interest in the media, and the taboo on death seems to be lifted. However, for children the taboo on death may take much more time to lift because parents often try to shield children from the reality of death by avoiding the topic. A number of death educators believe this is a legitimate topic for inclusion in the school curriculum.

Weiner, Hannah: Living experiences with death: a journey man's view through psychodrama, Omega **6:**251-274, 1975.

    Weiner provides basic psychodrama techniques and sample activities. She believes that psychodrama provides a valuable and flexible approach to the study of dying and death. This article provides a comprehensive discussion of psychodrama and represents a useful reference for the death educator.

White, E.A.: A description of kindergarten through fourth grade students; conception of death, doctoral dissertation, Stillwater, 1976, Oklahoma State University.

    This was designed to answer four basic questions: At what age or grade do children (1) see death as irreversible, (2) realize death is the cessation of life functions, (3) realize death is universal, and (4) develop a concept of life after death? In the discussion of findings, White makes a distinction between possessing a concept and understanding a concept. The majority of students in the grades studied possessed concepts of irrevocability, cessation, and universality. At the understanding level, the majority of children had not developed an understanding of cessation and irreversibility. It was found that understanding of cessation and irreversibility were a function of cognitive development.

Wittmaier, Bruce C.: Some unexpected attitudinal consequences of a short course on death, Omega **10:**271-275, 1979.

    Wittmaier measured the attitude toward death and dying of students who enrolled in a death course and compared them to an analogous group who wanted to take such a course but were unable to be accommodated. The author found that the students who completed the course had a higher fear of death score but that these same students felt more comfortable talking with a dying person.

Worden, J. William and Proctor, William: PDA: personal death awareness, Englewood Cliffs, NJ, 1976, Prentice-Hall, Inc., 196 pages.

    As the title implies, this text tries to make readers look at how they feel and interact with death. Readers are helped to assess their own personal death awareness, break their fear of death, and enhance their ability to cope with death and loss encounters across the life span. The text would provide an excellent supplemental text for a college level death education course. Many of the values clarification activities included in the text could be adapted for classroom use.

Yapundich, Eleanor F., and others: Health education packages: the human life cycle, Pub. No. ERIC #ED 202550, Washington, D.C., 1976, Resources In Education.

    This 70-page report of the Health Instruction Exchange presents four learning modules. The first module examines the biological, psychological, and social characteristics of various stages in the human life cycle. The second module examines the interrelationships of physical, social, emotional, and intellectual development in children. The third module examines the physiological changes that accompany old age. The fourth module examines psychological responses and coping techniques for dealing with these responses. This last module entitled, "Acceptance of Death," includes an introduction, learning activities, conclusion, posttest, and correct answers for the posttest.

Yarber, William L.: Death education: a living issue, The Science Teacher **43:**21-23, October 1976.

Yarber states that even though death is part of the natural aging process, it still remains a taboo topic. As a result children are growing up with a confused, unnatural image of death. The author believes that death education is interdisciplinary in nature, drawing on medicine, law, sociology, psychology, religion, and biology. Possible areas of study include definitions, causes, and stages of death; cross-cultural views and practices related to death; and the life cycle.

APPENDIX C

The development and validation of a Knowledge Test of Death and Dying

To successfully evaluate the effectiveness of death education programs and the effectiveness of related instructional activities, it is imperative that valid and reliable evaluative instruments be available. Appendix C outlines the procedures used to develop and validate a knowledge test for death and dying. This appendix serves as a guideline for death educators who need to tailor a measurement instrument to meet their specific needs.

For the Knowledge Test of Death and Dying several of Nunnally's suggestions were used to develop an eight-phase model (Chapter 3). Although there are a variety of ways to develop a standardized knowledge test, this eight-phase model provides an example of the procedures followed to develop a knowledge instrument. In additon, information on the reliability and validity scores for the knowledge test are provided.

PHASE I: DEFINING THE SCOPE

The initial task in the development of the knowledge test was to determine the parameters of the content related to death and dying. The knowledge test was originally designed to assess the knowledge of preprofessional death educators, but the instrument could be applicable in a variety of educational settings and for a variety of target populations. Within this phase of instrument development three stages were used to determine parameters. In the first stage, recent literature on death education was reviewed to delineate content areas recommended by various authors for inclusion in death and dying courses. Several authors have offered suggestions on content areas that should be included in a college level death education course. Sadwith[1] noted that the key elements of such a course should be classroom discussions focused on a wide range of topics. Leviton[2] suggested that a death education experience be divided into three basic components: (1) the nature of death, which would include its philosophical, religious, medical, and legal aspects, (2) attitudinal and emotional correlates of death and dying, which include attitudes of children, adolescents, adults, and death-defying athletes, and (3) coping with death and dying, which would include communicating with a terminally ill loved one, explaining death to children, and examining the nature of funerals in America. Yarber[3] provided a more complete list of possible content areas that could be included in a course designed to prepare instructors of death education (Table C-1). McMahon[4] suggested that an independent death education course for college students should consist of a variety of units ranging from biological, sociological, and psychological definitions of death to understanding the dying relative. The first four columns of Table C-1 provide a synopsis of the content areas listed by these four authors. As can be noted from the content areas specified by Sadwith, Leviton, Yarber, and McMahon, there is some overlap as well as obvious differences of opinion with regard to the information deemed essential for a course in death education.

To better understand the material that practicing health educators consider basic for a death education course, a death and dying content questionnaire was developed and mailed to 40 individuals professionally involved in the areas of death and dying and death education.

The purpose of the questionnaire was to determine the specific areas identified as essential or important for inclusion in a professional preparation course in death education. Based on a comprehensive review of the death and dying literature, 30 cognitive content areas were specified. Each participant in the survey was asked to rate each cognitive area according to the following criteria:

5, Very important; should be one of the main concepts of the course
4, Important; should be included in the course content
3, Slightly important; should be included if time permits, but would not be essential
1, Not important; has no relevance to the course; should not be included in the course content
N.O., No opinion

The returns (N = 38) included 26 respondents employed in college or university settings, 9 from public schools, and 3 from the public sector.

The results of the survey (Table C-1) delineated four broad categories of cognitive areas according to perceived importance. The first category consisted of cognitive areas thought to be essential concepts for a professional preparation course on death and dying. The five topical areas included in this category would provide the basic core of a death education course for prospective educators.

1. Understanding dying friends and relatives
2. The meaning of death in American society
3. Bereavement and mourning

Table C-1. Summary of death and dying content focus with mean scores, rank order, and author and content outline totals

Content areas* ($\overline{X}$)	Leviton (1969)	McMahon (1973)	Sadwith (1974)	Yarber (1976)	Eastern university	Small eastern college	Midwestern university	Southern university	Southeastern university	Midwestern university	Total
1. Understanding dying friends and relatives (4.800)	X	X	X	X				X	X	X	7
2. The meaning of death in American society (4.750)	X	X	X	X	X		X	X		X	8
3. Bereavement and mourning (4.686)		X		X	X	X	X	X	X	X	8
4. Explaining death to children (4.629)	X										1
5. Preparing for death (4.576)			X	X			X	X			4
6. Methods and materials of death education (4.444)											0
7. Definitions and causes of death (4.417)		X	X	X			X		X	X	6
8. Cross-cultural views of death (4.361)			X	X	X						3
9. Curricular development in death (4.333)							X	X		X	3
10. Religious view of death (4.314)	X		X				X	X	X	X	6
11. Legal aspects of death (4.306)	X		X			X	X	X	X	X	7
12. Euthanasia (4.250)			X	X	X	X		X		X	6
13. The life cycle (4.235)	X										1
14. Suicide (psychosocial aspects) (4.222)		X		X	X	X	X		X	X	7
15. Aging (psychosocial aspects) (4.171)											0
16. The role of the funeral home (4.114)	X	X					X	X	X	X	6
17. Aging (biological aspects) (4.056)											0

*Rank order as determined by the death and dying content questionnaire.

Table C-1. Summary of death and dying content focus with mean scores, rank order, and author and content outline totals

Content areas* ($\overline{X}$)	Authors				Colleges and universities						Total
	Leviton (1969)	McMahon (1973)	Sadwith (1974)	Yarber (1976)	Eastern university	Small eastern college	Midwestern university	Southern university	Southeastern university	Midwestern university	
18. Expressing condolences (4.028)				×							1
19. Suicide (referral aspects) (4.000)					×	×			×		3
20. The costs of funerals (4.000)	×	×	×					×		×	5
21. Organ donations and transplants (3.861)			×					×		×	3
22. The history of death and dying (3.853)									×	×	2
23. Alternatives to traditional funerals (3.743)			×								1
24. Memorial services (3.686)					×		×				2
25. Death portrayed in children's literature (3.611)					×		×			×	3
26. Cremation (3.611)			×	×	×						3
27. Embalming (3.500)											0
28. Death portrayed in music and literature (3.389)			×	×						×	3
29. Cryogenics (3.156)			×								1
30. Necrophilia (2.786)		×									1

4. Explaining death to children

5. Preparing for death

The second category consisted of those cognitive areas that should be included in a death and dying course but would not represent major concepts. It is obvious that several of these items relate closely to those key concepts identified in the first category.

1. Methods and materials of death education

2. Definitions and causes of death

3. Cross-cultural views of death

4. Curricular development in death education

5. Religious views of death
6. Euthanasia
7. The life cycle
8. Suicide (psychosocial aspects)
9. Aging (psychosocial aspects)
10. Role of the funeral home
11. Aging (biological aspects)
12. Expressing condolences to a friend or relative
13. Suicide (referral aspects)
14. Cost of funerals

The third category consisted of cognitive areas that should be included in a death and dying professional preparation course if adequate time was available:

1. Organ donation and transplant
2. History of death and dying
3. Alternatives to traditional funerals
4. Memorial services
5. Death and children's literature
6. Cremation
7. Embalming

The fourth category consisted of items that were thought to be of little importance in a professional preparation course:

1. Death portrayed in music and literature
2. Cryogenics
3. Necrophilia

Although the results of the questionnaire are subject to varying interpretations, they reflect the collective thinking of 38 professionals experienced in the field of death education.

The third stage was to review syllabi from death and dying courses. The 40 participants who were previously given the death and dying content questionnaire were asked to submit the course syllabus used for the death and dying course taught at their institution. Table C-2 provides a summary of death education and death and dying course content outlines gathered from a cross-section of institutions throughout the United States.

The selection of the content areas included in the knowledge test was based on the results of the death and dying content questionnaire, the content areas suggested by four authors (Leviton, McMahon, Sadwith, and Yarber), and content areas delineated by the six course syllabi.

Table C-2 provides the rank order of the content areas as determined by the death

Table C-2. Summation of the rank order interval scale and author-course outline scale

Cognitive area	Rank order interval scale	Author and course outline scale	Total
Priority areas			
The meaning of death in American society	10	8	18
Bereavement and mourning	10	8	18
Understanding dying friends and relatives	10	7	17
Definitions and causes of death	8	6	14
Legal definitions of death	7	7	14
Important areas			
Preparing for death	9	4	13
Religious views of death	7	6	13
Euthanasia	7	6	13
Suicide (psychosocial aspects)	6	7	13
Cross-cultural views of death	8	3	11
Role of the funeral home	5	6	11
Curricular development in death education	8	3	11
Explaining death to children	9	1	10
Methods and materials of death education	9	0	9
Cost of funerals	4	5	9
Marginal areas			
The life cycle	7	1	8
Organ donations and transplants	4	3	7
Suicide (referral aspects)	4	3	7
Expressing condolences to a friend or relative	5	1	6
History of death and dying	3	2	5
Memorial services	3	2	5
Cremation	2	3	5
Death in children's literature	2	3	5
Unimportant areas			
Alternatives to funerals	3	1	4
Death portrayed in music and literature	1	3	4
Embalming	2	0	2
Cryogenics	1	1	2
Necrophilia	1	1	2
Aging areas			
Aging (psychosocial aspects)	6	0	6
Aging (biological aspects)	5	0	5

and dying content questionnaire and a tally of the number of authors (the final column of Table C-2) and course outlines that included that particular content area. This table clearly ilustrates the varying philosophies that exist concerning which content areas should be included in a death and dying course. For example, the content area "explaining death to children" ranked fourth on the results of the death and dying content questionnaire and was felt to be an essential concept of a death and dying course, but "explaining death to children" was listed by only one of the four authors, and it did not appear on any course outline.

To equate the results of the death and dying content questionnaire with the opinion of the four authors and the course content outline, the rank order of the content areas from the questionnaire was divided into 10 equal intervals and assigned scores ranging from 1 to 10. Because of the broad scope of the questionnaire, the purpose of this procedure was to equate the questionnaire with both the opinions of the four authors and the suggestions of the course content outlines. Therefore by assigning scores from 1 to 10 among the 10 intervals of the questionnaire scores, each content area could receive a maximum of 10 points from the results of the questionnaire. Accordingly, a tally of the number of authors ($N = 6$) would allow for a maximum score of 10 for the combination of these two factors.

The interval scores were then added to the number of authors and content outlines that included that content area. The results of this procedure (Table C-2) determined the content areas of the knowledge test of death and dying. Those content areas with total scores ranging from 9 to 13 were considered important areas. Three items appeared on the knowledge test from each of these areas.

The content areas "methods and materials of death education" and "curricular development in death education," although scored as important areas, were not included on the knowledge test because of the difficulty in developing appropriate test items. The cause of this difficulty was twofold. First, the wide variety and varying availability of methods and materials related to death and dying make it difficult to write test items that can be generalized to all sections of the country. Second, the varying philosophies of curricular development coupled with institutional or instructor biases compounds the difficulty of developing items of a curricular nature in death education. In addition, because of local variation, items from the "cost of funeral" category were not included in the initial item pool.

The content areas with scores ranging from 5 to 8 were considered marginal areas. One item appeared on the knowledge test from each of these areas. Referral aspects of suicide fell into this marginal grouping. However, because of local differences in suicide counseling services, no items appeared on the knowledge test from this content area.

Also because of the variety of books on death and dying in the children's literature, this content area was ommitted from inclusion on the knowledge test.

The content areas "aging (psychosocial aspects)" and "aging (biological aspects)" created a special problem. The results of the death and dying content questionnaire showed that professionals teaching in the area of death education believed that aging (both biological and psychosocial aspects) should be included in a death and dying course if a separate course were not available. Therefore 10 supplemental items (five on biological aspects of aging and five on psychosocial aspects of aging) were included on the knowledge test.

The content areas with scores of less than 5 were considered unimportant content areas. No items appeared on the knowledge test from this grouping.

PHASE II: PREPARATION OF TEST ITEMS

The initial step in the preparation of test items was to select test items written by other authors. Multiple-choice test items were selected from a variety of references. In addition, a variety of questions were developed by the current investigators based on a review of literature. An initial pool of 141 items was reviewed by a local panel of four judges with expertise in death education. Fifty-one items were judged inadequate, leading to a pool of 90 items with which preliminary testing could begin.

PHASE III: PRELIMINARY RELIABILITY, ITEM DIFFICULTY, AND DISCRIMINATING DATA

Preliminary reliability, item difficulty, and discriminating data were gathered from students enrolled in one-credit health education classes at The Pennsylvania State University. The students were instructed to answer all items and to guess at items they did not know.

Kuder-Richardson's Formula 20 was used to determine the internal consistency of the preliminary instrument, and a difficulty rating was developed for each item. Finally, the discriminating power of each item was calculated.

The reliability test of the original 90-item form of the test yielded a Kuder-Richardson Formula 20 score of .714. Although there are several factors that affect reliability, Ary, Jacobs, and Asghar[5] state that researchers should be dissatisfied if they obtain reliability coefficients below .70. Ary and associates also mentioned that low reliability coefficients may result from tests that are either too easy or too difficult.

Therefore even though the reliability score for this form of test was above the level of acceptability of Ary and associates, it was expected that the elimination of inappropriate items would increase the reliability coefficient even more.

The acceptable difficulty rating range for the items on the preliminary group of questions was between 10% and 80%. Nunnally[6] believes that items above 80% and below 20% should be deleted. Nunnally also stated:

> The objectives of a particular unit of instruction and the nature of the subject matter should have precedence over statistical considerations in the development of test items. Some topics inherently are either easy or rather difficult for students as a whole, but teachers will not want to entirely avoid these topics.[6]

Death education is such a topic. With the relatively recent thrusts in the field coupled with the existing misconceptions, it was thought that not all difficult items (those below 20%) should be deleted. To compensate for these factors and the fact that the subjects used to gather this data were generally not knowledgeable in the area, the parameters for the difficulty ratio were set at 10% and 80%.

The discriminating power of individual items was also considered. Ahmann and Glock reported that "it is difficult to establish a minimum positive value below which the discriminating power of a test item is considered faulty."[7] Therefore only negative values, which means the item discriminates in the wrong direction, were deleted.

PHASE IV: CONTENT VALIDITY OF TEST ITEMS

The initial step in this phase was to identify a panel of judges. The panel of judges consisted of those participants (N = 30) of the death and dying content questionnaire who were actively teaching death and dying courses in college and university settings. To determine the content validity of the original test items, the judges were instructed to rate each of the test items on the following scale: 5, very good; 4, good; 3, fair; 2, poor; and 1, unacceptable. The judges were also asked to indicate a perceived need for revision of the stem or basic phase of each question by circling *SR* and a perceived need for revision of the alternatives by circling *AR*. The content validity scores indicated the collective opinions of 13 professionals actively involved in teaching death and dying courses or death education courses at colleges and universities throughout the United States.

316

PHASE V: DELETION OF POOR ITEMS

Three indexes were used to determine whether an item should be deleted from the initial group of 90 items. First, the acceptable difficulty rating range for the items on the preliminary group of questions was established at between 10% and 80%. Second, items with a negative discriminating power were deleted. Finally, the content validity of the individual items was analyzed. If the mean score of an item as determined by the panel of judges was below 3.00, it was deleted from the test.

From the 90 items that appeared on the initial form of the knowledge test, 28 items were eliminated. Five items with high or low difficulty ratings, four items with negative discriminating powers, and three items with low content validity scores were eliminated. An additional 16 items were eliminated because they did not achieve the necessary score on more than one of the indexes used to determine acceptable items.

PHASE VI: ITEM REVISIONS

The panel of judges was asked to indicate a perceived need for revisions in the stem phrase or the alternatives of individual test items. Once the unsatisfactory items were deleted, the suggestions of the panel of judges pertaining to item revisions were scrutinized, and appropriate corrections were made.

PHASE VII: RELIABILITY OF THE KNOWLEDGE TEST

Following the deletion of poor items (phase V) and item revision (phase VI), two reliability measures were gathered. First, Kuder-Richardson's Formula 20 was used to determine the internal consistency of this form of the knowledge text. These data were gathered from students (N = 252) enrolled in one-credit health education classes at The Pennsylvania State University. The result of this measure of reliability for the knowledge test was .742. Although there was a reduction in the number of test items from 90 to 62, the reliability coefficient increased from .714 to .742.

Second, a measure of the test-retest reliability of the knowledge test was gathered. To obtain an estimate of reliability using the test-retest method, the instrument was administered twice to the same group of students. Students (N = 36) enrolled in a three-credit teaching methods course at The Pennsylvania State University were used as subjects. The students were administered the knowledge test during the first and fifth weeks of the academic term.

The same procedure used in previous phases to administer the instrument was followed when gathering test-retest reliability data. The test-retest reliability for the knowledge test was .755. Although this test-retest reliability is relatively low, it should be noted that a small percentage of the students used to gather these data were involved with work on death education projects between treatments. This intervening factor may have altered their knowledge levels.

PHASE VIII: FIELD TESTING OF THE KNOWLEDGE TEST

The knowledge test was field-tested on three different student groups. First, the instrument was given as a pretest and posttest in a health education course (N = 85) entitled Perspectives of Dying at Kean College of New Jersey. Second, the knowledge test was administered in the first and tenth weeks of a sociology course entitled Psychological and Sociological Aspects of Dying at The Pennsylvania State University (N = 52). Third, the instrument was administered in the first and tenth weeks of a nursing course entitled Study of Death and Dying at The Pennsylvania State University (N = 66).

Two statistical procedures were used to analyze the data from the pretesting and posttesting of the knowledge test. First, a dependent t-test was used to determine whether a significant difference existed between the pretest and posttest scores. Second, the Pearson (r) Formula was used to determine the correlation coefficient between the pretest and posttest.

Table C-3 reports the t-test and Pearson r scores for the three field-test groups. All groups showed an increase in mean scores between treatments. Accordingly, the dependent t-test was statistically significant for all three groups at the .001 level. These data indicate the increase in scores between treatments was the result of student learning and not a chance occurrence. In addition, all three student groupings showed a high positive correlation (Pearson r) between test treatments. These data indicate that students scoring high on the pretest tended to score high on the posttest.

The knowledge test could prove useful in a variety of ways. It would provide a reliable evaluative instrument for research purposes. An instrument of this type could be useful in determining the effectiveness of various modes of instructional materials as well as in assessing differences in kowledge acquisition among various populations. Another use for the knowledge test would be to help standardize the course content for

Table C-3. t-Test scores, Pearson r scores, and mean scores for field-test scores

Student group	N	Pretest mean	Posttest mean	t-Test	Pearson r
Health education	85	31.50	35.74	8.75*	.73
Sociology	52	33.71	38.75	7.15*	.74
Nursing	66	34.47	38.66	9.47*	.88

*Significant at .001.

colleges and universities that offer multiple sections. The test could also prove useful for universities that wish to standardize course content with branch campuses and affiliated junior colleges.

The knowledge test could be used as a pretest in death and dying courses to determine the knowledge level of students. With the trend in many states toward competency-based teacher education, it has become important for educators to determine the current status or competency of individual students. The knowledge test could help educators determine such competencies. Finally, with the move toward accountabiity in education, death educators need to demonstrate that their instruction creates positive cognition and affect among the students enrolled. The knowledge test could assist death educators who wish to demonstrate an increase in student knowledge.

REFERENCES

1. Sadwith, J.: An interdisciplinary approach to death education, The Journal of School Health **44:**455-458, 1974.
2. Leviton, D.: The scope of death education, Death Education **1:**41056, 1977.
3. Yarber, W.: Death education: a living issue, The Science Teacher **43:**21-23, 1976.
4. McMahon, J.: Death education, an independent study unit, The Journal of School Health **43:**526-527, 1973.
5. Ary, D., Jacobs, L., and Asghar, R.: Introduction to research in education, New York, 1972, Holt, Rinehart & Winston.
6. Nunnally, J.: Educational measurement and evaluation, New York, 1964, McGraw-Hill, Inc.
7. Ahmann, J.S., and Glock, M.: Evaluating pupil growth: principles of test and measurement, ed. 4, Boston, 1971, Allyn & Bacon, Inc.

Knowledge Test of Death and Dying

The Knowledge Test of Death and Dying was developed and validated in 1979. The instrument contains 62 items. Items 1 to 52 pertain to cognitive areas of death and dying. Items 53 to 62 pertain to biomedical and psychosocial aspects of aging.

THE KNOWLEDGE TEST OF DEATH AND DYING, FINAL FORM (62 ITEMS)

1. In American society, the reality of death is largely
   a. accepted.
   *b. denied.
   c. exploited.
2. Much controversy revolves around the question of whether the medical care system should do which of the following:
   a. Allow mercy killing.
   b. Keep criminals alive.
   *c. Keep patients alive at all costs.
3. Cryogenics is
   a. an embalming process.
   *b. a freezing process.
   c. widely used in the United States.
   d. an inexpensive way of disposing of a body.
4. In American society denial of death is expressed through all of the following, except
   a. the tendency of funeral homes to add lifelike qualities to the dead.
   b. the adoption of euphemistic language for death.

*c. the inclusion of death education in the curriculum.
   d. the rejection and isolation of the aged.
5. When discussing the possibility of their own death, most people feel their death will be the result of
   a. terminal cancer.
   b. natural causes in old age.
   c. heart disease.
   *d. accidents.
6. A sign that grief is moving toward resolution is
   a. leaving the deceased person's belongings just as they were.
   b. practicing one-upmanship on other grievers.
   c. refusing to seek professional help.
   *d. reduced obsessional review.
7. After the death of his wife, an older man generally
   a. stays a widower.
   *b. remarries within 1 or 2 years.
   c. marries an older woman.

*Indicates the correct (or best) response.

d. marries someone he has just met.

8. Research shows that the people who are the most in need of grief therapy tend to be the survivors of victims who died as a result of
   *a. an accident.
   b. cancer.
   c. a prolonged heart condition.
   d. natural causes of old age.

9. The spouse of a terminally ill person begins the bereavement process some time before the event actually occurs. This phenomenon has been termed
   *a. anticipatory grief.
   b. grief therapy.
   c. obsessional review.
   d. preparatory mourning.

10. The events surrounding the death of a spouse may be relived over and over again. This phenomenon has been termed
    a. anticipatory grief.
    b. grief therapy.
    *c. obsessional review.
    d. prolonged bereavement.

11. In which stage of Kubler-Ross' stages of dying is the dying individual likely to seek other professional opinions?
    *a. Denial and isolation
    b. Anger
    c. Bargaining
    d. Depression

12. Kubler-Ross found that
    *a. most terminal patients wish to be told they are dying.
    b. most physicians are highly skilled in meeting the needs of dying patients.
    c. most families want a loved one to know that he or she is dying.
    d. a and b are correct responses.

13. Kubler-Ross found that dying patients
    *a. were usually willing and eager to discuss their own death.
    b. generally did not want to know their own fate.

c. usually did not want visits from friends and relatives.
d. seldom accepted their fate.

14. Research with dying patients has shown that
    a. they tend not to be aware of their terminal illness.
    b. they receive more attention from nurses and doctors than nonterminal patients.
    *c. they receive significantly less attention from nurses and doctors than nonterminal patients.
    d. there is no difference between terminal and nonterminal patients with regard to attention from nurses and doctors.

15. Research has shown that the older person's fear of death is
    a. greater than that of the remainder of the population.
    *b. less than that of the remainder of the population.
    c. approximately the same as the remainder of the population.

16. Scientists are beginning to define the parameters of death in terms of
    *a. cessation of brain waves.
    b. cessation of cardiac functions.
    c. lack of reflex response.
    d. lack of pulmonary functions.

17. Death is most reliably shown by a flat trace on what instrument?
    a. Electrocardiogram
    b. Electromyogram
    *c. Electroencephalograph
    d. Electron microscope

18. What is the study of death called?
    a. Euthanasia
    b. Hereafterism
    c. Pathology
    *d. Thanatology

19. Cellular death is manifested in which of the following?
    a. Cessation of heartbeat

*b. Rigor mortis
c. Cessation of urinary output
d. Cessation of pulmonary function
20. The absence of spontaneous breathing and a heartbeat is an example of
a. brain death.
b. cellular death.
*c. somatic death.
d. spiritual death.
21. An executor
a. is a lawyer who writes wills.
*b. administers the will after the death.
c. is a person who contests the will.
d. is a witness of the will.
22. A recent study found the average cost of securing legal assistance when writing a will was approximately
a. $20 to $35.
*b. $60 to $80.
c. $150 to $170.
d. over $200.
23. If you are insured under Social Security, when you die your spouse or whoever is responsible for your burial will receive
a. $150.
*b. $255.
c. $375.
d. $500.
24. In most states when a person dies without a will, an administrator to supervise the distribution of the property will be appointed by the
a. court of appeals.
b. district magistrate.
c. family court.
*d. probate court.
25. In which of the following cases is embalming legally mandated in all states of the United States?
a. If there is more than a 24-hour interval between death and burial or cremation.
*b. If the body is to be transported by public transportation.

c. If an autopsy has been performed on the body.
d. In all cases except cremation.
26. What is the name of the institution, building, or housing designed to deal exclusively with the dying patient?
a. Geriatric hospital
*b. Hospice
c. Nursing home
d. Thanatological spa
27. The Living Will is closely related to dying individuals' desire
a. to distribute their worldly possessions.
b. to dictate their method of burial.
*c. to be allowed to die a dignified death.
d. to donate their bodies to science.
28. Approximately what percentage of Americans make a will prior to their death?
a. 5%
*b. 25%
c. 50%
d. 75%
29. Which of the following religious groups strongly forbids cremation in all cases?
*a. Mormons
b. Reform Jews
c. Protestants
d. Roman Catholics
30. Which religion allows the greatest variation in funeral ceremonies?
a. Catholic
b. Jewish
c. Mormon
*d. Protestant
31. Which religion advocates burial within 48 hours of death?
a. Catholic
*b. Jewish
c. Mormon
d. Protestant
32. Administering a lethal dose of medicine to a dying patient to eliminate suffering is called

*a. direct euthanasia.
b. genocide.
c. indirect euthanasia.
d. thanocide.

33. Removing life-support systems of a terminally ill patient is called
    a. direct euthanasia.
    b. genocide.
    *c. indirect euthanasia.
    d. thanocide.

34. The nineteenth century practice of physician-induced death was referred to as
    a. passive euthanasia.
    b. indirect euthanasia.
    *c. iatrogenic death.
    d. corpus fatalis.

35. In which age group are the suicide mortality rates in the United States the highest?
    a. 15 to 24 years
    b. 25 to 36 years
    c. 36 to 50 years
    *d. 65 years and over

36. Suicide is most uncommon in which group?
    a. The elderly
    b. College students
    c. Adolescence
    *d. Children under 14 years of age

37. Overall, in the United States suicide is the
    a. fifth leading cause of death.
    *b. tenth leading cause of death.
    c. fifteenth leading cause of death.
    d. twentieth leading cause of death.

38. In cultures in which people are alleged to live to be 100 to 120 years old, the diet (by American standards) is low in what nutrients?
    a. Proteins and minerals
    b. Sugar and carbohydrates
    *c. Calories and animal fats

39. Which of the following groups has the longest life expectancy?

a. American Indians
*b. Black females
c. Black males
d. Mexican-Americans

40. In Great Britain, cremation accounts for approximately what average of all the dispositions?
    a. 5% to 10%
    b. 20% to 30%
    c. 40% to 50%
    *d. More than 50%

41. The traditional American funeral service
    a. is the costliest ceremonial expenditure made by most Americans.
    b. is not particularly appealing to poor people.
    *c. is thought to have social and therapeutic value for the bereaved.
    d. a, b, and c are all correct responses.

42. Funeral customs
    *a. have changed minimally over the past 20 years.
    b. have received little criticism in literature.
    c. are set by law.
    d. change constantly as the result of pressure from religious groups.

43. In the United States disposal of the body through cremation is used in what percent of all deaths?
    *a. 5% to 15%
    b. 20% to 30%
    c. 40% to 50%
    d. More than 50%

44. In what period do most children begin to think about death?
    *a. Preschool
    b. Lower elementary school
    c. Upper elementary school
    d. Junior high school

45. Which of the following is *not* a characteristic of the lower elementary school child?
    a. Seeks answers to questions about death

b. Denies that death is final

c. Views death as reversible

*d. Can distinguish between living and nonliving

46. Which of the following is usually a child's first reaction to the death of a loved one?

  *a. Denial

  b. Despair

  c. Guilt

  d. Hostility

47. What is the term for the educational approach to death education that depicts death in terms of birth, growth, aging, and death?

  a. The confluent approach

  *b. The life-cycle approach

  c. The maturation approach

  d. The systems approach

48. Which of the following statements is incorrect concerning the anatomical gift act?

  a. It allows you to designate your body to a physician, hospital, storage bank, or other medical institution.

  b. It allows you to designate an organ to a physician, hospital, storage bank or other medical institution.

  c. It must be signed with witnesses present.

  *d. It is legally binding in most states.

49. In American society the expression of condolences usually occurs during which of the following ceremonial functions?

  a. Burial

  b. Interment of the body

  c. Memorial service

  *d. Calling hours or wake

50. Which of the following situations did *not* exist or contribute to the more positive attitudes about death that prevailed in the nineteenth century?

  a. High childhood mortality

  *b. Use of hospitals for terminally ill patients

c. Large families

d. Shorter life expectancy

51. Which of the following statements concerning memorial services is correct?

  *a. The format for the ceremony is not uniform.

  b. The service is conducted before the body has been buried or cremated.

  c. There are extended hours for viewing of the body.

52. Cremation is an ancient custom dating from

  *a. prehistoric times.

  b. 1000 BC.

  c. the Roman Empire.

  d. the early fourteenth century.

53. Older people feel more valued in cultures that have

  *a. extended families.

  b. nuclear families.

  c. retirement benefits.

54. What percentage of the American population are over the age of 65?

  a. 3%

  *b. 10%

  c. 15%

  d. 20%

55. When Cumming and Henry asked people aged 50 and over about their social roles, the researchers found that

  *a. most people tended to have fewer social roles after the age of 65.

  b. women tended not to lose their formal roles.

  c. men had more social roles than women.

  d. poor people had more difficulty in dealing with changes in social roles.

56. The majority of old people consider sex to be

  a. dirty or unpleasant.

  b. impossible.

  c. unimportant.

  *d. a continuing valuable part of their lives.

57. Older people tend to
    a. spend more time in groups than alone.
    b. lose interest in religion.
    c. ignore politics.
    *d. continue with leisure activities they enjoyed earlier in life.
58. Which of the following is not a change that occurs in the older adult's skin tissue?
    a. Color change
    b. Increased dryness
    *c. Increased motility
    d. Loss of elasticity
59. In old age, the aging person's heart generally
    a. beats more rapidly.
    *b. has a reduced capacity for work.
    c. shows signs of some structural change.
    d. a, b, and c are all correct responses.

60. Which of the following is not true of the aging body?
    *a. Blood pressure lowers.
    b. Digestion becomes more difficult.
    c. Signals travel more slowly over motor nerves.
    d. Lung capacity decreases.
61. Perhaps the most characteristic thing about being older is being
    a. forgetful.
    *b. slower.
    c. less intelligent.
    d. poor in verbal skills.
62. Among the changes in sexual function experienced by older men is
    a. a decrease in the time it takes to reach a full erection.
    *b. an increase in the time an erection can be sustained without ejaculation.
    c. impotence.
    d. a and c are correct responses.

Summary of research related to death education

Author and source	Research method	Instrumentation	Results	Other comments
Bell, B.D.: The experimental manipulation of death attitudes: a preliminary investigation, Omega **6**:199-205, 1975.	Pretest and Posttest format. The experimental group (N = 24) consisted of students enrolled in an 18-week course on the social aspects of dying and death. The control group (N = 50) was randomly selected from the remaining population.	Investigator-developed cognitive and attitudinal scale was used.	The results showed a significant change in cognition for the experimental group. No significant difference was found in attitudinal measures between groups.	The experimental group engaged in more discussions about death although there was no difference between the groups related to fear of death.
Bolan, B.W.: The effects of a short course of death education on attitude toward death and suicide acceptability: an experimental study, doctoral dissertation, Denton, 1981, Texas Woman's University.	The purpose of the study was to determine if death education altered death attitudes and suicide acceptability. One hundred subjects were randomly assigned to experimental and control groups. Only a posttest design was used. The treatment consisted of a 10-hour course on death education.	The Hardt Death Attitude Scale and the Hoelter Suicide Acceptability Scale were used.	The death education experience had a positive effect on death attitudes. The levels of suicide acceptability were not altered by the treatment, and there was no relationship between death attitudes and suicide acceptability.	A follow-up was conducted 1 week after the posttest. The 7-day span did not change the effects of the treatment.
Combs, D.C.: The role of death education in increasing and decreasing death anxiety and increasing death acceptance, doctoral dissertation, Las Cruces, 1978, New Mexico State University.	This study examined the effects of an eight-session death education program on death anxiety and death acceptance. Didactic and experimental curricular models were examined. Undergraduate students were used as subjects. Nursing students were compared to other undergraduates.	The Templer Death Anxiety Scale and the Dickstein Death Concern Scale were used to measure anxiety. Death acceptance was measured by the Ray and Najman Death Acceptance Scale.	The results indicated that the experiential curricular model was more effective in decreasing death anxiety while the didactic model was more effective for undergraduates. The F-ratios for the Death Anxiety and Death Acceptance Scales proved not to be significant.	The author concludes that the denial of death prevented the participants from experiencing death fear or death anxiety. The author believes that curricular changes should be made to encourage students to confront death fears and anxieties.

Continued.

Author and source	Research method	Instrumentation	Results	Other comments
Davis, T.M.: The effect of the death education film *In My Memory* on elementary school students in the La Crosse, Wisconsin public schools doctoral dissertation, Bloomington, 1975, Indiana University.	The author assessed the effect of the Inside/Out film *In My Memory* on attitudes toward death of sixth through second grade students. Also the effects of allowing students to properly discuss death were measured.	The author designed an instrument to measure the death attitudes of students. This instrument was given as a pretest and posttest.	These data suggested that students who viewed the film and had an opportunity to discuss death were more accepting of the universality and irreversibility of death.	The *In My Memory* film is excellent if properly used. These data lend support to the notion that even a limited death education experience can have a positive affect on students' attitudes.
Freitag, C.B., and Hassler, S.D.: The effects of death education, Resources In Education, **16**(9):29, 1981.	The purpose of this study was to assess the effect of a death education course on reducing anxiety toward death. The control group (N = 116) consisted of students enrolled in a psychology course, and the experimental group (N = 60) were students enrolled in a death and dying course.	The Pandey Death Anxiety Scale and the Topics in Thanatology Scale were used.	The pretest showed similar levels of anxiety and similar feelings between the groups regarding death. The experimental group showed a significant decrease in death anxiety on the Pandey scale.	Between-treatment scores on the Topics of Thanatology Scale were not significant.
Hardt, D.V.: A measurement of the improvement of attitudes toward death, Journal of School Health, **46**:269-270, 1976.	Hardt pretested and post-tested 86 students aged 18 to 27. The attitude scale was administered on the first and last day of class between which 45 hours of instruction were given.	The author developed a reliable and valid death attitude instrument. The Thurstone Equal Appearing Internal Scale yielded a reliability of 0.87.	The subjects had positive increases in death attitudes. The researcher found that those students who tended to score low on the pretest tended to show the largest increase.	The author believes that these data support the notion that a death education course can have a positive influence in changing attitudes. However, he cautions that other factors, such as teacher qualifications, instructional strategies, and course objectives, may have influenced the

328

...ess, D.W.: An evaluation of a self-instructional program designed to reduce anxiety and fear about death and of the relation of that program to sixteen personal history variables, Memphis, 1974, Memphis State University.	...Rauer studied the effectiveness of the "Shaping Your Attitudes Toward Death: A Self-Instructional Approach" to a select group of 87 members of Presbyterian churches in Alabama and Tennessee. A pretest and posttest design was used.	The Templer Death Anxiety Scale and the Collett-Lester Fear of Death Scale were used.	The instructional approach was effective in reducing fear and anxiety concerning death. The only significant difference based on sex was that women showed a greater reduction of death anxiety between treatments.	The author also found that an increase in religious activities tended to lower fear and anxiety about death.
Male, N.S.: Effects of thanatology instruction on attitudes and fears about death and dying, doctoral dissertation, Philadelphia, 1978, Temple University.	The author conducted a study with high school students to determine if a death education experience would foster positive attitudes toward death and reduce the fear of death. The experimental group (N = 37) took an elective psychology course that included a 6-week module on thanatology. The control group did not receive the module.	The Collett-Lester Fear of Death Scale and the Hardt Death Attitudinal Scale were used. The Personal History Inventory was given as a pretest to provide background information.	The results of the Death Attitudinal Inventory failed to support the hypotheses that positive attitudes toward death would result from instruction and that there would be differences in attitudes and concepts between those who elected to take the course and those who opted otherwise.	Although the data showed no significant attitudinal change, the author and instructor of the course did believe that the 6-week course was a valuable experience for the students.

Continued.

Author and source	Research method	Instrumentation	Results	Other comments
McClam, P.A.: The effects of death education on fear of death and death anxiety among health-care and helping professionals, doctoral dissertation, Columbia, 1978, University of South Carolina.	A 2-day program of instruction using a pre-test and posttest follow-up design was used to determine the effects of a planned program of death education on death fears and anxieties of health care and helping professionals. Variables such as age, sex, religion, church attendance, early experience with death, and occupation were examined.	The Templer Death Anxiety Scale, Collett-Lester Fear of Death Scale and the Rotter Internal-External Locus of Control Scale were used.	The results indicated that only one variable, church attendance, accounted for a significant variation in fear of death of self, and death anxiety was not significantly related to any of the variables. There was no significant change in death fear as a result of the death instruction.	The results of the study highlight the need for research to be done in two areas. First, there is a need to examine two short-term effects of death education on belief systems, and second, there is a need for a reliable instrument in this area.
McDonald, R.T.: The effect of death education on specific attitudes toward death in college students, Death Education, 5:59-65, 1981.	The purpose of the study was to assess the effectiveness of death education on specific attitudes. The specific attitudes selected were those directly related to the following course goals: (1) information sharing, (2) values clarification, and (3) coping behaviors. The experimental group (N = 88) were students enrolled in an under-graduate course on death and dying. The control group (N = 80) were students not enrolled in the class but who expressed an interest in enrolling in the course	An investigator-developed attitude survey was given the first and last weeks of the semester. Items on the survey were placed on a Likert scale. The survey was designed to correspond with the major content areas of the course.	Significant changes in death attitudes occurred in the experimental group when compared to the control group. Students in the experimental group believed that they had become more comfortable in interacting with dying and bereaved persons. Also there was a significant change in preferences for means of body disposal, with the experimental group more likely to opt for more nontraditional means.	The author believes that most death education courses would have an immediate impact on attitudes toward death that are rooted in traditional and religious values. Long range follow-up studies need to be conducted in this area.

330

Miles, M.S.: The effects of a small group education/counseling experience on the attitudes of nurses and toward death and toward dying patients, doctoral dissertation, Kansas City, 1976, University of Missouri.	The purpose of the study was to assess the effects of a small-group educational experience in attitudes toward death and toward dying patients. The subjects were grouped in three categories: (1) registered nurses who worked in high-risk areas of hospitals who registered for the course, (2) a control group of registered nurses who did not register, and (3) freshman students from a local university.	Two instruments were used in this study: parts I and II of the Death Anxiety Semantic Differential and the Attitude Toward Dying Patients Questionnaire.	The author concluded that attendance at the small-group educational experience had an impact on changing attitudes toward death and toward dying patients for the nurses who enrolled in the course.	It would be of interest to examine whether a large group educational activity would have had a similar effect on changing the attitudes of registered nurses.
Murray, P.: Death education and its effects on the death anxiety level of nurses, Psychological Reports, 35:1250, 1974.	The author evaluated the effectiveness of a death education course designed for nurses. Thirty subjects were given a pretest and post-test and a 6½-hour class over a 6-week period. A follow-up was conducted 4 weeks later.	The Templer Death Anxiety Scale was used.	No significant difference was found between the pretest and posttest. However, a significant reduction in death anxiety scores was found between the posttest and the follow-up.	The author hypothesized that reflections on the course material and utilization of the knowledge gained in the course manifested itself in lower death anxiety scores of the follow-up.

Continued.

Author and source	Research method	Instrumentation	Results	Other comments
Nichol, J.C.: A study of the effects of a death education unit upon secondary students, doctoral dissertation, Fayetteville, 1980, University of Arkansas.	The study examined the effects of a death education unit on knowledge acquisition, attitudes toward death, and levels of anxiety for high school students. The experimental groups (N = 102) and control groups (N = 103) were given pretests and post-tests. The experimental group had a death education unit as part of a humanities or sociology course.	The Berg and Daugherty Fact Sheet, the Hardt Death Attitude Scale and Templer Death Anxiety Scale.	The result indicated that there was an increase in knowledge by the experimental group. Also the experimental group showed a significant change in death attitudes but there was no significant difference on the anxiety scale.	It would be interesting to correlate the relationship between knowledge increase and changes in death attitudes and death anxiety.
Pearson, A.L.: An investigation of the effects of a death education seminar on the attitudes of student practical nurses in Alabama toward death, doctoral dissertation, Auburn, AL, 1979, Auburn University.	The study sought to determine whether a death education seminar would change the death attitudes of student practical nurses. A pre-test and posttest experimental (N = 59) and a control group (N = 45) design was used. The groups were randomly assigned. The experimental group participated in a 2½-hour presentation on death education.	A personal data questionnaire, the Death Attitude Scale, and an attitude toward death scale were used.	The results indicated that there were no significant differences on the death attitude scale between groups and there were no significant differences between groups on the attitude toward death scale.	It seems that it may be unrealistic to assume that measurable attitudinal changes are going to result from a relatively short death education seminar.

Pennington, J.L.: Alterations in death attitudes as a function of formal instruction in death and dying, doctoral dissertation, St. Louis, 1978, St. Louis University.	This study sought to clarify the following questions: Will personal and personally desired attitudes toward death of others, death of self, dying of others and dying of self become more congruent as a result of death instruction? The control group took a course in psychology while the experimental group took a death and dying course.	The Collett-Lester Fear of Death Scale was used in this study.	The results of the study indicated that the experimental subjects' attitudes consistently became less congruent on all scales. Thus the results did not support the hypothesis.	The author believes that the study should be replicated using more highly developed operational definitions and using a battery of scales that measure death anxiety. In addition, a design that uses behavior change may provide supplemental measure on the effects of dying and death instruction.
Redick, R.: Behavioral group counseling and death anxiety in student nurses, doctoral dissertation, Pittsburgh, 1974, University of Pittsburgh.	Redick studied the use of behavior modification techniques to reduce death anxiety. Thirty nurses were randomly assigned to three groups: an experimental-treatment group, an attention-placebo group and a wait-list control group. The experimental group received eight 45 minute sessions on systematic desensitization. The placebo group received a similar number of lecture-oriented presentations. The wait-control group received no intervention.	The Boyar Fear of Death Scale and two parts of Death Anxiety Semantic Differential were given before and 4 days after the experiment.	On five of six comparisons, the experimental treatment group had significantly reduced their death anxiety.	The author notes that even though death anxiety was reduced, the experimental group still manifested death-related anxiety.

Continued.

Author and source	Research method	Instrumentation	Results	Other comments
Rochester, S. and others: Immediacy in language: a channel to care of the dying patient, Journal of Community Psychology **2**:75-76, 1974.	These authors analyzed the effect of therapy-discussion sessions on the communication patterns of nurses while they worked with dying patients. Twenty nurses served as the experimental group with the same number in the control.	Before and 3 months after the treatment each participant was asked what they would do and say in four situations involving dying patients. These responses were coded by raters as to directness in communication. These questions served as the evaluative instrument.	The results showed that the answers given by those nurses in the control group tended to indicate more communicative distance between the nurse and the dying patient.	The authors hypothesized that allowing nurses to express their fears and attitudes would enhance the nurses' ability to become more direct in their communications with their dying patients. Also nurses with no experience in dealing with terminal patients would tend to maintain communicative distance with their patients.
Snyder, M., and others: Changes in nursing students' attitudes toward death and dying: a measurement of curriculum integration effectiveness, International Journal of Social Psychiatry **19**:294-298, 1973.	The authors evaluated the effect of a 3-year nursing program on changing attitudes toward death. Sixty-five first-year students were compared to 65 third-year students.	The students were given a questionnaire to assess their conscious death concerns.	The study indicated that third-year students less often thought of their own death. Third-year students thought about the death of friends or relatives less often. First-year students tended to dream of being dead or dying more than third-year students.	These data indicate that nursing students who experienced the nursing program in death education manifested less death concern. Therefore these data lend support of the death education curriculum.

Watts, D.K.: Evaluation of death attitude change resulting from a death education instructional unit, Death Education 1:187-193, 1977.	The purpose of the study was to assess attitudinal changes of college students involved in a death education instructional unit within a personal health course. The experimental group (N = 39) and control group (N = 40) were given pretest and post-tests to assess attitudes.	The Hardt Death Anxiety Scale and the Watts-Andrews Death Attitude Questionnaire were used in this study.	The result showed that the experimental group had more favorable death attitudes than the control group.	The author believes that health educators can feel confident using death education strategies that require students to examine their personal attitudes and values.
Whelan, W.M.: The effects of a death awareness workshop on the cognitive, emotional and values orientation of participants, doctoral dissertation, 1978, University of Southern Mississippi. Hattiesburg,	The purpose of the study was to evaluate a death awareness workshop. Other variables, including death anxiety and attitudes toward death were also examined. Sixteen graduate students in counselor education were used as subjects. These students were randomly assigned to two groups (N = 8). The experimental group was given an 8-week workshop.	The subjects were given instruments designed to measure a variety of values, including death anxiety and attitudes toward death.	There was a significant difference between groups on death anxiety and attitudes toward death.	The author believes that the death awareness workshop was effective in helping students confront and become more comfortable with death.

APPENDIX F

Legislation regarding the Living Will and the right to die

In recent years many bills have been introduced in state legislatures. The three pieces of legislation included in Appendix F are examples of such bills. The following states have introduced legislation patterned after the California Natural Death Act: Alabama, Arizona, Colorado, Connecticut, Delaware, Florida, Georgia, Hawaii, Idaho, Illinois, Indiana, Maine, Maryland, Massachusetts, Minnesota, Mississippi, Missouri, Montana, Nebraska, Nevada, New Jersey, New Mexico, New York, Oklahoma, Texas, Utah, Vermont, Virginia, and Washington.

For further information a legislative manual may be obtained from Society for the Right to Die, Inc., 250 West 57th St., New York, NY 10019.

STATUTE OF THE STATE OF KANSAS

77-202. Definition of death. A person will be considered medically and legally dead if, in the opinion of a physician, based on ordinary standards of medical practice, there is the absence of spontaneous respiratory and cardiac function and, because of the disease or condition which caused, directly or indirectly, these functions to cease, or because of the passage of time since these functions ceased, attempts at resuscitation are considered hopeless; and, in this event, death will have occurred at the time these functions ceased; or

A person will be considered medically and legally dead if, in the opinion of a physician, based on ordinary standards of medical practice, there is the absence of spontaneous brain function; and if based on ordinary standards of medical practice, during reasonable attempts to either maintain or restore spontaneous circulatory or respiratory function in the absence of aforesaid brain function, it appears that further attempts at resuscitation or supportive maintenance will not succeed, death will have occurred at the time when these conditions first coincide. Death is to be pronounced before artifical means of supporting respiratory and circulatory function are terminated and before any vital organ is removed for purposes of transplantation.

These alternative definitions of death are to be utilized for all purposes in this state,

336

including the trials of civil and criminal cases, any laws to the contrary notwithstanding.

ARKANSAS LIVING WILL LEGISLATION

Act 879 (H.B. 826), enacted: March, 1977
Introduced by Representative Henry Wilkins III February 24, 1977
Passed by House (52-3) March 14, 1977
Passed by Senate (32-0) March 17, 1977
Signed by Governor David Pryor March 30, 1977

An act to permit an individual to request or refuse in writing medical or surgical means or procedures calculated to prolong his life; and to authorize such request or refusal by others on behalf of one incompetent or under 18; and for other purposes.

Be it enacted by the General Assembly of the State of Arkansas:

§1. Every person shall have the right to die with dignity and to refuse and deny the use or application by any person of artificial, extraordinary, extreme or radical medical or surgical means or procedures calculated to prolong his life. Alternatively, every person shall have the right to request that such extraordinary means be utilized to prolong life to the extent possible.

§2. Any person, with the same formalities as are required by the laws of this State for the execution of a will, may execute a document exercising such right and refusing and denying the use or application by any person of artificial, extraordinary, extreme or radical medical or surgical means or procedures calculated to prolong his life. In the alternative, any person may request in writing that all means be utilized to prolong life.

§3. If any person is a minor or an adult who is physically or mentally unable to execute or is otherwise incapacitated from executing either document, it may be executed in the same form on his behalf:

(a) By either parent of the minor;
(b) By his spouse;
(c) If his spouse is unwilling or unable to act, by his child aged eighteen or over;
(d) If he has more than one child aged eighteen or over, by a majority of such children;
(e) If he has no spouse or child aged eighteen or over, by either of his parents;
(f) If he has no parent living, by his nearest living relative; or

337

(g) If he is mentally incompetent, by his legally appointed guardian. Provided, that a form executed in compliance with this Section must contain a signed statement by two physicians that extraordinary means would have to be utilized to prolong life.

§4. Any person, hospital or other medical institution which acts or refrains from acting in reliance on and in compliance with such document shall be immune from liability otherwise arising out of such failure to use or apply artificial, extraordinary, extreme or radical medical or surgical means or procedures calculated to prolong such person's life.

§5. All laws and parts of laws in conflict with this Act are hereby repealed.

CALIFORNIA NATURAL DEATH ACT

The people of the State of California do enact as follows:

SECTION 1. Chapter 3.9 (commencing with section 7185 is added to Part 1 of Division 7 of the Health and Safety Code) to read:

Chapter 3.9 Natural Death Act

§7185. This act shall be known and may be cited as the Natural Death Act.

§7186. The Legislature finds that adult persons have the fundamental right to control the decisions relating to the rendering of their own medical care, including the decision to have life-sustaining procedures withheld or withdrawn in instances of a terminal condition.

The Legislature further finds that modern medical technology has made possible the artificial prolongation of human life beyond natural limits.

The Legislature further finds that, in the interest of protecting individual autonomy, such prolongation of life for persons with a terminal condition may cause loss of patients's dignity and unnecessary pain and suffering, while providing nothing medically necessary or beneficial to the patient.

The Legislature further finds that there exists considerable uncertainty in the medical and legal professions as to the legality of terminating the use or application of life-sustaining procedures where a patient has voluntarily and in sound mind evidenced a desire that such procedures be withheld or withdrawn.

In recognition of the dignity and privacy which patients have a right to expect, the Legislature hereby declares that the laws of the State of California shall recognize the right of an adult person to make written directive instructing his physician to withhold or withdraw life-sustaining procedures in the event of a terminal condition.

§7187. The following definitions shall govern the construction of this chapter.:

(a) "Attending physician" means the physician selected by, or assigned to, the patient who has primary responsibility for the treatment and care of that patient.

(b) "Directive" means a written document voluntarily executed by the declarant in accordance with the requirements of section 7188. The directive, or a copy of the directive, shall be made part of the patient's medical records.

(c) "Life-sustaining procedure" means any medical procedure or intervention which utilizes mechanical or other artificial means to sustain, restore, or supplant a vital function, which, when applied to a qualified patient, would serve only to artificially prolong the moment of death and where, in the judgment of the attending physician, death is imminent whether or not such procedures are utilized. "Life-sustaining procedure" shall not include the administration of medication or the performance of any medical procedure deemed necessary to alleviate pain.

(d) "Physician" means a physician and surgeon licensed by the Board of Medical Quality Assurance or the Board of Osteopathic Examiners.

(e) "Qualified patient" means a patient diagnosed and certified in writing to be afflicted with a terminal condition by two physicians, one of whom shall be the attending physician, who have personally examined the patient.

(f) "Terminal condition" means an incurable condition caused by injury, disease, or illness, which, regardless of the application of life-sustaining procedures, would, within reasonable medical judgment, produce death, and where the application of life-sustaining procedures serves only to postpone the moment of death of the patient.

§7188. Any adult person may execute a directive directing the withholding or withdrawal of life-sustaining procedures in a terminal condition. The directive shall be signed by the declarant in the presence of two witnesses not related to the declarant by blood or marriage and who would not be entitled to any portion of the estate of the declarant upon his decease under any will of the declarant or codicil thereto then existing or, at the time of the directive, by operation of law then existing. In addition, a witness to a directive shall not be the attending physician, an employee of the attending physician or a health facility in which the declarant is a patient, or any person who has a claim against any portion of the estate of the declarant upon his decease at the time of the execution of the directive. The directive shall be in the following form: [p. 340]

§7188.5 A directive shall have no force or effect if the declarant is a patient in a skilled nursing facility as defined in subdivision (c) of Section 1250 at the time the directive is executed unless one of the two witnesses to the directive is a patient advocate or ombudsman as may be designated by the State Department of Aging for this purpose pursuant to any other applicable provision of law. The patient advocate or ombudsman shall have the same qualifications as a witness under Section 7188.

STATE OF CALIFORNIA
Directive to Physicians

Directive made this _____ day of _____
(month, year).

    I _____,
being of sound mind, willfully, and voluntarily make known my desire that my life shall not be artificially prolonged under the circumstances set forth below, do hereby declare:

1. If at any time I should have an incurable injury, disease, or illness certified to be a terminal condition by two physicians, and where the application of life-sustaining procedures would serve only to artificially prolong the moment of my death and where my physician determines that my death is imminent whether or not life-sustaining procedures are utilized, I direct that such procedures be withheld or withdrawn, and that I be permitted to die naturally.

2. In the absence of my ability to give directions regarding the use of such life-sustaining procedures, it is my intention that this directive shall be honored by my family and physician(s) as the final expression of my legal right to refuse medical or surgical treatment and accept the consequences from such a refusal.

3. If I have been diagnosed as pregnant and that diagnosis is known to my physician, this directive shall have no force or effect during the course of my pregnancy.

4. I have been diagnosed and notified at least 14 days ago as having a terminal condition by _____, M.D., whose address is _____, and whose telephone number is _____. I understand that if I have not filled in the physician's name and address, it shall be presumed that I did not have a terminal condition when I made out this directive.

5. This directive shall have no force or effect five years from the date filled in above.

6. I understand the full import of this directive and I am emotionally and mentally competent to make this directive.

                Signed _____

City, County and State of Residence _____

The declarant has been personally known to me and I believe him or her to be of sound mind.

                Witness _____

                Witness _____

The intent of this section is to recognize that some patients in skilled nursing facilities may be so insulated from a voluntary decision-making role, by virtue of the custodial nature of their care, as to require special assurance that they are capable of willfully and voluntarily executing a directive.

§ 7189. (a) A directive may be revoked at any time by the declarant, without regard to his mental state or competency, by any of the following methods:

(1) By being canceled, defaced, obliterated, or burnt, torn, or otherwise destroyed by the declarant or by some person in his presence and by his direction.

(2) By a written revocation of the declarant expressing his intent to revoke, signed and dated by the declarant. Such revocation shall become effective only upon communication to the attending physician by the declarant or by a person acting on behalf of the declarant. The attending physician shall record in the patient's medical record the time and date when he received notification of the written revocation.

(3) By a verbal expression by the declarant of his intent to revoke the directive. Such revocation shall become effective only upon communication to the attending physician by the declarant or by a person acting on behalf of the declarant. The attending physician shall record in the patient's medical record the time, date, and place of revocation and the time, date, and place, if different, of when he received notification of the revocation.

(b) There shall be no criminal or civil liability on the part of the person for failure to act upon a revocation made pursuant to this section unless that person has actual knowledge of the revocation.

§ 7189.5. A directive shall be effective for five years from the date of execution thereof unless sooner revoked in a manner prescribed in Section 7189. Nothing in this chapter shall be construed to prevent a declarant from reexecuting a directive at any time in accordance with the formalities of Section 7188, including reexecution subsequent to a diagnosis of a terminal condition. If the declarant has executed more than one directive, such time shall be determined from the date of execution of the last directive known to the attending physician. If the declarant becomes comatose or is rendered incapable of communicating with the attending physician, the directive shall remain in effect for the duration of the comatose condition or until such time as the declarant's condition renders him or her able to communicate with the attending physician.

§ 7190. No physician or health facility which, acting in accordance with the requirements of this chapter, causes the withholding or withdrawal of life-sustaining procedures from a qualified patient, shall be subject to civil liability therefrom. No licensed health professional, acting under the direction of a physician, who participates in the withholding or withdrawal of life-sustaining procedures in accordance with the provisions of this chapter shall be subject to any civil liability. No physician, or licensed health professional acting under the direction of a physician, who participates in the withholding or withdrawal of life-sustaining procedures in accordance with the provisions of this chapter shall be guilty of any criminal act or of unprofessional conduct.

§ 7191. (a) Prior to effecting a withholding or withdrawal of life-sustaining procedures from a qualified patient pursuant to the directive, the attending physician shall determine that the directive complies with Section 7188, and, if the patient is mentally competent, that the directive and all steps proposed by the attending physician to be undertaken are in accord with the desires of the qualified patient.

(b) If the declarant was a qualified patient at least 14 days prior to executing or reexecuting the directive, the directive shall be conclusively presumed, unless revoked, to be the directions of the patient regarding the withholding or withdrawal of life-sustaining procedures. No physician, and no licensed health professional acting under the direction of a physician, shall be criminally or civilly liable for failing to effectuate the directive of the qualified patient pursuant to this subdivision. A failure by a physician to effectuate the directive of a qualified patient pursuant to this division shall constitute unprofessional conduct if the physician refuses to make the necessary arrangements, or fails to take the necessary steps, to effect the transfer of the qualified patient to another physician who will effectuate the directive of the qualified patient.

(c) If the declarant becomes a qualified patient subsequent to executing the directive, and has not subsequently reexecuted the directive, the attending physician may give weight to the directive as evidence of the patient's directions regarding the withholding or withdrawal of life-sustaining procedures and may consider other factors, such as information from the affected family or the nature of the patient's illness, injury, or disease, in determining whether the totality of circumstances known to the attending physician justify effectuating the directive. No physician, and no licensed health professional acting under the direction of a physician, shall be criminally or civilly liable for failing to effectuate the directive of the qualified patient pursuant to this subdivision.

§ 7192. (a) The withholding or withdrawal of life-sustaining procedures from a qualified patient in accordance with the provisions of this chapter shall not, for any purpose, constitute a suicide.

(b) The making of a directive pursuant to section 7188 shall not restrict, inhibit, or impair in any manner the sale, procurement, or issuance of any policy of life insurance, nor shall it be deemed to modify the terms of an existing policy of life insurance. No policy of life insurance shall be legally impaired or invalidated in any manner by the withholding or withdrawal of life-sustaining procedures from an insured qualified patient, notwithstanding any term of the policy to the contrary.

(c) No physician, health facility, or other health provider, and no health care service plan, insurer issuing disability insurance, self-insured employee welfare benefit plan, or non-profit hospital service plan, shall require any person to execute a directive as a condition for being insured for, or receiving, health care services.

§ 7193. Nothing in this chapter shall impair or supersede any legal right or legal responsibility which any person may have to effect the withholding or withdrawal of life-sustaining procedures in any lawful manner. In such respect the provisions of this chapter are cumulative.

§ 7194. Any person who willfully conceals, cancels, defaces, obliterates, or damages the directive of another without such declarant's consent shall be guilty of a misdemeanor. Any person who, except where justified or excused by law, falsifies or forges the directive of another, or willfully conceals or withholds personal knowledge of a revocation as provided in Section 7189, with the intent to cause a withholding or withdrawal of life-sustaining procedures contrary to the wishes of the declarant, and thereby, because of any such act, directly causes life-sustaining procedures to be withheld or withdrawn and death to thereby be hastened, shall be subject to prosecution for unlawful homicide as provided in Chapter 1 (commencing with Section 187) of Title 8 of Part 1 of the Penal Code.

§ 7195. Nothing in this chapter shall be construed to condone, authorize, or approve mercy killing, or to permit any affirmative or deliberate act or omission to end life other than to permit the natural process of dying as provided in this chapter.

SECTION 2. If any provision of this act or the application thereof to any person or circumstances in held invalid, such invalidity shall not affect other provisions or applications of the act which can be given effect without the invalid provision or application, and to this end the provisions of this act are severable.

SECTION 3. Notwithstanding Section 2231 of the Revenue of Taxation Code, there shall be no reimbursement pursuant to this section nor shall there be any appropriation made by this act because the Legislature recognizes that during any legislative session a variety of changes to laws relating to crimes and infractions may cause both increased and decreased costs to local government entities and school districts which, in the aggregate, do not result in significant identifiable cost changes.

APPENDIX G

Directory of funeral and memorial societies

A memorial society is a democratic, nonprofit association of people formed to obtain dignity, simplicity, and economy in funeral arrangements through preplanning.

Thoughtful people everywhere are turning to simplicity in funeral practices to emphasize the spiritual values of life and death rather than exalt the physical. They have learned by experience that simplicity can reduce both suffering and expense at the time of death and can more effectively meet the urgent social needs of the survivors.

Advance planning is necessary to obtain both simplicity and economy. Important also is understanding within the family, which can be developed by frank discussion and planning at a time when death is not imminent.

To facilitate preplanning, memorial societies have been formed in more than 175 cities in the United States and Canada. These societies welcome members without regard to color or creed. They charge modest membership fees and provide information and counsel. Most have helpful agreements with funeral directors. The societies listed here belong to the Continental Association of Funeral and Memorial Societies and the Memorial Society Association of Canada. The following pages tell where these societies are located.

For more information persons may contact their local society or write the Continental Association of funeral and Memorial Societies, Suite 1100, 1828 L St. NW, Washington, DC 20036, 202-293-4821. In Canada the address is the Memorial Society Association of Canada, Box 96, Station "A", Weston, Ontario M9N 3M6. For advice on organizing a society or preplanning without a society, one may send $2.50 plus 50¢ postage to the Continental Association for *A Manual of Death Education and Simple Burial*.

From A Manual of Death Education and Simple Burial, by Ernest Morgan. ($2.50 plus 50 cents postage from Celo Press, Route 5, Burnsville, NC 28714)

UNITED STATES

ALABAMA
Mobile: The Azalea Funeral and Memorial Council, 2601-A South Fla. Street, 36606, 205-653-9092.

ALASKA
Anchorage: Cook Inlet Memorial Society, P.O. Box 2414, 99510, 907-277-6001, 907-272-7801.

ARIZONA
Phoenix: Valley Memorial Society, P.O. Box 15813, 85060, 602-956-2919.
Prescott: Memorial Society of Prescott, 335 Aubrey St., 86301, 602-778-3000.
Tucson: Tucson Memorial Society, P.O. Box 12661, 85732, 602-323-1121.
Yuma: Memorial Society of Yuma, P.O. Box 4314, 85364, 602-783-2339.

ARKANSAS
Fayetteville: Northwest Arkansas Memorial Society, 1227 S. Maxwell, 72701, 501-442-5580.
Little Rock: Memorial Society of Central Arkansas, 12213 Rivercrest Dr., 72207, 501-225-7276.

CALIFORNIA
Arcata: Humboldt Funeral Society, 666 11th St., 95521, 707-822-1321.
Berkeley: Bay Area Funeral Society, P.O. Box 264, 94701, 415-841-6653.
Fresno: Valley Memorial Society, P.O. Box 101, 93707, 209-224-9580.
Los Angeles: Los Angeles Funeral Society, Inc., P.O. Box 44188, Panorama City, 91412, 213-786-6845.
Modesto: Stanislaus Memorial Society, P.O. Box 4252, 95352, 209-523-0316.
Palo Alto: Peninsula Funeral Society, 168 S. California Ave., 94306, 415-321-2109.
Ridgecrest: Kern Memorial Society, P.O. Box 2122, 93555.
Sacramento: Sacramento Valley Memorial Society, Inc., Box 161688, 3720 Folsom Blvd., 95816, 916-451-4641.
San Diego: San Diego Memorial Society, P.O. Box 16336, 92116, 714-284-1465.
San Luis Obispo: Central Coast Memorial Society, P.O. Box 679, 93406, 805-543-6133.
Santa Barbara: Channel Cities Memorial Society, P.O. Box 424, 93102, 805-962-4794.
Santa Cruz: Funeral and Memorial Society of Monterey Bay, Inc., P.O. Box 2900, 95063, 408-462-1333.
Stockton: San Joaquin Memorial Society, P.O. Box 4832, 95204, 209-462-8739.

COLORADO
Denver: Rocky Mountain Memorial Society, 4101 E. Hampden, 80222, 303-759-2800.

CONNECTICUT

Groton: Memorial Society of Southeast Connecticut, P.O. Box 825, 06340, 203-445-8848.
Hartford: Memorial Society of Greater Hartford, 2609 Albany Ave., W. Harford, 06117, 203-523-8700.
New Haven: Memorial Society of Greater New Haven, 60 Connelly Parkway, c/o Co-op, Hamden, 06514, 203-288-6463, 203-865-2015.
Southbury: Southbury Branch of Greater New Haven Memorial Society, 514A Heritage Village, 06488, 203-264-7564.
Stamford: Council Memorial Society, 628 Main St., 06901, 203-348-2800.
Westport: Memorial Society of southwest Connecticut:, 71 Hillendale Rd., 06880, 203-227-8705.

DISTRICT OF COLUMBIA

Washington: Memorial Society of Metropolitan Washington, 16th and Harvard Sts., N.W., 20009, 202-234-7777.

FLORIDA

Cocoa: Brevard Memorial Society, P.O. Box 276, 32922, 305-783-8699.
DeBary: Funeral Society of Mid-Florida, P.O. Box 262, 32713, 305-668-6587.
Destin: Okoloosa County Branch of Pensacola and Northwest Florida, P.O. Box 7, 32541, 904-837-6559.
Ft. Myers: Memorial Society of Southwest Florida, P.O. Box 1953, 33902, 813-936-1590.
Gainesville: Memorial Society of Alachua County, Box 13195, 32604, 904-376-7073.
Jacksonville: Jacksonville Memorial Society, 6915 Holiday Rd. N., 32216, 904-724-3766.
Miami: Miami Memorial Society, P.O. Box 557422, Ludlam Branch, 33155, 305-667-3697.
Orlando: Orange County Memorial Society, 1815 E. Robinson St., 32803, 305-898-3621.
Pensacola: Funeral and Memorial Society of Pensacola and Northwest Florida, P.O. Box 4778, 32507, 904-456-7028.
St. Petersburg: Suncoast-Tampa Bay Memorial Society, 719 Arlington Ave. N., 33701, 813-898-3294.
Sarasota: Memorial Society of Sarasota, P.O. Box 5683, 33579, 813-953-3740.
Tallahassee: Funeral and Memorial Society of Leon County, Box 20189, 32304.
Tampa: Tampa Memorial Society, 3915 N. A St., 33609, 813-877-4604.
West Palm Beach: Palm Beach Funeral Society, P.O. Box 2065, 33402, 305-833-8936.

GEORGIA

Atlanta: Memorial Society of Georgia, 1911 Cliff Valley Way, NE, 30329, 404-634-2896.

HAWAII

Honolulu: Funeral and Memorial Society of Hawaii, 200 N. Vineyard Blvd., Suite 403, 96817, 808-538-1282.

IDAHO

Boise: Idaho Memorial Association, P.O. Box 2622, 83705 (in process of joining).

ILLINOIS

Bloomington: McLean County Branch of Chicago Memorial Society, 1613 E. Emerson, 61701, 309-828-0235.
Carbondale: Memorial Society of Carbondale Area, 1214 W. Hill St., 62901, 618-549-7816.
Chicago: Chicago Memorial Association, 59 E. Van Buren St., 60605, 312-939-0678.
Elgin: Fox Valley Funeral Association, 783 Highland Ave., 60120, 312-695-5265.
Peoria: Memorial Society of Greater Peoria, 908 Hamilton Blvd., 61603, 309-673-5391.
Rockford: Memorial Society of Northern Illinois, P.O. Box 6131, 61125, 815-964-7697.
Urbana: Champaign County Memorial Society, 309 W. Green St., 61801, 217-384-8862.

INDIANA

Bloomington: Bloomington Memorial Society, 2120 N. Fee Lane, 47401, 812-332-3695.
Ft. Wayne: Northeast Indiana Memorial Society, 306 W. Rudisill Blvd., 46807, 219-745-4756.
Indianapolis: Indianapolis Memorial Society, 5805 E. 56th St., 46226, 317-545-6005.
Muncie: Memorial Society of Muncie Area, 1900 N. Morrison Rd., 47304, 317-288-9561 (evenings), 317-289-1500.
Valparaiso: Memorial Society of Northwest Indiana, 356 McIntyre Ct., 46383, 219-462-5701.
West Lafayette: Greater Lafayette Memorial Society, P.O. Box 2155, 47906, 317-463-9645.

IOWA

Ames: Central Iowa Memorial Society, 1015 Hyland Ave., 50010, 515-239-2421.
Cedar Rapids: Memorial Option Service of Cedar Rapids, 600 3rd Ave. S.E., 52403, 319-398-3955.
Davenport: Blackhawk Memorial Society, 3707 Eastern Ave., 52807, 319-326-0479.
Iowa City: Memorial Society of Iowa River Valley, 120 Dubuque St., 52240, 319-337-3019, 319-337-9828.

KANSAS

Hutchinson: Mid-Kansas Memorial Society, P.O. Box 2142, 67501.

KENTUCKY

Louisville: Memorial Society of Greater Louisville, 322 York St., 40203, 502-585-5119.

LOUISIANA

Baton Rouge: Memorial Society of Greater Baton Rouge, 8470 Goodwood Ave., 70806, 504-926-2291.
New Orleans: Memorial Society of Greater New Orleans, 1800 Jefferson Ave., 70115, 504-891-4055.

MAINE

Portland: Memorial Society of Maine, 425 Congress St., 04111, 207-773-5747.

MARYLAND

Baltimore: Memorial Society of Greater Baltimore, 3 Ruxview Ct., Apt. 101, 21204, 301-296-4657.

Columbia: Howard County Memorial Foundation, 100 Wilde, Lake Village Green, 21044, 301-730-7920, 301-9997-1188.

Greenbelt: Maryland Suburban Memorial Society, c/o Bruce Bowman, 1423 Laurell Hill, 20770, 301-474-6468.

Hagerstown: Memorial Society of Tri-State Area, 15 S. Mulberry, 21740, 301-733-3565.

MASSACHUSETTS

Brookline: Memorial Society of New England, 25 Monmouth St., 02146, 617-731-2073.

New Bedford: Memorial Society of Greater New Bedford, Inc., 71 Eighth St., 02740, 617-994-9686.

Orleans: Memorial Society of Cape Cod, P.O. Box 1346, 02653, 617-255-3841.

Springfield: Springfield Memorial Society, P.O. Box 2821, 01101, 413-733-7874.

MICHIGAN

Ann Arbor: Memorial Advisory and Planning Service, P.O. Box 7325, 48107, 313-663-2697.

Battle Creek: Memorial Society of Battle Creek, c/o Art Center, 265 E. Emmet St., 49017, 616-962-5362.

Detroit: Greater Detroit Memorial Society, 4605 Cass Ave., 48201, 313-833-9107.

East Lansing: Lansing Area Memorial Planning Society, 855 Grove St., 48823, 517-351-4081.

Flint: Memorial Society of Flint, G-2474 S. Ballenger Hwy. 48507, 313-232-4023.

Grand Rapids: Memorial Society of Greater Grand Valley, P.O. Box 1426, 49501, 616-459-4032.

Kalamazoo: Memorial Society of Greater Kalamazoo, 315 W. Michigan, 49006.

Mt. Pleasant: Memorial Society of Mid-Michigan, P.O. Box 313, 48858, 517-772-0220.

MINNESOTA

Minneapolis: Minnesota Memorial Society, 900 Mt. Curve Ave., 55403, 612-824-2440.

MISSISSIPPI

Gulfport: Funeral and Memorial Society of the Mississippi Gulf Coast, P.O. Box 265, 39501, 601-435-2284.

MISSOURI

Kansas City: Greater Kansas City Memorial Society, 4500 Warwick Blvd., 64111, 816-561-6322.

St. Louis: Memorial and Planning Funeral Society, 5007 Waterman Blvd., 63108, 314-361-0595.

MONTANA

Billings: Memorial Society of Montana, 1024 Princeton Ave., 59102, 406-252-5065.

Missoula: Five Valleys Burial-Memorial Association, 401 University Ave., 59801, 406-543-6952.

NEBRASKA

Omaha: Midland Memorial Society, 3114 Harney St., 68131, 402-345-3030.

NEVADA

Las Vegas: Las Vegas Funeral Society of Southern Nevada, P.O. Box 1324, 89101.
Reno: Memorial Society of Western Nevada, P.O. Box 8413, University Sta., 89507, 702-322-0688.

NEW HAMPSHIRE

Concord: Memorial Society of New Hampshire, 274 Pleasant St., 03301, 603-224-0291.

NEW JERSEY

Cape May: Memorial Society of South Jersey, P.O. Box 592, 08204, 609-884-8852.
East Brunswick: Raritan Valley Memorial Society, 176 Tices Lane, 08816, 201-246-9620, 201-572-1470.
Lanoka Harbor: Memorial Association of Ocean County, P.O. Box 173, 08734.
Lincroft: Memorial Association of Monmouth County, 1475 W. Front St., 07738, 201-741-8092.
Madison: Morris Memorial Society, P.O. Box 156, 07940, 201-540-1177.
Montclair: Memorial Society of Essex, 67 Church St., 07042, 201-338-9510.
Paramas: Central Memorial Society, 156 Forest Ave., 07652, 201-265-5910.
Plainfield: Memorial Society of Plainfield, P.O. Box 307, 07061.
Princeton: Princeton Memorial Association, P.O. Box 1154, 08540, 609-924-1604.

NEW MEXICO

Albuquerque: Memorial Association of Central New Mexico, P.O. Box 3251, 87190, 505-299-5384.
Los Alamos: Memorial and Funeral Society of Northern New Mexico, P.O. Box 178, 87544, 505-662-2346.

NEW YORK

Albany: Albany Area Memorial Society, 405 Washington Ave., 12206, 518-465-9664.
Binghamton: Southern Tier Memorial Society, 183 Riverside Dr., 13905, 607-729-1641.
Buffalo: Greater Buffalo Memorial Society, 695 Elmwood Ave., 14222, 716-885-2136.
Corning: Memorial Society of Greater Corning, P.O. Box 23, Painted Post, 14870, 607-962-2690.
Ithaca: Ithaca Memorial Society, P.O. Box 134, 14850, 607-272-5476.
New Hartford: Mohawk Valley Memorial Society, 28 Oxford Rd., 13413, 315-797-1955.
New York City: New York City Community Funeral Society, 40 E. 35th St., 10016, 212-683-4988.
New York City Consumers Memorial Society, 309 W. 23rd St., 10111, 212-691-8400.
New York City Memorial Society of Riverside Church, 490 Riverside Dr., 10027, 212-749-7000.

349

Oneonta: Memorial Society of Greater Oneonta, 12 Ford Ave., 13820, 607-432-3491.
Pomona: Rockland County Memorial Society, P.O. Box 461, 10970, 914-354-2917.
Port Washington: Memorial Society of Long Island, P.O. Box 303, 11050, 516-627-6590, 516-767-6026.
Poughkeepsie: Mid-Hudson Memorial Society, 249 Hooker Ave., 12603, 914-454-4164.
Rochester: Rochester Memorial Society, 220 Winton Rd. S., 14610, 716-461-1620.
Syracuse: Syracuse Memorial Society, P.O. Box 67, 13214, 315-474-4580.
Wellsville: Upper Genessee Memorial Society, 4604 Bolivar Rd., 14895, 716-593-1060.
White Plains: Funeral Planning Association of Westchester, Rosedale Ave. and Sycamore Lane, 10605, 914-946-1660.

NORTH CAROLINA

Asheville: The Blue Ridge Memorial Society, P.O. Box 2601, 28801.
Chapel Hill: Triangle Memorial and Funeral Society, P.O. Box 1223, 27514, 919-942-4427.
Charlotte: Charlotte Memorial Society, 234 N. Sharon Amity Rd., 28211, 704-597-2346.
Greensboro: Piedmont Memorial and Funeral Society, P.O. Box 16192, 27406, 919-674-5501.
Laurinburg: Scotland County Funeral and Memorial Society, P.O. Box 192, 28352.

OHIO

Akron: Canton-Akron Memorial Society, 3300 Morewood Rd., 44313, 216-836-8094.
Cincinnati: Memorial Society of Greater Cincinnati, Inc., 536 Linton St., 45219, 513-281-1564.
Cleveland: Cleveland Memorial Society, 21600 Shaker Blvd. 44122, 216-751-5515.
Columbus: Memorial Society of the Columbus Area, P.O. Box 14103, 43214, 614-267-4696.
Dayton: Dayton Memorial Society, 665 Salem Ave., 45406, 513-274-5890.
Elyria: Memorial Society of Lorain County (branch of Cleveland Memorial Society), 226, Middle Ave., 44035, 216-323-5776 ext. 441.
Toledo: Memorial Society of Northwest Ohio, 2210 Collingwood Blvd., 43620, 419-475-4812.
Wilmington: Funeral and Memorial Society of Southwest Ohio, 66 N. Mulberry St., 45177, 513-382-2349.
Yellow Springs: Yellow Springs Branch of Memorial Society of the Columbus Area, 317 Dayton St., 45387, 513-767-2011.
Youngstown: Memorial Society of Greater Youngstown, 75 Jackson Dr., Campbell, 44405, 216-755-8696.

OKLAHOMA

Oklahoma City: Memorial Society of Central Oklahoma, 600 NW 13th St., 73103, 405-232-9224.
Tulsa: Memorial Society of Eastern Oklahoma, 2942 S. Peoria, 74114, 918-743-2362.

OREGON

Portland: Oregon Memorial Association, 6220 SW 130th St. #17, Beaverton, 97005, 503-283-5500.

PENNSYLVANIA

Bethlehem: Lehigh Valley Memorial Society, 701 Lechauweki Ave., 18015, 215-866-7652.

Erie: Thanatopsis Society of Erie, P.O. Box 3495, 16508, 814-864-9300.

Harrisburg: Memorial Society of Greater Harrisburg, 1280 Clover Lane, 17113, 717-564-4761.

Philadelphia: Memorial Society of Greater Philadelphia, 2125 Chestnut St., 19103, 215-567-1065.

Pittsburgh: Pittsburgh Memorial Society, 605 Morewood Ave., 15213, 412-621-8008.

Pottstown: Pottstown Branch of Memorial Society of Greater Philadelphia, 1409 N. State St. 19464, 215-323-5561.

Scranton: Memorial Society of Scranton-Wilkes-Barre Area, 303 Main Ave., Clark's Summit 18411, 717-586-5255.

RHODE ISLAND

Providence: Rhode Island Memorial Society, 119 Kenyon Ave., E. Greenwich 02818, 401-884-5451. (In process of joining.)

SOUTH CAROLINA

Charleston: Memorial Society of Charleston, 2319 Bluefish Circle 29412.

Clemson: Clemson Funeral Society, P.O. Box 1132, 29631.

Myrtle Beach: Memorial Society of Eastern Carolina, P.O. Box 712, 29577, 803-449-6526, 803-449-3064.

TENNESSEE

Chattanooga: Memorial Society of Chattanooga, 1108 N. Concord Rd., 37421, 615-267-4685.

Knoxville: East Tennessee Memorial Society, P.O. Box 10507, 37919, 615-523-4176.

Nashville: Middle Tennessee Memorial Society, 1808 Woodmont Blvd. 37215, 615-383-5760.

Pleasant Hill: Cumberland Branch of East Tennessee Memorial Society, P.O. Box 246, 38578, 615-277-3795.

TEXAS

Austin: Austin Memorial and Burial Information Society, P.O. Box 4382, 78765.

Beaumont: Golden Triangle Memorial Society, Box 6136, 77705, 713-833-6883.

College Station: Memorial Society of Bryan-College Sta., P.O. Box 9078, 77840, 713-696-6944.

Dallas: Dallas Area Memorial Society, 4015 Normandy, 75205, 214-528-3990.

Houston: Houston Area Memorial Society 5210 Fannin St., 77004, 713-526-1571.
Lubbock: Lubbock Area Memorial Society, P.O. Box 6562, 79413, 806-792-0367.
San Antonio: San Antonio Memorial Society, 777 S.A. Bank and Trust Bldg., 771 Navarro, 78205.

UTAH

Salt Lake City: Utah Memorial Association, 569 S. 13th East 84102, 801-582-8687

VERMONT

Burlington: Vermont Memorial Society, P.O. Box 67, 05401, 802-863-4701.

VIRGINIA

Alexandria: Mt. Vernon Memorial Society, 1909 Windmill Lane, 22307, 703-765-5950.
Arlington: Memorial Society of Arlington, 4444 Arlington Blvd. 22204, 703-892-2565.
Charlottesville: Memorial Planning Society of the Piedmont, Edgewood Lane at Rugby Rd., 22901, 804-293-3323.
Oakton: Fairfax Memorial Society, P.O. Box 130, 22124, 703-281-4230.
Richmond: Memorial Society of Greater Richmond Area, Box 180, 23202, 804-355-0777.
Roanoke: Memorial Society of Roanoke Valley Inc., P.O. Box 8001, 24014, 703-774-9314.
Virginia Beach: Memorial Society of Tidewater Virginia, 2238 Oak St., 23451, 804-428-1804.

WASHINGTON

Seattle: People's Memorial Association, 2366 Eastlake Ave. E., 98102, 206-325-0489.
Spokane: Spokane Memorial Association, P.O. Box 14701, 99214, 509-838-4802.

WISCONSIN

Milwaukee: Funeral and Memorial Society of Greater Milwaukee, 2618 Hackett Ave. 52311, 414-332-0400.
Racine: Funeral and Memorial Society of·Racine and Kenosha, 625 College Ave., 53403, 414-634-0659.
River Falls: Western Wisconsin Funeral Society, 110 N. 3rd, 54022, 715-425-2052.
Sturgeon Bay: Memorial Society of Door County, c/o Hope United Church of Christ 54235, 414-743-2701.

CANADA

ALBERTA

Calgary: Calgary Co-op Memorial Society, P.O. Box 6443, Sta. D, T2P 2E1, 403-243-5088.

Edmonton: Memorial Society of Edmonton and District, 5904 109 B Ave., T6A 1S8, 403-466-8367.
Grande Prairie: Memorial Society of Grande Prairie, P.O. Box 471, T8V 3A7.
Lethbridge: Memorial Society of Southern Alberta, 924 20th St. South T1J 3J7.
Red Deer: Memorial Society of Red Deer and District, P.O. Box 817 T4N 5H2.

MANITOBA

Winnipeg: Funeral Planning and Memorial Society of Maintoba, c/o Dr. John Bond, 539 Manchester Blvd., R3T 1N7.

NEW BRUNSWICK

Fredericton: Memorial Society of New Brunswick, P.O. Box 622, E3B 5A6.

NEWFOUNDLAND

St. John's: Memorial and Funeral Planning Association of Newfoundland, 25 Hawker Crescent, A1E, 3W5.

NOVA SCOTIA

Halifax: Greater Halifax Memorial Society, P.O. Box 291, Armdale P.O., B3L 4K1, 902-429-5471.
Sydney: Memorial Society of Cape Breton, P.O. Box 934, B1P 6J4.

ONTARIO

Guelph: Memorial Society of Guelph, P.O. Box 1784, N1H 7A1, 519-822-7430.
Hamilton: Hamilton Memorial Society, P.O. Box 164, L8N 3A2, 416-549-6385.
Kingston: Memorial Society of Kingston, P.O. Box 1081, K7L 4Y5.
Kitchener: Kitchener-Waterloo Memorial Society, P.O. Box 113, N2G 3W9, 519-743-5481.
London: Memorial Society of London, P.O. Box 1729, Sta. A., N6A 5H9.
Niagara Peninsula: Niagara Peninsula Memorial Society, P.O. Box 2102, 4500 Queen St., L2E 6Z2.
Northern Ontario: Memorial Society of Northern Ontario, P.O. Box 2563, Sta. A, Sudbury, P3A 4S9.
Ottawa: Ottawa Memorial Society, 62 Steeple Hill Crescent, R.R. 7, Nepean, K2H 7V2, 613-836-5630.
Thunder Bay: Memorial Society of Thunder Bay, P.O. Box 501, Sta. F, P7C 4W4, 807-683-3051.
Toronto: Toronto Memorial Society, P.O. Box 96, Sta. "A", Weston, M9N 3M6, 416-241-6274.
Windsor: Memorial Society of Windsor and District, P.O. Box 481, N9A 6M6, 519-969-2252.

QUEBEC

Montreal: L'Association Funeraire de Montreal, P.O. Box 85, Dorion-Vaudreuil, J7V 5V8.

SASKATCHEWAN

Lloydminister: Lloydminister, Vermillion and Districts Memorial Society, 4729 45th St., S9V 0H6.

Saskatoon: Memorial Society of Saskatchewan, P.O. Box 1846, S7K 3S2.

A P P E N D I X H

Legislation regarding
the Uniform Anatomical Gift Act

Appendix H outlines the basic legal provision of the Uniform Anatomical Gift Act and identifies the statutory citations of the states that have adopted the statute. The act quoted in Appendix H was enacted by the Pennsylvania Legislature.

Table H-1. Jurisdictions Uniform Anatomical Gift Act has been adopted

Jurisdiction	Statutory citation
Alabama	Code, Tit. 22 § § 184(4) to 184(11).
Alaska	AS 13.50.010 to 13.50.090.
Arizona	A.R.S. § § 3-841 to 36-848.
Arkansas	Ark.Stats. § § 82-410.4 to 82-410.14.
California	West's Ann. Health & Safety Code, § § 7150 to 7158.
Colorado	C.R.S. '73, 12-34-101 to 12-34-109.
Connecticut	C.G.S.A. § § 19-139c to 19-139j.
Delaware	24 Del.C. § § 1780 to 1789.
District of Columbia	D.C.C.E. § § 2-271 to 2-278.
Florida	West's F.S.A. § § 732.910 to 732.919.
Georgia	Code § § 48-401 to 48-409.
Hawaii	H.R.S. § § 327-1 to 327-9.
Idaho	I.C. § § 39-3401 to 39-3411.
Illinois	S.H.A. ch. 3, § § 551 to 561.
Indiana	I.C. 1971, § § 29-2-16-1 to 29-2-16-9.
Iowa	I.C.A. § 142A.1 et seq.
Kansas	K.S.A. 65-3209 to 65-3217.
Kentucky	KRS 311.165 to 311.235.
Louisiana	LSA-R.S. 17:2351 to 17:2359.
Maine	22 M.R.S.A. § § 2901 to 2909.
Maryland	Code, Estates and Trusts, § § 4-501 to 4-512.
Massachusetts	M.G.L.A. c. 113, § § 7 to 13.
Michigan	M.C.L.A. § § 328.261 to 328.270.
Minnesota	M.S.A. § § 525.921 to 525.93

From Bissel, George T.: Purdon's Pennsylvania consolidated statutes annotated, St. Paul, 1975, West Publishing Co. Copyright © 1975 by West Publishing Co.

355

Table H-1—cont'd. Jurisdictions Uniform Anatomical Gift Act has been adopted

Jurisdiction	Statutory citation
Mississippi	Code 1972, § § 41-39-31 to 41-39-51.
Missouri	V.A.M.S. § § 194.210 to 194.290.
Montana	R.C.M.1947, § § 69.2315 to 69.2323.
Nebraska	R.S. Supp.1969, § § 71-4801 to 71-4812.
Nevada	N.R.S. 451.500 to 451.585.
New Hampshire	RSA 291-A:1 to 291-A:9.
New Jersey	N.J.S.A. 26:6-57 to 26:6-65.
New Mexico	1953 Comp § § 12-11-6 to 12-11-14.
New York	McKinney's Public Health Law § § 4300 to 4307.
North Carolina	G.S. § § 90-220.1 to 90-220.8
North Dakota	NDCC § § 23-06.1-01 to 23-06.1-09.
Ohio	R.C. § § 2108.01 to 2108.10.
Oklahoma	63 Okl.St.Ann. § § 2201 to 2209.
Oregon	ORS 97.250 to 97.295.
Pennsylvania	20 Pa.C.S.A. § § 8601 to 8607.
Rhode Island	Gen.Laws 1956, § § 23-47-1 to 23-47-7.
South Carolina	Code 1962, § § 32.711 to 32.720.
South Dakota	SDCL § § 34-26-20 to 34-26-41.
Tennessee	T.C.A. § § 53-4201 to 53-4209.
Texas	Vernon's Ann.Civ.St. art. 4590-2.
Utah	U.C.A.1953, 26-26-1 to 26-26-8.
Vermont	18 V.S.A. § § 5231-5237.
Virginia	Code 1950, § § 32-364.3 to 32-364.11.
Washington	RCWA 68.08.500 to 68.08.610.
West Virginia	Code, § § 16-19-1 to 16-19-9.
Wisconsin	W.S.A. 155.06.
Wyoming	W.S.1957, § § 35-221.1 to 35-221.11.

§ 8601. Definitions

As used in this chapter:

"Bank or storage facility." Means a facility licensed, accredited, or approved under the laws of any state for storage of human bodies or parts thereof.

"Decedent." Means a deceased individual and includes a stillborn infant or fetus.

"Donor." Means in individual who makes a gift of all or part of his body.

"Hospital." Means a hospital licensed, accredited, or approved under the laws of any state; includes a hospital operated by the United States Government, a state, or a subdivision thereof, although not required to be licensed under state laws.

"**Part.**" Means organs, tissues, eyes, bones, arteries, blood, other fluids and any other portions of a human body.

"**Person.**" Means an individual, corporation, government or governmental subdivision or agency, business trust, estate, trust, partnership or association, or any other legal entity.

"**Physician**" **or** " **surgeon.**" Means a physician or surgeon licensed or authorized to practice under the laws of any state.

"**State.**" Includes any state, district, commonwealth, territory, insular possession, and any other area subject to the legislative authority of the United States of America.

"**Board.**" Means the Humanity Gifts Registry.

1972, June 30, P.L. 508, No. 164, § 2, eff. July 1, 1972.

§ 8602. Persons who may execute an anatomical gift

(a) Any individual of sound mind and 18 years of age or more may give all or any part of his body for any purpose specified in section 8603 of this code (relating to persons who may become donees; purposes for which anatomical gifts may be made), the gift to take effect upon death. A gift of the whole body shall be invalid unless made in writing at least 15 days prior to the date of death.

(b) Any of the following persons, in order of priority stated, when persons in prior classes are not available at the time of death, and in the absence of actual notice of contrary indications by the decedent or actual notice of opposition by a member of the same or a prior class, may give all or any part of the decedent's body for any purpose specified in section 8603 of this code:

(1) the spouse;

(2) an adult son or daughter;

(3) either parent;

(4) an adult brother or sister;

(5) a guardian of the person of the decedent at the time of his death; and

(6) any other person authorized or under obligation to dispose of the body.

(c) If the donee has actual notice of contrary indications by the decedent or that a gift by a member of a class is opposed by a member of the same or a prior class, the donee shall not accept the gift. The persons authorized by subsection (b) of this section may make the gift after or immediately before death.

(d) A gift of all or part of a body authorizes any examination necessary to assure medical acceptability of the gift for the purposes intended.

(e) The rights of the donee created by the gift are paramount to the rights of others except as provided by section 8607(d) of this code (relating to rights and duties at death).

1972, June 30, P.L. 508, No. 164, § 2, eff. July 1, 1972; 1972, Dec. 6, P.L. 1461, No. 331, § 2.

§ 8603. Persons who may become donees; purposes for which anatomical gifts may be made

The following persons may become donees of gifts of bodies or parts thereof for the purposes stated:
(1) any hospital, surgeon, or physician, for medical or dental education, research, advancement of medical or dental science, therapy, or transplantation; or
(2) any accredited medical or dental school, college or university for education, research, advancement of medical or dental science, or therapy; or
(3) any bank or storage facility, for medical or dental education, research, advancement of medical or dental science, therapy, or transplantation; or
(4) any specified individual for therapy or transplantation needed by him; or
(5) the board.

1972, June 30, P.L. 508, No. 164, § 2, eff. July 1, 1972.

§ 8604. Manner of executing anatomical gifts

(a) A gift of all or part of the body under section 8602(a) of this code (relating to persons who may execute an anatomical gift) may be made by will. The gift becomes effective upon the death of the testator without waiting for probate. If the will is not probated, or if it is declared invalid for testamentary purposes, the gift, to the extent that it has been acted upon in good faith, is nevertheless valid and effective.

(b) A gift of all or part of the body under section 8602(a) of this code may also be made by document other than a will. The gift becomes effective upon the death of the donor. The document, which may be a card designed to be carried on the person, must be signed by the donor in the presence of two witnesses who must sign the document in his presence. If the donor is mentally competent to signify his desire to sign the document but is physically unable to do so, the doucment may be signed for him by another at his direction and in his presence in the presence of two witnesses who must sign the document in his presence. Delivery of the document of gift during the donor's lifetime is not necessary to make the gift valid.

(c) The gift may be made to a specified donee or without specifying a donee. If the latter, the gift may be accepted by the attending physician as donee upon or following death. If the gift is made to a specified donee who is not available at the time and place of death, the attending physician upon or following death, in the absence of any expressed indication that the donor desired otherwise, may accept the gift as donee. The physician who becomes a donee under this subsection shall not participate in the procedures for removing or transplanting a part.

(d) Notwithstanding section 8607(b) of this code (relating to rights and duties at death), the donor may designate in his will, card, or other document of gift the surgeon or physician to carry out the appropriate procedures. In the absence of a designation or if the designee is not available, the donee or other person authorized to accept the gift may employ or authorize any surgeon or physician for the purpose or, in the case of a gift of eyes, he may employ or authorize a funeral director licensed by the State Board of Funeral Directors who has successfully completed a course in eye enucleation approved by the State Board of Medical Education and Licensure to enucleate eyes for the gift after certification of death by a physician. A qualified funeral director acting in accordance with the terms of this subsection shall not have any liability, civil or criminal, for the eye enucleation.

(e) Any gift by a person designated in section 8062(b) of this code (relating to persons who may execute an anatomical gift), shall be made by a document signed by him or made by his telegraphic, recorded telephonic, or other recorded message.

1972, June 30, P.L. 508, No. 164 § 2, eff. July 1, 1972; 1974, Dec. 10, P.L. No. 293, § 18, imd. effective.

§ 8605. Delivery of document of gift

If the gift is made by the donor to a specified donee, the will, card, or other document, or an executed copy thereof, may be delivered to the donee to expedite the appropriate procedures immediately after death. Delivery is not necessary to the validity of the gift. The will, card, or other document, or an executed copy thereof, may be deposited in any hospital, bank or storage facility or registry office that accepts it for safekeeping or for facilitation of procedures after death. On request of any interested party upon or after the donor's death the person in possession shall produce the document for examination.

1972, June 30, P.L. 508, No. 164, § 2, eff. July 1, 1972.

§ 8606. Amendment or revocation of the gift

(a) If the will, card, or other document or executed copy thereof, has been delivered to a specified donee, the donor may amend or revoke the gift by:

(1) the execution and delivery to the donee of a signed statement; or

(2) an oral statement made in the presence of two persons and communicated to the donee; or

(3) a statement during a terminal illness or injury addressed to an attending physician and communicated to the donee; or

(4) a signed card or document found on his person or in his effects.

(b) Any document of gift which has not been delivered to the donee may be revoked by the donor in the manner set out in subsection (a) of this section, or by destruction, cancellation, or mutilation of the document and all executed copies thereof.

(c) Any gift made by a will may also be amended or revoked in the manner provided for amendment or revocation of wills, or as provided in subsection (a) of this section.

1972, June 30, P.L. 508, No. 164, § 2, eff. July 1, 1972.

§ 8607. Rights and duties at death

(a) The donee may accept or reject the gift. If the donee accepts a gift of the entir body, he shall subject to the terms of the gift, authorize embalming and the use of the body in funeral services if the surviving spouse or next of kin as determined in section 8602(b) of this code (relating to persons who may execute an anatomical gift) requests embalming and use of the body for funeral services. If the gift is of a part of the body, the donee, upon the death of the donor and prior to embalming, shall cause the part to be [1] removed without unnecessary mutilation. After removal of the part, custody of the remainder of the body vests in the surviving spouse, next of kin, or other persons under obligation to dispose of the body.

(b) The time of death shall be determined by a physician who tends the donor at his death, or, if none, the physician who certifies the death. The physician who certifies death or any of his professional partners or associates shall not participate in the procedures for removing or transplanting a part.

(c) A person who acts in good faith in accord with the terms of this chapter or with the anatomical gift laws of another state or a foreign country is not liable for damages in any civil action or subject to prosecution in any criminal proceeding for his act.

(d) The provisions of this chapter are subject to the laws of this State prescribing powers and duties with respect to autopsies.

1972, June 30, P.L. 508, No. 164, § 2, eff. July 1, 1972.

APPENDIX I

Medical schools of Canada and the United States that accept body donations

The need for bodies for anatomical studies varies among states and among institutions within states. To make a wise decision funeral consumers need to know the rules and regulations of the medical school to which they want to donate their bodies.

Appendix I identifies the medical schools in the United States and Canada that accept body donations. This appendix also indicates the relative need for the donation and approximate transportation responsibilities and costs.

Degree of need
U, Urgent need
M, Moderate need
A, Supplies ample
N, No bequeathals accepted

Transportation paid
W/S, W/P, Within state or province
150 miles, Within that radius
Local, Local area only
None, No transportation paid

	Phone	Need	Distance or amount school will transport or provide
U.S. MEDICAL SCHOOLS			
Alabama			
University of Alabama, Anatomy Department, University Station, Birmingham, AL 35294	205-934-4494	U	W/S
University of South Alabama, Department of Anatomy, Mobile, AL 36608	205-460-6490	M	None
Arizona			
University of Arizona, College of Medicine, Anatomy Department, Tucson, AZ 85724	602-626-6084	A	W/S
Arkansas			
University of Arkansas, College of Medicine, Anatomy Department, Little Rock, AR 72201	501-661-5180	M	W/S

From A Manual of Death Education and Simple Burial, by Ernest Morgan. ($2.50 plus 50 cents postage from Celo Press, Route 5, Burnsville, NC 28714)

	Phone	Need	Distance or amount school will transport or provide
California			
California State Polytechnic University, Pomona, CA 91768	714-598-4459 598-4444	M	50 miles
College of Osteopathic Medicine of the Pacific, 309 Pomona Mall E., Pomona, CA 91766	714-623-6116	U	50 miles
Loma Linda University School of Medicine, Anatomy Department, Loma Linda, CA 92354	714-796-7311 Ext. 2901	M	None
Stanford University, School of Medicine, Anatomy Department, Stanford, CA 94305	915-497-2404	M	10 miles
University of California at Davis, School of Medicine, Department of Human Anatomy, Davis, CA 95616	916-752-2100	M	30 miles
University of California at Irvine, College of Medicine, Anatomy Department, Irvine, CA 92717	714-833-6061 847-6716	M	50 miles
University of California at Los Angeles, School of Medicine, Anatomy Department, Los Angeles, CA 90024	213-825-9563	M	50 miles
University of California at San Diego, School of Medicine, Learning Resources Office, La Jolla, CA 92093	714-452-4536	M	County
University of California at San Francisco, School of Medicine, Anatomy Department, San Francisco, CA 94143	415-666-1981 666-9000	U	None
University of Southern California, School of Medicine, 2025 Zonal Ave., Los Angeles, CA 90033	213-222-0231 228-7825	A	50 miles
Colorado			
University of Colorado, School of Medicine, 4200 E. 9th Ave., Denver, CO 80260	302-394-8554 399-1211	M	Local
Connecticut			
University of Connecticut, School of Medicine, Farmington Ave., Farmington, CT 06032	203-223-4340	M	W/S
Yale University School of Medicine, New Haven, CT 06510	203-436-4219	U	W/S

	Phone	Need	Distance or amount school will transport or provide
District of Columbia			
Georgetown University School of Medicine, Anatomy Department, Washington, DC 20007	202-625-7521	M	25 miles
George Washington University, Anatomy Department, 2300 1 St., N.W., Washington, DC 20037	202-676-3511	U	Local
Howard University, College of Dentistry, 600 W. St., N.W., Washington, DC 20001	202-636-6400		
Howard University, College of Medicine, Washington, DC 2001	202-636-6555	U	Local
Florida			
Anatomical Board of Florida, University of Florida, College of Medicine, Gainesville, FL 32601	904-392-3588 372-0837	A	
University of Miami School of Medicine, Anatomy Department, Miami, FL 33101	305-547-6691 284-2211	M	
University of South Florida, College of Medicine, Anatomy Department, Tampa, FL 33620	813-974-2843 933-5415	A	None
Georgia			
Emory University, School of Medicine, Anatomy Department, Atlanta, GA 30322	404-329-6242	M	150 miles
Medical College of Georgia, School of Medicine, Anatomy Department, Augusta, GA 30912	404-724-7111 Ext. 8846	M	W/S
Hawaii			
University of Hawaii, Department of Anatomy, 1960 East-West Rd., Honolulu, HI 96822	808-948-7131	M	Local
Illinois			
Demonstrators Association of Illinois, 2240 W. Filmore, Chicago, IL 60612	312-733-5283	U	None
Indiana			
Indiana State Anatomical Board, Indiana University Medical Center, Indianapolis, IN 46223	317-264-7494 786-4256	M	None

	Phone	Need	Distance or amount school will transport or provide
Iowa			
College of Osteopathic Medicine and Surgery, Des Moines, IA 50309	515-274-4861	A	
University of Iowa, College of Medicine, Department of Anatomy, Iowa City, IA 52242	319-356-1616 353-5905	A	None
Kansas			
University of Kansas Medical Center, 39th and Rainbow Blvd., Kansas City, KS 66103	913-831-7000	M	Local
Kentucky			
University of Kentucky, College of Medicine, Lexington, KY 40506	606-233-5276 233-5811	M	W/S
University of Louisville, School of Medicine, Health Services Center, Louisville, KY 40201	502-588-5255	M	100 miles
Louisiana			
Louisiana State Anatomical Board, Department of Anatomy, Tulane University, School of Medicine, 1430 Tulane Ave., New Orleans, LA 70112	504-588-5255	M	W/S
Maine			
New England College of Osteopathic Medicine, 605 Pool Road, Biddefore, ME 04005	207-282-1515	U	W/S
Maryland			
Anatomy Board of Maryland, 655 W. Baltimore, Room B-026, Baltimore, MD 21201	301-547-1222	M	W/S
Coordinator of Anatomical Gifts, 55 Lake Ave. N, Worcester, MD 01605	301-856-2458	U	W/S
University of Health Sciences, Uniformed Services, 4301 Jones Ridge Rd., Bethesda, MD 20014	301-427-5199	U	150 miles
Michigan			
Michigan State University, Anatomy Department, East Lansing, MI 48823	517-355-1855	A	Local

	Phone	Need	Distance or amount school will transport or provide
University of Michigan, Medical School, 3726 Med. Science II, Ann Arbor, MI 48109	313-764-4359	M	150 miles
Wayne State University School of Medicine, 540 E. Canfield, Detroit, MI 48201	313-577-1188 577-1198	U	W/S
Minnesota			
University of Minnesota, College of Medical Science, State Anatomical Commission, 262 Jackson Hall, MInneapolis, MN 55455	612-373-2776	M	W/S
Mississippi			
University of Mississippi Medical Center, Jackson, MS 39216	601-987-4561	U	Local
Missouri			
In Missouri make bequeathals to individual schools, or to			
Missouri State Anatomical Board, University of Missouri, Columbia, MO 65212	314-882-2288	M	None
Nebraska			
Anatomical Board of Nebraska, 42nd & Dewey Aves., Omaha, NE 68105	402-541-7849	M	W/S
Nevada			
University of Nevada School of Medical Sciences, University of Nevada, Reno, NV 89557	702-784-6113	A	None
New Hampshire			
Dartmouth Medical School, Anatomy Department, Hanover, NH 03755	603-646-2820 646-2732	A	
New Jersey			
College of Medicine and Dentistry of New Jersey, 100 Bergen St., Newark, NJ 07103	201-456-4646 456-4648	M	W/S
Fairleigh Dickinson University, School of Dentistry, Hackensack, NJ 07601	201-863-6300 748-0240	U	100 miles
CMDMJ-Rutgers Medical School, P.O. Box 101, Piscataway, NJ 08854	609- or 201- 564-4580	M	W/S

	Phone	Need	Distance or amount school will transport or provide
New Mexico			
University of New Mexico, Anatomy Department, North Campus, Albuquerque, NM 87131	505-277-2555 843-2111	M	Local
New York			
Albany Medical College of Union University, Albany, NY 12208	518-445-5379	M	Local
Anatomical Gift Registry, P.O. Box 1664, New York, NY 10001	212-596-4444	U	
Anatomical Sciences, Health Science Center, Stony Brook, NY 11790	516-444-2420 444-2350	U	50 miles
Columbia University College of Physicians and Surgeons, 630 W. 168th, New York, NY 10032	212-694-3451	U	100 miles
Cornell University Medical College, 1300 York Ave., New York, NY 10021	607-472-6400	M	None
Downstate Medical Center, 450 Clarkson Ave., Brooklyn, NY 11203	212-270-1027 270-1053	U	
Mt. Sinai School of Medicine, Mt. Sinai Hosp., Madison Ave. Entrance, New York, NY 10029	212-650-7057	U	150 miles
New York Medical College, Basic Science Bldg., Valhalla, NY 10595	914-347-5630 347-5620	U	50 miles
New York University, College of Medicine, 550 1st Avenue, New York, NY 10016	212-679-3200 Ext. 2761	U	Local
State University of New York Upstate Medical Center Anatomy Department, 766 Irving Ave., Syracuse, NY 13210	315-473-5120	U	W/S
State University of New York at Buffalo, School of Medicine, Anatomy Department, Buffalo, NY 14214	716-831-2912	M	100 miles
University of Rochester, School of Medicine, 601 Elmwood Ave., Rochester, NY 14642	716-275-2591 275-2281	M	Local

	Phone	Need	Distance or amount school will transport or provide
Yeshiva University, Albert Einstein College of Medicine, Eastchester Road & Morris Park Ave., New York, NY 10461	212-430-2837	M	None
North Carolina			
Bowman Gray School of Medicine, Greenville, NC 27834	919-727-4368 723-5813	M	W/S or 200 miles
Duke Medical Center, Anatomy Department, Durham, NC 27710	919-684-4124	U	188 miles
East Carolina University School of Medicine, Greenville, NC 27834	919-758-6217 756-2644	U	W/S
University of North Carolina School of Medicine, Chapel Hill, NC 27514	919-966-2406	M	330 miles
North Dakota			
University of North Dakota, School of Medicine, Grand Forks, ND 58201	701-777-2101	U	W/S
Ohio			
Case Western Reserve School of Medicine, 2119 Abington Road, Cleveland, OH 44106	216-368-3430 221-9330	M	75 miles
Medical College of Ohio at Toledo, 3000 Arlington Ave., Toledo, OH 43699	419-381-4109	M	None
Northeastern Ohio College of Medicine, Rootstown, OH 44272	216-325-2511		
Ohio State University, Anatomy Department, 333 W. 10th Ave., Columbus, OH 43210	614-422-4831	U	W/S
Ohio University College of Osteopathic Medicine, Athens, OH 45701	614-594-6401	U	W/S
University of Cincinnati College of Medicine, Cincinnati, OH 45267	513-872-5611 481-4905	M	None
Wright State University School of Medicine, Dayton, OH 45435	513-873-3066	A	W/S
Oklahoma			
Oklahoma College of Osteopathic Medicine and Surgery, Tulsa, OK 74107	918-582-1972	M	W/S
University of Oklahoma, Health Sciences Center, Box 26901, Oklahoma City, OK 73190	405-271-2424	U	W/S

	Phone	Need	Distance or amount school will transport or provide
University of Oklahoma, Tulsa Medical College, Tulsa, OK 74105	918-749-5530		
Oregon			
University of Oregon, School of Medicine, Anatomy Department, Portland, OR 97201	503-225-8302 225-7888	M	None
Pennsylvania			
Humanity Gifts Registry of Pennsylvania, 130 S. 9th St., Philadelphia, PA 19107	215-922-4440	U	W/S
Puerto Rico			
University of Puerto Rico, Anatomy Department, School of Medicine, San Juan, P.R. 00936	809-767-9626 Ext. 390-482	U	W/S
Rhode Island			
Brown University, Division of Biology and Medicine, Providence, RI 02912	401-863-1000	M	W/S
South Carolina			
Medical University of South Carolina, 80 Barre St., Charleston, SC 29401	803-792-3521	M	W/S
South Dakota			
University of South Dakota, School of Medicine, Vermillion, SD 57069	605-624-2942 677-5321	M	300 miles
Tennessee			
East Tennessee State University, College of Medicine, Anatomy Department, Box 19960-A, Johnson City, TN 37601	615-928-6426	U	150 miles
Meharry Medical College, 1005 18th Ave. N., Nashville, TN 37208	615-327-6308 244-0375	U	300 miles
University of Tennessee, Center for Health Sciences, 875 Monroe Ave., Memphis, TN 38163	901-528-5965	U	500 miles
Vanderbilt University, School of Medicine, Anatomy Dept., Nashville, TN 37232	615-322-2134	M	200 miles
Texas			
Baylor College of Medicine, 1200 Moursund, Houston, TX 77025	713-529-4951	M	W/S

	Phone	Need	Distance or amount school will transport or provide
Baylor Dental School, 3302 Gaston, Dallas, TX 76226	214-824-6321 ext. 270	U	W/S
Texas A & M University Medical College, College Station, TX 77843	713-845-4913 845-3431		
Texas Chiropractic College, 5912 Spencer Hwy., Pasadena, TX 77505	713-487-1170	U	W/S
Texas College of Osteopathic Medicine, 3516 Camp Bowie Blvd., Ft. Worth, TX 76107	214-338-0982		
Texas Technical University School of Medicine, Anatomy Department, Lubbock, TX 79409	806-743-2700 743-3111	U	360 miles
University of Texas, Health Science Center, 5323 Harry Hines, Dallas, TX 75235	214-688-2221	M	50 miles
University of Texas, Health Science Center, 7703 Floyd Curl Dr., San Antonio, TX 78284	512-696-6533 534-0198	U	100 miles
University of Texas, Health Science Center at Houston, P.O. Box 20708, Houston, TX 77030	713-449-6511	U	W/S
University of Texas, Medical Branch, Galveston, TX 77550	713-765-1293 763-0200	U	300 miles
Utah			
University of Utah, College of Medicine, Salt Lake City, UT 84132	801-581-6728 582-3711	U	400 miles
University of Utah, Physical Therapy Program, Bldg. 206, Salt Lake City, UT 84112	801-581-8681	U	150 miles
Vermont			
University of Vermont, College of Medicine, Department of Anatomy, Burlington, VT 05401	802-656-2230 656-3131	M	Local
Virginia			
Department of Health, State Anatomical Division, Richmond, VA 23219	804-786-3174	U	W/S

	Phone	Need	Distance or amount school will transport or provide
Eastern Virginia Medical School, Department of Anatomy, Box 1980, Norfolk, VA 23501	804-466-5696		
Washington			
University of Washington, Department of Biological Structure, School of Medicine, Seattle, WA 98195	206-543-1860	M	Local
West Virginia			
Marshall University School of Medicine, Huntington, WV 25701	304-696-3615	M	W/S
West Virginia School of Osteopathic Medicine, 400 N. Lee St., Lewisburg, WV 24901	304-645-6270	M	W/S
West Virginia University Medical Center, Human Gift Registry, Morgantown, WV 26506	304-293-6322	M	W/S
Wisconsin			
The Medical College of Wisconsin, 561 N. 15th St., Milwaukee, WI 53233	414-272-5450 Ext. 301	M	Local
University of Wisconsin Medical School, 349 Bardeen Medical Labs, Madison, WI 53706	608-262-2888	M	W/S
CANADIAN MEDICAL SCHOOLS			
Alberta			
University of Alberta, Faculty of Medicine, Edmonton, ALTA	403-432-3355	U	Local
University of Calgary, Faculty of Medicine, 2920 24 Ave. NW, Calgary, ALTA T2N 1N4	403-284-6895	M	$125
British Columbia			
University of British Columbia, Faculty of Medicine, Vancouver, BC	604-228-2842 228-2578	M	Local
Manitoba			
University of Manitoba, Faculty of Medicine, Winnipeg, MAN R3E 0W3	204-786-3652	M	$50
Newfoundland			
Memorial University, Faculty of Medicine, St. Johns, NFLD A1B 3V6	737-6727	U	W/P

	Phone	Need	Distance or amount school will transport or provide
Nova Scotia			
Dalhousie University, Faculty of Medicine, Tupper Medical Bldg., Halifax, NS	902-		
Ontario			
McMaster University, Dept. of Anatomy, 1200 Main St., Hamilton, ONT L8S 4J9	807-525-9140	M	Local
Queen's University, Faculty of Medicine, Dept. of Anatomy, Kingston, ONT K7L 3N6	807-547-2600	M	W/P $120
University of Ottawa, Anatomy Dept., Faculty of Medicine, Ottawa, ONT K1N 9A9	807-231-3422 237-3680	M	None
University of Toronto, Anatomy Dept., Faculty of Medicine, Toronto, ONT M5S 1A8	807-978-2011 978-2692	M	None
University of Western Ontario, Medical School, Dept. of Anatomy, London, ONT	807-679-3741	M	None
Quebec			
McGill University, Anatomy Dept., 3640 University St., Montreal, P.Q. H3A 2B2	819-392-4898 873-2633	M	Local
Universite Laval, Department d'Anatomie, Quebec, P.Q. G1K 7P4	819-656-3090 681-6611	M	200 miles
Universite de Montreal, Faculte de Medicine, 2900 Blvd. Edward Montpetit, Montreal, P.Q. H3C 3J7	514-343-6290	M	100 miles
University of Sherbrooke, Faculty of Medicine, Sherbrooke, P.Q.	819-563-5555 873-2633	M	150 miles
Saskatchewan			
University of Saskatchewan, College of Medicine, Department of Anatomy, Saskatoon, SASK	306-343-2661	M	W/P

APPENDIX J

About eye banks

One important service we can render at death is to leave behind our eyes to relieve the blindness of others. In America alone there are about 30,000 blind people whose sight could be restored if enough corneas were available.

Eye donations are increasing, but the demand is increasing even more as new techniques are perfected and new uses are found for the donor-eye. Today the corneal transplant operation is effective in restoring sight in 90% of the most common corneal diseases. All vision defects cannot be cured by transplants. It is not possible to transfer the entire eye. To pledge your eyes, call or write the nearest eye bank. Carry a Uniform Donor Card and check the eye bank square. Let your physician know (in writing) and be sure to clear your plans with your family. No matter if you wear glasses, or what your age, race or blood type may be, your eyes may be pledged.

Eyes must be removed within 2 to 4 hours of death. This can be done in the hospital or at home, assuming eye bank personnel are available. An increasing number of funeral directors are being trained to do this. Eyes may not be bequeathed to specific individuals. They will be used on a first-come, first-served basis, regardless of ability to pay. Airlines fly them to their destinations without charge.

EYE BANKS IN THE UNITED STATES

ALABAMA

Birmingham: Alabama Lions Eye Bank, 708 18th St., 35233, 205-933-8251.
Tuskegee: Eye Bank of Central Alabama, 620 N. Water St., 36083, 205-727-6553

ARIZONA

Phoenix: Arizona Lions Eye Bank, P.O. Box 13609, 85002, 602-258-7373 ext. 568.

ARKANSAS

Little Rock: Arkansas Eye & Kidney Bank, 4301 W. Markham, 72205, 501-664-4990.

CALIFORNIA

San Diego: Eye Bank of San Diego, 4077 5th Ave., 92103, 714-294-8267.

From *A Manual of Death Education and Simple Burial* by Ernest Morgan ($2.50 plus 50 cents postage from Celo Press, Route 5, Burnsville, NC 28714.)

Torrance: Southern California Eye Bank & Research Foundation, Suite 380, 4201 Torrance Blvd., 90503, 213-540-5832.

COLORADO

Denver: Colorado Eye Bank, University of Colorado Health Sciences Center, 4200 9th Ave., 80262, 303-377-1087.

CONNECTICUT

New Britain: Connecticut Eye Bank, New Britain General Hospital, 06052, 203-224-5550.

DISTRICT OF COLUMBIA

Washington: Lions Eye Bank and Research Foundation, Suite 121, 919 18th St. NW, 20006, 202-393-2265.

FLORIDA

Gainesville: North Florida Lions Eye Bank, P.O. Box J-382, 32610, 904-392-3135.

Tampa: Central Florida Lions Eye Bank, P.O. Box 21, N. 30th St., 33612, 813-977-1300.

GEORGIA

Atlanta: Georgia Lions Eye Bank, Inc., 1365 Clifton Rd. NE, 30322, 404-321-9300.

Augusta: Georgia Lions Lighthouse Foundation, Inc., 30912, 404-724-1388.

ILLINOIS

Chicago: Illinois Eye Bank, Room 1435, 53 W. Jackson Blvd., 60604, 312-922-8710.

Chicago: Illinois Eye Bank Laboratory and Eye and Ear Infirmary, 1855 West Taylor St., 60612, 312-996-6507.

Bloomington: Watson Galley Eye Foundation Eye Bank, 807 N. Main St., 61701, 309-828-5241.

INDIANA

Indianapolis: Indiana Lions Eye Bank, Inc., 1100 W. Michigan St., 46223, 317-264-8527 or 635-8431.

IOWA

Iowa City: Iowa Lions Eye Bank, University Hospitals, 52242, 319-356-2215 or 356-1616.

KANSAS

Topeka: Kansas Odd Fellows Eye Bank, P.O. Box 1851, 66601, 913-233-4652.

KENTUCKY

Louisville: Kentucky Lions Eye Foundation, 301 E. Walnut St., 40202, 502-584-9934.

LOUISIANA

New Orleans: Southern Eye Bank, 145 Elk Place, 70112, 504-523-6343.

MAINE

See New England Eye Bank, Boston, MA.

MARYLAND

Baltimore: The Medical Eye Bank of Maryland, 505 Park Ave., 21202, 301-986-1830.
Bethesda: International Eye Bank, 7801 Norfolk Ave., 20014, 301-986-1830.

MASSACHUSETTS

Boston: New England Eye Bank, 243 Charles St., 02114, 617-523-7900.

MICHIGAN

Ann Arbor: Michigan Eye Bank, 1000 Wall St., Parkview Medical, 48109, 313-764-3262 or 764-4244.
Detroit: Michigan Eye Bank, 540 E. Canfield Ave., 48201, 313-577-1329.
Marquette: Upper Michigan Lions Eye Bank, 420 W. Magnetic St., 49855, 906-228-9440 ext. 438 or 800-562-9781.

MINNESOTA

Minneapolis: Minnesota Lions Eye Bank, Box 493, Mayo Hospital, 55455, 612-373-8425 or 373-8484.

MISSISSIPPI

Jackson: Mississippi Lions Eye Bank, Inc., 2500 N. State St., 39216, 601-987-3500 or 987-5899.

MISSOURI

Columbia: Lions Eye Tissue Bank, 404 Portland, 65201, 314-443-1471 or 443-1479.
Kansas City: Eye Bank of Kansas City, 3036 Gillham Rd., 64108, 816-531-1066.
St. Louis: Lions Eye Bank in St. Louis, 1325 S. Grand, 63104, 314-771-7600.
St. Louis Eye Bank, 660 S. Euclid, 63104, 314-454-2150 or 454-2666.

NEBRASKA

Omaha: Nebraska Lions Eye Bank, 42nd & Dewey Streets, 68105, 402-541-4039.

NEW HAMPSHIRE

See New England Eye Bank, Boston MA.

NEW JERSEY

Newark: New Jersey Eye Bank, Eye Institute of New Jersey, 15 S. 9th St., 07107, 201-456-4626.

NEW MEXICO

Albuquerque: New Mexico Lions Eye Bank, Suite 501, 201 Cedar S.E., 87106, 505-843-9211.

NEW YORK

Albany: Sight Conservation Society of Northeast New York, 628 Madison Ave., 12208, 518-445-5199 or 377-5761.
Buffalo: Buffalo Eye Bank and Research Society, Inc., 2550 Main St., 14214, 716-832-5448 or 835-8725.
New York City: Eye Bank for Site Restoration, 210 E. 64th St., 10021, 212-838-9155 or 838-9211.

Rochester: Rochester Eye and Human Parts Bank, 220 Alexander St., 14607, 716-546-5250.

Syracuse: Central New York Eye Bank and Research Corporation, P.O. Box 21, 13201, 315-471-6060.

NORTH CAROLINA

Winston-Salem: North Carolina Eye and Human Tissue Bank, 3195 Maplewood Ave., 27103, 919-765-0932.

NORTH DAKOTA

Williston: Williston Lions Eye Bank, Box 1627, 58801, 701-572-7661.

OHIO

Cincinnati: Cincinnati Eye Bank, Room 6004, 231 Bethesda Ave., 45267, 513-861-3716.

Cleveland: Cleveland Eye Bank, 1909 E. 101st St., 44106, 216-791-9700.

Columbus: Central Ohio Lions Eye Bank, Inc. 456 Clinic Dr., University Hospital Clinic, 43210, 614-422-1111.

Youngstown: Melvin E. Jones Eye Bank, 2246 Glenwood Ave., 44511, 216-788-2411.

OKLAHOMA

Oklahoma City: Oklahoma Lions Eye Bank, 608 Stanton L. Young Dr., 73104, 405-271-5691.

OREGON

Portland: Oregon Lions Sight and Hearing Foundation, Inc., 1200 NW 23rd St., 97210, 503-229-7523.

PENNSYLVANIA

Bethlehem: Northeast Pennsylvania Lions Eye Bank, 1916 Rockingham Dr., 18018, 215-867-9696.

Philadelphia: Eye Foundation of Delaware Valley, 1601 Spring Garden St., 19130, 215-569-3937.

Pittsburgh: Medical Eye Bank of Western Pennsylvania, 3615 5th Ave., 15213, 412-687-8828.

PUERTO RICO

San Juan: Lions Eye Bank of Puerto Rico, G.P.O. Box 5067, 00936, 809-763-8050.

RHODE ISLAND

See New England Eye Bank, Boston MA.

SOUTH CAROLINA

Columbia: South Carolina Eye Bank, 110 Lexington Medical Mall, 29169, 803-796-1304.

TENNESSEE

Knoxville: East Tennessee Eye Bank, 509 Cedar Bluff Rd., 37921, 615-693-4991.

Memphis: Mid-South Eye Bank, #215, 188 S. Bellevue, 38104, 901-726-8264.

Nashville: Lions Eye Bank, Suite 634, Research and Service Center, Medical Arts Bldg., 37212, 615-322-2662.

TEXAS

Amarillo: Lions Hi-Plains Eye Bank, P.O. Box 1717, 79105, 806-359-5101.
Dallas: Lions Sight and Tissue Foundation, Room G7-250, 5323 Harry Hines, 75235, 214-688-3908.
El Paso: West Texas Lions Eye Bank, 2901 McRae, 79925, 915-598-6306 or 598-5948.
Ft. Worth: Lions Organ and Eye Bank of District 2-E2, c/o Carter Blood Center, 1263 W. Rosedale, 76104, 817-335-4935.
Houston: Lions Eyes of Texas Eye Bank, Suite C-307, 6501 Fannin, 77030, 713-797-9270.
Lackland: Central U.S. Air Force Eye Bank, Lackland Air Force Base, 78236, 512-670-7841.
Lubbock: District 2-T2 Lions Eye Bank, P.O. Box 5901, 79417, 806-762-2242.
Midland: District 2-A1 Lions Eye Bank, P.O. Box 4283, 79701, 915-682-7381.
San Antonio: Eye Bank at Baptist Memorial Hospital, 111 Dalls, 78286, 512-222-8431 Ext. 2330.
Tyler: East Texas Regional Eye Bank, P.O. Drawer 6400, 75711, 214-597-0351.

UTAH

Salt Lake City: Lions Eye Bank of University of Utah, 50 N. Medical Dr., 84132, 801-581-6384.

VERMONT

See New England Eye Bank, Boston MA

VIRGINIA

Richmond: Old Dominion Eye Bank, 408 N. 12th St., 23219, 804-648-0890.
Roanoke: Eye Bank of Virginia, P.O. Box 1772, 24008, 703-345-8823.

WASHINGTON

Seattle: Lions Eye Bank of Washington and Northern Idaho, Department of Ophthalmology-RJ10, University of Washington 98195, 206-543-5394 or 223-3010.

WISCONSIN

Madison: Wisconsin Eye Bank, 600 Highland Ave., 53792, 608-263-6223.
Milwaukee: Wisconsin Lions Eye Bank, 8700 Wisconsin Ave., 53226, 414-257-5543.

CANADIAN EYE BANKS

BRITISH COLUMBIA-YUKON division
350 E. 36th Ave., Vancouver, V5W 1C6.

ALBERTA division
12010 Jasper Ave., Edmonton, T5J2L4.

SASKATCHEWAN division
2550 Broad St., Regina S4P3E1.

MANITOBA division
1031 Portage Ave., Winnipeg, R3G 0R9.

ONTARIO division
1929 Bayview Ave., Toronto, M4G 3E8.

QUEBEC division
1181 Guy St., Montreal, P.O. H3H 2K6.

MARITIME division
6136 Almon St., Halifax, Nova Scotia B3J271.

NEWFOUNDLAND & LABRADOR division
70 Boulevard, St. John's, Newfoundland, A1A 1K2.

Index